WITHDRAWN
UTSA LIBRARIES

3-4574

WITHDRAWN
ITSA LIBRARIES

ANATOMY OF A DICTATORSHIP

ANATOMY OF A DICTATORSHIP

INSIDE THE GDR

1949–1989

Mary Fulbrook

OXFORD UNIVERSITY PRESS

1995

Oxford University Press, Walton Street, Oxford OX2 6DP
Oxford New York
Athens Auckland Bangkok Bombay
Calcutta Cape Town Dar es Salaam Delhi
Florence Hong Kong Istanbul Karachi
Kuala Lumpur Madras Madrid Melbourne
Mexico City Nairobi Paris Singapore
Taipei Tokyo Toronto
and associated companies in
Berlin Ibadan

Oxford is a trade mark of Oxford University Press

Published in the United States
by Oxford University Press Inc., New York

© Mary Fulbrook 1995

All rights reserved. No part of this publication may be reproduced,
stored in a retrieval system, or transmitted, in any form or by any means,
without the prior permission in writing of Oxford University Press.
Within the UK, exceptions are allowed in respect of any fair dealing for the
purpose of research or private study, or criticism or review, as permitted
under the Copyright, Designs and Patents Act, 1988, or in the case of
reprographic reproduction in accordance with the terms of the licences
issued by the Copyright Licensing Agency. Enquiries concerning
reproduction outside these terms and in other countries should be
sent to the Rights Department, Oxford University Press,
at the address above

British Library Cataloguing in Publication Data
Data available

Library of Congress Cataloging in Publication Data
Data applied for

ISBN 0-19-820312-8

1 3 5 7 9 10 8 6 4 2

Typeset by Best-set Typesetter Ltd., Hong Kong
Printed in Great Britain
on acid-free paper by
Bookcraft Ltd., Midsomer Norton, Bath

LIBRARY
The University of Texas
At San Antonio

PREFACE

WRITING a book about the GDR at this time has not been easy. I first conceived the idea for this book in the early 1980s, when—as many historians took a delight in warning me—there was too little material to do more than hypothesize. Then came an entirely unexpected reversal of the situation: with the fall of the Wall and the opening of the abundant documentation of the East German archives, there is now almost too much material to do more than hypothesize.

With truly Prussian zeal and efficiency, the East German communists observed, collected, and collated the most extraordinary mountains of information in the interests of having total overview, total control, in a state where there was no open forum for gauging patterns of public opinion. As a result—and despite a number of problems of interpretation—there are fascinating sediments of unexpectedly rich material for the historian to explore. It will take decades of detailed archival research before the historiography of the GDR begins to attain the well-defined contours of debate which characterize earlier periods of German history.

It is not only the sheer quantity of archival residues which challenges the contemporary historian of the GDR. In a post-dictatorial society, and under the peculiar circumstances of social, economic, and political restructuring under the essentially benevolent but nevertheless quasi-colonial auspices of the West, any confrontation with the East German past is inevitably politically charged, laden with moral overtones, and coloured by implicit or explicit comparisons with the Third Reich. Who should be castigated for having sustained a dictatorship, whether through appeasement in the West, or acquiescence, complicity, or active support in the East? Who should be designated as 'oppressor', who as 'hero' or 'victim'? Who should reap the rewards of the new opportunities after 1990, and who condemned to remain the perpetual losers of history, under whatever system they happen to live? Given the betrayals of trust and friendship in the past, whom can one now trust? How should one live? Such are the—intrinsically existential as well as 'purely' historical—preoccupations swirling around in popular and political debates in Germany today.

This book is intended as a sober and to some extent provisional contribution to the analysis of the inner life and workings—the domestic anatomy—of the East German dictatorship. It seeks to understand, in their

own terms, the ways in which East Germans of different classes, generations, and political opinions perceived and played a role in the political
patterns of a state which existed for forty years. This state, which survived
for longer than the Weimar Republic and the Third Reich put together, was
for a long time regarded as a quintessentially successful communist state,
politically more stable and economically more productive than its immediate neighbours in the Soviet bloc. Despite the radical changes of perspective
and perception effected by the GDR's extraordinarily rapid collapse in
1989–90, this relative stability over four decades still remains to be explored
and explained: it is simply non-historical to see 1989 as a continuation of
1953. Moreover, in the course of forty years of major, politically directed
changes in economic and social structure, and with the inevitable passage of
generations, there were fundamental changes in society and identity in the
GDR which it is essential to explore and understand. The notion that
there was an undying, underlying, intrinsic German identity—encapsulated
in the slogan 'Wir sind ein Volk! (We Are One Nation)' of the winter of
1989–90—was one that was very soon challenged as Germans, East and
West, began to realize the extent to which they had grown apart over
nearly half a century of radically different experiences.

I have sought in this book to step outside the rather simplistic, black-and-
white stereotypes which tended, and still tend, to characterize debates on
the GDR both during and after the Cold War era. All historians of course
have their own personal political preferences and prejudices; but I affirm
Max Weber's view that it is both in principle possible, and indeed the
historian's distinctive task, to seek to understand the world-views of others,
and to explore the consequences of people's perceptions, beliefs, and values
for their actions, under the given historical circumstances in which they find
themselves. To understand and explain is neither to condone nor condemn.

In the course of exploring the GDR, and writing this book, I have been
aided and supported by many individuals and organizations, whose support
it is a pleasure to acknowledge here. My research trips to Germany have
been generously funded on a number of occasions by the British Academy
and by the Dean's Fund of University College London. A stint as Visiting
Fellow at the Forschungsschwerpunkt Zeithistorische Studien in Potsdam,
under the energetic leadership of Jürgen Kocka, provided an extremely
stimulating context in the closing stages of my research; the diversity of
views and approaches among colleagues at this research institute, and their
academic productivity regardless of political challenges and personal uncertainties, ensured a degree of liveliness and vigour to debates going beyond
anything experienced in more secure ivory towers. The contrasting tranquil-

lity of a sabbatical term as Visiting Bye-Fellow at Newnham College, Cambridge, provided the essential space for thinking and writing at one remove from the heat of inner-German controversies, and I would like to thank the Principal, Onora O'Neill, and the Fellows of Newnham, for making this possible. Colleagues and students at UCL have, as always, provided a supportive environment; the notion of separating the functions of teaching and research appears peculiarly inapposite when the mutually beneficial interaction, in a myriad of ways, is so clearly evident.

Among the archivists who helped me find paths into the labyrinthine remnants of the SED state, particularly in the early and often uncertain stages before archival reorganization and the opening up of different areas of material for research, there are a number of individuals whom I would like particularly to thank. Herr Braun of the then Johannes-Sassenbach-Stiftung archive of the trade union movement, before it was absorbed by the central party archives under the Bundesarchiv, took a great deal of time to introduce me to the revealing records of the FDGB (the GDR trade union organization), and to discuss, with the insights of an insider, some aspects of their style and problems of interpretation. Herr Lange and Frau Müller were very helpful at the former Institute for the History of the Workers' Movement at the Central Party Archive of the SED (IfGA, ZPA), which in the course of my research became the Foundation for the Archives of the Parties and Mass Organizations of the GDR in the Federal Archives (SAPMO-BArch). Herr Stang at the Federal Office for the Documents of the State Security Service of the former GDR (the so-called Gauck-Behörde for the Stasi archives, as it is more popularly known) was particularly helpful in locating a wide range of relevant documents, making available quantities of photocopies, and sending to me further material which only came to light at a late stage of my research. Frau Grünspek of the Federal Archive in Potsdam introduced me to the records of the State Office for Church Affairs in the GDR. The staff of the Forschungsschwerpunkt Zeithistorische Studien in Potsdam were invariably helpful under every circumstance. Under very different conditions on the other side of the Atlantic, the library of the Harvard Center for European Studies proved to be a stimulating location for surveying relevant secondary literature, and I would particularly like to thank the librarian, Loren Goldner, for his help in this connection.

Many East Germans have of course, in a wide variety of ways, contributed to my understanding of the GDR. I would like here particularly to mention Vera Wollenberger, whom I met when she was in exile in England after being arrested in January 1988, and whose very honest and insightful reflections were in marked contrast to the prevarications of her husband, later revealed as a Stasi informer. Christa Grengel of the Evangelical Churches of the GDR was very helpful in the early and mid-1980s, in providing me with the names of key people in the Protestant Church with whom I could discuss the role of the Church in the GDR. Among these, I would like particularly to thank Landessuperintendent De Boor of Schwerin, and Präses Wahrmann of Wismar, for their willingness to give up their time and to talk very frankly under rather circumscribed conditions in September 1986. Over the years, I have also had innumerable interesting informal discussions with other individuals in the GDR; to select further names for individual mention would be invidious.

Colleagues and friends in Britain have also helped me in the course of thinking about, researching, and writing this book. I owe particular thanks to Ian Kershaw, who has discussed these issues with me over many years, and whose own work on the Third Reich has constantly stimulated my thinking on the questions of conformity and resistance under dictatorial conditions. I would also like particularly to thank Mark Allinson for his close and careful reading of the full manuscript of this book, and his invaluable comments on both the contents and style of the text. Needless to say, I alone take full responsibility for the shortcomings which remain.

Finally—as always—I owe an immense and essentially immeasurable debt of thanks to my family. Without my husband's unstinting willingness to engage in childcare beyond normal measure, and in frequently less than ideal circumstances, this book could not have been written. My family have endured innumerable 'holidays' in the GDR, both before and after the collapse of the regime; their experiences have often led them to wonder why I could not be fascinated by the history of a more agreeable destination. But they have nevertheless unfailingly supported my endeavours, put up with my absorption in often disturbing material, and constantly reminded me that there is more to life than a reckoning with the past.

M.F.

London, July 1994

CONTENTS

LIST OF ILLUSTRATIONS

1. An official demonstration on the occasion of the 'First *Deutschland-treffen*', 25–9 May 1950.
   SED-Bildarchiv, SAPMO-BArch, Berlin

2. President Wilhelm Pieck at a 'Heroes of Work' ceremony on the 'Activists' Day', 13 October 1950.
   SED-Bildarchiv, SAPMO-BArch, Berlin

3. Referendum against the 'remilitarization of Germany', 3 June 1951.
   SED-Bildarchiv, SAPMO-BArch, Berlin

4. Suppression of the Uprising on 17 June 1953 by Soviet tanks.
   Bundesarchiv Koblenz

5. A ceremony inaugurating building works on 31 August 1955 at the lignite and coke works, 'Kombinat "Schwarze Pumpe"'.
   SED-Bildarchiv, SAPMO-BArch, Berlin

6. The National People's Army (*Nationale Volksarmee*) swearing the oath of allegiance, 30 April 1956.
   SED-Bildarchiv, SAPMO-BArch, Berlin

7. A *Jugendweihe* ceremony in March 1958.
   SED-Bildarchiv, SAPMO-BArch, Berlin

8. May Day demonstration, 1 May 1960.
   SED-Bildarchiv, SAPMO-BArch, Berlin

9. A *Roter Treff* meeting in a machine factory in Halle, 1960.
   SED-Bildarchiv, SAPMO-BArch, Berlin

10. A forcible removal in Bernauer Strasse on 24 September 1961.
    SED-Bildarchiv, SAPMO-BArch, Berlin

11. A parade of the National People's Army, 1 May 1962.
    SED-Bildarchiv, SAPMO-BArch, Berlin

12. Erich Honecker signing the Helsinki Final Declaration in August 1975.
    SED-Bildarchiv, SAPMO-BArch, Berlin

13. Young Pioneers on a holiday camp in Crimea in the 1970s.
    SED-Bildarchiv, SAPMO-BArch, Berlin

14. The 'summit meeting' (*Spitzengespräch*) between leaders of Church and state, 6 March 1978.
    Bundesarchiv Koblenz

1

INTERPRETING THE EAST GERMAN DICTATORSHIP

ON Wednesday, 21 September 1961, Sieglinde M., a sixth-form pupil in
Anklam, Neubrandenburg, came to school wearing a black pullover. For
this, she was expelled from school and forced to 'work in production'.

Sieglinde M. was not alone. The entire class 12*b* came to school on that
day wearing black. This was precisely the problem, as far as the East
German political leadership was concerned. Most teachers chose to ignore
this surprising display of uniformity. But in a break between classes, one
teacher asked the reason why the class was dressed in black. A pupil replied:
'We are bearing our future to the grave.'[1] The previous day the East German
parliament, the Volkskammer, had passed the defence law requiring all
young people to perform national service in the National People's Army (the
NVA); five and a half weeks earlier, on 13 August 1961, the last escape
route to the West had been sealed with the closing of the border around
West Berlin. The young people of the GDR were effectively imprisoned in
their own state, condemned to a life of militarization, of indoctrination to
hatred and fear. In a strikingly simple demonstration of their dissent, class
12*b* turned up to school dressed in black.

Sieglinde herself had not particularly supported the action: as her wid-
owed mother, a daily cleaner and home help, put it, 'My daughter's punishment is too harsh . . . That Wednesday, she was forced to put on a black
pullover.' The ringleader who had instigated the action appears to have
been one Rainer P., father a locksmith, mother a shop assistant and 'very
religious', although her son had no strong connections with the Church.
Rainer and a couple of friends persuaded all their classmates to wear black
clothes that day.

In a Western democracy, such an action would have been a minor,
passing incident in the tapestry of school life. In some schools it might
perhaps have been frowned upon, penalized; in others, such an action

---

[1] SAPMO-BArch, IV 2/905/27, report of 26 Sept. 1961 concerning 'reaktionäre Vorgänge in
der Erweiterten Oberschule in Anklam Bezirk Neubrandenburg'.

would have been applauded as an exemplary display of democratic initiative and political awareness among young people. Not so in the GDR of the early 1960s. For what was interpreted as a symbolic act of insubordination, indeed of treason against the state, the pupils involved were expelled from school, denied the chance to take the school-leaving exam, a prerequisite for university entry (the *Abitur*), and sent into manual labour. The two alleged ringleaders were arrested and imprisoned. A number of teachers were fired. Parents were brought to admit their own failings in the political education of their children, and were forced to agree that the sentences passed were the just and appropriate response to their children's grotesque and entirely unacceptable misdemeanours. The parents' obsequious and miserable admissions of failure in parenting, accompanied by professions of loyalty to the state and promises that their children would work hard to rehabilitate themselves and gain new chances in the future as loyal citizens of the GDR, were complemented by expressions of synthetic outrage on the part of apparently entirely unrelated 'members of the population' applauding the harsh measures meted out by the state. Meetings were called to mobilize teachers, party activists, and local pillars of the community to discuss and evaluate the incident and its implications. A report on the 'counter-revolutionary' demonstration of the sixth-formers was sent to the highest political decision-making body in the state, the centre of real power, the Politburo, with personal copies to the head of state and party, Walter Ulbricht, and to the former leader of the youth organization and later successor as head of party and state, Erich Honecker; the reverberations spread across the entire GDR.

An investigation by the district and regional party organizations and the State Security Police, the Stasi, revealed that political control within the school was slack and the teaching establishment unreliable. Three teachers who had taught there during the Third Reich, including the former Director, were still employed at the school; many other teachers were their former pupils, educated under Nazi auspices. The Communist Party (SED) organization within the school needed tightening up, while even the Secretary of the Free German Youth Organization, the FDJ, had played what was described as a 'politically negative role'. In early October, a strongly worded letter was sent to each and every regional and district party organization, instigating a major investigation into conditions in schools throughout the GDR. Not surprisingly, many another nest of pluralism and political unreliability was revealed, hitherto relatively untouched by the intrusive hand of the would-be all-pervasive state.

The incident reveals much about the GDR—and about its capture in documents. It reveals the difficult legacy with which the communist leadership had to grapple: the legacy of twelve years of Nazi rule and a less than committed subject population. It reveals the quite absurd and in principle unrealizable goal of attaining the total ideological subordination of this population, to be achieved by total party control of all aspects of social and individual life, reaching even into the sphere of the family and parenting as an instrument of political indoctrination and subordination to the higher collective purposes of the state. Against all the realities of individual differences—for which there was little or no respect—the party sought to achieve uniformity in pursuit of a better future: the higher end was deemed to justify the means, including the use of the secret police in conjunction with party discipline, afflicting the lives of millions of people. And in the process of seeking to sweep away the vestiges of Nazi rule and construct a new and better society, the party and its affiliated organizations observed, investigated, recorded, and sought to influence and control every last aspect of people's lives under what became known as 'actually existing socialism' in the GDR.

These records, collected and centralized with legendary Prussian efficiency, are now open: life under the surface of the apparently most successful and stable state in the communist bloc is now available for inspection. And even the most cursory exploration of these records reveals that there was a lot more seething under the surface than was ever suspected. This book seeks to open up some aspects of the range of popular opinion, of modes of accommodation, subordination, and dissent in the East German dictatorship; it seeks to explore the ways in which some East Germans came to terms with their regime and led what seemed to be normal lives, while others sought to challenge that apparent normality, to query the imposed rules of the game and explore the possibilities for change. And it analyses the conditions under which such challenges could make a contribution to effecting real and irreversible change, as the experiment of the first workers' and peasants' state on German soil was swept away by the first successful and peaceful revolution in German history.

The contested history of the GDR

The German Democratic Republic was a creation of the Cold War. In origins an artificial state, with a communist regime imposed in the Soviet zone of occupied Germany, it lacked indigenous legitimacy—whether national or political—from the outset. Created by Soviet power, the East German communist government floundered when the Soviet Union was no longer prepared to sustain its repressive regime. Predicated on military division, the German Democratic Republic collapsed when the precondition of division, the Wall, was breached. And throughout the forty years of its existence, the GDR was deeply influenced by the existence of a second German state, the vastly more affluent and democratic Federal Republic of Germany, in the West.

Yet prior to the collapse of communist rule in 1989, Western commentators had tended to consider the GDR a relatively successful communist state; indeed a surprisingly successful communist state, given the inherently unpromising conditions. (Who would have sought to found a communist regime on the ruins of Hitler's Germany?) In contrast to its neighbours in the Soviet bloc, the GDR did indeed seem to be performing very smoothly on a number of fronts. Overcoming the initial problem—peculiar to East Germany among Soviet bloc countries—of the lack of intrinsic legitimacy as a nation state, the GDR gained international recognition with the completion of *Ostpolitik* in 1972 and entry into the United Nations as a full voting member in 1973. In the course of the 1970s and 1980s, as the two Germanies pursued the new policy of '*rapprochement* through small steps', with a normalization of relations between what the West Germans now officially viewed as two German states in one German nation, the existence of a separate East German state came more and more to be viewed as a permanent feature of the political landscape. Particularly among the younger generation of West Germans who had no personal memories of Germany prior to division, the existence of two Germanies came to be taken for granted; and both politicians and scholarly analysts, while remembering the West German constitution's formal commitment to work for reunification, increasingly saw this as in reality a fading chimera, at worst a dangerous demand of the nationalist right.[2]

The apparent permanence of the GDR as a feature of the geopolitical landscape in the latter half of the twentieth century began to be reflected in the academic literature. Denunciations of communist political repression began to be complemented by more differentiated analyses of the character of GDR society. On the domestic front, it appeared, the East German regime had worked to establish an at least tenable form of implicit social contract.[3] The East German economy developed, despite a number of initial disadvantages and changes of course, to become, by the early 1980s, an

---

[2] See e.g. Richard J. Evans, *In Hitler's Shadow* (London: I. B. Tauris, 1989), 105–6.
[3] Cf. D. Staritz, *Geschichte der DDR, 1949–1985* (Frankfurt-on-Main: Suhrkamp, 1985).

economic pillar of the Soviet bloc. According to the World Bank in Washington, by 1984 it had become the twelfth most important economy in the world, having the highest per capita income of all the socialist bloc countries.[4] Under Honecker, social policies were pursued—such as improving housing conditions, pensions, maternity benefits—in combination with what has been called a form of 'consumer socialism', to allow East Germans an at least moderately comfortable material existence, certainly superior to that of their neighbours in Poland. While material deprivation undoubtedly did exist, there were no serious food shortages such as to provide the basis for food riots or mass political uprisings prior to 1989.

Indeed, it is this last feature which perhaps most clearly marked out the East German regime in comparison with neighbouring communist states. After the uprising of June 1953, the GDR experienced no mass political instability comparable to the upheavals which rocked Hungary in 1956, Czechoslovakia in 1968, or Poland at recurrent intervals, most notably in 1956, 1970, 1980–1, and intermittently throughout the 1980s. In political terms, the GDR appeared one of the most stable and quiescent of the Soviet bloc states.

Even in the cultural sphere, broadly defined, and despite the obvious constraints of censorship, modest successes had been achieved by the 1980s. East German writers such as Christa Wolf and Stefan Heym aroused considerable international interest and acclaim, while more critical cultural spirits were readily exported to the common language community, where they enjoyed automatic citizenship rights, of West Germany. As far as popular culture was concerned, international sporting successes were promoted to raise a sense of national pride; and while it can be scarcely credited as a 'cultural achievement' of the GDR, the near-universal watching of Western television was officially tolerated as a form of nightly collective political anaesthesia. Under Honecker's rule, it appeared that passive conformity was an acceptable compromise if outright ideological commitment was unattainable.

And then came the 'gentle revolution' (sanfte Revolution) of autumn 1989—which was met by almost universal surprise. It appeared momentarily that, for apparently the first time in their history, the Germans had experienced—indeed made—a successful revolution, making up for the alleged historical failures of 1525, 1848, 1918. This was, moreover, even a

[4] For the East German economy, see e.g. Stephen Frowen, 'The Economy of the German Democratic Republic', in D. Childs (ed.), *Honecker's Germany* (London: Allen and Unwin, 1985); Ian Jeffries and Manfred Melzer (eds.), *The East German Economy* (London: Croom Helm, 1987).

non-violent revolution, with remarkably little bloodshed. The old regime more or less dissolved itself. And yet, within a very short time, this very fact led to the querying of the notion of revolution. Doubts were raised as to whether the East Germans had indeed freed themselves, as to whether there had ever been any real revolution. Was it not rather that the Soviet Union had given up its puppet state—and, with the loss of Soviet force, the regime had simply imploded? And did this not mean, then, that the GDR was after all, for the whole of its history, simply an illegitimate state upheld solely by the use or threat of Soviet force?

Historical accounts of East German history written prior to 1989 by no means spoke with one voice.[5] There were certain notable cleavages, corresponding partly, but never very neatly, with disciplinary boundaries, political differences, and the broader context of writing.[6] Early emphasis on Soviet domination of a 'puppet regime' gave way, in the period of *Ostpolitik*, to a wide range of approaches to a regime that seemed to be here to stay. While Germanists explored the nuances of new variants of 'German inwardness', Western political scientists and 'Kremlinologists' of the GDR delineated institutional structures and sought to read between the lines on official policies and personalities. Right-wingers denouncing the GDR as 'totalitarian' appeared to be arguing from an increasingly embattled corner against the tendencies of neo-Marxists, left-wingers, and even moderate liberals to develop a more differentiated picture of a regime and a society which the governments of the Western world, and most immediately the Federal Republic of Germany, were treating as an acceptable partner irrespective of the fundamental denial of certain basic human rights.[7]

[5] For a range of Western accounts of the GDR written in what retrospectively appears to have been its heyday (if it ever enjoyed such a thing) see e.g. K. von Beyme and H. Zimmermann (eds.), *Policymaking in the German Democratic Republic* (Aldershot: Gower, 1984); D. Childs, *The GDR: Moscow's German Ally* (London: Allen and Unwin, 1985); M. Dennis, *German Democratic Republic* (London: Pinter, 1988); G. E. Edwards, *GDR Society and Social Institutions* (London: Macmillan, 1985) (a particularly rosy account); H. Krisch, *The German Democratic Republic* (Boulder, Colo.: Westview Press, 1985); M. McCauley, *The GDR since 1945* (London: Macmillan, 1983); K. Sontheimer and W. Bleek, *The Government and Politics of East Germany* (London: Hutchinson, 1975); Staritz, *Geschichte der DDR*. For my own general account of the GDR, see my *The Divided Nation: Germany 1918–1990* (London: Fontana, 1991; New York: Oxford University Press, 1992), part 2. A standard pre-*Wende* official East German history of the GDR may be found in H. Heitzer, *GDR: An Historical Outline* (Dresden: Verlag Zeit im Bild, 1981).

[6] For an overview of the state of research on the GDR and different approaches prior to 1989, see Hermann Weber, *Die DDR 1945–1986* (Munich: Oldenbourg, 1988), part 2: 'Grundprobleme und Tendenzen der Forschung'; see also my *The Two Germanies 1945–1990: Problems of Interpretation* (Basingstoke: Macmillan, 1992).

[7] For a post-*Wende* critique of these tendencies, see Jens Hacker, *Deutsche Irrtümer: Schönfärber und Helfershelfer der SED-Diktatur im Westen* (Frankfurt-on-Main and Berlin: Ullstein, 1992).

With the collapse of the GDR, the whole context of interpretation has dramatically changed. Not only has the empirical basis been expanded exponentially, beyond the wildest dreams (or nightmares) of any archival historian; the very terms of the debate, the categories of analysis, the political implications of the argument, have also been radically transformed. In the immediate aftermath of regime collapse, there are inevitably an infinite variety of factors complicating and cross-cutting any 'objective' historical debate. Not least among these are the multiple personal and political interests of participants and observers, which colour perspectives and concepts, explanations and justifications. Selective perceptions of facets of the past, often only implicit presuppositions about what was inevitable and what was accidental, carry an added freight in the context of the pressures of restructuring in a post-dictatorial society suffering, on some views, from a degree of 'colonization' by the West which complicates any 'coming to terms with the past'.[8] Additionally, a continuing stream of selective and partial revelations, often reflecting more on the interests of the present than the realities of the past, continually serves to transform both the interpretive framework and the ostensible 'knowledge base' on which any overall historical interpretation is constructed. The interests of journalists and politicians may both coincide and collide with those of the former subjects and alleged victims of history, and of historians from a wide range of theoretical and methodological traditions. Memories challenge reconstructions; personal experience queries documentary evidence; the sands on which any new interpretation is to be constructed are constantly shifting, as the archival remnants of the dictatorship are denounced as distortions, the memoirs as cover-ups, analyses as politically motivated and one-sided. The vehemence and heat with which debates are conducted, not only on the subject-matter of GDR history, but even on who should be permitted to undertake research into it, are quite striking.[9]

In any event, the current picture of the GDR is shifting. It is clearly too early to attempt any sort of definitive synthesis: it will take many years of intensive research on specific areas and topics to provide the empirical basis from which any such synthesis could emerge. But it is not too early to suggest some interpretive hypotheses, some conceptual categories, and lines of further inquiry. Contemporary historians must to some extent seek to

[8] Cf. Manfred Kossok, 'Im Gehäuse der selbstverschuldeten Unmündigkeit, oder, Umgang mit der Geschichte', in Dietmar Keller, Hans Modrow, and Herbert Wolf (eds.), *Ansichten zur Geschichte der DDR* (Bonn and Berlin: PDS/Linke Liste im Bundestag, 1993).

[9] Exemplified for example in the debates on the Institute for Studies in Contemporary History (Forschungsschwerpunkt Zeithistorische Studien) in Potsdam; cf. my article, 'New Historikerstreit, Missed Opportunity, or New Beginning?', *German History*, 12: 2 (1994), 203–7.

stand back from partial standpoints, selective and value-laden perspectives, in order to impose an analytical framework which does justice to the multiple meanings and motivations of contemporaries as they interacted in real historical processes to produce particular outcomes. In this somewhat provisional spirit, the current work seeks to explore and expose aspects of the inner workings of the GDR as they are now beginning to appear in the posthumous dissection of its domestic anatomy. The naming of the parts, the understanding of their interactions and effects, are processes which will engage the attention of historians and the wider public for many years; this is but a preliminary contribution to this process.

Explaining the East German dictatorship

The German Democratic Republic was 'democratic' only in the very specific, communist interpretation of that term: democratic centralism, as any cursory glance at the history of the Soviet bloc will reveal, was in practice more centralist than democratic, a dictatorship from above rather than government by (at least intermittent) consent from below.[10] The 'laws of history', as interpreted through the lens of Marxism-Leninism, implied that the party had to adopt a vanguard role, leading on behalf of a people who were not yet 'mature' enough to recognize and act on their own 'real' interests. The notion of 'false consciousness' neatly wrote off any need to legitimize party rule through free elections—at least once such elections had revealed the lack of majority support for communist rule. In what was effectively a one-party state, once the smaller parties and mass organizations had been coordinated within the communist-dominated 'National Front', there was no space for legitimate opposition. 'Total claims' were made on the people, in the attempt to achieve ideological conformity and compliance with party rule; and coercion was of course the other side of the political coin.

But to recognize that the GDR was a dictatorship is not to say very much about the specific character of this dictatorship. Dictatorships vary in a large number of respects. The Nazi dictatorship, to take a very immediate

---

[10] This is of course not the place to enter into debates on the character and shortcomings of Western 'representative' rather than 'participatory' democracies, or topics such as the alleged 'democratic deficit' in institutions such as the European Union. Here, as throughout this book, the attempt is made to understand the workings of the East German polity in its own terms, not as measured against (and found wanting in comparison with) some implicit idealized standard. The notion that 'West is best', which was deeply imbued in analyses from the Cold War period, may be one which it is hard to shake off; but for the purposes of sober historical analysis, the attempt must be made.

example for comparative purposes, was inaugurated with a large measure of popular approval; its 'totalitarian' claims were belied by somewhat chaotic, dualistic structures of rule; its legitimacy revolved to a high degree around a single, charismatic leader figure, Adolf Hitler; and it was ultimately brought down, not by revolution from within, but by massive defeat in total war. As we shall see in the course of this book, attempts to lump together the GDR and the Third Reich as instances of 'totalitarian dictatorship' may of course serve the purpose of political denunciation; but the differences between the two dictatorships prove in many respects to be infinitely more striking than any similarities evoked by the concept of dictatorship.[11] Some refinement of the analysis is clearly required.

Within any dictatorship, there may be larger or smaller numbers of people implicated in the processes of making decisions, executing policies, colluding in repressive practices. The people may be more or less willing subjects of dictatorial rule. As the debates over the role of Hitler in Nazi racial policies show, it may be very convenient, in post-dictatorial conditions, to criminalize a small gang of evil men at the top—effectively to elevate them to a plane of absolute evil—and implicitly to exonerate the larger masses of the passive population. But political convenience may not necessarily serve the purposes of historical clarification.

The experience of 1945, and the sediments of Cold War diatribes, have left their mark on current debates about the GDR. Many strands in these debates operate in mutually contradictory directions. On the one hand, there is currently something of a tendency to castigate large numbers of former GDR citizens for having been active accomplices or conformist fellow-travellers (*Mitläufer*) in the dictatorship; on the other, there is an equally ahistorical tendency to elevate an undifferentiated notion of 'the people' into heroes of opposition, or at least victims of oppression, in a brutal and repressive state. These gut reactions, widely prevalent in journalistic analyses and instant political interpretations, also inform key historical accounts of the dictatorship.

Political and moral attitudes inevitably colour perceptions in contemporary history (as they do, although perhaps with less immediacy or at least political effect, in all historical periods). Perhaps the most widespread perception about the GDR, deriving quite clearly from Cold War views, is that there is really very little to explain: the GDR was on this view quite simply an illegitimate state, created by and dependent on force, a pliant puppet of the Soviet Union.

---

[11] Some comparisons between the GDR and the Third Reich are drawn more systematically in the concluding chapter, below.

These issues and perceptions will be the subject of detailed analysis throughout this book, but the underlying principles deserve some preliminary discussion. A dictatorship implies of course that the bottom line of politics is force. In the wake of the GDR's collapse, a combination of factual revelations about the extent of security surveillance combined with a complex set of psychological processes to highlight this aspect to a far greater extent than in the period of *Ostpolitik*.

There is no doubt that coercion played a key role in East German history: the presence of Soviet tanks, the existence of the Wall, the less visible but no less insidious, frightening coercion exercised by the state security force, the Stasi, were all central features of GDR history. Because, in particular, of the highly symbolic division of Germany's former capital city, Berlin, repression was quite predictably emphasized in Western political histories prior to 1989, particularly in chronologically structured narratives of high politics which devoted little attention to the inner life of the GDR.[12] Perhaps somewhat surprisingly, it is also characteristic of more recent interpretations by East German social historians. A fascinating retrieval by Stefan Wolle and Armin Mitter of facets of popular opinion at key moments in the GDR's history repeatedly emphasizes that the GDR rested ultimately on, as they put it, 'Soviet bayonets'.[13] And among Eastern Europeans more generally, emerging from decades of oppression, the notion of 'totalitarianism'— for a long time discredited among Western academics—has been enjoying something of a revival.

But to refer to the threat or use of force alone—while a very real, and very important, factor—is not a sufficient explanation of the peculiar characteristics and pattern of development of the East German dictatorship, nor of its ultimate demise. For a number of reasons, a more differentiated analysis is required of the domestic workings of the GDR.

First, to refer to the threat or use of Soviet force does not help in distinguishing between, and explaining, differing degrees of stability and instability in different communist bloc states. True, the GDR was unique in having 300,000 Soviet troops stationed on its soil; it was also unique in representing the front line of the Cold War, the potential flashpoint of central Europe, in a way that Poland, and even Czechoslovakia (with its border with West Germany), were not. The GDR had a strategic military

---

[12] For a brief history of the GDR which both implicitly—for example, in its selection of illustrations—and explicitly emphasizes force as a major factor in the GDR's stability, see the first edition (written of course pre-1989) of Henry Ashby Turner, *The Two Germanies since 1945* (New Haven: Yale University Press, 1987).

[13] Armin Mitter and Stefan Wolle, *Untergang auf Raten* (Munich: C. Bertelsmann Verlag, 1993).

importance not shared by its immediate neighbours. But these differences did not prevent Soviet tanks from rolling into Hungary in 1956, or Czechoslovakia in 1968; nor did they prevent the installation of martial law under General Jaruzelski in Poland in 1981, to forestall the possibility of Soviet military intervention. The threat of repression by Soviet military might was common to all the Soviet bloc states, whether or not troops were permanently stationed on the soil of those states. It cannot in itself alone explain the apparently peculiar stability of the East German regime.

Secondly, the focus on repression is not actually very revealing. It does not tell us very much about degrees of political compliance, or acquiescence in their own domination, to be found among the East German population. A further, rather prevalent popular view of the GDR is that it was 'typically German': on this view, good German subjects—as always in German history—elevated the duty of obedience to the secular ruler, good or bad, above any form of civic courage. The sins of the oppressors were thus complemented by the sins of the oppressed. But how far was the East German dictatorship actually sustained by degrees of complicity and compromise? How far was it—perhaps—supported by belief in higher ideals, and a determination to tolerate imperfections and distortions in the difficult circumstances of the post-Nazi present, in the hope of building a truly better future? How should forms of compromise and collaboration, or indeed mere conformity and passive acquiescence, be interpreted, given the post-1989 witch-hunt and denunciation of those who had come to terms with the system? It is highly important that there should be a differentiated and sensitive understanding of the East German dictatorship if Germans are to come to terms, once again, with a difficult past.

Nor does a focus on repression alone tell us very much about modes of resistance—passive refusals, more active dissent, or opposition—and their effects on the regime. Why, for long periods, did there appear to be relatively little active dissent? Under what circumstances, as a result of what causes, and with what consequences, did more energetic challenges to the regime arise? How did emergent domestic political activism combine with changing external circumstances to help, ultimately, to bring down the communist regime? In recent years, the social history of the Third Reich has developed in extremely interesting directions, with increasingly sophisticated theoretical discussions of modes of nonconformity, dissent, and resistance to Nazi domination.[14] How do patterns of co-operation and

[14] For an outstanding analysis in English of the state of debate in the early 1990s, see Ian Kershaw, *The Nazi Dictatorship* (London: Edward Arnold, 3rd edn., 1993), particularly the new ch. 8 on the question of 'Resistance without the People?'

dissent in the GDR compare with popular political orientations under the preceding German dictatorship, that of Adolf Hitler? These are legitimate and highly important historical (and indeed also moral) questions, which are simply missed, or effectively dismissed, by a one-sided emphasis on repression.

More generally, approaches which stress repression and force as a sufficient explanation of the stability of dictatorial regimes cannot account for the conditions under which internal resistance and opposition may arise and be effective. Such approaches, rather fatalistically, tend to imply—however unintentionally—that people cannot affect the circumstances in which repression is sustained. In many ways, the particular manner in which the GDR came to an end—in the 'gentle revolution' of the autumn of 1989—itself proves the fallacy of this assumption.

But even the reverse assumption—that mass outright opposition necessarily leads to the downfall of dictatorships—must itself be examined more carefully. Many approaches to the GDR which do concede the notion of a revolution from within rather than merely the collapse of repressive force from without stress the fact of widespread discontent, evidenced dramatically in the rising tide of refugees once the Iron Curtain began to be riddled with holes in the summer of 1989. But discontent alone was not sufficient to fell the state from within: it had failed to do so in 1953, and had been a permanent, if fluctuating, factor in the history of the GDR. That a lot of people did not like the GDR is certainly true. But this alone is not sufficient to explain either its longevity and apparent stability over forty years, or its sudden and unexpected downfall within a matter of weeks. A more complex analysis is clearly required.

In short, there is more to the inner history of the GDR than the Cold War division of Europe and the presence of Soviet tanks. However illegitimate in origins, however repressive in practice, 'actually existing socialism' actually existed. People lived in the GDR, and in different ways they came to terms with the constrained parameters of their existence: they participated in the youth and trade union organizations, the women's and cultural leagues, the work brigades, they joined political parties, they played the system to further their own and their families' goals and aspirations. In the course of forty years, the society of East Germany diverged very considerably from that of West Germany; so far, indeed, that the cry of 'Wir sind ein Volk!', so prevalent in the heady days of late 1989, soon gave way to the surprised caricaturing and often mutual hostility of Ossis and Wessis in the more troubled months of 1990 and beyond.

With the opening of the East German archives, we are now for the first time able to dig a little below surface appearances, caricatures, and preconceptions, and explore some of the realities of everyday life in the German Democratic Republic. It may, however, be objected that the archives lie. This is certainly, in one very obvious sense, the case. All historical documents, from whatever historical context, are artefacts of particular motives and situations, written with certain intentions and audiences in mind; they must therefore be the subject of appropriate evaluation and interpretation. In some respects, the documentary evidence of the GDR may more easily be evaluated than that of more remote states, where there are fewer possibilities of comparing data from several sources, and of contextualizing fragments of evidence. In the case of the GDR, the political ideology is all too clear; even when the sources use words with almost the opposite meaning to that generally employed ('democratic forces', 'hostile-negative', and so on) it is generally abundantly clear to what is being referred. A more problematic facet of the East German sources is the way in which, over the years—and particularly from the late 1960s onwards—many sources are either so superficial and opaquely positive in tone as to say virtually nothing, or tend to exaggerate wildly in unpredictable directions (as in Stasi accounts which seek to overfulfil quotas by minimizing numbers of dissidents or exaggerating numbers of unofficial informers). Nevertheless, the sheer vastness of the documentary basis for analyses of the GDR provides tremendous opportunities for constructing plausible hypotheses which may turn out to be validated by appropriate further research; moreover, for all its potential pitfalls, the possibility of oral history provides additional avenues for social historical investigation.[15]

Using a wide range of sources, and exploring certain prevalent popular mentalities, patterns of political attitude, and behaviour at different stages of the GDR's history, it rapidly becomes clear that some reassessment of traditional views is required. Let me preview the approach of this book.

Towards an anatomy of patterns of power and political culture

To analyse the anatomy of the East German dictatorship means to examine the inner workings of the state and society: to look at the parts separately, at their functions, interrelations, and patterns of development. This book is not, then, a chronological life history of the GDR, its activities, and its

[15] For oral history carried out prior to 1989, see Lutz Niethammer, Alexander von Plato, and Dorothee Wierling, *Die volkseigene Erfahrung. Eine Archäologie des Lebens in der Industrieprovinz der DDR* (Berlin: Rowohlt, 1991); for recent research using a range of archival sources and methodological techniques, see Hartmut Kaelble, Jürgen Kocka, and Hartmut Zwahr (eds.), *Sozialgeschichte der DDR* (Stuttgart: Klett-Cotta, 1994); Jürgen Kocka (ed.), *Historische DDR-Forschung: Aufsätze und Studien* (Berlin: Akademie-Verlag, 1993).

relations with the outside world, but rather an exploration of its inner processes. Nor is it an attempt to present all facets of the inner life, but rather an attempt to highlight the most salient aspects of the ways in which the dictatorship was sustained and the manner in which it finally came to an end. It is an exploration of the character of power, conformity, and dissent in the GDR, seeking to delineate the structure and functioning of this particular dictatorship in comparison with others, and particularly in comparison with the Nazi dictatorship to which the GDR is often, implicitly or explicitly, equated.

To analyse an anatomy one must know what are the parts. Most accounts of the GDR presuppose a certain vocabulary. Prior to 1989, that vocabulary was largely determined by the character of what could be known, as far as Westerners were concerned; it tended, therefore, to be heavily institutional. Political scientists described in detail the structures of party and state, of constitutions and social organizations. Texts were illuminated—if that is not a misnomer in this case—with diagrams of hierarchical structures, of organizational tiers, of pyramids of power. Lists of abbreviations sought to provide a guide to the telephone-directory quality of the structures of life in a communist state.

This institutional analysis is by no means misplaced. As we shall see, the institutional invasion and control of society was highly developed in the GDR, which can be seen, as only the German language is capable of putting it, as a *durchherrschte Gesellschaft*, a *verstaatlichte Gesellschaft*—terms implying a society virtually drenched through by, in the sclerotic grip of, the state. But the conceptual framework determining the organization of this book is based not only on institutional structures of power and organizations, but also on patterns of political orientation. It seeks, in effect, to anatomize modes of political culture in changing structural conditions.

In the chapters which follow, an attempt is made to understand the ways in which different groups developed distinctive approaches to the regime, and to understand the peculiar features of the East German dictatorship which distinguished it, as far as patterns of popular political culture were concerned, both from other communist states and from the preceding Nazi dictatorship. In the process of this exploration, a specific theory of domination is developed: key factors are identified which help to explain the stages of development and ultimate demise of the East German dictatorship.

First of all, there was *some* change in at least the degree of outward conformity, and—not quite the same thing, and not quite to the same extent—of inner acceptance of the regime. But this partial acceptance (which is explored below) was achieved—to the extent that it was achieved at all—at best in the early to mid-1970s. The history of the GDR can be written neither as basically a history of constant, if for the most part suppressed, implicit civil war between rulers and ruled, as some recent East German authors, most notably Stefan Wolle and Armin Mitter, have sought to do; nor as essentially a quiet society of private niches, as popularized by a prominent West German observer of the 1970s, Günter Gaus.[16] It was more complex: it was both of these, and more; the relative proportions of the population in one or another form of orientation changed over time; and neither picture adequately explains the overall pattern of development over forty years.

It should be emphasized at the outset that there was a history to the GDR: in other words, it changed over time. Many interpretations are overly static in their assumptions: the 'people' were 'always' against the regime; the regime was always repressive; once given the chance, people got out; and so on. In fact, a curve of attitudes can be traced, with key generational shifts in orientation and behaviour. There does appear to have been a period of relative stability in the 1970s, when at least the system functioned rather more smoothly than either earlier or later. More people were at least outwardly compliant, the political structures operated relatively efficiently, the economy and domestic social policies appeared to give more grounds for hope than alarm. Yet, despite changes in the degree of willing or unwilling compliance with the regime over the years, a measure of discontent never-theless remained relatively constant: there was widespread dislike of living in an artificially created, intrusive police state, surrounded by a fortified border, with a relatively low standard of living compared to the affluent Western brother, throughout the history of the GDR. What changed were two other factors of major historical importance.

The first has to do with the political authorities and their modes of dealing with dissent. In determining the actual historical implications of widespread dissatisfaction, it is essential to examine whether the political and repressive authorities presented a united front, intervening decisively, and whether functionaries at the grass roots operated effectively or not. Here, some interesting developments emerge. The domestic capacity for control, intervention, and repression was relatively underdeveloped in 1953, allowing the June uprising to develop and spread; but the failings of the SED state were at that time ultimately compensated for by the Soviet Union's intervention. By 1968, the domestic system was far more effective. But in 1989, despite the extraordinary growth in the surveillance and

[16] Mitter and Wolle, *Untergang auf Raten*; Günter Gaus, *Wo Deutschland liegt* (Munich: dtv, 1986; orig. 1983).

security apparatus of the late GDR, for reasons we shall explore in detail below the political capacity to control and ultimately suppress dissent was no longer there.

Secondly, of major importance is the character of challenges to the system of domination. In particular, the growth of organized political activism for change within the system in the course of the 1980s was of great significance. It will be argued below that it was not so much *opposition* to the GDR as the attempt to *reform* and *improve* actually existing socialism which, ironically, ultimately led to its demise. In other words: the extent of disobedience throughout the history of the GDR, and of political expressions of discontent, is far greater than previously imagined. What changed in the 1980s was not the *fact* of political discontent, but rather the cultural flavour, the *goals,* and the forms of *organization* of new varieties of discontent. And, ironically, while dissent up until the 1980s had been largely oppositional in nature—that is, directed *against* the GDR—the dissent of the 1980s sought rather to effect reforms and influence policies *within* the GDR. To reformulate: opposition existed throughout the GDR's history; what was new about the 1980s was inner-GDR grass-roots organized political activism. Thus the story of the destabilization and ultimate demise of the GDR is *not* the story of 'the growth of opposition'; rather, it is the story of the displacement of opposition, or the growth, alongside opposition, of a reformist political activism.

Finally, what was crucial to the historical impact of that political activism was not only the collapse of the external support props of the GDR—the Iron Curtain between the Soviet bloc and the West, the willingness of the Soviet Union to intervene by force—but also, as far as the domestic situation was concerned, the disintegration of collusion as far as functionaries of the regime were concerned. The loss of the will to rule was a crumbling, faltering process; beginning as a series of attempts to retain power through limited and partial concessions, élite responses to challenges from below ultimately snowballed in a progressive loss of party control. Pressure from below was combined with a degree of lability at the top, in the context of wider international upheavals—the classic conditions for a political earthquake. And—last but not least!—the final outcome, the collapse not only of party rule but of the GDR itself as a separate state, was of course a consequence also of the dramatic changes in external circumstances, following the highly symbolic fall of the Wall.

This book, then, seeks to explore patterns of domination, complicity, and dissent in the GDR from its origins to its demise. It examines the mentalities of power, and the power of mentalities: the ways in which élites and subordinate groups viewed their political circumstances and sought to act in the light of their assumptions and goals, their perceived constraints and opportunities. The book attempts to analyse the anatomy of the peculiar contours of power and patterns of popular political culture under the changing economic, social, and political circumstances of the forty years of the GDR's existence. In so doing, it does not attempt to present any kind of complete history of the GDR, nor to rehearse the familiar highpoints of party politics or the articulate arguments of the dissident intelligentsia. Rather, it aims to explore wider patterns of popular experience: to clarify the ways in which a repressive dictatorship was often not actually experienced as such, and was in many ways sustained by a certain complicity within; and to explain the extraordinarily rapid implosion of the regime in the closing months, as rulers backed by guns and tanks capitulated to the demands of 'the people' in the guise of women and children, pastors and production workers, bearing candles and flowers.

PART I

THE CONTOURS OF DOMINATION

THE East German state was not, in intention, clearly separate from 'society'. There was to be *no* area of society uncontrolled by the state, the organization of which was to penetrate even to the most basic, fundamental level of society. The individual was subordinate to the whole: in very altered forms, and under different political colours, the notion of a *Volksgemeinschaft*, a collective entity and common good to which all individual aspirations and attributes must be subordinated, survived the transition from the Nazi dictatorship to the communist dictatorship surprisingly intact.

Because of this, the structures of domination, government, coercion, and control were to extend beyond the obviously political activities of the ruling communist party, and of the smaller, politically subordinate bloc parties and affiliated organizations, into all areas of life which, under a less invasive, more pluralistic form of state might be deemed to belong to a 'private sphere'. Education, the media, sports and leisure, even the family, were all to be controlled and manipulated by the state. Parents had a duty to bring their children up to become loyal, obedient, committed subjects of the communist state; trade unionists were there, not to represent the interests of the workers but to represent the interests of the party; even the Church was to be co-opted in the attempt to contain a potentially unreliable section of the populace. *All* areas of life were observed, manipulated, controlled, in the interests of the alleged greater good of the whole. The end justified the means; individual rights were subordinated to those of 'society', as conceived and defined by the leading force, the SED.

The first part of this book explores the contours of domination in the GDR, the ways in which the communist project led to a high degree of interpenetration of state and society. The regime was in part so stable for so long because of the very success of this intertwining, this sending of roots and tentacles into every area of social life. The 'carriers' of the regime were not merely the party bosses, the full-time functionaries; they were also the cadres and the fellow-travellers, the *Mitläufer*, and even, to some extent, those Protestant Church leaders of completely different moral and religious world-views who nevertheless made their compromises with the realities of power. Part I, in short, explores the structures and mentalities through which power was exercised and control exerted in the forty years during which the GDR appeared to be the most stable state in the communist bloc.

2

STRUCTURES AND MENTALITIES OF POWER

THE GDR was a repressive state. It was a dictatorship. In retrospect, in the moralistic terms of popular debate in united Germany, it has been widely dismissed as an *Unrechtsstaat*, a state operating beyond the realms of law (in implicit or explicit contrast to the West German *Rechtsstaat*). In the aftermath of the GDR's collapse and the opening of the Stasi files, the waves of revelations in the popular press about the extent of Stasi spying on friends and neighbours led to a demonization of all who were in any way involved with the apparatus of power in the GDR. 'Victims' were opposed to 'oppressors'; the world was painted in black-and-white terms, the forces of good pitted against the forces of evil. And in the confused struggle for restitution, rehabilitation, or survival through restructuring, personal bitterness and emotion often served to confuse an already muddy debate.

Yet many of those who lived in the GDR did not experience it in this way. As Mitter and Wolle have aptly pointed out, in the memories of East Germans there appear to have been two very different countries:

Listening to conversations between former citizens of the GDR, one sometimes gets the impression that the people speaking to each other had been living in different countries. Some of them remember the repression, subordination, surveillance, the inadequacies of the economy and the poor provisions, the countless restrictions on freedom, the stupid and dishonest SED propaganda and an education system which, from Kindergarten to University, was designed to elicit the obedience of corpses. The others think back to job security, clear professional prospects, individual welfare, crèche places guaranteed by the state, low rents and the bread roll costing five pennies.[1]

And in the GDR nostalgia that began to creep across eastern Germany in the early 1990s, as rising unemployment and psychological uncertainty cast shadows over the euphoria of the autumn of 1989, many began to see their former state more as a sheltered garden of innocence and security than a grey prison of repression and conformity.

[1] Armin Mitter and Stefan Wolle, *Untergang auf Raten* (Munich: C. Bertelsmann Verlag, 1993), 7.

What then were the realities of power in the GDR? Were all those who upheld the structures of domination really little better than state-sanctioned criminals, sustaining an evil regime of oppression comparable to the preceding Third Reich? Was the whole system and ideology implicitly evil—or was it rather a matter of a few men at the top, pulling the strings of the puppets who unwittingly and for the best of reasons did the bidding of their masters? Were these masters even evil, or merely well-meaning incompetents operating under adverse conditions, and increasingly running down blind alleys? What in fact were the motivations of those who played along with the rules of the game, and participated in the apparatus of power? How did they perceive and justify what they were doing? And how were the structures of domination presented to and experienced by the people?

The purpose of this chapter is not to write yet another history of the SED and affiliated parties and organizations, but rather to try to understand the ways in which the rulers conceived, presented, and legitimated their power, and to delineate the structures of domination in the context of which people came to express the different forms of political accommodation and resistance which form the subject of subsequent chapters. Without first understanding the landscape and images of domination, it is impossible to comprehend the ways in which people sustained, came to terms with, resisted, or sought ultimately to challenge, the edifice of power in the GDR.

Mentalities of power: paternalism and paranoia

The most characteristic feature of the mentalities of power in the GDR, throughout the entire period of its existence, was a curious combination of paternalism and paranoia. These characteristics were partly rooted in the theoretical foundations of communism, and considerably exacerbated by the circumstances in which East German communists had to act.

On the one hand, in principle—and certainly in the original vision of Karl Marx—communism was inspired by the desire to make things better for the mass of the people: to improve living conditions, to enhance opportunities for self-expression and self-realization for all, in a more just and egalitarian society. Once true communist society was attained, on Marx's view, all forms of alienation would have been abolished, and the condition for the free development of each individual would be the condition for the free development of all: there would be no more classes, inequalities, or oppression. On the other hand—and this difficulty, although recognized by Marx, was expressed most clearly in Marxism-Leninism—while the mass of the people were suffering from 'false consciousness' and could not recognize their own 'true' interests, the party had to adopt a 'leading role'. The bourgeois notion of 'democracy', in the sense of recording and acting on the alleged will of the majority of the people, was on this view simply a means of sustaining a system of oppression in which the 'ruling ideas of the age' were the 'ideas of the ruling class'. The party had therefore to adopt a 'vanguard role', which often entailed acting in the supposed 'real' interests of, but against the currently expressed will of, the majority of the people.

These theoretical considerations were given added weight by the experiences of German communists in the turbulent political conditions of early and mid-twentieth-century Germany. For those whose political faith had been forged in the experience of economic chaos and political disintegration in the Weimar Republic, or in the concentration camps of Hitler's Third Reich, there was little to recommend the virtues either of capitalism as an economic system or the capacity of the German people to vote for the right sort of government under a democracy. Just as the Western allies were initially suspicious—and rightly so—of what the West Germans might get up to if not strictly controlled, so too the East German government and its Soviet masters had little faith in the views of the people over whom they began to rule. The difference was, of course, that in the West the majority of people came to accept the system as one which worked and which, most importantly, proved very quickly that it could 'deliver the goods' as far as the economy was concerned, while the East German system never achieved a similar degree of material or political success.[2]

Given the conditions of the GDR's birth, its rulers never felt secure. But the degree of their insecurity is quite extraordinary. Paranoia lay at the root of many of the measures taken by the state. There was the justified fear, right after the collapse of the Third Reich, of the resurgence of former Nazis; this was soon overtaken by witch-hunts and purgings of former Social Democrats, communists who had spent the war years in the West, and others who might deviate from the neo-Stalinist line taken by Ulbricht in the early 1950s. Although from the later 1950s onwards active purging died down, there was a perpetual obsession with the search for the 'class enemy' allegedly undermining the state from within.

There was, more importantly in this non-national state, also the continuing fear of the other Germany in the West. The uncertainty surrounding the very existence, at all, of a separate East German state, and the continued

[2] Degrees of popular support, acquiescence, and discontent in the GDR will be analysed in detail in subsequent chapters.

claims made by the Federal Republic of Germany to speak on behalf of *all* Germans (even after the conclusion of *Ostpolitik*), informed the climate of decision-making, the justifications, prevarications, and aspirations of the élites of East Germany for nearly half a century. The fascist past and the divided, ever tentative, present were thus the two key features which served to sustain at least an outwardly united front.

There were of course different phases and degrees of paranoia, and it is also necessary to separate some of the rhetoric of paranoia from the emotional and rational evaluations of actual dangers and enemies.

The basic legitimation of the GDR was its status as the truly 'anti-fascist' state. For reasons of pragmatic politics as well as principle, the Soviet zone of occupation was subjected to more radical denazification in certain key areas, particularly politics, administration, and education, than were the Western zones. Having facilitated the dual processes of socio-economic transformation as well as communist seizure of key positions of control, denazification served a further function of effective whitewashing and the fostering of a collective amnesia for the allegedly innocent 'workers and peasants' who had been 'liberated' from 'fascist oppression' under the Nazis by the Red Army. The radical restructuring and turnover of personnel which occurred in the Soviet zone/GDR were contrasted with the allegedly lukewarm and incomplete processes of denazification in the West. The communists who ran the GDR in the 1950s could with some justification contrast their records of resistance to Nazi oppression (even if conducted from the relative safety of Stalin's Soviet Union) with the more dubious political pasts of individuals such as Hans Globke, Adenauer's chief aide in the Chancellery, and formerly official commentator on the Nuremberg Race Laws of 1935, or some of the former Nazis who held high cabinet positions (not least the Minister for Refugees, former SS-member Oberländer, and later, in 1966–9, the West German Chancellor and former NSDAP member Kurt Georg Kiesinger). In the official East German view, West Germany represented continuity with the Third Reich, allowing both the Nazi past and the Western present to be equally denigrated as 'fascist'.

In the post-1989 era of denunciation of a communist dictatorship, the attraction of the anti-fascist promise of the very early years of the GDR should not be overlooked. It was sufficient to bring back many left-wingers from exile abroad, not to the West but to the East: writers such as Bertolt Brecht and Stefan Heym initially held out higher hopes for a real break with the past and a better future under the red flag of communism than in the continued capitalism of the West, where those entrepreneurs who had benefited from the use of slave labour in the Third Reich were free to reinvest their profits and make further gains under continued conservative capitalism in the 1950s. The 'KZ generation', those who had suffered imprisonment, torture, exile for their left-wing views, were hence inclined to accept the difficulties of the present in the hopes of building a better Germany on the ruins of the Third Reich in the future.

But these hopes were very soon overtaken by the excesses of Stalinism in the early 1950s, when it became increasingly clear that one form of dictatorship was indeed being simply replaced by another. The transformation of the broad 'anti-fascist front' of 1945–6 into the clear domination of the SED, which officially became a Stalinist 'party of a new type' in 1948, marked this change; the handing in of party membership cards in 1950–1, and more particularly the increased repression and political show trials of 1952–3 and the purging of the party in the wake of the June 1953 uprising, consolidated the change. There were very few whose political faith survived the upheavals of 1956 unscathed.

The repression itself could be justified by the other element in the official paranoia: the fear of the West. The very existence of the GDR was never securely guaranteed. First of all, the GDR was essentially created as a pawn and servant of the Soviet Union, even though at times it appeared as if the apprentice had more freedom with the broom than the master. In the early 1950s, however, it was by no means clear that international circumstances would not in one way or another change sufficiently for the Soviet Union to consider giving up its pawn: this was certainly on the serious agenda at the time of the first Stalin Note in March 1952. Moreover, even when such a possibility appeared ever less plausible, the longing for German national unity was sufficiently strong—and not only in the minds of the majority of the population—to provide a destabilizing element. Even in the highest ranks of the SED, there were momentary flirtations with the idea that reunification might, after all, be a preferable goal to that of clinging on to communist power at all costs.[3] If nationalist sentiment could on occasion tempt even the highest of communist party officials, its lures were even more powerful when combined with the prospect of freedom, an enhanced standard of living, and automatic citizenship rights in the West for those who could escape from less privileged positions in the GDR. The open border

[3] This certainly seems to have been the case with Rudolf Herrnstadt, one of the dissident communists who lost his position in the wake of June 1953. Cf. Peter Grieder, 'Tension, Conflict and Opposition in the Leadership of the Socialist Unity Party of Germany (SED), 1946–58', Ph.D. thesis (University of Cambridge, 1995).

was a constant source of haemorrhaging of talent throughout the 1950s, until the last hole was closed with the erection of the Berlin Wall on 13 August 1961.

But even this did not get rid of the problem of the West. The competition of systems was a constant problem for the East German regime, particularly once it had become clear that all the economic promises of overtaking the West were impossible to realize. And the apparent attractions of the West, culturally and politically as well as economically, were a constant challenge to the legitimacy of this non-national state, this drabber part of a divided nation.

Moreover, the problem was not one purely of competition in the popularity stakes with respect to economics, domestic politics, or popular culture: in the Cold War context, the two Germanies were on the front line of potential international conflagration. The remilitarization of the two Germanies and their incorporation into opposing Western and Eastern military alliances symbolized the division of the world between the superpowers in the Cold War era; the clash of world systems and world-views was experienced most acutely on German soil. The West Germans were not only the 'brothers' of the East Germans: they also had to be presented as their bitterest potential enemies. And written into the West German constitution (or 'temporary' Basic Law) was the goal of German reunification—at the expense of the total disappearance of the East German state. The GDR was hence imbued from the start by a sense of massive, existential insecurity.

The insecurity of the East German regime both informed and exacerbated the inculcation of a 'friend/foe' mentality. There was an all-pervading, constant fear of fifth columnism: the 'class enemy' was deemed to be everywhere. Every sign of hostility to the state, every indication that people did not applaud and laud the actions of the rulers, that they dared to think differently, was crudely interpreted as the result of the activities of enemy agents, 'hostile-negative forces' working to undermine the GDR from within. Given this mental frame, it was very hard to accept that there might be genuine reasons for people to raise well-founded criticisms of the workings of East German communism.

The less than perfect circumstances in which the rulers were seeking to transform the GDR into a more perfect society provided the context and legitimation for all the inadequacies of the means. The end might justify the means: but if the starting-point and the conditions of the attempt were particularly unfavourable, the means would have to be all the more nasty. Thus the building of the Wall was justified by the bleeding of manpower:

although humanly unpleasant (some might say, unacceptable in terms of human rights), it was deemed to be the essential prerequisite if conditions were to improve for those who remained. This sort of logic was subsequently used for all measures of dishonesty and deceit, the extent of which will become more apparent when the mechanisms of Stasi repression and manipulation are considered.

As time went by, and the very existence of the GDR appeared less under threat, the paranoia became, in a sense, more institutionalized. From a genuine fear of 'fascists', 'class enemies', and the like in the early years there developed a ritualized rhetoric or demonology, in which very few can have really believed any more. Nevertheless, denunciations of 'imperialist agents' continued to deflect attention from genuine shortcomings at home. Particularly in the later Honecker years, there was ever less willingness to analyse the real causes of distress within the GDR. Living effectively in the centre of an ideological hall of mirrors, with witches and demons painted on the windows, Honecker increasingly refused to recognize the causes, and sought only to suppress the manifestations, of popular discontent under actually existing socialism. Reports from the provinces were increasingly bland depictions of alleged popular support for the regime and its ruler; and those, such as Hans Modrow, First Secretary of Dresden, who sought to draw Honecker's attention to the social realities which lay below the mounting discontent, were disciplined for their pains. Even at the high point of his career in 1986–7—which in retrospect was also the beginning of the end—Honecker still saw the West in relatively paranoid terms: the preparations for Berlin's 750th anniversary reveal the depth of the fears about the 'political line being followed by the West Berlin Senate in preparation for the anniversary celebrations' and the distortions of historical representation which were necessary to present an alternative view of Berlin and East German history.[4] In what were to be the closing months of the regime, the top party leadership appeared to prefer to discard the accounts they received of rising popular unrest, and to ignore the roots of dissatisfaction.

Throughout forty years of separate existence, the GDR was deeply affected by the competition of systems and by the leadership's fear of the GDR's collapse if it were genuinely compared with, or opened to, the West (and events of course were to prove this fear to be well founded). These

---

[4] Cf. IfGA, ZPA, IV 2/2.040/21, 'Zwischenbericht an das Sekretariat des ZK der SED über die Vorbereitung des 750. Jahrestages von Berlin' (31 Jan. 1986); Ministerium für Staatssicherheit, 'Information über den Stand der Vorbereitungen des westberliner Senats auf die 750-Jahr-Feier 1987' (29 Jan. 1986). ·

features, uniquely accentuated in East Germany, exacerbated patterns of party discipline which were common to communist parties elsewhere in the Soviet bloc. The party line was above any individual pangs of conscience or differences of intellectual viewpoint, to an extent virtually unknown in more democratic parties. (The notion of democratic centralism again meant, in the party as in the state, the effective dictatorship of the centre.) The communists had developed a set of disciplinary techniques and psychological means of ensuring iron party discipline, of controlling individuals to make the system of domination work more effectively. These included the preliminary selection and training of cadres—those who could be entrusted with the party's work—and their subsequent manipulation and control. In formalized procedures and sessions of 'criticism and self-criticism', in disciplinary measures and in more drastic sanctions, the party sought to keep those who did its bidding within strict limits, ensuring that orders from above were carried out by those in subordinate positions. The rewards for good behaviour were privileges, promotion, career opportunities; and many party members were also committed to the ultimate goals and ideals. Careerism and opportunism were often complemented by a desire to do a good job, to carry out party work in a more friendly and humane manner than others might do so, to put personal expertise to the service of improving conditions.[5]

But however humane the motives of individual carriers of the system might have been, the system itself was not. The problem in practice was that party ideology and goals were elevated above individuals, above the rights of people in the here and now. If individuals dared to speak out against the system—if they dared to constitute spokes in the works, blocking inexorable progress towards ultimate goals—their value as human beings was to be utterly disregarded. There was, at the heart of the system—however much individual party members might disavow this—an essential disregard for human worth, for the rights of people to hold different views. In its more malign modes, the communist regime utterly despised the human beings over whom the SED ruled: the apparatus of repression was prepared to destroy not just careers, but trusting human relationships and whole lives, in its quest for a mirage in the future.[6]

---

[5] Cf. e.g. *OhnMacht. DDR-Funktionäre sagen aus* (Berlin: Verlag Neues Leben, 1992).

[6] It was partly the discovery that their faith, and all the difficulties this had entailed, had been founded on an unattainable mirage that led to the extraordinary collapse and exhaustion of many former communists in the years after 1989. Some would of course argue that the quest for a better future was not a mirage: that the goal was in principle realizable, and that it was force of unfortunate circumstances which deflected them from its attainment. The argument depends partly on the issue of the viability or otherwise of a planned economy in principle. This case will no doubt remain contentious for many years to come.

The party was inherently manipulative, coercive. Everything was designed to achieve certain ends; and the ends justified the use of virtually any means. There is no doubt that this approach offended, and offends, deeply against any genuine sense of respect for others, recognition of the right to differ and the value of open debate. The Machiavellian tactics of the party were carried to quite inhumane extremes, which were justified in principle with reference to the unfortunate circumstances of the present, as interpreted by the relatively paranoid leadership. In such a system there could be no real trust—or such trust as there was had to be in a sense provisional, aspiring, based on a vision of a better future.[7] Appearances of the present were managed for effect, for intended consequences; they did not reflect any realities.

The regime sought to achieve the *appearance* of popular support and consensus: it sought to claim nearly 100 per cent support for its policies. The party allegedly ruled on behalf of an eternally grateful, if subordinate, *Volk*. And, for all the repressive character of its methods, the ultimate goal was essentially to create a better, more just, and equal society. The problem appeared to be that the conditions of the present were militating against this goal; and that therefore unpleasant means were essential to achieve the ultimate ends.

At the same time, the party was genuinely—if this does not contradict too much what has just been said about its essentially manipulative and inherently dishonest character—paternalistic. It was paternalistic as far as its own members and functionaries were concerned, looking after the interests of its own people. But it was paternalistic too in the much wider sense of seeking to act (at least sometimes) in the perceived interests of the people. 'Alles zum Wohle des Volkes (Everything for the Benefit of the People)' was not a completely empty or cynical slogan.

Most policies were at the least double-edged: designed to gain popular approval and promote a sense of community and a faith in the all-providing state, to be sure; but also with at least a degree of desire to improve the living conditions of the working people so far as political and, particularly, economic constraints allowed. Swimming pools provide a nice illustration

---

[7] It was thus the general cause and ultimate goals, rather than the specific means, which might evoke loyalty even among people who had themselves suffered at the hands of the system. The quasi-religious aspects of communism as an institutionalized belief system with parallels to certain periods of Christianity (such as the Inquisition) have often been noted; just as those branded as 'heretics' were often able to keep their faith through periods when they felt the Church had lost its original Christian mission, so too did many communists even in the worst periods of Stalinist distortion of Marxist visions. The point about trust will be taken further, below, when we consider the intrinsic dishonesty built into the system of Stasi informants.

of this point: the party archives hold a file of detailed correspondence about the construction of swimming pools in the mid-1970s, showing how important it was for the development of a sense of community that the people should participate in the planning and construction of their pools, and the care and management of their premises, in addition to the obvious health benefits to individuals and the social functions of community sports in *Volksfeste*.[8]

One of the party's favourite words was *Geborgenheit*—a sense of security, but a word with connotations which are hard to render in English (there are religious overtones in the German which find no parallel in Anglican theology). The *unmündige* subjects—those who had not yet come to full maturity—were to bask in the care of their well-meaning, all-powerful state. The image is perhaps one of a totally authoritarian parent, who is prepared to engage in the pretence of consulting the child but who will from the outset refuse to value the child's opinions—for the omniscient and omnipotent parent always, in principle, knows better. The authoritarian parent will of course seek to act in the best interests of an immature child who does not really understand, and who should to some extent be protected from full knowledge of the facts so as not to get unduly upset about things which it is too immature to comprehend. The child will be bought sweets and toys on occasion, be given outings and treats—but also be smacked and sent to bed if behaviour starts to get out of control. In the same way, the East German leadership always sought to achieve a *vertrauensvolle*, a trusting, relationship with members of the population—which unfortunately many were naïve enough to enter into. But behind all the good intentions, the paternalism, and the real desire for improvement, there lay a deep and manipulative cynicism which must in principle undermine any possibility of real trust. A better image than that of parent might be that of evil stepmother or stepfather, so common in German fairy tales: for, ultimately, there was no real relation of love involved.

The characteristics just outlined pervade the entire history of the SED, although with different degrees of emphasis at different times. They were, however, not universally distributed among communists, and many privately harboured qualms about the party's general *modus operandi*. Nor was the party without disputes over specific issues of policy. Nevertheless, for the best part of forty years the principle of party unity prevailed.

---

[8] IfGA, ZPA, IV B 2/2.028/40. Not even splashing around in the water could be an apolitical activity in the East German state.

The unity of the Socialist Unity Party

In the beginning was the party. One of the reasons that for nearly forty years the East Germans appeared—at least to the Western world—so docile was that, in comparison to Poland and Czechoslovakia, the apparatus of domination in East Germany was more effective. This does not mean that people were more afraid, and therefore did nothing (the 'Soviet tanks on German soil' argument discussed in Chapter 1, above). What was unique about the GDR, as we shall see in exploring the patterns of popular disobedience and insubordination in subsequent chapters, was that from the later 1950s until the later 1980s élite groups were relatively united and lacking in any outwardly visible factional splits which might have provided the political space, the 'opportunity structure', for exploitation by dissent from below. And after the experience of 1953—when domestic repressive forces were inadequate, and Ulbricht had to appeal to Soviet tanks for help—the East German police state became peculiarly efficient in diverting, controlling, and suppressing most spontaneous popular unrest.

To the outside world, the East German Communist Party appeared a model of efficiency and discipline—communism with a Prussian complexion. This appeared to contrast with the capers of Polish communists, who in the face of the Solidarity challenge of 1980–1 were in effect ousted in favour of military rule under General Jaruzelski, and with Czech communists who, in the period leading up to 1968, tolerated a greater diversity of view in their ranks. The monolithic outward face of East German communism for the best part of its history—at least from the late 1950s to the later 1980s—was one of the keys to the successful repression of opposition in the GDR.

There were two major periods in which the SED's monolithic character, and hence its iron grip on power, was somewhat tenuous. The first was from the formation of a separate East German state in the later 1940s to the mid-1950s; a convenient cut-off date, important for more than purely symbolic reasons, was then provided by the building of the Berlin Wall on 13 August 1961. The second was in the latter part of the 1980s. In the first period, and in the face of the widespread popular protests of June 1953, the hard-line SED leadership was nevertheless able to retain and indeed strengthen its hold on power; in the latter case, it was crucially and ultimately fatally weakened by a combination of factors, not least the loss of support from the Soviet Union under Gorbachev.

During the period from the occupation of *Mitteldeutschland* by the Red Army in the closing months of the war, through the formation of the SED in April 1946, to the foundation of the GDR in 1949, it was by no means certain that there would indeed be any communist state on German soil. The permanence of this state was not guaranteed even in the 1950s, when many alternative scenarios appeared at least possible, if not plausible. As far as the SED itself was concerned, there were a number of internal tensions and difficulties: there were differences of opinion among German communists themselves, and also between the position of certain German communists on key issues and their masters in Moscow.

The major tensions within the party in the very early years ran along fairly well-defined fault-lines. In the first place, recognizing their relative lack of popularity in electoral terms, the KPD very rapidly reversed their initial line, held in the summer of 1945, of opposition to any proposed merger with the SPD, which was first suggested by the Social Democrats themselves in the light of the bitter experience of the consequences of division in the years of Weimar and the Third Reich.[9] By late 1945—and with the evidence of the Austrian elections to confirm their fears—the KPD had come to the view that merger with the SPD was essential to any success at the polls and hence to popular legitimization of their claim to power. But the acknowledged leader of the SPD in the Western zones, Kurt Schumacher, was bitterly opposed to this line, as were many Social Democrats in the Soviet zone by this time. The story of the road to 'Socialist Unity', completed in April 1946 in the merging of the KPD and SPD to form the SED in the Soviet zone only, is in fact one of coercion and concession— the coercion enacted by the KPD and the Soviet Military Administration (SMAD), the concessions made by the Social Democrats, some of whose number chose to flee or were otherwise written out of the official script of harmonious marriage.[10] Many of those Social Democrats who remained in the SED were purged in the following years: there was, for example, a major 'cleansing' operation in 1948, with mass arrests as well as loss of party membership for many former Social Democrats. A further purge was undertaken in the first half of 1951.

[9] For some classic general accounts of this early period, see e.g. J. P. Nettl, *The Eastern Zone and Soviet Policy in Germany 1945–50* (London: Oxford University Press, 1951); Gregory Sandford, *From Hitler to Ulbricht: The Communist Reconstruction of East Germany, 1945–6* (Princeton: Princeton University Press, 1983); D. Staritz, *Geschichte der DDR, 1949–1985* (Frankfurt-on-Main: Suhrkamp, 1985); Hermann Weber, *Die DDR 1945–1986* (Munich: Oldenbourg, 1988), 'Vorgeschichte der DDR 1945–49'. Although recent research may be refining the details, it has not so far altered the gist of the story of communist take-over to any significant degree as far as the view from the centre is concerned. It is, however, increasingly clear that forthcoming local studies will be able to shed new light on different patterns of relations between Social Democrats and communists in different local areas, although ultimately all were eventually subjected to the same pressures from above.

[10] Some were arrested, imprisoned, even murdered: cf. Wolfgang Buschfort, *Das Ostbüro der SPD* (Munich: Oldenbourg, 1991), 11–15, esp. 14.

It was not only former Social Democrats who were suspect in the eyes of the SED leadership. Ulbricht had come back to Germany in late April 1945 from Moscow, at the head of a small group of élite Moscow-trained communists.[11] Well-versed in Stalinist theory and tactics, these communists were deeply suspicious of those who had spent their Third Reich years exposed to allegedly dangerous influences in exile in the West, or even in the prisons and camps of the Third Reich itself. Western émigrés such as Paul Merker and Franz Dahlem held more 'all-German' views than did Ulbricht. Additionally, all across Eastern Europe in the early 1950s there were moves to 'expose' and isolate those who had allegedly been associated with the American Noel H. Field, and in a series of show trials those communists who did not adhere to the Moscow line were dealt with in often quite draconian fashion. Although purges were not quite as drastic in either extent or degree of punishment (the death penalty) in the GDR as in, for example, Czechoslovakia, there was nevertheless a concerted process of stigmatization and exclusion which was exceedingly unpleasant—a grotesque understatement in many cases—for those affected.[12]

Many disagreements were based in matters of principle rather than pre-1945 experiences. Some differences were dealt with by processes of party discipline: Anton Ackermann, for example, who in February 1946 had propagated the notion of a specifically 'German road to socialism', was brought into line in the winter of 1948–9.[13] Other tensions were only resolved as a result of larger political upheavals. The genuine political differences between Wilhelm Zaisser and Rudolf Herrnstadt on the one hand, and Ulbricht on the other, were only brought to a conclusion—in favour of Ulbricht—as a result of the June Uprising in 1953.[14]

[11] See the classic account by Wolfgang Leonhard, *Child of the Revolution* (London: Collins, 1957); and his revisiting of the past in id., *Spurensuche. Vierzig Jahre nach 'die Revolution entlässt ihre Kinder'* (Cologne: Kiepenheuer and Witsch, 1992).

[12] In addition to the references given above, see Grieder, 'Tension, Conflict and Opposition in the Leadership of the Socialist Unity Party of Germany'.

[13] A. Ackermann, 'Gibt es einen besonderen *deutschen* Weg zum Sozialismus?', *Einheit*, 1 (Feb. 1946), 22–32. (*Einheit* was at this time the 'Monatsschrift zur Vorbereitung der Sozialistischen Einheitspartei', of which only 3 issues were produced, not to be confused with the restarted numbering, under the rubric of the 'Theoretische Monatsschrift für Sozialismus', from Heft 1, June 1946.) Ackermann's view had in fact been the official line in the spring of 1946; Ackermann subsequently stood out largely because he was genuinely committed to this historically and theoretically well-argued view, and was not prepared to change instantly, for political purposes, at the behest of Moscow.

[14] Cf. Nadja Stulz-Herrnstadt (ed.), *Das Herrnstadt-Dokument. Das Politbüro der SED und die Geschichte des 17. Juni 1953* (Hamburg: Rowohlt, 1990). See particularly Grieder, 'Tension, Conflict and Opposition', for new material from the East German archives which suggests a need for some revision of older views put forward by Weber, *Die DDR 1945–1986*, and M. Jänicke, *Der dritte Weg* (Cologne: Neuer Deutscher Verlag, 1964). This paragraph is largely based on Grieder's recent interpretation.

Zaisser and Herrnstadt had criticized Ulbricht's dogmatism and leadership cult, and had argued in favour of a more collective leadership, a more conciliatory stance towards former Social Democrats and the bloc parties, and the need to achieve more popular support for the party's policies, if necessary by reversing such policies as enforced collectivization. They also had a more open mind with respect to the German question than did Ulbricht. In the wake of the June Uprising, there was considerable weight of opinion against Ulbricht within the top echelons of the SED leadership, and on 7 July 1953 a majority in the Politburo revealed their lack of confidence in Ulbricht (one of the notable exceptions being Erich Honecker, already perhaps preening himself in the role of crown prince). But this nascent opposition was itself lacking in an alternative leadership candidate, and following a trip to Moscow on 8–10 July Ulbricht was able to garner sufficient support to quell the anti-Stalinist tide in the GDR leadership. By 22–3 July, Herrnstadt and Zaisser had been forced into the disciplinary process of self-criticism. Condemned in the longer term to exclusion and ill-health, their influence for a degree of democratization or at the very least a real change of social and economic course, was lost: having reasserted his authority, Ulbricht reverted to hard-line policies including not only a return to the collectivization of agriculture but also massive political repression in the wake of the June Uprising.

Ulbricht's line was not, however, completely secured from further challenges at this early stage in the GDR's history. There was a further period of factionalism and incipient opposition in high places in 1956–8. In the context of the denunciation of Stalinism by the CPSU (Communist Party of the Soviet Union) at its XX Party Congress, and with moves towards political liberalization in both Hungary and Poland in 1956, there were rumblings of change too in the GDR. In different ways, individuals such as Merker and Dahlem, Karl Schirdewan and Fred Oelssner, presented potential alternatives to Ulbricht's recalcitrant refusal to engage in any genuine destalinization. Schirdewan in particular presented a potential alternative leader, standing for greater openness, increased democratization in the party, a more conciliatory stance towards the Church and the bloc parties. He and others in the Politburo argued that it was necessary, not simply to denounce alleged 'Western agents' for the mass exodus to the West, but to consider the domestic causes of widespread distress and dissatisfaction sufficient for people to risk uprooting themselves and fleeing their homeland for an uncertain future. Such views found considerable support among a number of members of the Central Committee at this time, and the changed climate in Moscow following the XX Party

Congress of the CPSU lent some hope to those critical of Ulbricht's hard-line approach.

But events elsewhere in the summer and autumn of 1956 dashed the expectations of East German communist reformers. The strikes and political unrest in Poland, the suppression by Soviet tanks of the Hungarian uprising, and the international tensions occasioned by the Suez crisis, transformed the situation. In Moscow, there was renewed support for Ulbricht, whose situation was once again saved by the threat of popular unrest and the danger of destabilizing the situation by any change of leadership. The position of the East German hard-liners was confirmed, allowing, as it were, a crackdown before events could roll out of control in a manner comparable to Poland or Hungary. Thus inner-communist opposition to Ulbricht was ultimately able to make little headway. The Minister for State Security, Ernst Wollweber, was deposed in favour of Erich Mielke in October 1957 because of what were perceived as over-lenient views; the Minister for Industry Gerhart Ziller failed to resolve serious differences over economic policies and committed suicide in December 1957; others were expelled from the Central Committee at the V Party Congress in 1958.

Although there were articulate alternative policies enunciated, with detailed reference to political, social, and economic matters, individuals such as the political economists Friedrich (Fritz) Behrens and Arne Benary, or the group around Wolfgang Harich, were not able to gain sufficient support in the Central Committee or Politburo to put across a coherent alternative to Ulbricht's strategies and leadership. In widely publicized show trials in the course of 1957, Wolfgang Harich and others, including Walter Janka of the Aufbau publishing house and Gustav Just, chief editor of *Sonntag*, were tried and sentenced; the humiliation and subordination of East German intellectuals were confirmed as former friends and colleagues were intimidated and silenced. Broader processes of criticism, self-criticism, and party discipline effectively suppressed other voices for reform within the party. Thus, while in the early and mid-1950s there was a somewhat heterogeneous and fragmented, but nevertheless articulate, opposition to Ulbricht's line within the SED, by the late 1950s this had effectively been purged to such an extent that, at least outwardly, the Socialist Unity Party of Germany presented a remarkably united front to the outside world.

In the course of the 1960s, the profile of the higher echelons—at least as high as the Central Committee, although not perhaps the Politburo itself—began to change. The West German scholar Peter Christian Ludz was quick to discern the rise of what he chose to call an 'institutionalised counter-elite': a group of people who owed their position more to technical expertise rather than to an anti-fascist record or blind loyalty to party dogmatism.[15] Nevertheless, Ludz's label was a little exaggerated. Intelligence, education, expertise had to be combined with party loyalty if individuals were to gain entry to the party élite: this was no 'counter-elite', but rather the fostering of a new generation of technocrats within the loyal party élite. Insider accounts tend to stress rather the grey conformity of the new generation of apparatchiks, who were prepared to swallow many a personal scruple or private disagreement in pursuit of the common higher goal.

Even when Ulbricht was ultimately deposed, on 3 May 1971, in favour of his long-term crown prince Erich Honecker, this deposition was executed in a remarkably smooth and ameliorative manner. Differences of policy over Ostpolitik—in particular, Ulbricht's resistance to Moscow's favoured line of rapprochement with the West—were disguised under the convenient umbrella of retirement on health grounds, and Ulbricht held a relatively revered position in the party, retaining his position as formal head of state, in his capacity as Chair of the National Council of State (the political functions of which were somewhat curtailed, it should be noted), for a further two years until his timely death on 1 August 1973.

The lack of visible political opposition or factionalism within the SED from the late 1950s should not be held to imply that otherwise there were no changes in the outlook or composition of the party in the 1960s and 1970s. The introduction of the New Economic System in 1963, and the more general emphasis on science and technology in the 1960s, were associated with the rise of a new breed of technocrats in the party. Despite the reassertion of ideology from the later 1960s (the New Economic System was brought to an end, not because of any economic inefficiency, but as a result of the political fall-out following the suppression of the Czech Prague Spring), the trend towards higher educational and technical qualifications in the higher reaches of the party continued into the 1970s and constituted something of a cultural and generational, if not political, fault-line in the party.[16] There was at this stage a degree of optimism: the resolution of Ostpolitik, the acceptance of the GDR as a full voting member of the UN, the participation in the Conference on Security and Co-operation in Europe (CSCE) and the signing of the Helsinki Declaration concluding

[15] Peter Christian Ludz, The Changing Party Elite in East Germany (Cambridge, Mass.: MIT Press, 1972).

[16] Cf. ibid.; see also e.g. Ilse Spittmann (ed.), Die SED in Geschichte und Gegenwart (Cologne: Verlag Wissenschaft und Politik, 1987); Martin McCauley, Marxism-Leninism in the GDR: The Socialist Unity Party (London: Macmillan, 1979); and most recently, for a detailed study of the Honecker period, Gerd Meyer, Die Machtelite in der Ära Honecker (Tübingen: A. Francke Verlag, 1991).

this in 1975—all seemed to augur well for the GDR's secure international status.

But, as time went by, older party functionaries who held their high positions by virtue of their political records under Nazism and their dogged loyalty to the leadership were increasingly confronted by a rising generation with less personal experience of opposition to Nazism and a greater concern with enhancing efficiency and increasing productivity. This is not to suggest that the rising generation was in any way disloyal; they respected the anti-fascist credentials of their elders, and owed their own rapid promotion to positions of responsibility to the selection and training opportunities provided through the FDJ and other communist party organizations in the early years of the GDR.[17] While in the early 1970s the new generation was still relatively young and prepared to wait, a decade later frustrations were mounting.

The second major period of instability began in the later 1970s, and gathered strength in the course of the 1980s. It was occasioned partly by the succession question, given the inexorably advancing age of Honecker and his immediate entourage; it was fuelled by mounting evidence of serious economic, environmental, and associated political problems with which an increasingly remote leadership appeared unable or unwilling to deal; and it was exacerbated finally by the adoption of the new policies of openness and restructuring favoured by the new leader of the Soviet Union after 1985, Mikhail Gorbachev.

From the mid- to later 1970s, there were rising real problems facing an apparently inflexible and ageing leadership. The oil crises of 1973 and 1979 began to put increasing strains on the East German economy. Despite the extraordinary credit agreements fixed up with West Germany following a visit in 1983 by that most implausible friend of the communists, the deeply conservative leader of the Bavarian CSU, Franz Josef Strauß, it began to appear to many East German functionaries who held sufficiently high positions to have a relatively accurate picture that all that was in fact being bought was time, certainly not final salvation. As the GDR's chief statistician, Professor Dr Arno Donda, later put it:

... I began to realize this around 1982/83. It was quite clear, on the basis of all the material known to me at the time ... that we were heading for economic collapse. But the so-called Strauß-credit and the following agreements ... managed to allay these fears to a considerable extent. So then I began to think, well maybe the GDR

[17] Cf. Lutz Niethammer, 'Erfahrungen und Strukturen. Prolegomena zu einer Geschichte der Gesellschaft in der DDR', in H. Kaelble, J. Kocka, and H. Zwahr (eds.), *Sozialgeschichte der DDR* (Stuttgart: Klett-Cotta, 1994), 104–8.

will not fall like a rotten plum from the tree, but all the same, slowly but surely, it will eventually collapse.[18]

By the later 1980s, the picture was considerably grimmer, but the reality was withheld from even the higher echelons of the party. Manfred Uschner, former chief assistant to Hermann Axen in the Politburo, tells of the glimpse he and his colleagues had into the real financial situation when the figures were finally dragged out of Günter Mittag in 1988:

The overview had been intentionally presented in an almost unreadable format, the rows of numbers contained no gaps after three figures, on purpose. We had to strain ourselves, and in great haste, to try to read off the magnitude of the indebtedness. Then it was crystal clear to us: the GDR was totally bankrupt, and there was no way it could get out of the now fatal circle of indebtedness, renewed indebtedness, new credits, and the growing burden of interest payments.[19]

Moreover, short-term goals with respect to economic productivity were having ever more apparent deleterious effects on the environment—a matter of concern not only to the unofficial ecological groups sprouting in every parish in the 1980s, but also to some of the functionaries responsible for their repression.

The East German economy, still being held up in Western textbooks as a model of efficiency and productivity, was to the insider view visibly creaking and groaning in the 1980s: and the economic leaders, notably Günter Mittag, appeared to have no clear formula for its transformation. Planning chief Gerhard Schürer's proposals, developed after he was given the task in May 1986 of seeking a solution to the GDR's economic difficulties, would have effectively sabotaged Honecker's sacred cow of the 'unity of economic and social policy' in favour of reduced subsidies to consumers and increased investment in modernizing sectors such as microelectronics. Whether or not these proposals would have represented a feasible route to salvaging the East German economy remains a purely academic question; Schürer's suggestions of April 1988 were firmly swept off the table by Mittag's entirely unrealistic counter-proposals, supported at the highest political level by Erich Honecker.[20]

This episode was merely illustrative of the shift in power which had been slowly developing at the very top of East German politics. Increasingly, Honecker appeared to rely ever more heavily on a few very close advisers:

[18] Arno Donda in *OhnMacht. DDR-Funktionäre sagen aus*, 37.
[19] Manfred Uschner, *Die zweite Etage. Funktionsweise eines Machtapparates* (Berlin: Dietz Verlag, 1993), 59.
[20] See Peter Przybylski, *Tatort Politbüro. Band 2: Honecker, Mittag und Schalck-Golodkowski* (Berlin: Rowohlt, 1992), 66 ff.

particularly Erich Mielke and Günter Mittag, and to a lesser extent one or two others, taking on more and more of the key decision-making into this small circle and away from the political functionaries, offices, and ministries who were ostensibly responsible for different areas. This appears to have been particularly the case with respect to foreign policy, where Honecker increasingly took the initiative alone. The most important strategic discussions appear to have gone on, not in meetings of the Politburo, let alone the Central Committee of the party, but rather between Honecker and Mielke on private hunting expeditions and walks, and in small groups of individuals *outside* Politburo meetings.[21] Despite grumblings from those around, however, the rarefied atmosphere of obsequious subservience to the party boss and party discipline ensured the lack of open opposition within the top ranks of the party. Meanwhile, the top functionaries and their families were effectively locked away in the luxury ghetto of Wandlitz (commonly known as 'Volvograd', since all residents had a personal Volvo at their disposal), a high-security settlement north of Berlin, where they remained sheltered from the realities of everyday life among the East German people.[22]

At the same time, however, there was a crucial shift of generations occurring. The political leadership—the gerontocracy—constituted the generation of horny-handed sons of toil (or so they liked to believe) whose crucial experiences and outlook had been forged in opposition to Hitler. But forty years after the end of the war, a new generation—those who had been, not exiles or concentration camp inmates, but rather innocent children, often of communist or social democractic families but perhaps equally often former members of the Hitler Youth organization—were rising towards the peak of their political careers. The gerontocracy at the top began to appear increasingly out of touch, even old-fashioned: the anti-fascist battles of yesterday were not the pressing economic and technical issues of today. A more highly qualified, educated political élite of the middle generation

[21] For insider views of the atmosphere at the top, see e.g. Günter Schabowski, *Das Politbüro* (Hamburg: Rowohlt, 1990); Egon Krenz, *Wenn Mauern fallen* (Vienna: Paul Neff Verlag, 1990); Manfred Gerlach, *Mitverantwortlich. Als Liberaler im SED-Staat* (Berlin: Morgenbuch Verlag, 1991).

[22] Cf. e.g. the accounts in Krenz, *Wenn Mauern fallen*, and V. Klemm, *Korruption und Amtsmißbrauch in der DDR* (Stuttgart: Deutsche Verlags-Anstalt, 1991), 71–4. Corruption among the East German political élite was on a very modest scale in comparison with Western standards of comfort, let alone luxury; the popular outrage that was unleashed by the revelations of November and December 1989 related more to the dissonance between the frustrations of everyday life endured by the population over many years and the now visibly hypocritical exhortations of an allegedly super-moral leadership selflessly pursuing the higher cause.

began to jockey for position in anticipation of the inevitable leadership contest when Honecker would finally see fit to retire.[23]

The frustration with mounting economic problems, the generational shift, and the uncertainties over the succession question were mightily fuelled with the accession to power in the Soviet Union of Mikhail Gorbachev in March 1985. Those regional party bosses who no longer believed much of the myth and imagery of the 'class enemy' saw real hopes of enhanced flexibility and reform in Gorbachev's notions of restructuring and increased openness (perestroika and glasnost). Although only a little of this is apparent in the often tedious sediments of bureaucratic rule deposited in the bland reports amassed in the central party archives, there is sufficient to see that something approaching a leavening (though not quite a ferment) was under way under the disciplined outer shell of East German communism in the later 1980s. Many memoirs and analyses produced after the collapse of the GDR also provide some indications of the internal rifts—though never open splits—beginning to develop within the SED in the later 1980s.[24] But for all the growing tensions and hesitations, it was clear to leading members of the SED that the time was not yet ripe for any dramatic moves. Even in Moscow, it was felt that reforms could yet be effected under a continuing Honecker leadership. When, at a secret meeting at his country retreat in Dierhagen in February 1989, Schürer confronted Krenz with the urgency of a change in the leadership and a proposal for deposing Honecker, Mittag, and propaganda chief Hermann, Krenz allegedly replied that they would have to wait for a 'biological solution' to the problem.[25] For the time being, party loyalty and discipline prevailed: the palace revolution was deferred for a moment of greater political crisis.

This palace revolution—the ousting of Erich Honecker—finally took place in face of the mounting refugee crisis and the growing demonstrations on the streets in the early autumn of 1989. Honecker's clear incapacity to deal with a situation of rising national and international tension was based partly in very real ill-health—he was absent from the political stage for a few crucial weeks during the summer for an operation and a period of convalescence—but also in a fundamental unwillingness to recognize the reality that life was not perfect in his beloved GDR. With some support from Moscow, a coup was engineered: and faced with the effective vote of no confidence in the Politburo on 17 October, on the following day

[23] Cf. Uschner, *Die zweite Etage*, for an intriguing insider depiction of the different prevalent types of functionary, and of the frustrations experienced by many who felt that their promotion was being blocked for an unnecessarily long period of time.

[24] Cf. e.g. Schabowski, *Das Politbüro*, 36–7.   [25] Przybylski, *Tatort Politbüro*, 74.

Honecker announced his resignation to the Central Committee, ostensibly on grounds of inadequate health and strength to deal with the tasks faced by the party.[26] For a few brief weeks in the autumn of 1989, Honecker was replaced by Egon Krenz, who appears to have thought initially that by a careful series of apparent concessions and measures of liberalization, he would ultimately be able to regain control of the situation.

Retrospective accounts by key players in this drama are of course full of fascinating, but often unreliable, details. After 1989, many top communists sought to represent themselves as having been closet reformers for the best part of their lives—although they left precious little evidence of this at the time. The contemporary records clearly also have to be evaluated very carefully, produced as they were in a world operating according to quite different assumptions. Nevertheless, they may be rather more revealing in certain respects.

Some intriguing evidence of the internal differences within the higher reaches of the SED is provided in the stenographic report of the discussion on 1 November 1989 between Egon Krenz and Mikhail Gorbachev in Moscow. This discussion took place before the collapse of the GDR, when it was thought it would be merely a question of making appropriate adjustments and reforms, retrenching and regrouping. The two leaders exchanged remarkably frank views about members of the SED, although Krenz was clearly trying to cast himself in a favourable light *vis-à-vis* the Soviet leader. Gorbachev allowed himself some preliminary critical remarks with respect to Erich Honecker:

If [Honecker] had, on his own initiative, introduced basic policy correctives two or three years ago, then such losses and difficulties would have been neither necessary nor possible. Comrade Erich Honecker obviously considered himself to be Number One in Socialism, perhaps even in the whole world. He no longer saw clearly what was really going on.[27]

Krenz responded that Honecker changed when Gorbachev was elected General Secretary in the Soviet Union:

Suddenly Honecker found himself confronted with a young, dynamic leader, who tackled new questions in a very unconventional way. Until this time he had seen himself in this role. Gradually he lost his sense of reality. The worst thing about it

---

[26] Retrospective accounts may be found in Krenz, *Wenn Mauern fallen*; G. Schabowski, *Der Absturz* (Berlin: Rowohlt, 1991); R. Andert and W. Herzberg, *Der Sturz: Erich Honecker im Kreuzverhör* (Berlin and Weimar: Aufbau Verlag, 1990). For further details see Ch. 9 below.

[27] IfGA, ZPA, IV 2/2.039/329, 'Niederschrift des Gesprächs Egon Krenz, Generalsekretär des ZK der SED und Vorsitzender des Staatsrates der DDR, mit Genossen Michail Gorbatschow, Generalsekretär des ZK des Obersten Sowjets der UdSSR, am 1.11.1989 in Moskau', 8.

was, that he increasingly ceased to rely on the collective, but only on Comrade Günter Mittag.[28]

Allegedly, Mittag was a bad influence: he sowed 'a climate of suspicion against other members of the Politburo'. Many comrades recognized the extent of real economic problems in the GDR, but did nothing: Krenz claimed that 'many Comrades had long ago recognized the problems. But they kept quiet, in order to preserve the unity and closed ranks of the party.'[29]

Gorbachev revealed that certain comrades with whom he sympathized had not been treated well by Honecker. Stoph had been 'really humiliated', and Gorbachev had been 'particularly upset ... by the way in which Modrow had been messed around'.[30] Krenz then alleged that he had himself been sent by Honecker, two years earlier, to dispose of Modrow (in what way is not made explicit); but that he had found a tactical means to criticize Modrow without relieving him of his party functions. No doubt Krenz was seeking to represent himself as a Gorbachev sympathizer in this story; all the same, it reveals quite clearly the publicly suppressed tensions within the ranks of the SED in the closing years of the Honecker era. Nevertheless, until the rising challenges from below in the autumn of 1989, these tensions were not permitted to erupt into public differences of opinion or give rise to purges comparable to those of the 1950s. Almost to the end, SED functionaries maintained the priority of the appearance of *Einheit und Geschlossenheit* over any honest confrontation with economic realities or other painful truths.

So much for the mentalities of power in the GDR: despite the passage of generations, an embattled sense of party unity was embedded in the processes of political socialization, cadre selection, and party discipline, and prevailed for forty years, until finally events overtook the strategies forged in an earlier historical era. But to rest content with a focus on the top echelons of the party would be to concede the view of a dictatorship as the repression of the many by the few. Although it is certainly true that in the later years Honecker increasingly isolated himself even from close associates at the top, one of the key features of communist domination in the GDR was its very deep penetration of society. The dictatorship was not simply sustained by a troika of 'wicked men' at the top—nor yet by a band of demons acting at the behest of the wicked (and apparently nameless and faceless) Stasi, although much of the post-*Wende* literature

[28] IfGA, ZPA, IV 2/2.039/329, 9.   [29] Ibid. 10.   [30] Ibid. 11.

tends to imply such interpretations. It is time now to turn from key aspects of the mentalities of power at the top to examine the ways in which this power was exerted, actualized, and structured through a series of institutions and activities, to extend into almost every corner of East German life.

The party state

It is a platitude of analyses of communist states in general, and the GDR in particular, that they were organized and structured according to the dictates of democratic centralism, which ultimately meant the dictates of the higher echelons of the communist party. This was of course true, and any cursory analysis of the structures of power will very easily turn into a description of the party hierarchy and the ways in which the party sought to control and direct the structures of government, administration, and coercion.

This was certainly, in principle, the case in the GDR. From the moment of Ulbricht's arrival from Moscow into the ruins of Nazi Germany in the last days of the war, the communists sought to take over and control all organs of state, and to exert their influence throughout every area of society. From being a clandestine band of underground activists, the communists became the 'leading force' transforming the character of East German society. In 1968, this role became enshrined in the new constitution, which threw out the fiction—maintained for nearly twenty years—that the GDR was essentially some form of pluralist democracy in which all parties were equal.[31]

Yet a degree of duality—perhaps multiplicity—remained. The duality of structures of power was certainly not as great as that in the Third Reich, to which the notion of 'polyarchy' has been applied. Nor was it based on the same reasons. In the case of the GDR, parallelity of structures was not a hangover from the past, an indication of the growth of party structures alongside those of a relatively unscathed bureaucracy and judiciary. There was not an increasingly chaotic, hydra-headed monster, in which the only ultimate source of authority and arbitration was the final word of a Führer.

---

[31] In 1949, when the German Democratic Republic was proclaimed, its constitution was in principle quite similar to that of the Federal Republic. In practice, the political realities were of course already quite different: the multi-party system played quite a different role from that in the West. Constitutional realities continued to diverge with, for example, the abolition of the *Länder* in 1952 and the subsequent rather belated abolition of the upper chamber of parliament, and in 1960 the replacement of the role of President with a collective head of state in the Council of State.

The East German state was ordered along far more rational lines, without the overlapping of spheres of competence that increasingly characterized the brief history of the Third Reich.

To some extent the duality of structures in the GDR reflected a double need for legitimation and efficiency. The fiction of separation of party and state was helpful in a number of respects. It was certainly the case that the SED (and behind the SED, of course, the voice of the Communist Party of the Soviet Union, fluctuating in intensity but never entirely absent) determined policy, and that the functions of parliament and administration were to transmit policy decisions, to publicize them, and to carry them out in practice. The hierarchical system of government and administration was thoroughly drenched with party control, but was nevertheless somewhat separate from the obvious and direct lines of party politics. Local citizens, members of parties other than the SED, pastors and others, might all find dealing with state functionaries, who could maintain a façade of some separation from the SED, more acceptable than dealing with the SED (let alone the Stasi).[32] In any event, state officials were often deployed as the first line of influence by the SED.

The extent to which party and state worked in any way at odds with each other, or that the state acted as some form of brake on party aspirations, will no doubt form a subject for serious research, now that some of the decision-making processes are more open to analysis.[33] But any brush with the evidence—from almost any sphere of GDR life and activity—only serves to emphasize the deep intermeshing of party and state in the GDR. Although it is possible to describe the separate institutions and their spheres of competence and activity, it is virtually impossible to suggest that any of these were beyond the control of—or even in any serious respect 'separate' from—the SED. SED membership was a prerequisite for any position of responsibility, and indeed was increasingly taken for granted as a not unacceptable fact of life by large numbers of people. Already in the early 1950s, SED membership and evidence of willingness to work for the future could redeem the sins and infelicities of the recent past; and, by the 1980s,

---

[32] As we shall see, it was the recognition that such separation was in the main mere façade that led certain individuals, such as Manfred Stolpe, to consider that there was little to choose between contacts with representatives of the SED, the state, or the Stasi, as far as access to centres of power was concerned.

[33] But see Stefan Wolle, 'In the Labyrinth of the Documents: The Archival Legacy of the SED-State', *German History*, 10: 3 (1992), 352–65, for cautions against the view that key processes of decision-making at the very top will have left adequate documentary traces. Certainly the links between Honecker and Mielke were primarily oral, as the testimonies of Krenz, Schabowski, and others suggest. Protocols of private conversations after Politburo meetings or on the hunt are highly implausible.

as many as one-fifth of the adult population were members of the party. The SED party organization itself was primarily based, not on place of residence, but on workplace organizations.

It was not so much the visible one-party control of the government and administration of the GDR as the more insidious practices of its organs of surveillance and coercion that have dominated public debate since the collapse of the dictatorship. If effective party discipline and unity, and rational administration and bureacratic organization, were features distinguishing the East German dictatorship from its predecessor and from such contemporaneous communist states as Poland, the efficiency of the organs of repression was an even more important characteristic of its domestic anatomy.

Coercion and control: Stasi, police, and military

The GDR was a police state. By the late 1980s the GDR had spawned a vast apparatus of repression. In proportion to its population, the GDR had far more unofficial informers, informal spies, and paid officials of the secret police than the terroristic Third Reich ever enjoyed. And in contrast to other communist states (including the Soviet Union) at different times, the secret police, the military, and other repressive forces worked in close harmony with the party: there were no visible antagonisms, rivalries, and differences of policy as were evident at times in other Soviet bloc states. The apparatus of repression in the GDR was exceedingly efficient. Yet in the end, it failed—and even in some respects appeared to have played a part in its own ultimate undoing.

The visible organs of coercion were directed both inwards and outwards. The East German army, the Nationale Volksarmee (NVA), was founded in 1956 and constituted a highly important element in the Soviet bloc military alliance, the Warsaw Pact, to which it was officially subordinated. Conceived and presented as the ultimate defensive force, protecting the workers' and peasants' state against all enemies abroad, the NVA participated in the prevailing friend/foe mentality which was as quick to perceive enemies within as enemies without. Nor did the NVA initially have many supporters within the East German population; from 1962, conscription had to be introduced, to ensure an adequate supply of recruits into the army. At the higher levels, officers were highly trained and technically qualified, in addition to sustaining total party discipline and ideological conformity. There could be no splits between military and party as were evident in Poland in 1980–1, or in the closing years of the Soviet Union.

The police forces in the GDR held a range of functions, with related branches and specialized forces. It was from the paramilitary Kasernierte Volkspolizei (KVP, people's police in barracks) that the NVA was originally formed. Other branches of the police included not only the criminal police which dealt with crime as conventionally understood (theft, murder, and so on—although it should be noted that the definition of 'crime' is socially and historically variable), but also specialized branches dealing with border protection, passport and identity controls, transport control, and the protection of sensitive buildings and areas. Police functions were extended beyond the official, paid forces into elements of society, through the categories of *Kampfgruppen der Arbeiterklasse*, organized units within factories and workplaces numbering around 400,000, and through voluntary helpers (*Freiwillige Helfer der DVP*), who numbered around 126,000 in the later 1970s.[34]

The ubiquity of the East German military and police forces by the 1970s and 1980s could not be overlooked, and their visible presence clearly constituted something of a brake on people's willingness to overstep the very narrowly defined boundaries of 'legality' in the GDR. (The prospect of being shot was a potent deterrent to anyone wanting to approach too closely the border with the West.) On the other hand, the external perception of an efficiently policed society should not be allowed to detract attention from the fact that this was something of a historical achievement—and, as it was to prove, a passing achievement at that. As we shall see, in the early 1950s the political reliability of the police and paramilitary forces in the GDR was questionable at best, and the lack of politically reliable forces of repression played an important role in the evolution of the June Uprising of 1953. In the autumn of 1989, a similar picture—but for different reasons and in different ways—began to emerge.

Less visible, but more insidious and potentially more frightening, was the State Security Service (Staatssicherheitsdienst, or Stasi, as it was popularly known). This has been the subject of intense public interest since the collapse of the GDR. A spate of revelations about the roles played by particular individuals accompanied more general accounts of this hydra-like enterprise, which was identified as the epitome of all evil. Reputations and careers were smashed in an instant once Stasi connections were so much as adumbrated, let alone proven. It became the ultimate litmus test of complicity or defiance, being on the side of the devils or the angels, under the old

[34] Cf. *DDR Handbuch* (Cologne: Verlag Wissenschaft und Politik, 2nd edn., 1979), 579 and 257. Research into the East German police forces is just beginning to open up, with the work of scholars such as Thomas Lindenburger and Richard Bessel.

regime. The witch-hunt caused a great deal of anguish for individuals, whether accusers or accused, as people discovered the secret workings of a police state in which friends, relatives, and partners had spied and informed on each other in ways which victims often never suspected. The emotional strains of the revelations were intense.[35] But the witch-hunt also threw the role of the Stasi into a wider prominence, to some extent deflecting public attention from the primary iniquities of the system as a whole.

The Stasi was established by a law of 8 February 1950—a mere four months after the foundation of the GDR itself. The first head of the State Security Service was Zaisser, who lost his job in the wake of the June Uprising, and was replaced by Ernst Wollweber. On his own request, Wollweber was pensioned off on grounds of ill-health in the autumn of 1957; in February 1958 he and Karl Schirdewan were disciplined for factionalism and expelled from the Central Committee. Thereafter, the leadership of the Stasi became somewhat more stable. Erich Mielke became the Minister for State Security on 1 November 1957, a position he held until the very end. Mielke became a candidate member of the Politburo in 1971, and a full member in 1976. Although Mielke officially presided over the MfS, he ultimately presided only in a very indirect manner: below him were twenty-seven Generals heading different, specialized, divisions, each of which constituted virtually a secret service in itself.[36]

Until the uprising of 17 June 1953, the Stasi employed around 4,000 people. Given the apparently dismal failure of its intelligence-gathering and intervention functions on this occasion, it was drastically overhauled and strengthened in the following years. By 1955, its size had more than doubled to 9,000 employees. In the *Richtlinie Nr. 1/58* (Guideline no. 1/58) of 1958, the Stasi's central function was defined very precisely: 'The Ministry of State Security is entrusted with the task of preventing or throttling at the earliest stages—using whatever means and methods may be necessary—all attempts to delay or to hinder the victory of socialism.'[37] This entailed discerning even the most nascent potential simmerings of unrest, and intervening to suppress potential opposition even before it had become open. To this end,

---

[35] Cf e.g. the personal account by the former dissident, subsequently a member of parliament in united Germany, Vera Wollenberger, whose own husband spied on her and ultimately betrayed her, apparently regardless of the consequences for their two children: *Virus der Heuchler: Innenansichten aus Stasi-Akten* (Berlin: Elefanten-Press, 1992).

[36] Ibid. 22.

[37] 'Das Ministerium für Staatssicherheit ist beauftragt, alle Versuche, den Sieg des Sozialismus aufzuhalten oder zu verhindern—mit welchen Mitteln und Methoden es auch sei—, vorbeugend und im Keime zu ersticken.' Quoted in Karl Wilhelm Fricke, *MfS Intern* (Cologne: Verlag Wissenschaft und Politik, 1991), 13.

the organization embarked on a cancer-like process of growth, spreading its tentacles into every last corner of East German life.

Although the functions and activities of the Stasi were very clearly defined in the Ulbricht era, an extraordinary process of mushrooming growth took place under Honecker. The opening of the GDR to increased permeation from the West as a consequence of *Ostpolitik* in the early 1970s in some ways meant that internal surveillance was perceived as even more important. By 1975, the number of paid Stasi employees had grown to 59,458; and along with increasing numbers went increasing specialization. From the mid-1970s, a phenomenal expansion of the MfS took place, with ever-increasing specialization, the creation of ever new sections and divisions, as well as an almost exponential increase in numbers. By 1989, the number of *paid* employees of the Stasi had swollen to somewhere between 85,000 and 105,000, in addition to whom there was a vast network of unofficial collaborators and informers of varying levels of activity, observation, and intervention.[38]

The internal organization of the Stasi was hierarchical and increasingly specialized. By 1989, Erich Mielke had four deputies: Generaloberst Rudi Mittig, Generalleutnant Dr Wolfgang Schwanitz, Generalleutnant Dr Gerhard Neiber, and Generaloberst Werner Großmann. There were thirteen major departments (*Hauptabteilungen*) and twenty independent departments (*selbständige Abteilungen*), in addition to several central working groups, sectors, and administrative units. Hauptabteilung XX was the most important as far as the observation and control of the domestic population was concerned. Within this, the section XX/4 was responsible for the observation and control of the Churches; section XX/9 was charged with suppressing underground political activities (*Bekämpfung politischer Untergrundtätigkeit*).

The Stasi owned a huge, forbidding complex of high-security buildings in Berlin-Lichtenberg, in addition to regional Stasi headquarters and other property throughout the GDR. The budget was massive: in 1989, it was around 4 billion Marks, according to the report made to the Round Table on 15 January 1990. The Stasi's supply of weapons was allegedly enough for a small army, and its own dedicated military unit, the Wachregiment 'Feliks Dzierzynski', boasted 10,992 men.[39] Its technical armoury of infor-

---

[38] The higher figure is given by Manfred Schell and Werner Kalinka, *Stasi und kein Ende: Die Personen und Fakten* (Frankfurt-on-Main and Berlin: Ullstein, 1991), 15. The lower figure is that preferred by Fricke, *MfS Intern*, 21, based on the figures given to the Round Table on 15 Jan. 1990 by Manfred Sauer, and a few days earlier by Peter Koch.

[39] See Fricke, *MfS Intern*, ch. 2.

mation collection and storage, while outdated by the standards of Western computer technology, was formidable in extent; it has been estimated that files were kept on around six million individuals by the closing years.[40] And, as Mielke is alleged to have commented, cards and paper have the edge over computers when there is a power failure—an important consideration under actually existing socialism. The usual other technical prerequisites of the big brother state were of course also in full operation: telephone tapping, bugging devices, postal controls, personal and video surveillance. Even the *smells* of individuals were collected (for example, from the seats of chairs in police stations when they had been held for questioning) and preserved in jars, to assist tracker dogs in pursuit of their quarry.[41]

It was not only the resources and the bureaucratic organization of the Stasi which increased in complexity and specialization. The Stasi developed an entire system of terminology, based in an increasingly rigid and typically paranoid view of the world. 'Hostile-negative forces' (*feindlich-negative Kräfte*) were subjected to various processes of observation, control, and discrediting, even destroying, with each process—whether aimed at an individual or a group—possessing its particular label, its *operativer Vorgang*, its *Bearbeitung*. Both observed and observers worked under code-names, *Decknamen*, to disguise their real identities. Stasi informers worked within a system with a large number of different status appellations: IM, IMS, IME, IMB, IMK, HIM, FIM, IMV, IMF, GMS, OibE, UM, depending on their particular role and degree of operational leeway.[42] While simple informers (IMs) might be 'led' by the seniors to whom they reported, and act in a purely informative role, others, such as IMBs (*Inoffizielle Mitarbeiter Bearbeitung*) were allocated more proactive roles in the penetration of opposition groups, the attempted control of social and political processes, or in the effective demolition (through so-called *Maßnahmen der Zersetzung*) of individual lives and careers. *Offiziere im besonderen Einsatz* (OibEs) were the élite, active in high positions in all important institutions and organizations, while UMs spied on the Stasi itself. In retrospect, the childlike proliferation of codes and secrets, the guidelines and procedures, and the files of trivial observations couched in the self-important jargon of bureaucracy, could on occasion almost appear quite

[40] Joachim Gauck, *Die Stasi-Akten. Das unheimliche Erbe der DDR* (Hamburg: Rowohlt, 1991), 11.

[41] See Bürgerkomitee Leipzig (ed.), *Stasi Intern. Macht und Banalität* (Leipzig: Forum Verlag, 1991), 147–53.

[42] Cf. Fricke, *MfS Intern*, 41–2; Gauck, *Die Stasi-Akten*, 61–8; David Gill and Ulrich Schroeter, *Das Ministerium für Staatssicherheit. Anatomie des Mielke-Imperiums* (Berlin: Rowohlt, 1991), ch. 4, for details.

comic, were it not so tragic for those whose lives and careers were blighted in the process.

Estimates of the number of informers active in the closing years of the GDR vary from around 109,000 to perhaps 180,000; one expert considers that even the latter figure is probably too low.[43] Given that informers were often only active for a few years, turnover was relatively high. It has been estimated (with what accuracy it is impossible to judge) that, over the forty years' existence of the GDR, over half a million people—or something approaching every thirtieth citizen of the GDR—may have acted at one time or another as an informer.[44] What motivated the Stasi informers? There is no single answer to this question. Some were undoubtedly motivated by base considerations of greed for money, privileges, or promotion.[45] Others might have felt they were reporting relatively harmless details about colleagues for the benefit of the greater good to which they were ideologically committed.[46] Some might have felt this was a means of seeking to influence the state, and had a spurious sense of personal empowerment in the process.[47] Others, particularly in prominent positions, who engaged in such discussions, might not even be aware that they had been classified as an IM.[48] Some were not entirely willing to enter into an agreement to engage in conspiratorial discussions: they might have suffered a degree of coercion, through blackmail or threats relating to past misdemeanours or the desire to gain an exit visa.[49] But using this as a blanket excuse does not entirely excuse; for, as others who resisted both the temptations and the pressures have pointed out, it was perfectly possible to lead a relatively unharmed life without engaging in the compromise of having secretive discussions with the Stasi. This was not a situation where there was no other choice: one merely had to tell the Stasi that one had confided in another person, and the conspiratorial nature of the contact was broken, the informer free.[50]

[43] Fricke, MfS Intern, 44.

[44] L. Wawrzyn, Der Blaue. Das Spitzelsystem der DDR (Berlin: Wagenbach, 1990), 7–8.

[45] e.g. Oberkirchenrat Lotz of Thuringia, referred to in more detail in a subsequent chapter.

[46] This was probably the case with the young and rather naïve Christa Wolf when she reported to the Stasi in the period 1958–61.

[47] This was at least the way in which Vera Wollenberger's husband, Knud ('Donald'), sought to represent his original motives in betraying his wife and endangering his children.

[48] This may possibly have been the case with Church leader Manfred Stolpe, who made little distinction in principle between discussions with representatives of party, state, and Stasi in his attempts to be a serious political actor in a non-democratic state (see further below, Ch. 4). Cf. Manfred Stolpe, Schwieriger Aufbruch (Munich: Siedler, 1992), 12; and Erich Mielke, 'Spiegel-Gespräch', 50. It is, however, extremely unlikely that many individuals designated by the Stasi as unofficial informers were themselves unaware of this.

[49] Cf. Gauck, Die Stasi-Akten, 28–9, and 36; Gill and Schroeter, Das Ministerium, 109–10.

[50] Cf. e.g. Gill and Schroeter, Das Ministerium, 112.

A word should perhaps be said here about the curious issue of the relatively large number of Stasi informers who were involved in opposition groups, often holding leading roles, in the final period of the GDR. Following the collapse of communist rule and the beginnings of a wave of revelations from the Stasi archives, individuals who had played very prominent roles in the downfall of the dictatorship were suddenly revealed as Stasi spies. Stasi informers who seem to have been central in destabilizing the state they were supposedly working to uphold include Ibrahim Boehme, who played a formative role in the creation of an East German SPD; Wolfgang Schnur, a lawyer who had long defended dissidents and was a founding member of the conservative Democratic Awakening (DA); and aspersions were also cast on the first and last democratically elected prime minister of the GDR, Lothar de Maizière, who from March to October 1990 played the role of puppet to Helmut Kohl's string-pulling in respect of rapid unification with the West. Such extraordinary prominence of former Stasi informers led to some speculation, not least among sensation-seeking journalists, that the autumn revolution was partly instigated by the Stasi, perhaps on the KGB's bidding, in order to get rid of Honecker.

At the moment this speculation remains a little far-fetched. It is clear that Gorbachev was anxious to see a more reform-minded successor to Honecker; and no doubt the effect of burgeoning dissent in the GDR was to destabilize the situation and underline the need for greater dialogue and reform. But against the view of a simple conspiracy to destabilize the GDR a few sober considerations should be adduced. There is no evidence of any such intentions or direction in the evidence 'from above', that is, from Erich Mielke, as far as is currently known. There are also other quite good reasons why Stasi informers should have attained such prominent roles in dissident groups, which make their pre-eminence in the autumn events less surprising. Many Stasi informers attained quite high profiles in the dissident groups of the 1980s as a result of their need to establish their oppositional credentials within the group. Perhaps unintentionally, they often pushed groups into more extreme positions than they might otherwise have adopted; and lack of caution was also a useful means of trying to create the conditions for the arrest of dissidents which might otherwise have been avoidable. Once the balance tipped, and the situation rolled out of control (something which few would have predicted prior to 9 November 1989), these former loyal Stasi supporters no doubt sought to cover their tracks and maintain their democratic credentials into the new era for as long as they could. They were, after all, hardly new to the art of political dissimulation.

The relations between party, state, and Stasi have been the subject of considerable discussion. Several prominent analyses have referred to the Stasi—authors perhaps to heighten dramatic effect and hence publicity (and sales figures), communist politicians to exonerate themselves from a degree of blame—as a 'state within a state'.[51] Others chose to underline rather its official role, that of 'sword and shield of the party (*Schwert und Schild der Partei*)'.[52] What then, on balance, was in fact the role of the Stasi in the GDR?

On the one hand, it is quite clear that the Stasi built up a quite extraordinary apparatus of surveillance and intervention, on a scale without parallel in recent German history. The comparison with the Gestapo in Nazi Germany is quite revealing. This earlier apparatus of terror was able to make do with a relatively small number of official personnel and the willingness of ordinary Germans to inform on neighbours for personal reasons of spite or private vendettas.[53] The Stasi, by contrast, had a far higher degree of specialization and a far more organized system of unofficial informers. The size of the operation alone is quite staggering, and led to a degree of visible distance from party organizations, and arguably perhaps increasing control of party and state decisions by the better-informed Stasi. Certainly Stasi reports often concluded with suggestions for political and state officials. There certainly was a degree of institutional difference and predictable friction. While the Stasi reported directly to the SED at all levels—local, regional, and central—many SED leaders (not least Honecker himself in the closing months of his regime) chose to ignore or refused to believe particularly negative information, leading to a degree of frustration among those Stasi officials who had compiled the reports.[54] On the other hand, however, the Stasi was quite clearly the creation of the SED, and was run by committed SED members in the service of ensuring the continued domination of the party within the GDR against all potential threats and opposition. For all the individual frictions, inevitable between different elements in a highly bureaucratized state, to suggest that the Stasi

[51] Cf. e.g. Christina Wilkening, *Staat im Staate* (Berlin and Weimar: Aufbau Verlag, 1990)—although some of the testimonies actually emphasize not so much autonomy, as political interference, in the affairs of the Stasi. Seeking to exonerate the SED, former SED leader Egon Krenz used the assertion that the Stasi was a 'state within a state' when speaking to the Round Table on 22 Jan. 1990. Cf. Fricke, *MfS Intern*, 12.

[52] Cf. Fricke, *MfS Intern*; Schell and Kalinka, *Stasi und kein Ende*; Gauck, *Die Stasi-Akten*—although Gauck uses both labels consecutively.

[53] Cf. R. Gellately, *The Gestapo in German Society* (Oxford: Oxford University Press, 1990).

[54] Cf. Schell and Kalinka, *Stasi und kein Ende*, 63–4; Fricke, *MfS Intern*, 68; Andert and Herzberg, *Der Sturz*, 312; Gill and Schroeter, *Das Ministerium*, 21–2.

constituted a 'state within a state' is to miss the point and manner of its operations.

It would seem to me that a more appropriate metaphor than *either* 'sword and shield' *or* 'state within a state' is that of 'nerve system and brain centre' of the GDR. The Stasi gathered information, sorted it, evaluated it, sent messages to instigate action, and acted of its own accord. Thus in the most literal sense it acted as the intelligence centre of the GDR, both analysing and acting. But it did this in collaboration with the organs of both party and government. If one analyses any specific instance of attempted control of potentially dissident activities, the closely intermeshing circles become readily apparent. Stasi informers would report to their superiors on dissident activities; decisions would be taken at higher levels as to the most appropriate mode of intervention; and depending on the circumstances, influence would be brought to bear on key individuals by whichever level of party, state, or social institution was deemed most appropriate to the particular case under the circumstances.[55]

What is most striking, perhaps, is not the independence of the Stasi but rather the high degree of coordination between the Stasi, the party, and the other instances of coercion in the GDR. The People's Police (Volkspolizei), the National People's Army (Nationale Volksarmee), and the Stasi all co-operated under the local, regional, and central leaderships of the party, under the overall control of the National Defence Council. As we shall see in subsequent chapters, this relatively smooth co-operation was not present from the beginning (indeed, its absence was a notable feature permitting the 1953 June Uprising to snowball out of control) but was rather built up over time. The effective coordination of the repressive forces was subsequently a key factor in ensuring the rapid suppression of potential unrest at all times in the GDR, and particularly in moments of crisis such as August 1961 and August 1968. The efficiency of the coercive forces of the GDR and their close co-operation with the organs of state and party was a key factor throughout the period from 1953 to 1989 in maintaining the outward semblance of stability and docility in the GDR, in contrast to its more turbulent eastern neighbour, the People's Republic of Poland.

The beginnings of a split, or at least of a greater degree of frustration and difference over tactics, between Stasi and SED was evident only in the autumn of 1989. There are some (not wholly convincing, but certainly

---

[55] Church leaders, for example, might be used for purposes of intervention and control, after they had been spoken to by party or government officials, on the prior advice of Stasi personnel. Some of the circles of information and intervention will be considered in more detail below, in the chapters on the Church and on the growth of political activism in the 1980s.

suggestive) indications of changes of view within lower echelons of the Stasi apparatus from the mid-1980s, closely related to the shifts in view discernible within the SED at lower levels in the Gorbachev era. As in the party apparatus, so too in the Stasi there appear to have been at least a handful of individuals who began to think it would be worth examining the causes of opposition, rather than seeking merely to suppress the symptoms.[56] At the higher levels—in the gerontocracy, as it were—the close partnership appears to have continued almost to the last. Honecker's close political ally, Erich Mielke, only appears to have become increasingly irritated over the way in which technical efficiency and operational principles had to founder on the rocks of political unacceptability in what were to be the closing weeks and days of communist rule.[57] And, even then, Mielke's criticisms of the political leadership's handling of the situation were not exactly evidence of a split between party and Stasi, but rather the reverse: Mielke was irritated at the way in which individuals appeared, by action or inaction, to be endangering the cause of the party in the longer term. Even if rumours of KGB-supported plots by the Stasi to undermine Honecker were ultimately substantiated, they would do little more than reinforce the view that the Stasi acted in the perceived interests of the survival of the party and the party state. Party and Stasi worked hand in hand throughout Mielke's period in office; it was only as the party lost its hold on power that the Stasi began to founder in its wake.

What were the effects of this massive machinery of observation and control on the everyday life of people in the GDR? There can be no doubt that for those who were likely to be affected—the politically active, whose nonconformity or criticisms of the state rendered them particularly visible—it led to a climate of fear and suspicion. The suspicions might be entirely misplaced: one of the favourite techniques of the Stasi to discredit people was to cast aspersions that they might themselves be Stasi informants (as happened to Vera Wollenberger), thus losing the trust of their friends. The Stasi developed insidious methods: ascertaining intimate details of a person's private life, in order to build up and propagate distorted stories with enough of a kernel of truth to sow suspicion and discredit the individual. Photographs taken and doctored to appear as if the subject had been caught

---

[56] Cf. e.g. Ulrich von Saß and Harriet von Suchodoletz (eds.), 'Feindlich-negativ'. Zur politisch-operativen Arbeit einer Stasi-Zentrale (Berlin: Evangelische Verlags-Anstalt, 1990), 125–30. Retrospective self-justification on the part of former Stasi workers cannot of course be discounted here.

[57] Cf. Armin Mitter and Stefan Wolle (eds.), 'Ich liebe euch doch alle!' Befehle und Lageberichte des MfS Jan.–Nov. 1989 (Berlin: BasisDruck, 1990); Mielke, 'Spiegel-Gespräch', 38–53.

in compromising circumstances, and the spreading of rumours, were common techniques of distorting a person's reputation and destroying their relationships. No one and nowhere could be deemed to be safe; friendships inevitably had a shadow of distance and doubt. Nor were there necessarily fixed criteria or predictable patterns in life: efforts might go entirely unrewarded, people might be cast up or down at will, hopes might be raised or dashed as the Stasi had a mind to play with people's fates. A particularly vicious element in the Stasi's mode of operation was the threat, not directly and openly to the physical well-being or otherwise of the victim (imprisonment or torture on Gestapo lines), but rather, more insidiously, to the health, security, and future of other members of the victim's family. There can be little that is potentially more frightening for a parent than the prospect of one's own child being harmed.

Many East Germans lived with a sense of oppression and fear, although—perhaps even because—they did not know the extent of surveillance and interference in their lives. But for the vast and apolitical masses of the East German population, such considerations were for the most part, consciously or unconsciously, consigned to irrelevance. From an early age, it was instilled into East German citizens that they must conform, obey the written and unwritten rules of behaviour, and never stand out in any way that might attract attention.[58] And as we shall see in subsequent chapters, it was possible to keep one's head down and lead a quiet life, ignoring the fact that this was only within given parameters, given constraints, on the condition that one neither enquired nor criticized too much. The climate of fear was the outer parameter of existence within the total *Überwachungsstaat*; it did not have to be a feature of everyday life.

The genuine aspirations which lay at the root of at least the original Marxist vision, if deformed by the Leninist and Stalinist mutations of the twentieth century, lead one to have to ask: were these distortions, in particular the political repression, a necessary and inherent element of communism, or were they rather—as many committed communists themselves believe—'merely' an unpleasant consequence of the circumstances in which communists sought to achieve their goals? And in either case, was such a system of dishonesty, inhumane repression, and cynical manipulation of other human beings by persons in positions of power morally justified (particularly since the end, which was held to justify the means, in the event never came and arguably could never come)? These questions lead us away

---

[58] For an intriguing, if overgeneralized, account of the impact of East German conditions on individual psychology and personality structures, see Hans-Joachim Maaz, *Der Gefühlsstau* (Berlin: Argon, 1990).

from the realms of history into deeper issues of philosophy, ethics, morality. But they cannot entirely be evaded. These issues will resurface as we proceed to examine the ways in which different human beings came to collude or collide with the system in which they had to live.

3

COLLUSION: PATTERNS OF COMPLICITY

IN the aftermath of the collapse of the GDR, accusations and counter-accusations were flung about with abandon concerning degrees of complicity in sustaining a dictatorial regime. Who had been a Stasi informer? Who had made what compromises in order to further his or her career? Would the regime have collapsed much sooner, had the people not fitted into its patterns of pressure, participation, and conformity? To what extent was the successful exertion of domination by a narrow political élite actually predicated on the deep penetration of society, the monitoring of, and interference in, a whole range of everyday social processes, by the multiple, ubiquitous tentacles of the Stasi? What, in short, was the role played by the vast masses of the East German people in allowing the East German dictatorship to reproduce itself and develop over such a considerable period of time?

The state relied heavily on widespread participation at lower levels, right down to organizational strategies in the workplace and residential areas, to put across its messages and implement its policies. This heavy reliance on grass-roots participation meant a considerable interpenetration of 'state' and 'civil society'. In the process, many strategies were diverted, diluted, rendered ineffectual, or had consequences other than those intended. The state—or more particularly, the ruling party and the key political decision-makers—had to seek to establish a radically different form of society and political system from that which had existed in Germany previously, and they had to do so on intrinsically unpromising soil. (Marx had never envisaged the implausible prospect of creating communist society in a post-Nazi state governed by an imposed regime after total military defeat.) That the system was established, and functioned relatively effectively, is testimony to a degree of willingness to co-operate with whatever regime happened to be in power on the part of a considerable number of people, irrespective of their ideological understanding or commitment to proclaimed goals—in other words, testimony to the historical importance of the *Mitläufertum*.

Reaching the parts the party cannot reach: bloc parties and mass organizations

Not all the structures of power in the GDR were characterized by the degree of deceit and implicit terror which were the hallmark of the Stasi. The East German dictatorship was sustained by an open edifice of affiliated bloc parties and mass organizations, which co-operated with the SED and the Stasi to seek to incorporate every last citizen in the organized life of state and society. There was to be no area of 'civil society', no 'public sphere' beyond the reach of state control: every aspect of life, work, and leisure in East Germany was to be under the control, ultimately, of the communist state.

The bloc parties were in origin somewhat independent of the SED. The conservative-Christian party, the CDU, and the liberal party, the LDPD, had formed themselves alongside the SPD and KPD after the end of the war. Initially quite independent, they had increasingly been brought into line with the SED, until they were effectively no more than 'puppet parties' translating the SED's policies into language intelligible to their distinctive constituencies.[1] As we shall see, although this bringing into line was effected by 1948 at the latest at the national level, at the grass roots it took somewhat longer to put into practice. The other two bloc parties, the nationalist NDPD and the peasants' DBD, had by contrast been founded by communists during the occupation period precisely in order to encompass and contain segments of the population to which communist ideas could not be expected to appeal. A pamphlet circulated by the NDPD in the summer of 1952, for example, entitled 'Ruf an die deutsche Frontgeneration des zweiten Weltkrieges', which employed evocative language to appeal to the sense of 'Liebe und Treue zu unserem gemeinsamen Vaterland (love for and allegiance to our common fatherland)', listed among its signatories such former Nazi stalwarts as a 'former district leader of the NSDAP', a 'former SA-troop leader and lieutenant', and a 'former member of the NS-women's organization and war widow'; clearly political salvation for ordinary former Nazis was possible if they were prepared to put their love for the fatherland to the new common purpose.[2] All four bloc parties co-operated at the national level, and were effectively mouthpieces for the SED facing in different directions only as far as target audiences were concerned.

---

[1] On the CDU, see e.g. the rather heated condemnation by C. V. Ditfurth, *Blockflöten. Wie die CDU ihre realsozialistische Vergangenheit verdrängt* (Cologne: Kiepenheuer and Witsch, 1991).

[2] IfZ, fg 44/2.

Membership of these parties was extremely useful for those East Germans who could not bring themselves to join an avowedly communist party, but who nevertheless wished to show their commitment to building a better, anti-fascist German state. Conversely, party organizations, newsletters, and meetings were extremely useful to the SED as a channel of communication to people who would be highly sceptical of anything with an openly communist stamp on it. The CDU, for example, could be used as a means of seeking to reach Christians with views rather at odds with those of the state. CDU members might be more conversant with appropriate phraseology and argumentation to seek to influence other Christians than would atheist members of the SED. The problem, of course, lay in the degree of cynicism with which individuals came to view the bloc parties if they were not themselves committed supporters of the GDR.

The mass organizations similarly became effectively organs of the SED. The largest of the mass organizations was the trade union body, the FDGB (Freier Deutscher Gewerkschaftsbund), which in the late 1980s boasted a membership of 9.6 million people—virtually the entire adult population of the GDR (it should not be forgotten that around 50 per cent of the workforce was female).[3] Formally founded in February 1946, following the initial establishment of a functioning organization as early as June 1945, the FDGB experienced a comparable process of being brought into line with communist policies. By the time of the FDGB's third congress in 1950, the principles of democratic centralism and the leadership role of the SED had been firmly established. In effect representing not the interests of the workers to the employer, but rather the interests of the party and state to the workers, the FDGB sought to encompass no less than the whole of the working population of the GDR. It was of key strategic importance in seeking to effect and implement the social and economic policies of the state, and to ensure work discipline and political obedience. To this end, the FDGB was also engaged in detailed processes of monitoring mood and popular opinion, as well as engaging in active political work on the ground.[4] In addition to monitoring and controlling, the FDGB provided certain

[3] An extensive monograph on the FDGB is greatly to be desired: the archival basis for such work is certainly excellent. A rapid representation, concentrating on the 'blank spots (*weisse Flecken*)' in the history of the FDGB, and written in the period of the '*noch-DDR*' in 1990, can be found in Wolfgang Eckelmann, Hans-Herman Hertle, and Rainer Weinert, *FDGB Intern. Innenansichten einer Massenorganisation der SED* (Berlin: Treptower Verlagshaus GmbH, 1990).

[4] The records of the FDGB are often less paranoid in tone than those of the SED and Stasi, and for the 1950s and 1960s at least provide a very valuable source of information on popular opinion and social processes at the grass roots.

benefits for its members: for example, it owned holiday accommodation and at least some members could look forward to a week or two at a mountain spa or Baltic coast resort which they would otherwise be unlikely to experience. Although clearly subordinate to the SED, the FDGB was of immense strategic importance in seeking to implement, monitor, and contribute to the revision of SED policies.

The communist youth movement was of similar strategic importance to the SED. The Free German Youth organization (Freie Deutsche Jugend, FDJ) had its origins in the months immediately following the end of the war, and was formally founded on 7 March 1946 under the leadership of a then more youthful Erich Honecker. Initially ostensibly non-political, the FDJ increasingly developed into an instrument of communist rule, and became a member of the 'democratic bloc' in 1950. The leading role of the SED was formally recognized at the FDJ's fourth parliament in 1952, when the principle of democratic centralism was also adopted, and in 1957 it was officially declared a 'socialist' youth organization. The FDJ played a major role in the political indoctrination of young people, in cadre selection and leadership training; it also sought to cater for the leisure interests of youth, and held overall responsibility for the organization for younger children, the Pionierorganisation 'Ernst Thälmann'. Like the FDGB, although somewhat less extensively, the FDJ sought to incorporate, monitor, and control; it was of pivotal importance in the SED's youth policies and more general attempts to win the hearts and minds of the rising generation. Like the FDGB, too, the FDJ was not necessarily experienced as a one-sided instrument of coercion: many young people greatly enjoyed the camps and hikes, the music and camaraderie involved, provided they were willing to swallow, or at least outwardly acquiesce in, the ideological conformity required.

There was virtually no social group, no area of life or leisure, which was not in some way contained or captured by a relevant SED-controlled organization. Women were catered for by the DFD (Demokratischer Frauenbund Deutschlands), which in the 1980s claimed a fairly constant membership of around 1.3 million women. The DFD particularly sought to encompass and attract into political life women who might otherwise remain impervious to the attractions of the traditionally male and proletarian image of the SED. The Kulturbund similarly attempted to reach members of the intelligentsia who might have rejected the working-class and non-intellectual image of communist traditions. With a little over 200,000 members, this was perhaps of less importance in seeking to influence the population than the other mass organizations, but it nevertheless enjoyed representation in the parliament (Volkskammer). A variety of societies fostered special interests and outlooks which were of importance to the state. The largest of these, with around 5.5 million members, was the Gesellschaft für Deutsch-Sowjetische Freundschaft, which claimed the second largest membership after the FDGB. The élite youth organization, the Gesellschaft für Sport und Technik (GST), was founded in 1952 as a paramilitary training society closely related to the National People's Army (Nationale Volksarmee, NVA).

The point here is not so much to construct a directory of organizations and their initials as to make a more general point. The East German dictatorship cannot be adequately conceived in terms of a thin layer of evil SED and Stasi officials at the top constantly repressing a cowering population which lived in a state of terror. The GDR was not in a perpetual state of implicit civil war; it cannot be simply written off as a repressive regime pitted against a heroically oppositional people. The edifice of the dictatorship was constructed with and through the vast majority of the population, who participated in its workings in a multiplicity of organizations and activities. As we shall see in the chapters which follow, participation did not preclude grumbling and dissenting; but grumbling and dissenting does not amount to incipient opposition.

The GDR was not a pluralist state, nor an open society. There was one official line, to which the population had to conform. The peculiar combination of paternalism and paranoia described above led to a comparable combination of coercion and the desire to achieve a genuine consent below. With the benefit of hindsight, we know that the experiment failed. But we should not read back from that failure to assume that the whole of existence, in forty years of communist control, was unredeemably black. Even from within the ideological confines of a communist youth organization, the pine trees and mountains may look beautiful, friendships may be fulfilling, the camp-fire, the songs, and the supper a source of enjoyment.

The penetration of society? Functionaries at the grass roots

It is one thing to describe the formal, institutional structures of power: the plans and personalities at the centre, or top, of the state, the party, the governmental institutions. It is quite another to extrapolate from this to the situation on the ground. How far, and in what ways, did the people in the hamlets, villages, and small towns of eastern Germany—the people who in living memory had been adulating their Führer, Adolf Hitler—actually experience the East German dictatorship? How was the communist project extended into the factories, the housing estates, the working-class culture of cities and larger towns, formerly often strongholds of Social Democracy or other political perspectives? Who brought the state to the people, and how successfully?

A key intermediary in the state's projected total penetration of society was of course the political or economic functionary: the member of regional and district party leaderships, of the basic organizations (*Grundorganisationen*), the trade union groups, or the housing block representative. The smooth functioning and successful transition of party ideology from the very top to every last individual subject depended on a succession of intermediary stages, finally coming down to individual representatives of party and state in their local workplace or residential setting.

The party aimed at total penetration and control of social processes, total persuasion of all the people, total conformity and outward support. This was of course an essentially ludicrous aim: inherent in the very attempt to achieve universal acclaim for the goals and methods of the state was absolutely certain failure. It was simply an impossible and unrealizable project (which was in any event to some extent abandoned in the early 1970s—or at least, the limits were set somewhat wider than before). But in the process of pursuing this project, and in registering the degrees of approval, 'ideological confusion' (*Unklarheiten*), and dissent or opposition (*Feindtätigkeit*), the party built up a tremendous apparatus of penetration, observation, and control. It was the ever smoother functioning of this system, rather than any major growth in positive commitment to official ideology—although there was perhaps some, as we shall see in Chapter 7, below—that led to the development of more widespread behavioural patterns of at least outward conformity in the 1970s, which must be distinguished from genuine changes in popular attitude. And, in turn, the ever more taken for granted patterns of outward conformity reinforced the smoother functioning of the system. The 'normality of everyday life' became unquestioned, the parameters of the system internalized, the rules of the game understood and obeyed—by both rulers and ruled.[5]

District and local SED and bloc party officials, workplace functionaries in the mass trade union organization, the FDGB, and other institutional 'carriers' of the system, such as teachers, were of course crucial to the maintenance and reproduction of the system of domination. The SED leadership devoted considerable time and attention to organizational and ideological work among these groups. *Kaderpolitik* was always of vital importance: the

[5] The key change in the autumn of 1989, as we shall see, was that people came to realize that they could actually question and challenge the previously accepted rules of the game.

selection, training, control, and disciplining of the party cadres who carried the system on the ground was a constant feature of life in the GDR. Anyone who sought to play an active role in the political life of the GDR had to reckon with incessant meetings, *Parteiaktivtagungen*, and playing an uncomfortable role in the crossfire between superiors exerting pressure from above and the grumblings and criticisms from those whom the functionary was there to influence and control below. It is not surprising that the records are constantly full of complaints about the inadequate ideological and organizational work of these grass-roots representatives of the state, and of suggestions and strategies for improvement.

Inadequacies arose partly because of disagreement with, or lack of understanding of, whatever constituted the current party line; lack of skills in organizational work; and also because these functionaries were themselves human beings, members of local society, and wished to avoid serious conflicts in their own local communities. Frequently they were simply tired, and wanted to avoid undue pressures and tensions among neighbours, work colleagues, and friends. The efficiency of the streamlined communist state often crumbled on the rock of local humanity.

Very roughly, one might divide the history of functionaries in the GDR into four stages. In the 1950s, the state's penetration of society by functionaries was precarious, tentative, often unreliable. In the 1960s, party discipline and procedures were improving, the mechanisms for control (and expulsion) of functionaries were becoming more routinized and efficient. By the 1970s and 1980s, the system of *Kaderpolitik* had been perfected to such a degree that organizational procedures were for the most part very smooth and efficient. Although there were some intimations of change in preceding years, the functionary system of sustaining the dictatorship in every last corner of the Republic only began to collapse in mid-November 1989, when it crumbled very rapidly indeed in the face of capitulation at the centre combined with revelations of corruption in high places.

To start with, the population had lived through twelve years of Nazi rule—and many former Nazis had exchanged their brown shirts for other colours with the change in political fortunes in 1945. This did not mean that former Nazis could not be pillars of the new state, and indeed many were only too willing to put their energies at the disposal of the state. A report on preparations for the 1954 SED district delegates' conference in Dippoldiswalde, Bezirk Dresden, for example, reveals the scale of the problem. For 325 places at the conference, only 312 nominations had been received. Of these, 30 individuals had belonged to the NSDAP, 18 to organizations affiliated to the NSDAP, 37 to the Hitler Youth organization (HJ) and the

League of German Girls (BdM), 5 to other 'groups hostile to the [communist] Party (*parteifeindliche Gruppierungen*)', 37 had held low-ranking positions in the Nazi *Wehrmacht*, and 3 had been *Wehrmacht* officers.[6] It was with this sort of human material that the SED had to build up the ranks at the grass roots. Some former members of the NSDAP, such as the SED party functionary who had been a concentration camp guard at Mauthausen, should not perhaps have been allowed to squeeze through; others argued that they had only been 'nominal' Nazis. In 1962, for example, there were numerous complaints to the SED department concerned with leading organs of the party and mass organizations, querying why, even after ten years' or more loyal service to the SED, 'they could no longer hold leadership positions in the SED merely on account of previous nominal NSDAP membership', and adding that they now felt like second-class citizens (*Menschen zweiter Klasse*).[7]

A very much larger group within the SED ranks was of course that of former Social Democrats, many of whom had continual problems not only with specific SED policies but also with the communist forms of organization and party discipline. Throughout the early years of the GDR these former SPD members were subject to difficulties and periodic purges, particularly in the wake of the June Uprising of 1953. Difficulties were in any event frequent and inevitable, given the way in which the party line was subject to rapid change and often quite unpalatable at first sight. Moreover, in the early years there were constant frictions between hard-line Soviet-style neo-Stalinist communism and the views of more humanistic Marxists as well as members of the former SPD. It took some considerable time to purge the party of those principled socialists who refused to toe the line, and to ensure submission to party discipline, including willingness to change tack and tactics at a moment's notice, on the part of the less recalcitrant.

There were also more general factors which rendered difficult the implementation of party strategies at the grass roots, including the following: personal disagreement with whatever was the current official line, the desire to avoid conflicts in the local community, sympathy with one's neighbours and friends, and common sloth or incompetence. These factors were evident among a wide variety of people who were in one way or another representatives of the state, such as teachers, functionaries of the bloc parties, trade union officials, and even functionaries (not just grass-roots members) of the SED itself.

    [6] SAPMO-BArch, Nachlass Walter Ulbricht, NL 182/1096, 'Kurzbericht der Vorbereitung der Kreisdelegiertenkonferenz im Kreis Dippoldiswalde Bezirk Dresden' (30 Jan. 1954).
    [7] IfGA, ZPA, IV 2/5/250, report of 30 Aug. 1962.

When functionaries were not adequately prepared in advance to put across the party line and counter popular views, they were often themselves confused and more sympathetic with the opinions of their immediate friends and colleagues than with a new line coming unexpectedly from above. In 1953 this was a major reason why the demonstrations against the raised work norms were able to snowball so rapidly into a mass popular uprising. Already prior to the uprising the local functionaries were unsure of the official line, given the extraordinarily rapid and unprepared changes in the latter. Reactions to the Politburo communiqué of 9 June, which suddenly announced the 'New Course' overturning the earlier (and unpopular) decisions of the II Party Conference of the previous summer, were already somewhat rattled:

It is clear from a large number of party reports that, on publication of the communiqué, the majority of local party leaders and members were shocked, uncertain, and in the main helpless (the same story comes across in all reports, particularly from comrades working right at the grass roots) . . .

This response on the part of party leaders and members is explicable by the fact that, in recent weeks, many comrades have had a hard time trying to defend and justify the [previous] resolutions (travel costs, foodstuffs, prices, etc.), in often stormy confrontations . . .

It is often suggested that the party has isolated itself from the masses, that too many rose-coloured reports had been given to the top party leadership and that the latter was therefore unaware of the real mood among the population.[8]

This uncertainty led directly into the confused and often quite ameliorative responses to the demands of demonstrators on 17 June. As a central party report of 7 a.m. on 18 June 1953 put it, collating all the local reports that had been coming in during the preceding night:

On 17 June 1953 functionaries and party members in the factories often gave in to the *provocateurs* and simply capitulated. In a number of cases party members even took on leadership roles in hostile activities, or were active in leading groups . . . The trade unions have failed to exert any real influence . . .

The report concludes:

A stop must be put to the general phenomenon of 17 June, that people merely observed, withdrew, or allowed themselves to be ignored or disarmed (as in the case of the Volkspolizei).[9]

[8] IfGA ZPA, IV 2/5/530, report of 20 June 1953.
[9] IfGA, ZPA, IV 2/5/530, report of 18 June 1953, 7 a.m., 'Zusammenfassende Information und Schlußfolgerungen aus Erfahrungen, die die Berichte in der Nacht vom 17. zum 18.6.1953 ergeben'.

There were similar difficulties with understanding the SED party line in the tumultuous year of 1956, with the Soviet Union's renunciation of Stalinism and the personality cult, as well as the upheavals in Hungary and Poland. In October 1956, certain anonymous 'leading economic functionaries *(führende Wirtschaftsfunktionäre)*' in the Magdeburg area are alleged to have commented that 'the political line of the party is like a rudderless ship, sometimes steering to the left, sometimes to the right'.[10] Many German communists appear to have sympathized with the notion of a 'national' path to communism, independent from the Soviet Union, and to have viewed events in Hungary and Poland with a degree of sympathy. Others thought the hour of the SPD might soon be coming, or that the time was in any event ripe for change. Even 'responsible functionaries *(verantwortliche Funktionäre)*' are making comments 'along the following lines: German unity, yes, but not with the Russians, and not like it is here, but only like in the West. After all, things are blowing up everywhere *(es knallt jetzt doch überall)* and something is going to have to change here too very soon.'[11] Others were simply trying to cover themselves in the event of yet another political upheaval. As one comrade in Rohrberg, Kreis Kloetze, expressed it, rather inelegantly but with obvious feeling: 'What on earth is going to come of it all, I really don't want to go on, just so long as they don't pull the wool over our eyes, like the Nazis did, they were always trying to build a better future too and afterwards we got the stick for it.'[12] Uncertainty about the future appears to have led to a considerable neglect of party work, which 'manifested itself in poor attendance at party schools and members' meetings, low participation in brigade group training, and marked reluctance when political candidates or recruits for the auxiliary police are being sought'.[13]

For many functionaries, the official interpretation of events was simply beyond their grasp. One report to the Central Committee bemoans the fact that 'despite the agreed measures, there is still no evidence of any stronger motivation on the part of the broader membership. One reason is that even many functionaries have not yet adequately acquainted themselves with the materials of the 28th Plenum.'[14] It seems that many functionaries 'cannot

[10] SAPMO-BArch, IV 2/5/732, 'Bericht über weitere Diskussionen der Bevölkerung im Bezirk zu den Ereignissen in Volkspolen und Ungarn' (25 Oct. 1956).

[11] Ibid., report of 27 Oct. 1956.

[12] 'Wie soll das bloß noch werden, ich habe keine Lust mehr, wenn sie uns bloß nicht hinters Licht führen, wie es die Nazis getan haben, die haben auch immer aufgebaut und nachher haben wir es auch bekommen.' SAPMO-BArch, IV 2/5/732, report of 3 Nov. 1956.

[13] Ibid., IV 2/5/732, report of 7 Nov. 1956.

[14] Ibid., IV 2/5/731, Informationsbericht of 22 Aug. 1956.

argue properly, retreat in the face of false interpretations or even to some extent support them'.[15] Others, particularly members of the bloc parties, seem simply to have continued in their traditional views and activities, irrespective of their new political colours. The District Leadership (*Bezirksleitung*) of Frankfurt-on-Oder, for example, complained in November 1955, in a report which was sent, among others, to Ulbricht himself, that 'on 20 November 1955, in Müllrose Kreis Fürstenberg, there was a commemorative service in the cemetery at the graves of unknown soldiers of the fascist *Wehrmacht* who had fallen in the Second World War . . . The people responsible for organizing this ceremony were several CDU members and the NDPD local group.'[16]

Many SED members and functionaries were simply not willing to engage in local confrontations which might endanger good neighbourly relationships. There were complaints that SED members did not speak up in meetings, but rather left 'the field open for the enemy'.[17] In February 1955, for example, directions were requested as to the best means by which to deal with the party leadership of Cottbus Stadt, where the local SED was trying to avoid a *Kirchenkampf* and was not requesting that local comrades should give up their church membership. The First Secretary of the area, Comrade J., was particularly ameliorative.[18] Similar respect for the religious views of neighbours was evidenced in Kreis Bad Salzungen, for example, where schools in Catholic areas were in 1955 still observing twenty-one days of (religious) holidays above and beyond those days officially designated as public holidays. As the SED district leadership's report explains, 'school directors have everywhere gone along with the Church's requests, in order, as they say, to avoid unnecessary trouble. Even today there are still crucifixes and religious pictures in classrooms in a number of schools.'[19] Local functionaries of the bloc parties were not entirely reliable either when it came to the question of religion. This was of course particularly the case with respect to the CDU in the early years, but neither the CDU nor the LDPD appear to have been wholly supportive of the SED's introduction of the *Jugendweihe*, the state alternative to confirmation, as we shall see in the following chapter.

Occasions for a non-confrontational stance were not always on such moral high ground, nor always peacefully resolved. On 24 October 1961,

---

[15] Ibid., IV 2/5/732, Informationsbericht of 7 Dec. 1956.
[16] IfGA, ZPA, IV 2/5/322, report of 24 Nov. 1955.
[17] FDGB, file no. 2672, Information No. 10, p. 2.
[18] IfGA, ZPA, IV 2/5/322, report of 21 Feb. 1955.
[19] Ibid., report of 6 Sept. 1955 quoting report of 25 Aug. 1955.

for example, eight workers in the VEB Energie-Versorgung Görlitz took an extended breakfast break at 9 o'clock, 'which they did not keep to, but rather a drinking session with fisticuffs ensued'. Comrade G., the local Party Secretary, arrived on the scene at 11 o'clock. Far from ordering the workmen back to work, he joined in with a beer and schnapps himself. Not that this fraternization did the Party Secretary much good: in due course, the ringleaders of the downing of tools, a father and his two sons with a prior reputation for violence, physically assaulted Comrade G., accompanied by the comment, 'there, you party swine (*Parteischwein*), now you've got your reward'.[20] Some simply could not face the jeers of their neighbours: in Wernigerode, many functionaries excused their failure to talk politics on the grounds that 'they would be whistled at by the peasants'.[21] Others feared more dramatic consequences: one comrade refused to take party office on the grounds that 'he would rather stay neutral, so that he won't be hung one day, like the workers' functionaries in Hungary'.[22]

Even in the highly charged atmosphere of 1956, party functionaries often had more mundane reasons for failure to fulfil their party tasks. As a report of 18 August put it: 'In some areas there is inadequate leadership . . . There are particular difficulties in country areas because of the increased need for labour to bring in the harvest. The *Kreisleitung* in Stendal even says that people are getting weary of attending meetings (*Versammlungs-müdigkeit*).'[23] Four months later, the harvest might be safely in, but the situation appeared to be little better in Stendal in the run-up to Christmas: 'As far as political work with the masses is concerned, at the moment the activity of our party organizations has declined . . . In Stendal they explain this by the fact that most people are busy with preparations for Christmas right now. Other districts give similar reasons.'[24] Clearly the traditional seasonal rhythms of life had to go on, irrespective of political ructions in high places. But the normality of everyday life could not remain resistant to political intrusion for ever.

During the 1950s, there were constant efforts to improve party work on the ground. The Berlin party organization, for example, made strenuous attempts to deal with such misdemeanours as 'the discovery of sloppiness

[20] Archiv der Gewerkschaftsbewegung Berlin, FDGB Bundesvorstand, 15/1470/6447, report from the FDGB Bezirksvorstand Dresden of 15 Nov. 1961.

[21] SAPMO-BArch, IV 2/5/732, report of 21 Dec. 1956.

[22] Ibid., report of 14 Nov. 1956.

[23] Ibid., IV 2/5/731, report of 18 Aug. 1956, 'Zwischenbericht über den Stand der Mitgliederversammlungen zum Beschluß des ZK der KPdSU zur Überwindung des Personenkultes'.

[24] Ibid., IV 2/5/732, Informationsbericht of 21 Dec. 1956.

(*vorgefundene Schlamperei*) in the Unified Membership and Statistics Sector of the district leadership of Berlin-Mitte', or the fact that 'the district leadership of Pankow has absolutely no idea as to whether and where organized groups of party activists exist in their factories'. Further investigations into the Berlin party revealed 'many errors' or 'ideological confusions' (euphemistically known as *Unklarheiten*), particularly about the concept of Social Democracy (which was used in a pejorative sense, upsetting former SPD members), not to mention 'pacifist conceptions'. Last but not least were moral transgressions: 'There are serious weaknesses in the moral behaviour of some members of the party organizations. The majority of party disciplinary proceedings have to do with the moral shortcomings of individual comrades. The Volkspolizei has a particularly large proportion of party disciplinary measures and punishments relating to excessive drinking and womanizing (*Frauengeschichten*).'[25]

Fortunately for historians (and possibly for some contemporaries who escaped the interventions of the party, although less fortunately for the rain forests), one of the reasons given for inadequate political-ideological-organizational work on the ground was the excess of paperwork. As one reporter wearily noted:

One of the reasons is the ponderous and bureaucratic style of working which is still[!] very prevalent. An extraordinary number of analyses, commentaries, and reports are compiled, which obviously take up a lot of the time and energy of colleagues, at the expense of the immediate running of the basic organizations here and now . . . One can easily imagine just what mountains of paper (*Papierwulst*) comrades have to contend with . . . That prevents comrades from devoting themselves more to party work at the grass roots.[26]

The most cursory acquaintance with an East German archive will readily substantiate the truth underlying this comrade's complaints. But despite such protests, the paperwork did not lessen. In the mid-1980s, the apparently very hard-working and energetic First Secretary of Bad Salzungen was complaining of the tensions between merely keeping up with reading the paperwork prepared by his subordinates and making the time for meetings and talking to people.[27]

In the meantime, efforts to improve party work on the ground continued. In the tense days after the erection of the Berlin Wall in August 1961, a particularly wary eye was kept on political work and the influencing of

[25] Ibid., IV 2/5/975, reports of 12 Mar. 1954, 26 Apr. 1955, 20 May 1955.
[26] Ibid. (n.d., *c.*22 Aug. 1955).
[27] Landolf Scherzer, *Der Erste. Eine Reportage aus der DDR* (Cologne: Kiepenheuer and Witsch, 1989; 1st pub. 1988), 26–7.

popular opinion at the grass roots. But the functionary system was still not entirely reliable. Many SED functionaries in Berlin appear to have fallen prey to sudden illness, or had to leave their posts on urgent business (seeing to a problem with the car, or a country cottage, or a relative).[28] In Karl-Marx-Stadt (Chemnitz), many in the party organization had apparently failed to understand 'that, with the realization of the measures of the Council of Ministers of 13 August 1961 in the fight against militarism and imperialism in West Germany, we have gone on to the offensive and rescued the prospect of peace in Europe'. Some had the temerity to suggest that the measures were 'too severe', and that the division of Germany would be accentuated in this way.[29] In the Leipzig area it was apparent 'that a number of comrades do not have the appropriate political concerns, and that a proportion of party members are retreating and not engaging themselves in the party's cause'.[30] In some Leipzig factories party functionaries were failing to put across a strong or clear line: there was 'an obvious avoidance of confrontations', and 'no consensus about the expulsion of a *provocateur* from the ranks of the party'. One *Abteilungsleiter*, a Genosse Kurt W., had even been heard to say that 'the 17 June only came about because of mistakes made by the party and the government'.[31] Another party comrade, working in the administration of Kreis Wurzen, dared to suggest that 'our people, particularly in the state apparatus, are put under too much political pressure and that is why they beat it to the West'.[32] The chairman of the CDU in Dahlenberg/Torgau had made similarly inappropriate comments: 'When people keep talking of peace, then war is not far off. The situation is coming to a head, everything is ordained from above. If you say anything, you get done for it, that's why no one says anything in meetings about it.'[33] This last comment reveals the kind of pressures functionaries felt themselves under. A decrease in their 'unreliability' probably reflected less any real growth in inner conviction than a rising sense of pressure under ever more effective party discipline, as well as a turnover in the personnel and a new generation of functionaries.

The situation among trade union functionaries in 1961 appears to have been no better. A report of 18 August 1961 to the FDGB executive committee started in the customary glowing tones: 'In all *Bezirken* of

[28] SAPMO-BArch, IV 2/5/673.
[29] Ibid., IV 2/5/961, 'Einschätzung der Kampfkraft der Parteiorganisation im Staatsapparat' (11 Sept. 1961).
[30] Ibid., IV 2/5/919, report of 18 Aug. 1961.
[31] Ibid., IV 2/5/919, telegram of 16 Aug. 1961, Leipzig.
[32] Ibid., report of 17 Aug. 1961.
[33] Ibid.

our Republic honorary and full-time functionaries lead the way in discussions with our members. They glow with optimism and bestow new strength on our members for ever greater tasks.'[34] But the report loses little space before recording complaints that many, far from beaming optimism, are spreading 'negative views and disagreements', 'hesitations . . . and an attitude of defeatism (*kapitulantenhaftes Verhalten*)'. One *Vertrauensmann* is quoted as saying 'that the government itself has forfeited the trust of the population, and that, when difficulties arise, one can no longer use the excuse (*Ausrede*) that it is the fault of [enemy] agents'. (Note the use of the word *Ausrede*—an implicit admission of mendacity.) Under the difficult circumstances of being pressurized to defend the indefensible, many functionaries either lost their positions, or simply gave up of their own accord. The tendency to 'defeatism is expressed, among other ways, in the fact that representatives try to avoid discussions, trade union committee members resign from their positions or are suddenly stricken with unexpected illnesses'. And, as one put it, 'if we are not ourselves convinced that the measures were right, then we cannot stand up and support what has happened'.

Discussions on the *National Document* in 1962 similarly reveal the extent of doubts and hesitations among even functionaries of the FDGB. A report of 2 June 1962 again begins by reporting allegedly positive reactions: people supposedly recognize that 'it is the duty of all working people, through their productivity, to struggle for the greater strength and security of the GDR, so that she can fulfil her historical mission' and that 'the militarists and fascists who are exercising power once again in West Germany represent the greatest threat to peace and to the nation'.[35] But again, it does not take long to come to the question of 'political-ideological misunderstandings (*Unklarheiten*)', particularly apparent in demands for free elections and freedom of travel, and failure to understand why the two Germanies are supposed to be enemies to each other. And even many FDGB functionaries share the view that conditions in the West are much better, that the Wall is only to stop people fleeing, and so on. 'Confused and negative interpretations of the National Document are even being expressed by some trade union functionaries. This includes BGL chairs and members, functionaries of the AGL, of the trade union groups and also some honorary members of the district executive committees.' The appropriate organizational conclusions were drawn: 'Our trade union leaders have confronted

[34] Archiv der Gewerkschaftsbewegung Berlin, FDGB Bundesvorstand, 2677 (1961), report of 16 Aug. 1961, Informationsbericht No. 6.
[35] Ibid. 2678 (1962), 16, Information (2 June 1962), 3.

the relevant functionaries and, where necessary, they have been relieved of their functions.'[36]

The signs of inadequate party work become less frequent in the records in the course of the 1960s and 1970s. There are of course instances in moments of crisis, such as the summer of 1968, when 'intensive party discussions' and 'disciplinary investigations' are necessary.[37] For example, among the transport police of Bad Salzungen many comrades showed signs of defeatism in face of enemy arguments (*Zurückweichen vor gegnerischen Argumenten*). 'Investigations revealed that the comrades had been inadequately prepared for such discussions by their superiors at work and by party organizations, and had been only superficially armed with our arguments. Measures to alter this situation are being carried out.'[38] The extent to which measures could go to combat inadequate application to party work sometimes verged on the ludicrous. One report on the Volkspolizei—in the situation of heightened tension at the beginning of September 1968, shortly after the invasion of Czechoslovakia—complains that 'among some comrades there are certain signs of tiredness and a decline in readiness to intervene'. Lack of energy had less to do with disagreements of principle than simple lack of sleep: comrades had been heard to make such comments as 'we really need to get a decent night's sleep for once'. Ever eager to impress their superiors in Berlin, local officials could not allow such biological needs to get in the way of the higher cause: 'The basic organizations, political organs, and duty officers are combating this tendency, but have not so far been able to overcome it.'[39]

What is striking, however, about 1968 in comparison to 1953 (and even 1956 and 1961) is the relative paucity of such complaints. By the later 1960s, many of the major organizational difficulties of the 1950s appear to have been ironed out. There are of course still cases of individual human failings: specific examples could readily be adduced. Nor did functionaries always maintain an appropriate public presence: in 1967, for example, on the occasion of a visit from a French delegation, a number of FDGB dignitaries indulged in an unrestrained drinking session in the Hotel Elefant in Weimar, entailing the imbibing of considerable quantities of French cognac. This eventuated, at around midnight, in fisticuffs; the subsequent

---

[36] Archiv der Gewerkschaftsbewegung Berlin, FDGB Bundesvorstand, 2678 (1962), 16, Information (2 June 1962), 9.
[37] IfGA, ZPA, IV A 2/12/27, Sonderinformation No. 15/68, 23 Aug. 1968.
[38] Ibid. 18/68, 25 Aug. 1968.
[39] Ibid. 26/68, 1 Sept. 1968, 12 midnight. Clearly the report writer, given the time of this report, did not suffer as much from the need for sleep as did the colleagues about whom he was complaining.

investigation occasioned by the incident came to the conclusion that the entire district organization was basically corrupt, enjoying their privileges and covering up their own incompetence.[40] But the more general pervasion of party and trade union reports with generalized complaints of incompetence, inadequate argumentation, insufficient ideological and political work among the masses, at least appears to decline.

There is something of a methodological problem here, to which attention should be drawn. In the 1970s, the reports from the FDGB and from the SED regional and district party organizations to their respective executive or central committees become what the Germans call *verschönert*, representing what report writers clearly thought their superiors wanted to hear. A fairly safe generalization that can be made is that, the better the technical quality of the reports—better paper, an electric rather than a manual typewriter, xeroxes rather than fragile and often virtually illegible multiple carbon copies—the less 'reality' the reports seem to reflect. The rhetoric of reporting becomes ritualized: the structures are standard, the phrases jargonized, the contents increasingly predictable. A general statement full of optimism and success is accompanied by stock quotations from representative individuals, all supporting and repeating the official party line. Very occasionally a modest note of criticism is put into someone's mouth, perhaps as a mild hint from the regions that policy might be amended in some minor respect. The vivid sketches of incidents and people in the reports of the 1950s and early 1960s, offering rich and fascinating insights into real social processes, are gone; instead, we are left with beautifully produced, centrally collated, and meticulously filed mountains of paper, full of sycophantic adulation, signifying nothing.[41]

Or next to nothing. For one interpretation that can be put on these ritualized reports, particularly of the 1970s, is that the very fact that they reveal so little is in itself revealing, or at least suggestive. It suggests that the system was functioning relatively smoothly, that for the most part the structures were in place, the wheels well oiled, the functionaries performing their allotted roles. There are only occasional and striking illustrations of when things had gone wrong in particular organizations. Let us take two examples, one from the SED and one from the FDGB.

In 1975, an investigation into troubles at the VEB Kombinat Schwarze Pumpe in Hoyerswerda came to conclusions couched in no uncertain terms:

[40] See FDGB, file no. 3023, report of 20 July 1967. See also reports of 5 Sept. 1967 and 27 Feb. 1969 for other examples.

[41] See e.g. IfGA, ZPA, IV B 2/5/999; IV B 2/5/763.

In the factory, as in our Republic, there are no objective reasons why anyone should engage in hostile and malicious discussions aimed against the policies of the party, the government, and the trade unions ... The class enemy's ideological invasion for the purposes of hostile activities, and the handing in of membership books of the FDGB in such large numbers, were caused by fundamental inadequacies in political-ideological work ...[42]

The result was, that the ideological influence of the class enemy, nationalistic conceptions, and patterns of thought and action hostile to socialism, were not discovered in time, and their proponents were not firmly and actively opposed.[43]

Those on the ground could not be trusted to carry out their work properly. The root causes lay in inadequate vigilance and neglecting the cadre principle:

The *Vertrauensleute* were politically not properly qualified and nor were they given adequate direction. The *Tribüne* is not read by the *Vertrauensleuten* ...[44]

The working group had to conclude that the influence of the party in the factory trade union organizations ... had not been secured ...[45]

[Finally], over the last few years a lot of grievances had been piling up as far as working and living conditions were concerned ... Trade union leaders did not pay proper attention to quite justified suggestions, tips, and criticisms.[46]

There are similar expressions of outrage about some local conditions uncovered by the SED Leipzig district leadership in 1975, worth quoting at some length to give a flavour of the problem and the ways in which it was conceptualized:

... in the basic organizations of the 'terra' shoe factory and the 'Hermann Matern' forge there were grotesque infringements of the Leninistic norms of party life, a tendency to disregard the unity and purity of the party, and leading cadres engaged in behaviour inappropriate to party members, even going so far as punishable offences and unprincipled behaviour as far as class alertness and combating the influence of bourgeois ideology was concerned ... Similar liberal[47] behaviour inappropriate to party members was evident on the part of comrades in the Roßwein town council ... In the secretariat [of Kreisleitung Döbeln] an uncritical atmosphere developed, leading to an aura of self-satisfaction, routine work, and superficial analyses of the situation ... Because of the egoistic and oversensitive behaviour of the First Secretary there were liberal positions in the secretariat. The secretariat did not exert its influence on the First Secretary, in order to overcome his evidently

---

[42] FDGB, file no. 5414, 'Abschlussbericht der Arbeitsgruppe des Sekretariats des Bundesvorstandes des FDGB zur Unterstützung des Kreisvorstandes der IG Bergbau/Energie im VEB Kombinat Schwarze Pumpe' (12 Dec. 1975), 2.

[43] Ibid. 3.

[44] Ibid.

[45] Ibid. 4.

[46] Ibid. 6.

[47] 'Liberal' is of course used in a pejorative sense here and elsewhere in SED jargon.

subjectivistic (*unsachliches*) approach, which was accompanied by arrogance, infallibility, and a tendency towards administrative traits in his work.[48]

Clearly a den of iniquity—or at least infringement of the high moral rules of party behaviour—had been uncovered, in which local party functionaries' attempts to lead relatively normal lives of incompetence and self-importance aroused great moral indignation on the part of their superiors.

There were of course also other intimations of disquiet about the party's mode of operating on the ground. The 'Analyses of the petitions of the population (*Eingaben der Bevölkerung*)', for example, reveal that *Kreisleitungen* often did not deal effectively and rapidly with mundane problems as they arose, or reacted in an overbureaucratic and insensitive manner.[49] But for the most part, the *system* at least appears to have been functioning, even if particular individuals occasionally failed to live up to its expectations and rules. Those that fell short of party expectations stood out and were the focus of very specific outrage and investigation, in comparison to the much more generalized complaints of the 1950s and early 1960s, where the impression is given that there was only minimal and faltering penetration of society through a very much less than adequate apparatus of power at the grass roots.

Nor is it only the system that seems to have functioned more smoothly in the 1970s. There was also a marked improvement in the level of educational achievement and qualifications of functionaries by this time. In the early years of the GDR, social and political background and ideological credentials were the key attributes of functionaries; but this did not necessarily mean that they were also intelligent, capable, efficient. (A widely current joke in the GDR ran as follows. Of the three possible personal attributes of intelligence, honesty, and party membership, only two were ever mutually compatible: if you were intelligent and honest, you could not be a party member; if you were intelligent and a party member, you could not be honest; and if you were honest and a party member, you could not be intelligent.) The remedy was sought in education. The GDR education system initially focused, in the 1950s and early 1960s, on the promotion of people from previously underprivileged backgrounds: in other words, it fostered intergenerational social mobility, as children from working-class and peasant backgrounds were advantaged at the expense of those traditionally more privileged children of the middle classes. These new, upwardly mobile young people had of course also to prove their political

---

[48] SAPMO-BArch, Büro Erich Honecker, J IV A 2/2.030/258, report of 16 May 1975.
[49] Cf. e.g. SAPMO-BArch, vorl. SED 27310; SAPMO-BArch, vorl. SED aus 27310.

commitment, their willingness to conform. If they evinced the appropriate combination of talent and conformity, their career prospects were good. And by the 1970s, the harvest was beginning to be evident in the rising general levels of educational qualifications among state and party functionaries. By this time, too, the goals of the education system had been shifted away from the fostering of social mobility to a primary focus on talent irrespective of background.[50] But once the GDR had produced its own functionaries, who had been socialized into the appropriate modes of operation, the wheels of the system were far better oiled.

Does this picture of a smoothly operating system, with functionaries socialized into the rules of the game, focusing primarily on technical efficiency and accepting the price of ideological conformity—even feeling genuinely grateful to a system to which they owed their own rapid promotion—change at all in the mid- to later 1980s, as some contemporaries have suggested? Or is the perception of the creeping shades of glasnost rather a retrospective recasting of party history, a clutching at straws of alleged previous political reformism despite all outward appearances?

There is some evidence of rising unease among functionaries at the grass roots in the 1980s; but this unease was at most expressed in veiled, oblique language—the insertion into reports of comments allegedly arising from other quarters, the increasing prevalence of undercurrents of unrest expressed in political jokes and unofficial asides. The prevailing assumption was that the system was here to stay; nor was it necessarily the system, in a very general sense, that was wrong. It was more a question of identifying how the system could be made more flexible to meet changing needs, or respond to changing pressures.[51] Part of the problem lay in the way in which, in the late Honecker period, there were no institutionalized avenues for relatively open, but still inner-party, debate along the lines introduced in the USSR under Gorbachev. To some extent there was a sense among many functionaries that it was a question of *überwintern*, surviving through the winter, pending a change in the leadership at the top.

---

[50] 'Workers' and peasants' faculties', which had offered courses to prepare people from manual backgrounds for admission to higher education, were dissolved in 1963, and the quota of 60% of sixth form and university students to be of worker and peasant origin was dropped; the system of more generous scholarships for workers' and peasants' children was terminated in 1968.

[51] Cf. Scherzer, *Der Erste*, for insights into the frustrations felt by well-meaning and hardworking local functionaries who simply could not square the visible needs of their constituents with partially contradictory pressures and directives from above (as in the case of building prestige construction projects where they were not needed while hundreds were without adequate housing in other areas).

A single example, typical of innumerable party reports from the provinces in the 1980s, must suffice to illustrate the double game played by regional party functionaries, who wished both to express a degree of disquiet and the need for change, while at the same time distancing themselves from it and reasserting their loyalty to the current leadership line. A report from Bezirksleitung Schwerin in March 1986, as summarized for the information of the Politburo, comments that: 'Many people express the view . . . that our party should discuss things a lot more openly. But they do not take into consideration the fact that our level of development is quite different, and cannot be simply compared to the situation in the Soviet Union.'[52] The latter sentence, of course, described the official view from the gerontocracy; the former suggested that there might perhaps be room for change in the future.

In the event, however, the functionaries appear to have remained at least outwardly loyal until the autumn of 1989. There was clearly a degree of crumbling in the last year or two before the autumn revolution; but it took the demonstrations on the streets to begin to break the outward appearance of uniformity in the ranks that had so arduously been constructed in the preceding decades. And, as we shall see, it was not until the week or so *after* the opening of the Wall that the functionary system began to collapse massively. For whatever combinations of personal motives—commitment, self-interest, internalization of the rules of the game—the ruler's staffs remained outwardly loyal to the system virtually to the end.

The importance of bureaucracy, of the preparedness of rulers' staffs to uphold a system of domination, irrespective of their personal motives, was emphasized in the classical analysis by Max Weber. It was perhaps this, rather more than the evil repression of a thin layer of individuals at the top, which anchored the stability of the East German dictatorship for so long.

The co-option of the intelligentsia

A similar anchoring of the system through the assumption of longevity and the serendipity of change is evident when one considers, more broadly, the professional classes in the GDR. However, once again generalization is not easy, and the attempt must be made to draw a qualified picture with an eye to some of the ambiguities and complexities of the situation.

What is meant by the intelligentsia? Westerners might immediately think of prominent individuals—novelists, poets, playwrights. The usage in

[52] SAPMO-BArch, J IV A 2/2.030/240, Büro Erich Honecker, 'Information über einige Probleme aus dem Monatsbericht des Genossen Ziegner, Bezirksleitung Schwerin' (20 Mar. 1986).

the GDR was wider, to refer in effect to all those groups which might in Western societies be thought of as professionals or 'bourgeois'. The latter term of course has connotations suggesting a particular set of social positions in capitalist society ('bourgeois society' *par excellence*), and is therefore not entirely appropriate in relation to a state where, increasingly, private property in the means of production was being squeezed out of the system. Discussions of communist states have therefore preferred the term 'intelligentsia', using it to cover not only the cultural intelligentsia (intellectuals in a loose Western sense) but also the technical intelligentsia (including occupations such as engineering) and members of a rather wider range of professional groups (such as medicine).

The pinnacles of the cultural intelligentsia were of great significance in the history of the GDR. Returning exiles such as Bertolt Brecht or Stefan Heym, if restrained and doled out to the public in selective, limited doses, were highly important in establishing a degree of legitimacy for the anti-fascist state; critical writers of a slightly younger generation, who were themselves to a greater degree products of the GDR itself, such as Christa Wolf, for all their veiled and partially self-censored critical comments nevertheless similarly lent the GDR a degree of international acclaim and credibility. The extent to which prominent writers who made their compromises with the regime should be castigated for their complicity in sustaining a dictatorship has been the subject of furious debate in the years since the GDR's collapse.[53]

There were of course also many others who refused to engage in the necessary self-censorship and critical conformity. The songwriter and guitarist Wolf Biermann, the writer and daughter of a high-placed communist official Monika Maron, the poet and writer Reiner Kunze, and many others, were either forced or persuaded into exile in West Germany.[54] In an

[53] The belated, post-*Wende* publication of Christa Wolf's brief account of a day under light Stasi surveillance, *Was bleibt*, was the immediate occasion for the controversy, sparked by a highly critical review of this book in *Die Zeit*. The ensuing *Literaturstreit* illustrated the lack of mutual understanding of privileged *Wessis* who had never experienced the constraints of life under a dictatorship, such as the literary reviewers of the establishment press in the West, and privileged *Ossis* who had come to terms with the compromises necessary for survival, and was enlivened by the ideologically pure sniping from the sidelines of those who had escaped or been expelled, such as Wolf Biermann.

[54] Wolf Biermann was not allowed to return to the GDR following a concert tour in the West in 1976. The critical insights of Reiner Kunze, who left for the West in 1977, are published in his collection entitled *Die wunderbaren Jahre* (Frankfurt-on-Main: Fischer Verlag, 1976), which provides marvellous vignettes of the everyday pressures on youth towards militarism and conformity in the GDR. Karl Maron, Monika Maron's stepfather, was variously deputy editor of *Neues Deutschland*, chief of the East German police force, Interior Minister, a member of the division of the National Defence Council responsible for the Berlin

almost regular cycle, waves of hope and quasi-liberalization were repeatedly followed by periods of clamp-down and censorship. Those dissident spirits who attempted to continue their work in the GDR were often only able to perform in protected niches, such as the singer Bettina Wegner giving concerts under the auspices of church services. The articulate few who continued to voice their concerns were a constant thorn in the flesh of the East German authorities, striving as the latter were to present a view of a monolithic, contented, subordinate population.

These literary stars, twinkling critically in the firmament of actually existing socialism, are, however, not the sole representatives of the intelligentsia, even though they may have previously attracted the most attention in the West. It is important to consider too the political attitudes and activities of the East German intelligentsia in a much broader sense, referring to all those professionals in a wide range of cultural, scientific, and technical occupations: schoolteachers, university teachers, researchers, journalists, media people, doctors, dentists, engineers, lawyers, and so on. If one considers this far broader spectrum of society, using essentially the definition of intelligentsia employed by the regime itself to cover what Westerners like to call the 'middle classes', then an interesting pattern of development emerges.

In the 1950s, it was particularly from the ranks of the professional classes that the *Republikflüchtlinge*, those fleeing to the West, were drawn. While the Western Church sought to persuade pastors to stay in the GDR, there was no such pressure on doctors, who often left for the West themselves or sent their children to study at Western universities where they would not be discriminated against. Similarly, other highly trained professionals felt there would be better prospects for themselves and their children in the Federal Republic. This was a constant source of concern to the state, and Ulbricht adopted a number of measures to seek to secure a more privileged position for the intelligentsia, including differential pay rates and other privileges. Nevertheless, it was only the building of the Berlin Wall that finally put a stop to the haemorrhage. After 13 August 1961, *Republikflucht* was no longer of such concern. Doctors and nurses no longer had to fear that when they came to work yet more colleagues would be missing from hospital wards and surgeries; technical and scientific projects would no longer founder on the unexpected departure of crucial boffins; the work of factories and offices would no longer falter through

Wall, and Director of the Institute for Public Opinion Research of the Central Committee of the SED. Monika Maron ran into trouble for the publication in 1981 of her critical novel about environmental pollution in the GDR, *Flugasche*, and left Berlin for Hamburg in 1988.

sudden loss of expertise in key places. But a number of concomitant developments ensured the greater conformity of the vast bulk of the East German intelligentsia from the 1960s in any event.

For the most part, members of the professional classes had evinced a rather withdrawn or critical attitude in the 1950s. They were certainly not at the forefront of movements of popular unrest, such as the 1953 June Uprising, and the FDGB opinion and mood reports of the 1950s repeatedly refer to members of the intelligentsia as withdrawn, unwilling to express their opinions: as one report of 1956 put it, 'in the circles of the intelligentsia a somewhat negative, wait-and-see attitude still prevails. People do not express their opinions openly.'[55] There were clusters of more openly critical intellectuals, particularly in research institutes and establishments of higher education: there are, for example, extensive Stasi reports on groups in the Martin-Luther University Halle, the Deutsches Institut für Zeitgeschichte, the Institut für Gesellschaftswissenschaften at the Humboldt University of Berlin, at Leipzig University, in the Medical Academy in Magdeburg, at the Technical University of Dresden, and elsewhere.[56] These attitudes of critical withdrawal were hardly improved by the erection of the Berlin Wall. But the individuals involved generally limited their dissent to private discussions, tending on the whole to adopt conformist attitudes in public. In the words of the Stasi report on the Halle group, 'it is notable that . . . all the above-named individuals are negatively disposed towards the socialist development of the GDR, its government, and particularly the leaders of the SED, but despite this their behaviour in [public] consultations and in their practical activities is quite differentiated'.[57]

Over time, both the situation and the composition of the East German intelligentsia began to change. For one thing, the new social and economic policies of the 1960s and 1970s had an impact on the role of the intelligentsia in East German society. The New Economic System of 1963–70 was associated with an enhanced role for technocrats, while the concern with improvements in the here and now of Honecker's early focus on the 'unity of economic and social policy' had similar consequences for the well qualified. At the same time, the composition of the intelligentsia was increasingly that of a younger generation, selected and trained according to the communist cadre principles, with an emphasis on party discipline as well as techni-

---

[55] FDGB 2672, Information No. 10 (1956).

[56] Cf. e.g. MfS, ZAIG, Z 119 (11 Apr. 1958); MfS, ZAIG 137 (28 June 1958); MfS, ZAIG 158, No. 89/58 (5 July 1958); MfS, ZAIG 169, No. 12/59; MfS, ZAIG Z 1671, No. 261/69 (13 June 1969).

[57] MfS, ZAIG, Z 119, 'Staatsfeindliche Gruppierung von bürgerlichen Professoren an der Martin-Luther-Universität Halle' (11 Apr. 1958).

cal expertise. Only the ideologically sound could in any event proceed to study the subject of their choice (dissident youngsters with intellectual talents found themselves pointed only in the direction of theology). Those who subsequently failed to conform were disciplined or expelled: teachers who propagated 'bourgeois' attitudes, journalists who allowed a voice to the 'class enemy', scientists who tolerated pluralist views in their institutes, soon found themselves out of a position of leadership and influence, possibly even out of a job. Cadre training and party control eventually came to mean that the intelligentsia constituted in effect conformist pillars of the system, rather than containing a series of potentially oppositional groups. The contrast with the more critical and independent roles of the technical and cultural intelligentsias in Czechoslovakia and Poland would bear further analysis. It may turn out to be less a matter of differences in any 'national political culture' than in the structural determination of the composition of these classes in each case.

There were of course differences within the general category of intelligentsia which should not be overlooked. It was infinitely easier to distance oneself from the regime, and to maintain a separation between technical expertise and political opinions, in the fields, for example, of natural science, medicine, and engineering than it was in the social sciences and the humanities.[58] Moreover, different subject areas started from different baselines in terms of political and social background, and in terms of the perceived usefulness of the expertise to the regime. Medicine had been very thoroughly Nazified during the Third Reich; but it was also, clearly, a key area where professional expertise was more important than ideological credentials. Doctors were subject to very light denazification because of the priority of public health issues in the post-war years: as many as 80 per cent of doctors in Thuringia, for example, had been members of the NSDAP.[59] In 1954, 45.8 per cent of professors of medicine in the GDR were former members of the NSDAP. And medicine remained the most 'bourgeois' profession into the 1960s, while the politically more sensitive area of law became much more rapidly 'proletarianized': by 1965 51.3 per cent of law professors were of proletarian or peasant background (in striking contrast

[58] On the technical intelligentsia, see particularly the older study of Thomas Baylis, *The Technical Intelligentsia and the East German Elite* (Berkeley and Los Angeles: University of California Press, 1974), which emphasizes the *lack* of any uniform political outlook, let alone sense of class consciousness and capacity for common political action, among the disparate groups which constituted the technical intelligentsia.

[59] Christoph Kleßmann, 'Relikte des Bildungsbürgertums in der DDR', in Hartmut Kaelble, Jürgen Kocka, and Hartmut Zwahr (eds.), *Sozialgeschichte der DDR* (Stuttgart: Klett-Cotta, 1994), 258.

to the Federal Republic, where the post-1945 legal profession evinced striking continuities).[60]

Even within the social and historical sciences—which have often been written off as little more than 'legitimatory sciences' for the regime—there were more or less distant islands. In history, for example, it was less difficult to escape the constraints of ideology and politically determined distortion in the fields of ancient history or even medieval history than in recent or contemporary history.[61] Many commentators nevertheless argue that East German historians did not fully use the spaces which *were* available to them, in contrast to, say, Polish historians. It appears that East Germans successfully internalized the relevant walls and censorship scissors, and did not respond only to external pressures and constraints. The same might be said of much of the cultural intelligentsia.

On the other hand, even the writings of many relatively conformist intellectuals in the politically most sensitive areas did succeed—to a greater or lesser extent at different times—in sustaining a kind of critical intellect, a form of at least implicit dialogue about the character of the society in which they lived. Writings may have a critical impact somewhat separate from the political roles of their authors; works may serve to sustain a critical consciousness and debate among the population, even if the authors were relatively subservient servants of the regime (as with the long-time Stasi informer Hermann Kant, or the rather less tainted Christa Wolf). An extraordinary phenomenon is that of the supposedly radically critical alternative poets of Prenzlauer Berg, many of whom—most notably Sascha Anderson—were subsequently revealed to have been deeply implicated as Stasi informers.

There always existed an uneasy relationship between the regime and its intellectuals. Hopes of liberalization were periodically squashed, relaxation of censorship gave way to a tightening up. But in each phase of liberalization seeds were sown which would grow, in however constrained and distorted a fashion, in subsequent periods. So, for example, during the early Honecker years, when the official view was that of 'no taboos under socialism', new cultural currents and groups began to emerge. At the level

[60] Ralph Jessen, 'Professoren im Sozialismus. Aspekte des Strukturwandels der Hochschullehrerschaft in der Ulbricht-Ära', ibid. 226, 224.

[61] On East German historiography, see e.g. Alexander Fischer and Günther Heydemann (eds.), *Geschichtswissenschaft in der DDR*, i (Berlin: Duncker and Humblot, 1988); Konrad Jarausch (ed.), *Zwischen Parteilichkeit und Professionalität. Bilanz der Geschichtswissenschaft in der DDR* (Berlin: Akademie Verlag, 1991); Georg Iggers (ed.), *Marxist Historiography in Transformation: New Orientations in Recent East German History* (Oxford: Berg, 1991).

of individual writers and more critical voices, this was evident, for example, in the publication of Ulrich Plenzdorf's *Die neuen Leiden des jungen W.* (1973), or Christa Wolf's *Kindheitsmuster* (1976); but it also had a wider subcultural resonance among people who did not attain such individual or international renown.

In Jena, from around 1973, a group discussing alternative ideas and cultural productions began to develop, initially under the roof of the Kulturhaus Jena-Neulobeda.[62] In 1976, this group was forced out of the Kulturhaus and continued its discussions under the wing of the Church, in the shape of the protection of the *Jugenddiakon* Thomas Auerbach. In East Berlin, a circle developed around Klaus Schlesinger and Bettina Wegner, in the Haus der jungen Talente. The productions of this group, under the title *Eintopp*, were, however, forbidden on 22 July 1975. Less organized circles sprang up elsewhere, discussing the unorthodox ideas of anti-Stalinists such as Trotsky. While some of these unofficial discussion groups were associated with university circles—particularly around the Humboldt University of Berlin, and the universities in Halle and Leipzig—there were also informal groupings associated with the 'alternative scene' based in cafés and pubs.

The enforced exile of the guitarist and singer Wolf Biermann in late 1976 came as a considerable shock to many people involved in the cultural life of the GDR. Twelve prominent authors, including Christa Wolf—formerly a candidate member of the Central Committee of the SED—openly protested against Biermann's expulsion. Many other writers supported their protest. So too did many quite ordinary people. Comrade M. of the state theatre in Dresden reported that reactions in Dresden were 'highly differentiated': 'Basically people are asking:—How could our government do such a thing?—Our international reputation will suffer from this', and, ironically, 'up to now 80 per cent of our citizens knew nothing about him, now he has become a hero'.[63] A more general report of 17 December 1976 summarized reactions thus: a significant number of people 'support B., or refuse to take a position and remain withdrawn. This is primarily true of members of the cultural, pedagogical, and to some extent the scientific intelligentsia and among youth. Here are to be heard the majority of confused conceptions (*unklaren Auffassungen*). And they often support their mistaken views very obstinately.' The report continues: 'A far smaller proportion express

---

[62] This paragraph is based on Wolfgang Rüddenklau, *Störenfried. ddr-opposition 1986–89* (Berlin: BasisDruck, 1992), Introduction.

[63] FDGB, file no. 3023, 'Information über weitere Meinungen von Gewerkschafts-mitgliedern zur Aberkennung der Staatsbürgerschaft von Biermann' (2 Dec. 1976), 6.

themselves openly, cynically, and provocatively against the decisions of the government and engage themselves in favour of B. in the worst possible ways . . .'[64] Activities expressing protest include declarations against the state's policy, collections of signatures by young people (*Jugendliche*), the spreading of leaflets, writing letters expressing solidarity to Mrs Biermann, writing open letters on *Wandzeitungen* (wall newspapers), making and circulating tape-recordings of Biermann's concerts in the West, and, among schoolchildren, singing the Deutschlandlied.[65] Clearly protests were not limited to a handful of intellectuals.

But cultural revolt did not eventuate into much by way of political activism; rather, in the following years there were many intellectuals who followed Biermann to the West, whether willingly or unwillingly. Others maintained a marginal existence within the GDR, whether through the 'alternative scene' of the Prenzlauer Berg, or on the fringes of the Church. These individuals were able to contribute to a mood of critical disaffection with the nature of life in the GDR; they were, however, less important organizationally, as forces for change. As we shall see in a later chapter, a more active leaven in the body politic were the currents seeking actually to affect policy: seeking not merely to interpret the world, but to change it.

Meanwhile, the vast masses of the professional classes in the GDR—those who were not internationally prominent authors, songwriters, and poets, but rather humdrum teachers, nursery nurses, engineers, dentists, journalists—did their best to fulfil their professional duties, to make life bearable, efficient, workable for those who actually lived under actually existing socialism. The history of these social groups in the GDR has yet, for the most part, to be written. Like the vast majority of GDR citizens, most of them sought to come to terms with the system within which they had to make their lives. Professionalism took precedence over political risk-taking—as it does for most people, most of the time, over most of the world.

Sustaining subordination: the *Mitläufertum*

Many East Germans—and not only professionals—went a little further than simply keeping their heads down and avoiding unnecessary confrontations. For a variety of reasons, they played a more active part in the everyday reproduction of the system of domination. Many were card-carrying party

---

[64] FDGB, file no. 3023, 'Information über die ideologische Situation in den gewerkschaftlichen Grundorganisationen zur Aberkennung der DDR-Staatsbürgerschaft Biermanns' (17 Dec. 1976), 2.
[65] Ibid. 5–6.

members; some worked as unofficial informers (IMs) for the Stasi. What were the motives for, and implications of, this more active support of the system?

Party membership, and membership of the mass organizations, was very widespread. One in five of the adult population was a member of the SED in the early 1980s; virtually all the adult working population belonged to the FDGB; around half belonged to the Gesellschaft für Deutsch-Sowjetische Freundschaft, and substantial proportions belonged to the other bloc parties and mass organizations depicted at the start of this chapter. Mass participation was for a wide variety of motives, ranging from genuine commitment through unthinking conformity to pragmatic self-interest. Members of the older generation—a generation among which many were not able to have a genuine memory of their participation in the Nazi past—often were driven by a desire to indicate their commitment to the new system, to provide outward evidence of an alleged change of heart, to prove their willingness to conform. Party or organizational membership was a suitable alibi, with possible personal advantages. Members of younger generations, socialized in the GDR, often simply took it for granted that this is what life was like: one took the sociopolitical structure for granted, knew the rules of the game, and played according to these rules. In some senses, the retrospective condemnation of all such alleged complicity in the supposedly heinous crimes of an *Unrechtsstaat* is misplaced. The capacity to conform, without enquiring too closely, the capacity to live within apparently immutable parameters, is less difficult to explain than the emergence of a willingness to think differently, to have the courage of one's convictions and accept the related risks and disadvantages, and to dare to mount an active challenge to the rules of the game.[66]

Given the current climate of moralizing—however out of place this might seem in a historical text—it is worth explicitly posing the question of whether these *Mitläufer* should be the object of castigation or condemnation for their complicity in sustaining a dictatorial regime.[67] Neither the Third Reich nor the GDR could have functioned without the millions of

[66] This latter is much more difficult to explain, and will be considered in detail in Ch. 8 below.

[67] One of the problems of much German writing on the GDR, whether from East or West, is that it is so closely embroiled in political and personal commitments that it is often very difficult to separate out what is historical explanation and what is moral castigation. This is evident not only in the language and terminology of description used, but also in the prior assumptions structuring accounts. See e.g. Armin Mitter and Stefan Wolle, *Untergang auf Raten* (Munich: C. Bertelsmann Verlag, 1993). Outsiders of course are less personally affected, but as with any contemporary history there is a degree of political presupposition involved.

Germans who made the system work. But unlike the Third Reich, there was in the GDR no sense of enthusiasm for nationalist expansionism, nor were there disturbing intimations of the disappearance of large groups of people, selected on 'racial' grounds, and their non-return from rumoured places of death in the East. There can be no doubt that the GDR was a dictatorship based on party domination, and ultimately deceit and repression, as described in the previous chapter. But it was not, at least after the worst excesses of the Stalinist period in the late 1940s and 1950s, a state in which mass murder was not only condoned but actively encouraged. This is not the place to engage in an exercise of comparative political moral philosophy, but on any common-sense scale of humanitarianism the GDR would have to score at an infinitely less abysmal level than the Third Reich. Without wishing to enter into inappropriate apologetics, it should also be pointed out that many East Germans were genuinely surprised and perturbed at the excesses of deceit and repression practised by the SED and the Stasi, when the scale of their activities was revealed after the GDR's collapse. If ignorance is any defence, then a significant proportion of East German *Mitläufer* should not be treated too harshly in the judgement of history. It should also be remembered that the vast majority of the East German population, who effectively fell in with the rules of the game imposed from above, did so from a position of relative exposure and personal weakness. And they did so at a time when, from a contrasting position of strength, the leaders of the West were also treating the GDR government with a degree of respect and an assumption of permanency. Honecker was, after all, received by the West as a much-honoured guest in 1987.

There were, of course, also a much smaller number of East Germans who were complicit in more serious ways, who engaged more consciously in practices of deceit and repression. Somewhere in the order of 180,000 people were active as unofficial informers for the Stasi by the later 1980s. Some of these so-called IMs might not have been aware of the fact that they were being 'led'; most would, however, have entered into an agreement to inform for the Stasi, and signed a written agreement to maintain secrecy. The leading of a double life which this activity often (but not always) entailed, the transgression of common bounds of behaviour and norms of decency and honesty in human relationships, is clearly a subject not only for further research but also a degree of personal agonizing for those involved.

4

RENDER UNTO CAESAR?

THE PIVOTAL ROLE OF THE PROTESTANT CHURCHES

IT may seem a little strange to include a chapter on the Protestant Churches under a section entitled 'The Contours of Domination'. The Churches were, after all, hardly part of the communist state apparatus; a legacy of centuries of Christian history, they were institutional standard-bearers of a very different world-view from that of Ulbricht and Honecker. The Church appeared to have acted as a haven for dissidents in the course of the 1980s, leading up to the climactic events of the autumn of 1989; moreover, in the months following the fall of the Wall, many commentators were surprised at the prevalence of pastors in the political landscape of that short-lived transitional state, the 'noch-DDR'. It seemed to many that the Protestant Church had played more of a role in undermining than sustaining the system of domination in the GDR.

But it did not take long before this view was challenged, as the extent of Stasi infiltration into, and exploitation of, the Protestant Church for communist purposes began to be revealed. The concerted public attacks on the Social Democrat Prime Minister of Land Brandenburg and former senior Church functionary, Manfred Stolpe, for his alleged close links with the Stasi, opened up an apparent can of Stasi worms crawling in the innards of the Protestant Church. Moreover, as part of the awkward process of 'coming to terms' with a divided past, and measuring the extent to which East and West Germans, popular proclamations notwithstanding, hardly felt like 'one Volk', these attacks on the Church to some extent paralleled the concomitant debates on the complicity of the cultural intelligentsia in the person of Christa Wolf.

Thus, heralded by some commentators as a form of political opposition paving the way for the 'Protestant Revolution' of 1989, denounced by others as pusillanimous and self-serving, the Protestant Churches have been the focus of considerable controversy with respect to their political role under actually existing socialism. But, as always, the reality is more complex than the simplicities of public debates in the media sometimes allow. As we shall see, the role of the Protestant Churches in the GDR was, paradoxically, simultaneously both conducive and detrimental to the stability of communist rule.[1] While this chapter considers aspects of the highly ambiguous and changing Church–state relations over the years, a later chapter will explore the subcultural undercurrents, the swirls and eddies that washed around the ecclesiastical edifice, which ultimately helped to contribute to the demise of the state with which the Church had effectively come to terms. Whatever the ultimate historical verdict on its political role in the GDR, the Protestant Church cannot be ignored as a major factor in the landscape of power.

The GDR was predominantly Protestant. In some areas, there were substantial Catholic congregations (for example, in the Eichsfeld), but in general the Catholic Church was not as relevant to the political development of the GDR as were Protestants. Catholics tended on the whole to retain a lower political profile, and to adopt a policy of retreat and hibernation (*Überwintern*) which was for the most part of less direct relevance to the concerns of this book, and will therefore not be the subject of explicit discussion here.

It should be emphasized at the outset that the Protestant Church in the GDR was not a monolithic entity, but rather a league of eight different regional Churches, which differed from one another in terms of their historical, theological, and political traditions.[2] Five of the regional Churches combined Lutheran and Reformed traditions, merged under Prussia in the Old Prussian Union (subsequently Evangelical Church of the Union) in the nineteenth century; three were purely Lutheran. Pre-1945 differences were compounded subsequently by the varying degrees of success of the SED and the Stasi in seeking to infiltrate Church structures and

---

[1] Sections of this chapter are also published, in slightly different form, as parts of an article in Michael Geyer and Robert von Hallberg (eds.), *Cultural Authority in Contemporary Germany: Intellectual Responsibility between State Security Surveillance and Media Society* (Chicago: University of Chicago Press, forthcoming).

[2] For overviews researched before 1989, see e.g. Frederic Spotts, *The Churches and Politics in Germany* (Middletown, Conn.: Wesleyan University Press, 1973); Horst Dähn, *Konfrontation oder Kooperation? Das Verhältnis von Staat und Kirche in der SBZ/DDR 1945–1980* (Opladen: Westdeutscher Verlag, 1982); Reinhard Henkys (ed.), *Die evangelischen Kirchen in der DDR* (Munich: Chr. Kaiser Verlag, 1982); Robert Goeckel, *The Lutheran Church and the East German State* (Ithaca, NY: Cornell University Press, 1990). For a more recent analysis of the early years, based on extensive study of the documents now available, see Gerhard Besier, *Der SED-Staat und die Kirche* (Munich: C. Bertelsmann Verlag, 1993).

to influence the leading personnel of the regional Churches, effectively hijacking democratic procedures and placing compliant churchpeople in positions of authority where possible. In some areas such processes were more, in others less, successful. Moreover, there was great variability from area to area, parish to parish, *within* any of the regional Churches, depending on the views and personalities of particular pastors and their support or otherwise from regional leaders. So to speak in the singular of 'the Church', although entirely legitimate, should not be allowed to entail the assumption that this was a uniform and single political actor. Nevertheless, certain generalizations can be made.

On the one hand, some members of the Protestant establishment, whether advertently or inadvertently, undoubtedly aided the regime's capacity to monitor, interfere with, and channel social processes in directions desired by the SED. The state pursued a systematic, single-minded policy—whatever the twists and turns in appearance—of seeking both to undermine Christianity as a living force in society while at the same time attempting to infiltrate and increasingly control the leadership of the Church. For all the ostensible changes in state attitudes to the Church, the ultimate aims remained the same: to reduce the impact of Christian beliefs in society; and to make use of the institutional Church as an important means of often hidden social control, an indirect means of exerting coercion. Even the Church–state agreement of 6 March 1978, previously heralded as a sign of incipient liberalization in the GDR, must now be interpreted as a further step—which ultimately backfired very badly for the state—in seeking to co-opt and take over what should in the end have become a subservient state Church in classical Lutheran tradition. The regime's project of effective *Gleichschaltung* was, however, subverted by irrepressible forces from within and around the Church, ironically to some degree as a direct result of the state's policies.

By denying political nonconformists and committed Christians chances of higher education outside theology, and hence career prospects in a range of secular professions, the regime itself unintentionally *produced* a relatively cohesive group of disaffected activists: pastors, theologians, and people unable to pursue other career paths who gained employment in some capacity with the Church. It was primarily these people who became politically very active in the changing circumstances of the 1980s and in the unfolding of the revolution of 1989. Moreover, in seeking to co-opt and make use of the Church—in the process according it the anomalous status of an officially permitted autonomous social institution—the state actually *created* the structural preconditions for the growth of organized grass-roots dissent, among non-Christians as well as Christians, on a scale never pre-viously possible in the GDR.

Protestantism was in many respects a most formidable partner for the state to take on. It was the only intact institutional structure in post-Hitler Germany, other organized bases for a potential 'civil society', such as trade unions, social, and cultural organizations, having been destroyed or co-opted under Nazism, and their short-lived successors after 1945 being relatively easily *gleichgeschaltet* for a second time under different political colours. Moreover, Christianity had two thousand years of history: of persecution, of courage and martyrdom in the face of adversity, of belief in the will of the Lord and the transcendence of the spirit. This was no mere passing intellectual ideology which might or might not be rejected on purely rational or pragmatic grounds: centuries of belief and religious practice could arouse very powerful and deep emotions in people. The fundamental belief in (and fear of) God was a factor often underestimated by secular communists (not to mention many academic commentators). This was a quite different cultural habitus for many people, and religious communities often constituted 'cultural islands' (*Kulturinsel*) which proved remarkably resistant to communist infiltration. Despite declining church-attendance figures, a resilient localized Christian culture and active Church-related social activities remained a perpetual problem for the political authorities, while even in secularized form certain fundamental values were counter-posed to the constraints of life under communism.

Realizing that it could not destroy the cultural power of Christianity, the state sought instead to co-opt the Church as, to some degree, an extended arm of the state. This could not, of course, be done in quite such an obvious and crass manner as the achievement of political control over the other political parties and mass organizations in the late 1940s and early 1950s; nor could it be quite as complete. The trick seemed to be to grant consider-able concessions to the Church in pursuit of its narrowly defined *religious* aims, and then to pressurize Church leaders to adopt a line of political loyalty and to curb the more turbulent spirits in their midst by reminding them of the possibility of endangering the state's apparently uniquely toler-ant and concessionary stance towards the Church. Political obedience was the price to be paid for freedom of the spirit—a concept of what Thomas Mann called 'machtgeschützte Innerlichkeit', not unfamiliar with Germans since Luther and Kant.

Thus, the Church was in a sense caught in the crossfire: on the one hand used, to a degree infiltrated, by the state (particularly through the Stasi), on the other hand also made the vehicle of protest and discussion, such that by the later 1980s it constituted a highly contested political terrain and played a significant role in the domestic balance of power.

A number of phases of development of Church–state relations may, very broadly, be distinguished. Of course, there were overlaps between, and ambiguities within, each of these phases, but a periodization is nevertheless apparent. First, there was the phase of open hostility, combined with rather crass attempts at control and eventually more subtle *rapprochement*, which lasted until the late 1960s. Then there was the period of the growth of a cautious, unequal, and arguably rather cynical partnership, mightily aided by the institutional separation of the East German Churches from their West German counterparts in 1969, which culminated in the Church–state agreement of 1978—an agreement which was subject to quite different interpretations on the part of the state, the more conformist members of the Church leadership, and more radical Christians. Finally there was the phase of simultaneous compromise and contention, which lasted from 1978 to 1989. Within each of these periods, significant shifts can be discerned.

Antagonism and *rapprochement*, 1945–1969

Certainly in the early years of the GDR, the Church seemed to provide one of the major social—and institutional—bases of 'immunity' to the regime. In the immediate post-war period, the Churches enjoyed a sudden rise in public support and popularity, as they provided an anchor of faith and forgiveness, and a sense of eternity, in the maelstrom, confusion, and chaos of current events.

At the end of the war, the Churches occupied a relatively strong position in Germany, for a number of reasons—moral and cultural, as well as institutional and economic. First of all, the Churches had considerable institutional and numerical weight. In the Soviet zone, with a total population of around 17 million, there were just under 15 million Protestants and around 1 million Catholics. While Hitler had succeeded in abolishing or co-opting virtually all other social institutions in Germany, the Churches had—despite their compromises with the Nazi regime—retained their institutional structures intact. Along with the newly created Christian political party, the CDU, the Churches were a massive force to be reckoned with in seeking to exert communist control over German life in the Soviet zone.

Furthermore, there were outstanding individuals—such as those active in the Confessing Church (*Bekennende Kirche*)—who had taken a firm stand against Hitler. The relatively rapid issue by Protestants of a 'Declaration of

Guilt' in the *Stuttgarter Schuldbekenntnis* of October 1945 confirmed the view that the Protestant Churches had a strong sense of moral and political responsibility, despite their deep internal divisions at this time. Moreover, the existence of Christian opposition to Hitler, as well as many personal friendships formed in concentration camps between persecuted communists and Christians, made it difficult for the 'anti-fascist' regime of the early post-war years to take any dramatic action against either the institutional status or the personnel of the Churches. Moreover, for many Social Democrats there was no conflict in principle between Christianity and socialism.

In the Soviet zone, Church possessions were exempted from the land reform of 1945 and the nationalization measures of 1946. The Churches were also left to engage in their own (lukewarm) denazification. Much later, official defences of the lack of any real denazification in the East German Church included the somewhat ahistorical and apologetic comment, made in 1986 by an Ecumenical Officer of the Evangelical Church, to the effect that 'there were no real Nazis among the pastors in the Soviet zone any-way'.[3] In the event, however, there were very real and bitter splits within the Church between those who had opposed Hitler and those who had made their compromises with the Nazi regime. These animosities were sub-sequently exploited by the state in its efforts to undermine the influence of the Church in the 1950s, as we shall see.

The Soviet administration and the East German communists initially propagated the notion of a partnership, in which Christians and commu-nists could work together in a broad, democratic, anti-fascist front. But appearances belied realities. While the CDU was gradually being co-opted into a puppet party within a communist-dominated bloc, broader policies were pursued to exclude Christianity from public life and reduce the ac-tivities of the Churches to a purely religious sphere.

The battle for ideological influence over the rising generation was opened only a year after the defeat of Hitler. On 31 May 1946 the Law for the Democratization of German Schools (Gesetz zur Demokratisierung der deutschen Schule) stated in section 2 that 'The education of children in schools is exclusively the prerogative of the state. Religious instruction is the prerogative of religious associations...'[4] Church opposition to the secularization of education was to little effect: denominational schools were abolished in the Soviet zone, and there were mounting difficulties in connec-tion with making religious instruction available within secular schools,

---

[3] Interview with Christa Grengel in East Berlin, 4 Sept. 1986.
[4] See Dähn, *Konfrontation oder Kooperation?*, 30–2.

including problems with timetabling, lack of appropriate rooms, and the fact that many teachers of religious education had been Nazis. Excluded from the classroom, in the following years Christians were to find their influence over youth the focus of contention in virtually all areas of social and cultural life as well.

Anti-Christian policies became more forceful under Ulbricht in the 1950s. Reading through documents relating to this decade, a number of features are very striking. It is quite clear that there was a major clash of two very strong, opposing, all-encompassing world-views—Christianity and Marxism-Leninism—both of which at this time made quite incompatible and total claims on the rising generation. Both enjoyed considerable organizational and institutional strength: the Church through its inherited structures and hierarchy; the state through emerging organizations and on the basis of overwhelming political and coercive power. The Church, however, was to some extent weakened by internal divisions between individuals of the Confessing Church persuasion and former pro-Nazi German Christians—divisions which the state sought to identify, exacerbate, and exploit. The state similarly was not as yet fully established, its own internal structures of command and control were still nascent and developing. As a report of 1958 put it, in some areas the difficulties of establishing appropriate structures and procedures, and the weakness of certain functionaries, meant that party work 'is threatened with suffocation by trivialities'. Furthermore, 'connections between localities and the coordination of measures within the state apparatus are similarly still inadequate'.[5]

The whole situation was furthermore overwhelmingly influenced by the international context of the time. The issue of separation from the West was of overriding concern to SED leaders; pro-Western, pro-Adenauer views in the Church were the epitome of fifth columnism as far as the East German leadership was concerned. A lengthy document, undated but clearly compiled in the mid-1950s, represents the state's attempt to understand the structure and mentality of the Church hierarchy, which is viewed in quite paranoid terms. In the Cold War view of the anonymous compiler of this official report, the Church hierarchy sees itself 'as God's appointed opponent' of the GDR, entirely dependent on the 'financial, political, and ideological support of the Western world'. The 'highest principle of this Western-coloured (*westlerischen*) politics is deadly hostility against the German Democratic Republic, against the Soviet Union and against Social-

---

[5] BP, O-4 2377, 'Bericht über die Dienstreise vom 19.5 bis 24.5.1958 in die Bezirke Erfurt, Gera und Suhl'.

ism'.[6] In view of this evaluation of the political role of the Church, it is hardly surprising that the Church was initially treated so harshly by the newly established, as yet insecure (and in any event always paranoid) communist state. On the other hand, Church leaders appear to have seen the duration of division as still undetermined, the current political circumstances as perhaps merely temporary. They appeared to be willing to enter into major ideological confrontations at this time, refusing to budge on key issues. This stands, as we shall see, in stark contrast to the later willingness to compromise and to seek small measures of improvement in the 1980s when, paradoxically, the GDR appeared to be a much more permanent entity on the political landscape, likely to last for the foreseeable future. While major opposition and ideological confrontation achieved virtually nothing in the 1950s, more subtle attempts to pressurize from within while entering into compromises in the 1980s were to produce much more dramatic effects by way of ultimate destabilization of the regime. We shall return to these musings at a later juncture.

In January 1951, the Central Committee reached the decision that teachers must be impregnated with a materialist, atheist world-view of Marxism-Leninism, entailing an inevitable conflict with children from Christian homes. The latter were systematically discriminated against at school. From 1952, there was a concerted campaign against the Junge Gemeinde (groups of young Christians in the Church), which was designated as a 'criminal' organization because the only officially permitted organization for young people was the Free German Youth (FDJ). Many members of the Junge Gemeinde were expelled from school, or blocked from entering higher education. Characteristically, however, this explosively oppositional policy did not last long.

In the uncertain political conditions of early June 1953, the state sought to come to some form of agreement with the Church. At a meeting on 10 June—a bare week before the mass uprising—the government acknowledged that it had made certain mistakes, and a number of pupils who had been expelled from schools because of their activities in the Junge Gemeinde were readmitted. On 11 July 1953, in the aftermath of the June Uprising, the then youth leader Erich Honecker officially conceded that the Junge Gemeinde should not be viewed as an illegal organization, and even that a belief in Marxism-Leninism was not a necessary prerequisite for membership in the FDJ.[7] In the event, the attempt at compromise turned out to be more a matter of appearance, of tactics, than a long-term change in strategy.

[6] BP, O-4 1918, 'Analyse der Kirchen-Hierarchie und ihre Tätigkeit nach 1945', 6.
[7] See Dähn, Konfrontation oder Kooperation?, 50.

The state was still determined that membership in the FDJ should take precedence over young Christian social activities. But the new approach was to improve the attractiveness of the FDJ offerings, rather than condemn and forbid the Junge Gemeinde. As a report of September 1955 noted, it was well known that the Junge Gemeinde was able to grow in strength and importance 'in those areas and quarters . . . in which the work of the FDJ is miserable, there is inadequate support from the party and the other mass organizations, and clerics are able, off their own bat, to organize "happy times for youngsters"'. The FDJ would have to improve their own activities and organizational strategies; one could not simply 'liquidate' the pastors' youth activities 'by administrative means'.[8]

Open conflicts between Church and state intensified dramatically in 1954 with the introduction of the *Jugendweihe*, the state's secular alternative to the Church's confirmation ceremony. The *Jugendweihe* represented a resurrection of a socialist tradition dating back to the Weimar Republic, but in its new form was allegedly—according to its new communist proponents—not anti-religious in intent. It was merely intended to mark the transition to maturity of young people who should be educated to be active citizens of socialist society. In preparation for the ceremony, there were lessons in what was essentially an atheist world-view. In a characteristically long-winded, optimistic official description, the *Jugendweihe* contributed 'to the process of imparting to young people useful knowledge in basic questions of the scientific world-view and socialist morality, of raising them in the spirit of socialist patriotism and proletarian internationalism, and helping them to prepare themselves for active participation in the construction of developed socialist society and the creation of the basic preconditions for the gradual transition to communism'.[9] This 'scientific' world-view and contribution to the building of communism entailed, of course, digging the grave of Christianity: religion, it must be recalled, was but the 'sigh of the oppressed creature' under capitalism, and was officially scheduled to 'wither away' with the transition to truly communist society. Not surprisingly, the Churches reacted accordingly, saying that induction into such a world-view was in principle incompatible with Christian confirmation in church.

As Bishop Dibelius put it, in a circular letter of 2 August 1955 which was to be read out to all members of the Junge Gemeinde: 'A person who has committed himself or herself to God cannot at the same time support and

---

[8] IfGA, ZPA, IV 2/5/322, letter from W. Barth to Genosse Kleinert, Abteilung Leitender Organe (28 Sept. 1955).
[9] *Kleines Politisches Wörterbuch* (Berlin: Dietz Verlag, 3rd edn., 1978), 416.

profess such a [materialist] world-view.' There was a clear conflict between the duties of obedience and the demands of conscience: 'Of course there are many people to whom we owe a duty of obedience: parents, teachers, superiors. But this obedience has its limits. None of these people has the right to dispose over our consciences.'[10]

The introduction of the *Jugendweihe* unleashed a storm of reaction and protest. Innumerable pastors made vigorous public representations.[11] Even the (subsequently rather conciliatory and pro-regime) Bishop of Thuringia, Bishop Mitzenheim, emphasized in a circular letter to teachers that it was unacceptable to have an atheistic-materialistic world-view built up as a cult, with its own ceremony, particularly since the latter conflicted with Easter and with church preparations for confirmation. Since the state had indicated that the *Jugendweihe* was purely voluntary in nature, teachers should not support it.[12] Even as late as 3 November 1957, this on the whole politically compliant bishop was preaching the duties of political disobedience if the commands of the state were at odds with those of God, in which context the *Jugendweihe* received specific mention. In a sermon delivered in front of around 1,500 people, Mitzenheim asserted that 'Apostle Paul has already said that Christians must obey secular authority and obey laws which do not entail sinning. If they had to obey laws which would entail committing a sin, then there is only one possibility, to obey God alone.' Mitzenheim repeatedly stressed that 'it is more important to obey God than human beings'.[13]

Nor was it only pastors who protested against the *Jugendweihe*. As late as February 1955, for example, there are indications that party functionaries in the bloc parties of the CDU and the LDPD had not yet been completely *gleichgeschaltet* (pulled into line) as far as their Christian beliefs

---

[10] BP, O-4 1918, letter of 2 Aug. 1955.

[11] See e.g. IfGA, ZPA, IV 2/5/322, 'Wochenbericht der Stadtleitung Plauen' (27 Sept. 1955); BP O-4 2377, 'Bericht über Gespräche mit Pfarrern in Kreis Zeulenroda' (22 June 1957); cf. also more generally the circular letter from Bishop Dibelius to all members of the Junge Gemeinde on the fundamental clash between a religious and an atheist world-view, to be read out by all pastors to their groups and congregations (BP, O-4 1918).

[12] IfGA, ZPA, IV 2/5/322, Informationsbericht der BL Suhl, 2 Nov. 1955, with copy of Bishop Mitzenheim's letter of 20 Oct. 1955.

[13] BP, O-4 2377, report on the 'Greiz Gottesdienst in der Stadtkirche am 3. Nov. 1957, 20.00–22.00 Uhr'. Bishop Mitzenheim was preaching on the theme of 'die Freiheit eines Christenmenschen'. The writer of the report notes that the service finished with an emotional rendering of the hymn 'Eine feste Burg ist unser Gott', 'wovon die dritte Strophe: "Und wenn die Welt voll Teufel wär, und wollt uns gar verschlingen" solo d.h. ohne Orgel gesungen wurde, damit es auch richtig gehört wurde' ('A Safe Stronghold our God is still', 'of which the third verse, "And were this world all devils o'er, And watching to devour us" was sung solo, i.e. without the organ, so that it could be heard properly').

were concerned. One of the SED weekly reports from the Bezirk Gera complains that pastors are being supported by members of the 'bourgeois parties': 'In Eisenberg the CDU Chairman G. said in a gathering of members that his party was not yet[!] opposed to the government, but that it would definitely fight against the *Jugendweihe* with whatever means were necessary. Meetings of LDPD members in the Landkreis Pößneck ran more or less along the same lines.'[14]

In the event, however, the conflict over the *Jugendweihe* eventually simmered down. Talks between Church and state in the course of 1956 did not achieve any real change in the character of the *Jugendweihe*, despite some discussion of whether it could be turned into a less stridently atheistic, more purely ceremonial school-leaving celebration, a neutral rite of passage.[15] In 1957, Ulbricht still insisted on its importance and its continuity with Weimar traditions. Having essentially lost the battle of principle, the Church had to make the best of a bad job in practice. In the following years, the Church implicitly renounced its absolute claims in this area, and ceased to insist on the fundamental incompatibility of confirmation in church and participation in the *Jugendweihe*. Ever-increasing numbers of East German young people came to take the *Jugendweihe* as an accepted fact of adolescent life. While only 17.7 per cent of the age group took the *Jugendweihe* in 1954–5, the figure had reached over 90 per cent by the late 1960s.

Nevertheless, a more general battle for the souls of the people continued to be waged. Ulbricht began to modify his policies of overt confrontation in favour of more muted attempts to exploit and develop a wedge between 'positive' (i.e. pro-state) and 'negative' forces within the Church from the later 1950s. (These policies of political interference in the internal affairs of the Church continued right through to 1989, despite apparently major changes in visible tactics and outward forms of the relationship.) A document of 6 September 1955 sought to differentiate between those pastors who were in principle friendly to the regime, and the pro-Western, anti-GDR politics of the Church hierarchy under Bishop Otto Dibelius of Berlin.[16] This line of enquiry was to be pursued further, and essentially

[14] IfGA, ZPA, IV 2/5/322, 'Abteilung Leitende Organe der Partei und Massenorganisationen', report of 14 Feb. 1955.

[15] The various texts of the *Jugendweihe* (1955, 1958, and 1969 versions) are reprinted in Christoph Kleßmann, *Zwei Staaten, eine Nation: Deutsche Geschichte 1955–1970* (Göttingen: Vandenhoek and Ruprecht, 1988), Doc. 64, 573–4. Despite changes in wording and emphasis, reflecting changes in the political situation of the GDR over the years, the text to which young people were required to give their assent remained—and was intended to remain—highly political in character.

[16] BP, O-4 1918, document of 6 Sept. 1955.

formed the basis of the Church politics of the subsequent three and a half decades.

The Stasi also began to extend its poisonous tentacles into the realms of the Church, perhaps most successfully in Thuringia, which over the following years spearheaded the process of accommodation with the regime. In 1955, Oberkirchenrat Lotz was approached by the Stasi. In return for personal favours and not inconsiderable sums of money, Lotz both reported to the Stasi on confidential internal Church affairs and sought to influence the Church in Thuringia in the directions desired by the Stasi.[17] Over a period of many years, he influenced the so-called 'Red Bishop' of Thuringia, Mitzenheim, on matters concerning the personnel as well as the politics of the Thuringian Church. Lotz was instrumental in laying the groundwork for the split in 1969 from the West German Churches, and in ensuring more positive state–Church relations within the GDR. He furthermore helped to ensure that the successor to Bishop Mitzenheim was Ingo Braechlein, who was himself a Stasi informant (IM).[18] Not that Lotz himself was a committed communist; it seems rather that he was merely a practised informer and political time-server under dictatorships of any persuasion. He had quite cynically ('with a nonchalant flexibility') joined the CDU in 1946, after a period of apparently faithful service to the Nazi regime. As one commentator observed: 'This Herr Lotz was at one time a died-in-the-wool German Christian [i.e. pro-Nazi] of the Thuringian variety, and a forceful advocate of National Socialism within the Thuringian Church . . . [Lotz] co-operated with the Gestapo to cleanse the Church from pastors of the Confessing Church persuasion'.[19] And Lotz was of course not the only character of this kind.[20] Although Thuringia clearly led the way, it appears

[17] See e.g. BP, O-4 2377, 'Aussprache mit Oberkirchenrat Lotz, Landeskirchenrat Eisenach, am 8.11.57', in which it is revealed that Lotz has a daughter who has fled the GDR (*republikflüchtig*) and who has been refused permission to come and visit him; and, in the same file, the confidential letter of 17 Dec. 1959 from Staatssekretär Eggerath to Comrade Kother of the Rat des Bezirkes Erfurt, informing him that a sum of 1,000 Marks has been sent to the 'special account (*Sonderkonto*)' and asking Kother 'to put this sum into the enclosed greetings card to Herr Oberkirchenrat Lotz and to hand it over to him in a sealed envelope'.

[18] 'DDR-Kirche. "Opposition bringt nichts". Das geheime Leben des ostdeutschen Oberkirchenrats "Karl" alias Gerhard Lotz', *Der Spiegel*, 46: 26 (1992), 122–41.

[19] Letter quoted in G. Besier and S. Wolf (eds.), *'Pfarrer, Christen und Katholiken'. Das Ministerium für Staatssicherheit der ehemaligen DDR und die Kirchen* (Neukirchen: Neukirchener Verlag, 2nd edn., 1992), 18–19 n. 94.

[20] One pastor Behr, for example, a former member of the NSDAP 1933–45 and interned in Buchenwald 1945–8 for his Nazi past, was now evincing positive attitudes towards the new regime. In June 1957 he came under active consideration for co-option although the state was slightly hesitant with respect to the question 'as to whether it is advisable to win over former (*abgetackelten*) Nazi pastors, which would probably be successful in the case of Behr'. BP, O-4 2377, 'Bericht über Gespräche mit Pfarrern in Kreis Zeulenroda' (22 June 1957).

that at least four Landeskirchen were successfully infiltrated by the Stasi in the mid-1950s.

An important analysis of late May 1956, in preparation for a discussion of the *Abteilung Kirchenfragen* of the Central Committee of the SED, emphasized the need to identify 'progressive' (i.e. pro-regime) forces in the Church hierarchy, with a view to using these people to exert influence over the less willing forces among the leadership. 'This must be done with the aim of using differentiation cleverly and skilfully, in order to persuade other Church leaders to change their attitudes.' At lower levels of Church personnel, it was necessary to win over 'wavering pastors who are still undecided' through a variety of means: individual discussions, small acts of helpfulness in respect of one matter or another. 'In particular, the little wishes and concerns of pastors are ignored by bureaucratic behaviour. . . . The possibility of financial and material help and support has not so far been exploited sufficiently, in a skilful and fruitful manner, to create good relationships.' The Central Committee would need to discuss in more detail the role of the National Front and in particular of the CDU in influencing pastors. There were still many difficulties at the parish level. The document reached the following conclusion:

The view may be confirmed that the inadequacies which have appeared in work so far may be traced back, in large part, to the fact that a number of organs or bodies and organizations are working to some extent separately from one another. Only a coordination of all questions concerning Church politics under an organ of state will be able to overcome this problem and enable better work.[21]

The following year, the Ministry for Church Affairs was established, to exercise just such a function of coordination, oversight, and direction. This subsequently became the Staatssekretariat für Kirchenfragen (State Secretariat for Church Questions) in 1960. As with all state bureaucracies, it worked very closely with the SED hierarchy and with the Stasi. The overlap between the records of Stasi, SED, and state documents is quite striking, as we shall see in exploring the treatment of dissent in the 1980s. To suggest that Church leaders were somehow less tainted if they dealt solely with party or state functionaries, and refused to enter into dialogue with Stasi representatives, is to ignore the realities of the structure of power in the GDR.

Meanwhile, with the introduction of military conscription in the Federal Republic of Germany, and the use of the Church to minister to NATO

---

[21] BP, O-4 1918, undated and untitled document, probably late May 1956, in preparation for 'Termin beim ZK/Abt. Kirchenfragen, 29.5.56 abends, spät am 30.5.56 mittags'.

soldiers (the *Militärseelsorgevertrag*), the political implications of an un-divided Church in a divided nation were becoming ever more problematic. The Western Churches were officially denigrated as the 'NATO-Kirche' and more concerted efforts were devoted to seeking to split the Churches in the GDR from their pan-German organization. In 1958, the Bund evangelischer Pfarrer in der DDR was founded, as an organization designed explicitly to split the Church, separating pro-regime and dissenting pastors. Rather too visibly and obviously a state stooge organization to enjoy much credibility or genuine support, the Pfarrerbund was eventually officially dissolved in 1974 (five years after the East German Church had separated organizationally from the Western Churches), although a rump organiz-ation of pro-regime pastors remained. Also in 1958, the pro-regime Christliche Friedenskonferenz (CFK, Christian Peace Conference) was founded in Prague, again essentially a front organization designed to co-opt compliant pastors to support the state's official peace policies. This too was treated with appropriate distance by many more independent-minded Christians.

By 1958, the more subtle politics of influence from within rather than overt confrontation received official expression. In June and July 1958, there was a series of meetings between Church and state representatives seeking to reduce the areas of controversy and to reach some sort of *modus vivendi*. Although there were clear differences of political emphasis among the Church leaders who participated in the discussions, a compromise formula (which seems to have been the result of some considerable covert Stasi influence) was agreed.[22] The communiqué of 21 July 1958 announced that the East German Church representatives had conceded that they were not bound by the *Militärseelsorgevertrag*, that they were in favour of peace among nations, and that they essentially supported the peace policies of the GDR. 'In accordance with their faith Christians fulfil their duties as citizens on the basis of law. They respect the development towards socialism and contribute to the peaceful construction of the life of the community

---

[22] Cf. BP, O-4 588, 'Einschätzung der Tätigkeit von Vertretern der Evangelischen Kirche nach Verhandlungen zwischen Staat und Kirche im Juni und Juli 1958'. Berlin Bishop Dibelius was characterized as evincing 'negative' views: 'as long as the state in the GDR is atheist, there is no freedom there. The state must immediately give up enforcing a particular world-view, if it wants Christians to become loyal citizens.' The *Rat der EKU* was similarly on the whole negative: 'Here, particular emphasis is laid on the fact that the GDR government continues to do everything possible to hinder the work of the Church and that there is as yet no sign of any improvement in conditions.' Mitzenheim was, however, singled out for praise for his 'positive' responses: 'He particularly emphasized a respect for socialism in the GDR and challenged Christians to participate actively in the construction of socialism and the struggle for the maintenance of peace.'

(*Volksleben*).' In return for this major concession, the state confirmed freedom of belief and conscience for Christians in the GDR: 'Every citizen enjoys full freedom of belief and conscience. The undisturbed practice of religion is protected by the Republic.'[23] The state nevertheless refused to make concessions with respect to the *Jugendweihe*, and its concurrent educational policies stressed an atheistic world-view which was incompatible with Christian teachings.

From 1959, the Church leadership effectively gave up its battle over the *Jugendweihe*, softening its stance and renouncing the earlier view that taking the *Jugendweihe* and confirmation were absolutely and for all time completely incompatible. This shift in emphasis was justified by some Church leaders, who felt that the people were simply not behind their own interpretation of the matter as an either/or question. The masses after all had to live in the real world, and to find their own forms of compromise with the prevailing political conditions; and a continued adamant stance on the part of the Church leadership might ultimately have led to the *Volkskirche* finding itself without a *Volk*. It seemed pointless to give a lead where few would follow.

What then was the meaning of Christianity for people at this time, a little over a decade after the defeat of the Third Reich? Although there were clearly difficulties with respect to political frictions, religious values and practices were still very important as an alternative belief system and source of social and psychological support for large numbers of people. Religious communities were to some considerable degree 'resistant' to communist infiltration and control, particularly where there was a strong pastor and a wide range of active church-based social organizations (women's groups, brass bands, choral groups, and so on). It is important also not to lose sight of the more passive aspects of the role of religion in East German society: the ways in which it provided a source of strength in retreat.

Religious faith was clearly a powerful emotive force. In the weekly report of March 1955 from the local SED leadership in Stalinstadt, for example, we hear that the local Evangelical church on 12 April had 210 people present. Pastor B. included in his sermon the comment 'that those who fell in the war ... only went to Heaven if they had faith. On hearing this, several of those present started to cry.'[24] A kindergarten teacher in Waren, Bezirk Neubrandenburg, was able to influence a girl against going to the state *Jugendweihe* ceremony, with the following argument: 'anyone who

[23] The communiqué is reprinted in Kleßmann, *Zwei Staaten, eine Nation*, Doc. 69, 578–9.
[24] IfGA, ZPA, IV 2/5/322, report of Apr. 1955.

participates in the *Jugendweihe* will not be confirmed, nor married in church, and when that individual dies, he or she will not be buried in the churchyard, but will be thrown into the ground like a dog on the other side of the cemetery walls'—whereupon the girl in question prudently decided in favour of confirmation in church.[25]

Concern about one's destination in the afterlife was not the only source of strength of the Church. Often activities organized by the Church in the here and now were highly popular, and took up a great deal of the leisure time of local communities. In January 1956, the SED district leadership of Plauen compiled a detailed analysis of the activities and strength of the Protestant churches in its area.[26] The six parishes were able to boast 16 youth groups (Junge Gemeinde), with 420 members, 14 women's groups, with around 720 members, and 11 men's groups with around 200 members. The church wardens were mainly 'petty bourgeois persons' or 'business people who also support the church financially'. In the parish of Theume, the Junge Gemeinde covered around 80 per cent of young people, and enjoyed similar strength in the parishes of Fröbersgrün and Rodau. The pastors in these parishes provided a large number of activities and fun for the young people—an offering with which the local FDJ groups found themselves unable to compete. The women's organizations were similarly active. In Leubnitz, the women's evenings were very lively, whereas the official communist women's organization, the DFD 'in contrast exists only on paper and is utterly non-viable'. Nearly every woman in the parish of Theuma participated in the church's *Frauenkreis* (women's circle), and, as the SED report sourly noted, their attitudes were in general 'negative' as far as the GDR's 'progressive development' was concerned. In the SED view, parish pastors were in the main 'reactionaries', who propagated anti-Soviet views, supported Adenauer and the USA, and gained great local support because they invited people in for coffee and home-made cake. In the face of all this, the relevant SED organizations could barely gain a foothold.

Nor was it only a question of organized activities. Christianity could provide a set of alternative values, to be held up against the prevailing norms of everyday life under the communist regime. In October 1957, for example, a placard on the noticeboard of a Lutheran church in Karl-Marx-Stadt (Chemnitz) presented two contrasting lists under the headings 'Soll' (what should be) and 'Haben' (what is), along the following lines:[27]

[25] IfGA, ZPA, IV 2/5/322, report of 20 Oct. 1955.   [26] Ibid., IV 2/5/968.
[27] BP, O-4 2377, letter of 16 Nov. 1957.

SOLL	HABEN
Truth	Lies, Deceit
Love	Hatred
Trust	Doubt
Patience	Haste, Nervosity
Courage	Cowardice
Faith	Fear
Hope	Resignation

Without openly criticizing the state as such, this sort of list reminded people of what sorts of social relationships and orientations they should strive to value and maintain, even in the face of structural circumstances which pressurized them into feeling and behaving in very different ways. In altered forms, a comparable clash of values and beliefs about the right ordering of relationships between human beings was to reappear more openly in the 1980s, as will become clear when examining the emergence of the reformist movements of the closing years of the GDR.

Nevertheless, for the next two decades the Church appeared to be fighting a losing battle as far as its hold over the population was concerned. Official statistics ceased to be collected after the census of 1964, but it was widely apparent that church-attendance figures were declining and that organized Christianity was becoming of decreasing relevance to the lives and concerns of increasing numbers of people in the GDR. Processes of secularization were particularly evident in cities, larger towns, and among younger people: given continuing processes of urbanization and generational change, the prospects for religious faith and practice were in any event not promising. Rural communities became less cohesive, as young people left for jobs in the towns and cities; new residential areas were constructed on the outskirts of towns, without churches or other visible religious presence; the squeezing out of religious education from schools began to have the expected effects of reduced exposure to the teachings of Christianity among young people; and the pressures to conform inexorably made their mark with the passage of time. By the late 1960s, the East German sociologist Professor Olof Klohr was able to observe with some satisfaction (in a lecture hopefully entitled 'The process of the withering away (*absterben*) of religion and the Church in the GDR') that the percentage of non-religious citizens had gone up from 7.6 per cent in 1950 to nearly a third of the population (31.5 per cent) by 1964. The percentage of Protestants had declined from 80.5 per cent to 59.3 per cent and of Catholics from 11.0 per cent to 8.1 per cent during the same period (the difference of 1.1 per cent being comprised of other religious communities).[28] Generation clearly made a major difference. Proportions of non-religious individuals decreased with age: as many as 41.6 per cent of the under-14 age group were without religious affiliation, compared to a mere 13.5 per cent of the over-70s, with a sliding scale in between.[29] Another survey of young people carried out in 1969 for the SED found that only 14 per cent of young people professed to be religious, whereas 43 per cent were firmly of an atheist persuasion.[30] The 'socialist big city' was, not surprisingly, found to be the most secularized location, and the working class the most secularized socio-economic group, while men tended to be less religious than women.[31] These findings confirmed tendencies of secularization general to the Western, urbanized, industrial world; nevertheless, several millions of East Germans still had active religious affiliations, which, in the view of the SED, 'demand . . . our greatest mass-political interest and appropriate state measures'.[32] The SED, therefore, characteristically sought to help the inevitable path of historical progress on its way with a little political intervention.

The state's policy of attempted *Gleichschaltung* continued: Ulbricht's new, publicly ameliorative stance was expressed to the Volkskammer in a speech on 4 October 1960, when he pronounced that 'Christianity and the humanistic goals of Socialism are not opposed to each other'.[33] In the course of the 1960s the state staged a series of rather artificial 'Christian–Marxist dialogues' with compliant theologians, including Emil Fuchs and the by now rather favourably inclined Bishop Mitzenheim of Thuringia. By 1967, the SED sought to make use of the 450th anniversary of the Lutheran Reformation to present a new image of the GDR, 'which is . . . the heir and protagonist of all progressive and national traditions of our history'. At the same time, the celebration was 'to use a basically religious occasion to confirm the common ground between Christians and Marxists and, on the basis of this particular occasion, to further the sense of citizenship (*Staatsbewußtsein*) of confessionally committed individuals . . . [and] to continue the process of differentiation within the leadership of the Church'.[34] A major issue here was the *Alleinvertretungsanspruch* (claim to

[28] BP, O-4 459, Information No. 4, 'Der Prozeß des Absterbens von Religion und Kirche in der DDR' (Information aus der Vorlesung von Gen. Prof. Dr. Olof Klohr auf der Schulung in Brandenburg in Feb. 1968), 3.   [29] Ibid. 9.

[30] IfGA, ZPA, IV A 2/2021/370, 'Kurzfassung über Probleme und Folgerungen zur Bewußtseinsentwicklung Jugendlicher in der DDR, die vom Zentralinstitut für Jugendforschung anläßlich der "Umfrage 69" vorgelegt wurden'.

[31] Ibid. 7, 5, 9.   [32] Ibid. 11.

[33] Quoted in Dähn, *Konfrontation oder Kooperation?*, 75.

[34] BP, O-4 458, Information No. 2/68, 'Analyse der Vorbereitung und Durchführung des 450. Jahrestages der Reformation 1967'.

be able to represent all Germans) of the West, and particularly the all-German organizational framework of the Church. This latter was in any event not to last for much longer; but the state prided itself on the way in which it had successfully navigated the issue on the occasion of the Luther celebrations.

The Church nevertheless fought back with respect to influence over the East German population, particularly seeking to retain its crucial foothold among youth. The Church always held a hand out to 'oppositional cultures'. It sought to protect those who, for reasons of conscience, felt unable to render military service after the introduction of conscription in 1962, and was instrumental in the formation of alternative service as 'construction soldiers (*Bausoldaten*)' in 1964. Around 80 per cent of *Bausoldaten* in 1964–6 were Christians, and this was to prove a key avenue for the formation of a distinctive dissident network in the later 1970s and 1980s. The Church also sought to extend its appeal and modernize its image with the introduction of aspects of popular youth culture in religious services: in the mid-1960s, for example, in an effort to counteract falling church attendance, churches in Karl-Marx-Stadt (Chemnitz) introduced *Gottesdienste einmal anders* (services which are different for once), 'with Jazz music, Negro spirituals, and Blues', while a 1968 report on churches in the Bezirk Frankfurt-on-Oder notes sourly that religious services are now 'framed' by 'Beatmusic' and dances. By 1968, *Gottesdienste einmal anders* had spread to Leipzig, Erfurt, Dresden, Schwerin, and Rostock. State officials complained that the majority of young people attending these services 'have few if any links with the church and in no way possess religious sensibilities. These youngsters come purely out of interest in modern music . . .'.[35]

But, in the late 1960s and 1970s, it seemed that the Church was fighting a losing battle for the souls of youth in an increasingly secular society. Not that secularization was necessarily a direct result of the SED's policies; levels of religious observance and church attendance were as much on the decline in the West as the East at this time. However, the determination of the Church to maintain programmes of outreach, accessibility, and relevance was to stand it in good stead from the late 1970s, when its structural location thrust it into a controversial position of social and political relevance, as we shall see. The maintenance of certain cultural traditions was later to prove extremely important.

On the organizational front, resistance to state pressures was less success-

---

[35] BP, O-4 458: undated report (*c.* late 1966), and report of 31 May 1968; also BP, O-4 459.

ful and the efforts by the Church to retain its links with the West were ultimately in vain. The new constitution of 1968 made it quite clear that any all-German organization was not only essentially outlawed, but also quite impracticable. There simply would be no possibility of any effective and genuine all-German organization of Church affairs, when the state had total control of entrance and exit visas and could ensure the non-viability in practice of any planned all-German gatherings of Church functionaries. At the same time, the constitution confirmed the state's earlier, very important, concession to the Churches by explicitly asserting the freedom of religious practice in Article 20. In 1969, recognizing the realities of the situation— and of the new winds of *Ostpolitik* which were beginning to blow, suggesting that a policy of 'hibernation' pending reunification was a relic of another era—the GDR Churches finally broke away from the all-German EKD and formed the specifically East German Bund der Evangelischen Kirchen. Not all Church leaders were entirely convinced of the necessity or the desirability of these moves, and many were critical of the new flavour of *Anpassung*, or political accommodation, which they reflected. But by now the forces in the Church leadership who were in favour of coming to terms with political realities, as they saw them, had attained dominance in the Church. The organizational separation heralded a new era of uneasy compromise and co-operation of a Church which had, to a large degree, come to recognize that if it wished to be a meaningful actor in the world, it would have to find its role within actually existing socialism.

Co-option, 1969–1978: a Church within socialism?

The new stance of the Churches was very soon summarized in the oft-quoted phrase of Bishop Schönherr: 'We want to be a Church not alongside, not against, but rather a Church within socialism.' This formula was convenient in part because of its vagueness. It was clear that it meant the Churches would not see themselves in the role of opponents of the regime, nor as irrelevant to life in the GDR; less clear was what precisely was meant by the arguably most important, positive part of the self-identification, in the phrase 'Church within socialism (*Kirche im Sozialismus*)'. Did this mean that the Church officially accepted, and hence implicitly supported, even legitimized, the prevailing political conditions? Did it—less contentiously— appeal rather to a notion which many but by no means all pastors could accept in principle, namely that of a 'socialism which could be improved (*verbesserlicher Sozialismus*)'? In this case, there were in fact many Christians who believed that, for example, the Sermon on the Mount was compatible with (even directly entailed) socialist, although not Marxist-Leninist and atheist, political beliefs. Or did 'within socialism' merely mean that this was geopolitically where the Church happened to find itself, and it had to come to terms with its surroundings and act accordingly? Given the wide range of possible interpretations, despite a degree of unease in certain quarters the principle gained widespread acceptance in the new climate of the 1970s.

There were, in any event, many fronts where Christians and Marxists could 'walk hand in hand', as the official SED propaganda put it. Church hospitals, old people's homes, orphanages, day care centres, institutions for the mentally ill and people with disabilities, played a vital role in the social infrastructure of the GDR. Finances from the West German Churches for a wide range of projects, including, for example, the restoration of church buildings which were often also historic monuments of national importance (such as the Berlin cathedral), also aided the GDR with significant injections of Western hard currency. Ecumenical work in the World Council of Churches served to lend the regime a degree of international legitimacy, as did the later prominence of the East German Churches in the international anti-nuclear movement (particularly in so far as this contributed to under-mining NATO rather than Warsaw Pact forces).[36] Recent discussions aris-ing from the German parliament's investigation into GDR history (the Enquete-Kommission) have suggested that the East German Churches also played what was certainly an important, and perhaps even a key, role in gaining international recognition for the GDR and its acceptance as a full voting member of the United Nations in 1973.

Moreover, from the Church's point of view, the new partnership was in line with the West German post-*Ostpolitik* policy of 'small steps'; abandon-ing an apparently ever more futile stance of outright opposition and denunciation, and seeking instead, through a policy of accommodation, to achieve realizable improvements in conditions for people living in the here and now. It seemed that the price for concessions on humanitarian matters was a degree of political pliability; the pay-off appeared to be visible in 1975 when Honecker was a signatory to Basket Three, covering human rights, of the Helsinki Declaration.

This policy of *Gratwanderung*—tightrope walking—was not entirely easy, nor without its casualties. On 18 August 1976 Pastor Oskar Brüsewitz publicly set himself alight in front of the Michaeliskirche in Zeitz, and died

---

[36] Cf. Henkys (ed.), *Die evangelischen Kirchen in der DDR*; Mary Fulbrook, 'Co-option and Commitment: Aspects of Relations between Church and State in the GDR', *Social History*, 12: 1 (Jan. 1987), 73–91.

in hospital four days later from his burns. His suicide note drew attention to the deep chasm between the public peace apparently obtaining in the Church, while 'between the forces of Light and Darkness a mighty war' was raging. There were others, too, who in less dramatic fashion registered a degree of unease about the apparently ever more harmonious relations between Church and state; or who sought to make use of the prevailing leeway to pursue certain activities more energetically.

In the 1970s, 'outreach' to drug addicts, 'asocials', alcoholics, homosexuals, and others who seemed to have no real home in actually existing socialism became a regular feature of Christian activities in some areas, with Church groups in the university town of Jena perhaps leading the way. Such outreach and openness to alternative cultures continued and arguably expanded in the late 1970s and 1980s, with the introduction of *Bluesmessen* in certain Berlin churches, and with the appearances of oppositional singers and songwriters, not always themselves Christian, such as Bettina Wegner. It should be emphasized that, in contrast to the mainstream Church youth work of the 1950s and 1960s, some of these more specifically subcultural activities were highly localized, restricted to individual churches where the pastor was favourably inclined, and—depending on the political implications of the activity—may have been frowned upon by Church authorities. Eppelmann's willingness to open his Berlin parish church to an 'alternative scene', for example, was a constant thorn in the flesh of his superiors in the Church hierarchy. While on the one hand seeming to condone, even foster, dissenting voices, such activities under the wing of the Churches at the same time offered the possibility of the Churches acting as a safety-valve for the regime. These considerations played a role, along with the developments of previous years, in the changing visible policies of the state with regard to the Church in the later 1970s.

There was also something of a generational change occurring which affected the SED's view of the Churches. The older generation of communists had been in large part working class in background, often ill-educated, and with an instinctive distrust of the Churches and religious intellectuals whom they viewed as intrinsically conservative. They had, however, also often been brought up in a religious environment, perhaps even been confirmed in church themselves, and might have spent time in concentration camps with Christians, giving them a degree of insight into, and often respect for, religious faith in the most adverse circumstances. The younger generation of communists were in the main better educated, more capable of intellectual dialogue with Church leaders, functionaries, and pastors; they had, on the other hand, little sympathy with, or understanding for, their religious faith.[37] There was similarly a generational shift in the Church: a new generation was coming to prominence which had been to a larger degree socialized in the GDR, and tended to see it as a relatively enduring entity rather than, essentially, an illegitimate Soviet imposition which should be only of short historical duration and resisted in principle.[38] These generational shifts, although hard to define with precision, played something of a role alongside the more obvious considerations in the changing Church–state relations of the 1970s.

The period from 1949 to the 1970s can be interpreted as one of a constantly shifting, constantly changing, but effectively never resolved battle between Protestantism and the state, with partial concessions and partial triumphs on both sides. For the most part during this period, the triumphs appeared to be on the part of the state, the concessions on the part of the Church: the *Jugendweihe* won out against church confirmation, with Church leaders finally forced to renounce active opposition and retreat from the view of mutual incompatibility; the East German Churches were forced to separate institutionally from their West German counterparts and establish the League of Protestant Churches in the GDR in 1969; and, by the early 1970s, the official view of East German Protestant Church leaders (articulated by Bishop Schönherr) was that theirs was a Church *within* socialism, which shared common humanistic goals with the state. At the same time, processes of secularization appeared to be at work rendering Christianity ever less relevant to ever larger numbers of the population. Honecker had good reason to believe that policies of co-option rather than overt confrontation were beginning to bear some fruit when the historic compromise of 6 March 1978 was agreed. In the event, however, this proved to be the beginning of the end.

Attempted *Gleichschaltung*: the agreement of 6 March 1978

The Church–state agreement of 6 March 1978 meant a number of quite different things, depending on perspective. These different interpretations were pivotal to the highly ambiguous political role of the Churches in the 1980s. In a sense, the meeting between Church leaders and Erich Honecker proved to be an important turning-point in the history of the GDR.

[37] These ideas partly arise from the author's discussions in Sept. 1986 with Landessuperintendent de Boor in Schwerin, and Präses Wahrmann in Wismar; they would no doubt bear further systematic exploration and research.

[38] A point emphasized by Manfred Stolpe in his opening address to a conference on GDR history organized by the Forschungsschwerpunkt Zeithistorische Studien, Potsdam, June 1993.

The officially more harmonious relations between Church and state embodied in the high-level meeting between Honecker and Church leaders appeared at first to outside observers to represent an interesting and progressive experiment in a degree of liberalization in the GDR, opening the way to a limited pluralism, or 'a limited partnership'.[39] It was nevertheless apparent to Western analysts that a somewhat risky strategy was being employed, with unforeseeable consequences for both Church and state.[40] As the Western academic expert Hartmut Zimmermann put it in 1979: 'It remains an open question as to whether the Church really will be able to fulfil the allotted tasks of providing social services and integrating marginal groups in a manner that will not, after all, entail social and political changes tending in the direction of a tolerated ideological pluralism.'[41]

It is now absolutely clear that a limited experiment in genuine liberalization or pluralism was certainly *not* what was intended by the East German leadership at the time. Recognizing that religion in the GDR was—contrary to Marxist theory—not going to wither away so soon, the SED leadership sought to co-opt Christians for their own purposes.[42] The agreement of 6 March 1978 was entered into at a time when, privately, the state remained extremely cynical about the political implications of even the more 'progressive' (in the SED's sense of the term) forces in the Church. As an official report of January 1978 on the differences in conceptions of human rights among churchpeople put it:

But the more the Churches develop their own particular viewpoints on the question of human rights, the more differences emerge between well-defined positions. This even goes as far as open opposition between extremely reactionary and anti-communist forces on the one hand, and on the other hand those who are more realistic and flexible, and do not counterpose the questions of human rights and the policy of peaceful coexistence, but rather want to link the two in order to further a gradual

[39] Reinhard Henkys's phrase in the article on churches in *DDR-Handbuch* (Cologne: Verlag Wissenschaft und Politik, 1979), 590.

[40] Cf. my article, 'Co-option and Commitment'.

[41] H. Zimmermann, '"Kirche im Sozialismus"—Zur Situation der evangelischen Kirche in der DDR', *DDR-Report*, 12: 1 (1979), 9.

[42] While there had certainly been a process of secularization in the sense of a decline in the numbers attending church services or being confirmed, for example, the Church nevertheless remained a key social institution whose organizational importance and potential could not be overlooked. There were also indications of an increase in certain indices of religiosity—in other words, a resistance to the trend of secularization—in the late 1970s and 1980s, such as increasing numbers of baptisms and confirmations; for a detailed and thoughtful analysis, see Detlev Pollack, 'Von der Volkskirche zur Minderheitskirche. Zur Entwicklung von Religiosität und Kirchlichkeit in der DDR', in Hartmut Kaelble, Jürgen Kocka, and Hartmut Zwahr (eds.), *Sozialgeschichte der DDR* (Stuttgart: Klett-Cotta, 1994).

process of 'liberalization' and ideological change in socialism, *a refined form of anti-communism*[!].[43]

It was the intention of the state functionaries to seek to influence these more 'progressive' forces:

On the whole, the BEK and the *Landeskirchen* of the GDR currently maintain a realistic position on the question of human rights, and refuse to let any controversies in this area become an object of the Cold War. Nevertheless, in no way can it be assumed that, as yet, clarity obtains on this question, either in general or as far as details are concerned. Therefore it is essential to be prepared for further discussions.[44]

Less than two months later, the main framework for these 'further discussions' had been established.

The actual meeting of 6 March 1978 ran according to a very well-prepared plan. Polite speeches were delivered by Honecker and, on behalf of the Church leadership, by Bishop Schönherr.[45] In addition to the usual remarks about the importance of securing peace, and references to the Helsinki process, Honecker made complimentary comments about the role of the Church: 'The engagement of the Church for the maintenance of peace, for *détente* and understanding between nations deserves general recognition.' Church and state could co-operate on a 'politics of growth, of welfare and stability . . . [and of a] raising of people's cultural *niveau* . . .' and the like.[46] In his reply, Bishop Schönherr emphasized that 'ideological differences, which should be neither papered over nor played down, should not form insuperable barriers'.[47] There then followed discussions of specific policy issues concerning the place of Christians in actually existing socialist society.

The contributions of the Church representatives present did not seek to disguise the difficulties experienced by Christians on the ground. Präses Wahrmann sought to ensure that residents of elderly persons' homes would have the chance to attend worship services. Präsident Domsch pointed out in the most diplomatic terms that state policies were not always translated into practice on the ground:

[43] BP, O-4 1943, Staatssekretär für Kirchenfragen, Information No. 2/78 (Jan. 1978), 1. Emphasis added.
[44] Ibid. 3.
[45] Previous analyses of this meeting were based on the brief snippet—the official press release—in *Neues Deutschland* (7 Mar. 1978). The complete report of the meeting can now be read: BP, O-4 970, 'Bericht über das Gespräch des Generalsekretärs des ZK der SED und Vorsitzenden des Staatsrates, Erich Honecker, mit dem Vorstand der Konferenz der Evangelischen Kirchenleitungen in der DDR am 6. März 1978'.
[46] Ibid. 2, 3. [47] Ibid. 4.

It was, however, the case that the experiences of Christian citizens must be mentioned which did not correspond to the official principles of state policies on Church questions . . . He was aware that there was no lack of good intentions, but 'there was often friction (*oft knirscht es*) at the grass roots' . . . A commitment to Marxism-Leninism . . . often became the sole measure for the evaluation and the availability for service of a citizen. He was of the firm conviction that this was not the intention of the state leadership, but this opinion often did not get through to those below.[48]

Bishop Krusche pointed to the need for some positive and practical development of the Helsinki principles, particularly relating to improvements in travel opportunities and the lifting of restrictions; and while the Church supported the position that 'We are staying here (*Wir bleiben hier*)', Krusche argued that the state should not deal so harshly with those who wished to leave. Frau Schultheiß raised the problem of those Christians who were blocked from following their chosen professions. Stolpe's somewhat anodyne contribution to this discussion was to mention that the GDR had a large number of individuals working in the World Council of Churches.[49]

In reply, Honecker failed to engage with the serious points of criticism. Further relaxation of travel restrictions was impossible, because the Federal Republic of Germany was still engaging in anti-communist diatribes, and had broken the Basic Treaty through the Constitutional Court's decision that the border between the two Germanies was legally the equivalent of a border between two federal *Länder*. State control of who entered what profession (*Berufslenkung*) was necessary because of constantly changing economic and social conditions and related occupational demands, but all children had equal opportunities. Honecker particularly wished to thank the Churches for their 'unstinting activity in diaconical institutions looking after the elderly, the ill and the mentally retarded . . . which our state values very highly and supports'. Finally, Honecker emphasized the importance of the fact that the East German Churches had made a decisive organizational break from the West. 'With the formation of the BEK recognition has been given to the fact that there are two independent sovereign German states.

---

[48] BP, O-4 970, 6.

[49] These issues were clearly not resolved: they were raised again at a meeting of Church leaders (including Stolpe, Wahrmann, Schultheiß, and Bishop Hempel and OKR Ziegler) with the State Secretary for Church Affairs, Klaus Gysi, nearly seven years later, on 18 Dec. 1984. BP, O-4 968, 'Information über das Gespräch des Staatssekretärs für Kirchenfragen mit dem Vorstand der Konferenz der Evangelischen Kirchenleitungen am 18.12.84'. The non-resolution of these points of concern did not, however, appear to have had adverse effects on the atmosphere: 'The five-hour meeting proceeded in a very trusting (*vertrauensvollen*), constructive and relaxed atmosphere.'

This step . . . has created the precondition for the evangelical Churches to be able to concentrate on service within socialist society.'[50]

This was really the crux of the matter. Notwithstanding the appendix of ten specific points which had been resolved—dealing with issues ranging from the restoration or construction of church buildings, the transmission of monthly church information bulletins on radio and television, and religious provisions in prisons and old people's homes, to the arrangements concerning Church-owned kindergartens, farming enterprises, and cemeteries—the real significance of the meeting was the fact of mutual recognition. Both sides had officially recognized that the other was not going to go away: the GDR was, so it seemed, here to stay, and so was Christianity. The two partners must now agree on a *modus vivendi*.

What this meant in practice was interpreted rather differently, however, depending on the different values and ultimate goals of the two parties to the agreement. Moreover, what the Church leadership understood by the new partnership was not necessarily shared by more radical Christians at the grass roots, or by non-religious members of East German society.

Bishop Schönherr's speech at the meeting summarized well the concerns of the Church leadership. He stressed the need for peace, the improvement of life for individuals, the protection of the freedom to practise one's faith. He emphasized the importance of a relationship of trust, and the translation of policy into practice: 'Openness and transparency are the barometer of trust. The relationship between Church and state is only as good as the ways in which it is experienced by the individual citizen in his social situation on the ground.'[51] And he articulated his own view of the role of Christians in this particular state. As Schönherr put it:

Christian faith is not bound to a particular state or political form because the One in whom Christians believe is bound to no one. The Christian will, accordingly, have an easier or more difficult time of it, but under no circumstances can he see himself freed from the responsibility in which the love of humankind and the world has placed him.[52]

As we shall see, this Christian sense of responsibility for God's creation, human and natural, was very soon to clash headlong with the state's social and environmental policies.

Many in the Church saw the agreement as enhancing not only their physical space for religious observance and activity, but also their political freedom of manoeuvre. When, within weeks of the agreement, the introduction of military education as a compulsory school subject was announced,

[50] BP, O-4 970, 10.   [51] Ibid., Anlage, 6.   [52] Ibid. 2.

many Christians objected vociferously. Nor did the Churches suddenly endorse wholeheartedly the state's one-sided peace policies. Rather, they appeared to have gained in confidence in explicitly opposing such policies and articulating alternative views.

That the nature of the new partnership may have been 'misunderstood', and the experiment may even have started to backfire, was apparent to state functionaries within less than a year. In a typically complex linguistic formulation (perhaps only possible in the German language) the different understandings of what had been implied by '6.3.78' were expressed in a state paper of January 1979 analysing the developments of the preceding months. Having reviewed the Church's apparent 'misinterpretations' of the meaning of the agreement, the functionary comes to the conclusion:

In practice, the developments outlined here concerning the attitude of the Protestant Churches in the GDR to the question of peace following the meeting of 6.3.78 indicate the need to be wary that a continuing misinterpretation with verbal reference to the sixth of March does not take place, pursuing substantially different goals, namely, instead of contributing to a strengthening of the loyalty of the Churches [to the state] rather orientates itself in a struggle for perpetual extension of the rights and role of the Churches in socialist society and against the state, and in this way relativizes its policies and allows the impression to arise that there is an alternative conception of peace policies in socialist states.[53]

While the state had conceived the meaning of 6.3.78 as committing the Church to a strengthening of socialism, many Church members perceived it rather as strengthening the Church's role in socialism: in the words of the anonymous bureaucrat, there was a tendency 'to misinterpret [it] as a weakness of the state' and 'confront the state with far-reaching demands . . . and to bring to bear . . . on the state a modified form of the "office of watchman" and "partnership" '. Even 'realistically inclined forces' see it as a 'strengthening of the position of the Church'.[54] The report notes with some misgivings that Church communities are being mobilized to a more

[53] This extraordinary sentence is worth reproducing in German, indicating the tortuous character of the thought: 'In der Tat ergibt sich aus der hier dargelegten Entwicklung der Haltung der protestantischen Kirchen in der DDR zur Frage des Friedens nach dem Gespräch vom 6.3. die Notwendigkeit, darauf zu achten, daß nicht unter verbaler Berufung auf den 6.3. eine fortgesetzte Fehlinterpretation geschieht, die substanziell andere Ziele verfolgt, nämlich statt zu einer Bekräftigung der Loyalität der Kirchen beizutragen, auf den Kampf um ständige Erweiterung der Rechte und Rolle der Kirchen in der sozialistischen Gesellschaft und gegenüber dem Staat zu orientieren und dabei seine Politik zu relativieren und den Eindruck eines alternativen Angebotes zur Friedenspolitik der sozialistischen Staaten entstehen zu lassen.' BP, O-4 1942, 'Zu den bisherigen Auswirkungen des Gesprächs des Staatsratsvorsitzenden, Genossen Erich Honecker, mit dem Vorstand der Konferenz der Evangelischen Kirchenleitungen in der DDR' (Jan. 1979), 9.

[54] Ibid. 11; but cf. also Stolpe's views, BP, O-4 1943 (Feb. 1981), 21.

critical stance towards socialist society and the state; that there is a new mood of self-confidence in the Churches; and that they are testing and stretching the boundaries. 'The Churches are, to be sure, constrained to respect the limits of citizens' loyalty, but they are seeking to expand these limits and to exploit them to the utmost. As a result, ideological disputes are refined, but quite clearly they will be no less intensive and complicated in the future.'[55] In this prediction, the unknown functionary was to be proved correct.

The porous rock: between God, state, and society, 1978–1989

The Churches were torn in a number of directions in the 1980s, the narrative of which will be recounted in greater detail in relation to the growth of political activism (Ch. 8, below). Here, it is important to highlight the structural location of the Church in this period, and to raise for discussion some of the key questions surrounding its overall role in the stabilization and ultimate destabilization of the GDR.

First, it is important to emphasize once again that the East German Churches were *religious* institutions: the Church leaders felt their primary responsibility was to God, not to any particular political cause. It is certainly the case that there were Stasi informers who had been actively inserted into the Church by the Stasi, rather than having been won over by the Stasi from existing religious personnel. But when we come to consider the contentious issue of relations between Church, state, Stasi, and dissidents it is nevertheless essential not to lose sight of the paramount importance of the propagation of the Christian Gospel for the vast majority of churchpeople, of whatever political persuasion.

The primacy of the propagation of Christian faith did not, however, entail any particular, uncontested political strategy. There was a vast gulf between, for example, the former Superintendent and Konsistorialrat of the Berlin-Brandenburg Church, Reinhard Steinlein, who resigned his position in protest against the March 1978 agreement, and, at the other extreme, the politically highly compliant Manfred Stolpe, on whom more in a moment.[56] On the other hand, the importance of religious faith provides something of a motive for political actions which must remain separate from the evaluation of the ostensible effects of these actions. The issue is an extremely complex one, in which it is important to be sensitive to criteria which one may not always share oneself.

[55] Ibid. 14.   [56] Cf. Reinhard Steinlein, *Die gottlosen Jahre* (Berlin: Rowohlt, 1993).

In a number of respects, the uneasy partnership of the preceding years was continued. In 1983 the state and the Church co-operated on the quincentenary Luther celebrations, which even overshadowed the centenary of Marx's death in the same year. The peace movements of the late 1970s and early 1980s saw the Church adopt a difficult balancing act, seeking not to upset the state while at the same time allowing more radical voices a degree of shelter under Church protection. The SED, for its part, sought to make use of the Church hierarchy as an extended arm of the state. The main miscalculation on the part of the SED here, however, was to assume that the Church operated according to the same hierarchy of command—in other words, that it was essentially characterized by the same democratic centralist structures—as the SED itself. To the SED's dismay, it discovered too late that it could not rely on the leadership of the Church to contain unruly spirits below; that 'turbulent priests' had greater leeway in the Church than did their secular counterparts under the iron hand of communist party discipline. The attempt to use the apparently compliant Church was to backfire very badly in the longer term.

In the meantime, however, the Church was a key partner in a subtle mechanism of attempted control. There was essentially a circle of interrelating (and overlapping) actors: the Stasi, the SED, the state functionaries, Church leaders, and political activists—and the circle of course met at both ends.[57] There were many versions of short-circuiting this circle: as well as directly and indirectly influencing higher levels of the Church hierarchy, the Stasi intervened directly in the internal affairs of dissident groups, seeking to sow distrust and affect decision-making. In the mid-1980s, they scored a number of successes in splitting the environmental movement, where personal animosities were exacerbated and policy differences—for example, over the issue of whether to seek Western contacts and media publicity— were exploited.[58] In what was effectively the longest chain of information-gathering, decision-making, commands, and consequent action, the circle would run as follows. Unofficial Stasi informers (*Inoffizielle Mitarbeiter*, or IMs) would report to their controlling officers; the latter would report to more senior levels in the Stasi hierarchy, who would report to the SED; the SED leadership would issue instructions to local state functionaries, who would meet with responsible Church leaders; and finally the latter, in the

---

[57] A few paragraphs from the preceding sections of this chapter, and the bulk of the following section, are also published, in slightly different form, as part of an article in Geyer and von Hallberg (eds.), *Cultural Authority in Contemporary Germany*.

[58] See e.g. Wolfgang Rüddenklau, *Störenfried* (Berlin: BasisDruck, 1992).

interests of maintaining harmony between Church and state 'in the spirit of 6.3.78', would seek to control the dissident spirits in their midst and ensure a more limited 'purely religious' function to politically potentially explosive gatherings. This was the strategy adopted in relation to the annual 'peace weeks' (*Friedensdekaden*), which were effectively kept under such firm control by Church leaders, under constant pressure from the state, that by the mid-1980s SED and Stasi reports began to crow over static or declining attendance figures, the apparent aimlessness of many discussions, and the ease with which unwelcome literature or placards were disposed of. Church leaders were being used very much as an extended arm of the state, whether or not they were aware of the long line of strategic and tactical decision-making behind their own roles.

A variant tactic was that of direct co-option of groups by the state. As we shall see in a subsequent chapter, this seems to have worked relatively successfully with the Church-run environmental centre at Wittenberg (Kirchliche Forschungsheim Wittenberg, KFH) under the direction of Dr Peter Gensichen. Over a period of time, he and many of those involved in regional Christian environmental workshops became amenable to the idea of co-operating with state functionaries and technical experts on specific projects. In this way, the SED sought to channel relevant energies and contain the political implications of a sense of environmental responsibility, even to divert Christians to positive support of state initiatives. By 1988, the KFH appeared to be under firm political control, and Gensichen was reported to be making critical utterances against the less readily co-optable Environmental Library in Berlin.[59]

Infiltration of groups was not only by Stasi informants. 'Positive societal forces'—pro-regime Christian members of the CDU, for example—were encouraged to join and raise their voices to put the state's point of view in any particular discussion. A constant strategy was to seek to separate and isolate 'negative' forces, although this proved in the long run to backfire as far as party control of developments was concerned.

A key turning-point was reached in the autumn of 1987. There was a dramatic shift from a 'softly-softly' policy of controlled co-option, infiltration, and control—no less despicable, inhumane, and immoral for its secretive, manipulative, and dishonest nature—to one of open and visible repression. This shift is symbolized by two closely occurring events: the Olof Palme Peace March of October 1987 and the raid on the Environmental

[59] Cf. e.g. BP, O-4 799, report dated 24 May 1988 of a discussion on 19 May 1988.

Library in Berlin the following month. The former—in which the banners of the unofficial peace initiatives were flanked by the official banners of the state—was seen, almost euphorically, as signalling the possibility of a Gorbachev-style process of liberalization in the GDR. But within weeks, the Stasi had engaged in a draconian raid on the Environmental Library in Berlin, accompanied by arrests and seizure of Church-owned printing equipment.

Thereafter, open repression became a more constant and visible response of the authorities. The SED and Stasi had long feared that the Church leadership was not capable of exerting effective control, but reports frequently mention the need to continue to allow them to try. From 1987–8, it became ever more clear to the political authorities that this strategy was becoming ever *less* effective; the formation of the Church from Below (*Kirche von Unten*) in the summer of 1987 was merely one sign of a developing deterioration of relations between the most cautious and conservative Church leaders at the top, and more self-confident and organized (if often also dejected and pessimistic) currents from below. Church leaders themselves were ever less sure of their own capacity to influence the activities of grass-roots activists. They also appear, to some extent, to have been shifting fronts in view of the rising uncertainties of the Gorbachev era.[60]

How one evaluates the political role of prominent Church functionaries during this period is a difficult question. There was a wide range of Protestant responses to the regime, from—at one extreme—those unofficial Stasi informants and others who appear to have acted primarily in the interests of the state or of their own self-interest, to—at the other—those who adamantly resisted and opposed any state co-option of the Church and made a strong personal stand against compromise. In between the two polar extremes are the vast expanses of mottled shades of grey: from those who prevaricated, trimmed, and conformed, in the perceived interests of the survival of the Church and the protection of religious faith and practice under communism, to those who sought one or another tactic of passive resistance or subversion. The Weberian contrast between an ethics of responsibility and an ethics of morality would at first sight appear apposite here; but this is essentially too simple, and begs a number of questions about the limits of political possibility, and the perceptions and assumptions of those involved.

[60] Cf. Stolpe's typically clever political egg-dancing in 1988–9, summarized by Ralf Georg Reuth, *IM 'Sekretär'. Die 'Gauck-Recherche' und die Dokumente zum 'Fall Stolpe'* (Frankfurt-on-Main and Berlin: Ullstein, 1992), 74.

Church, state, and Stasi

Perhaps the most prominent and ambiguous case is that of Manfred Stolpe, which also serves to illustrate some of the problems involved in seeking to evaluate the evidence. In 1992, when his Stasi files were opened, Stolpe was the very popular SPD Prime Minister of Brandenburg—one of the very few East German politicians remaining in a prominent political position, who had even made a considerable impression upon West German colleagues. Before the collapse of the GDR, he had been a powerful functionary and former *Konsistorialpräsident* of the Evangelical Church. At the same time, it transpired, he had entered into regular meetings with Stasi officials, and engaged, quite consciously, in frequent conversations with them under 'conspiratorial conditions'. On Stolpe's account, this was in order to protect and further the interests of the Church, and he allegedly had the full authority of the Church to act in any way he deemed appropriate to pursue Church affairs in this way; on the view of his critics, Stolpe had in the process—whether intentionally or otherwise—done considerable harm to the cause of opposition groups in the GDR, and dramatically affected the lives of many individuals, with often highly undesirable consequences. The case of Manfred Stolpe vividly illustrates the moral and political dilemmas faced by active Christians in the GDR, and the difficulties and ambiguities faced in any attempt to evaluate the political role of the Protestant Churches.

It is very difficult to reach a definitive conclusion on the Stolpe case, in large measure *not* because of lack of documentation or evidence, but rather because of the shifting criteria by which his actions might be evaluated. It is quite clear, beyond any shadow of doubt, that Stolpe consciously, conscientiously, and promptly reported—in other words, was not simply 'milked' for information without being aware of this—to the Stasi a very wide range of confidential discussions, including the internal proceedings of church committees and synodal debates, conversations with Western politicians and dignitaries, and other matters which participants had deemed to be relatively private.[61] He thus quite clearly was of major help to the state and the Stasi. It is also clear that although Stolpe does not appear to have had to sign the regular form for Stasi informants (which Erich Mielke conceded was not essential in any event for high-placed informants, or, more neutrally, 'conversation partners'),[62] Stolpe nevertheless was aware of, and

---

[61] See e.g. the introductory essay and supporting documentation in Reuth, *IM 'Sekretär'*.

[62] Erich Mielke, 'Spiegel-Gespräch', *Der Spiegel*, 46: 36 (31 Aug. 1992), 50: 'Stolpe did not work for the MfS. There were of course conversations between the Church and us, which, among others, Stolpe conducted on behalf of the Church.'

adhered to, the basic ground rules of conspiratorial endeavours. He agreed to meet in Stasi-designated safe locations, and observed the confidentiality of his Stasi contacts. These contacts were sustained over more than two decades of fruitful collaboration, as Stolpe gradually rose to ever more influential and prominent positions in the Church hierarchy.

The real issue, then, is not *whether* Stolpe had conscious conspiratorial contacts with the Stasi, but what interpretation one is to put on these. Was he primarily acting in the interests of the state, using his insider status in the Church to aid the state's policies of seeking to exert control over Church personnel and policy, and to tip off the Stasi in its efforts to contain dissent; or was he rather employing his good relations with the state to safeguard the essentially religious interests of the 'Church within socialism'? Did he perhaps consider that he was—uniquely—doing both at the same time, as a Christian socialist seeing no conflict in principle between the two endeavours, despite the communist state's essentially atheistic stance and appalling record on humanitarian issues? As far as Stolpe's own motives are concerned, the latter seems the most likely: Stolpe was seeking both to further the interests of the Church, which he understood as most readily realized through harmonious accommodation with the state, and at the same time using all available channels of intervention and mediation in order to improve—as he saw it—the character of the state itself. But the debate revolves not only around Stolpe's imputed motives, but also around the morality, and more particularly, the consequences of Stolpe's actions for those on whose behalf he seems to have empowered himself to act.

Stolpe is and was clearly an astute and skilled politician. On his version, he freely entered into conspiratorial discussions with Stasi officials as well as state functionaries, in the best interests of the Church.[63] The furies whipped up in the media, unleashed by pre-publication extracts from his memoirs in *Spiegel*, were accompanied by a constant stream of selective revelations seeking to establish a guilt that Stolpe himself refused to concede. The official investigative commission of the Land Brandenburg parliament, chaired by a representative of the PDS (the SED's successor party), Lothar Bisky (who was widely expected to give a sympathetic hearing to Stolpe), ground on over a lengthy period; its report, finally published at the end of August 1993, eventually came to the expected conclusion that Stolpe was to be exonerated.[64] Even the unofficial alternative report, however, compiled by the east German theologian and historian Ehrhart Neubert on the basis of a study of around 10,000 pages of relevant documents, was not able to

[63] Manfred Stolpe, *Schwieriger Aufbruch* (Munich: Siedler, 1992).
[64] *Frankfurter Allgemeine Zeitung* (30 Aug. 1993), 6.

:each any really damning conclusion (notwithstanding *Spiegel*'s typically
sensationalist use of the adjective *vernichtend*).[65] Despite the fact that
Stolpe clearly revealed personal and political confidentialities to the Stasi,
and arguably acted in ways which were on occasion detrimental to the
interests of dissident individuals and groups, it could not be shown that he
had tipped over the balance from acting in what he perceived to be the long-
term interests of the Church to acting primarily in the interests of Stasi or
state.[66]

A major element in Neubert's critique of Stolpe is that the latter perceived
the conspiratorial methods of the Stasi as a purely 'technical' matter, a
necessary concession to the constraints of political reality if one were to
engage in a fruitful dialogue—in which Stolpe conceived himself to be an
important and equal, indeed irreplaceable, partner. For Neubert and others,
however, this concession was not a matter of 'technical detail', but rather an
essential, ethical and political capitulation: the whole point of many of the
reformist endeavours of political activists in the 1980s was to seek to create
a more open atmosphere, the conditions for free discussion and dialogue, a
'public sphere' or 'civil society'. This difference is essentially one of political
perception of constraints, possibilities, and strategies: for Stolpe, the SED
regime was there to stay for the foreseeable long-term future, and he
apparently thought it was in the best long-term interests of the Church to
maintain a harmonious relationship with the state, thus protecting a limited
degree of freedom within the Church; for the more radical political activists,
it was more important to seek to test and stretch the limits of political
constraints, to expand the boundaries of the possible rather than to accept
them as given.

The other major point of contention is not so much about the means, as
the consequences of Stolpe's actions. Here, there is a clear problem in
evaluating the documentary evidence. Again and again it appears that in
meetings with Stasi and state officials Stolpe made critical or denigratory
remarks about particular individuals within the Church. Thus, for example,
Stolpe perpetually agreed with SED criticisms of the radical pastor Rainer
Eppelmann, explaining on one occasion that in the long term he (Stolpe)
saw 'in the case of Pastor Eppelmann two possible solutions: first, Pastor
Eppelmann leaves Berlin, and secondly, Pastor Eppelmann leaves the Republic . . .'.[67] But, when Eppelmann came out in a vicious tirade against

---

[65] 'Stolpe's Verrat an der Kirche', *Der Spiegel*, 47: 35 (30 Aug. 1993), 33.
[66] Ibid. 34: 'Neubert concedes that Stolpe maintained and extended his Stasi contacts in the
interests of the Church.'
[67] BP, O-4 766, note of 26 Nov. 1982 on a discussion of 24 Nov. 1982.

Stolpe on precisely this point in the autumn of 1992, Wolfgang Thierse pointed out in Stolpe's defence that in fact, despite what were considered to be repeated outrageous political provocations, Eppelmann enjoyed the retention of his Berlin pastorate throughout the 1980s. Eppelmann was *not* expelled. In many other cases too, the effect of Stolpe's discussions seems to have been the leaving of disciplinary measures to internal Church procedures, which more often than not seem then to have been lengthy and ultimately ineffective (from the state's point of view, at least).

What was it, then, that these dissident pastors were doing, which occasioned such irritation on the part of the state? While Stolpe was in effect safeguarding Eppelmann's position by ingratiating himself to such a degree with the state that the state was prepared to leave disciplinary procedures to such an evidently trustworthy Church leadership, Eppelmann was repeatedly engaging in activities which tested the state to its very limits. Eppelmann first caught public attention with his joint appeal with the dissident intellectual Robert Havemann, the so-called *Berliner Appell* (Berlin Appeal) of 1982. While many in the Church sympathized with the urgency of this call for peace, the Berlin-Brandenburg Church leadership was quick to withdraw their support, suggesting that it failed to give adequate consideration to the 'actual political and military constellation'.[68] Many pastors rejected it as endangering the new Church–state relationship; but others, such as Pastor Wonneberger of Dresden, continued to try to collect signatures for the Appeal, with the consequence that ever larger numbers of GDR citizens were given the impetus to think more directly about the nature of their state and its policies. The Berlin Appeal was but a prominent symptom of growing co-operation between Christians and non-Christians in unofficial peace initiatives and other activities relating much more broadly to human rights, the environment, the character of East German society—and hence, inevitably, the character of East German politics.

It was extraordinarily difficult to remain 'purely' religious in such an all-intrusive political context with the ruling party claiming total hegemony over all aspects of life. Many of these activities were on a far more local scale than the Berlin Appeal, but no less irritating to the state. Eppelmann, to remain with this example, repeatedly held 'worship services' targeted at young people, many of whom had never previously had much contact with the Church. These services were often very critical of the character of

[68] MfS, ZAIG, Z 3201, No. 82/82 (16 Feb. 1982), which includes a copy of the *Stellungnahme* of the Berlin-Brandenburg Church of 13 Feb. 1982.

ontemporary East German society, including not only alternative music but also sketches and plays highlighting problems such as the pressures to conformity and achievement (as in the play about a character called Lustlos, who ultimately drops out as a result of multiple pressures to conform).[69] What the Stasi termed 'provocative-demonstrative' acts might take all sorts of forms. On 6 June 1984, at 13.50 hours, a *Müllberg* (mountain of rubbish) was found by the Stasi on the grounds of the Samariterkirche in East Berlin, studded with environmentalist slogans such as 'Umweltschutz statt Umweltschmutz (Environmental protection instead of pollution)' and 'Radfahren statt Autofahren (Cycle a bike instead of driving a car)'. The Stasi were infuriated by Eppelmann's legalistic insistence that he had no authority to remove this rubbish tip, because the decision had to be taken by the *Gemeindekirchenrat*. The offending heap was finally removed at 18.15 in the evening, having clearly made some public impact in the course of the afternoon.[70]

In the interplay between Stolpe and Eppelmann, we can see the two polar positions: the close (even obsequious) partnership with the state on the one hand, and the testing to the limits of what the state would tolerate, on the other. But before considering these as alternatives to be evaluated *against* each other, it may be worth asking whether in fact they were rather *symbiotic*: the former being the essential precondition for the latter. Many meetings and events, from *Friedensdekaden* to *Bluesmessen*, could not have taken place without the Church leadership accepting certain state-imposed conditions; and the development of dissident ideas and organizational forms could not have happened had it not been for such organizational frameworks and (sometimes admittedly only limited or ineffective) Church protection. As we shall see, one of the most important factors in the growth of grass-roots dissent in the course of the 1980s was the growth of networks across groups and regions. Such networks were only possible, at least at first, in the context of gatherings controlled by the Church, and sanctioned by the state on the basis of relevant promises by Church leaders. Perpetual interventions by the conservative Church leadership in both directions— between state and activists—may have helped to gain the time during which an alternative culture of dissidence could develop, and its organizational networks and strategies be formed.

[69] Cf. BP, O-4 766, report of 23 Apr. 1982.
[70] MfS, ZAIG, Z 3370, Information No. 245/84 (8 June 1984), 'Information über eine provokatorisch-demonstrative Handlung auf dem Außengelände der Samariterkirche in Berlin-Friedrichshain'.

It is clear that, ultimately, the state's policies of co-opting the Church to control dissent ultimately failed. But should the preceding caution of the Church leadership therefore, in retrospect, be castigated as essentially serving to sustain unnecessarily an illegitimate and dictatorial regime?

This is a complex question to answer. It must be remembered that the ultimate crumbling of the domination of the SED in the autumn of 1989 was predicated on a combination of other, external factors, in the context of which domestic dissent was able to make a more immediate impact: the opening of the Iron Curtain, the Soviet Union's renunciation of the doctrine of intervention in the domestic affairs of Warsaw Pact states, and indeed Gorbachev's active desire to encourage reform and change in the GDR. It was only in the context of the massive regime crisis caused by the flood of refugees leaving for the West that domestic reform movements were able to exert sufficient pressures to ensure real and irreversible change (although this ultimately did not eventuate in the desired direction of a continuing socialist but democratic GDR). But, within this context, the growth of organized voices pressuring for reform was crucial to the snowballing process of regime capitulation and eventual renunciation of the party's claim to domination.

It will be argued below that, without the protective umbrella of the co-opted state Church throughout the 1980s, these dissenting voices could not have developed to the degree that they did by the time external conditions were ripe for a challenge from below. It was, for many people, only in the context of church discussion groups that they learned to voice their real opinions at all, and to respect and tolerate the opinions of others with whom they disagreed. It was also only through a relatively long process of tactical manœuvring and strategic thinking that certain organizational forms were developed and practised which then bore fruit in the rapid growth of New Forum and other groups in the autumn of 1989. Had Church leaders not maintained an admittedly restricted space, such a process of development during the 1980s would hardly have been possible.

It was, however, a learning process in which only a very tiny minority of the population participated. Most of the gatherings and grouplets of the 1980s involved often only dozens, at best hundreds, of individuals. As we shall see in the following chapters, the vast majority of the East German population developed strategies of coping, of coming to terms with an often repressive but not always unpleasant regime (or a regime the unpleasantness of which it was possible to ignore). The limited 'public sphere' which developed under the constraints of Church protection in the 1980s was not ultimately sufficient to counteract the massive influence of Western media, political propaganda, and consumer attractions in the context of a rapidly collapsing East German economy and totally discredited state when it came to the winter and spring of 1989–90. The oppositional cultures which had been nurtured under the partially protective wing of the co-opted state Church were ultimately sufficient to help to explode the brittle shell of the moribund regime, but not to determine decisively the transition to a stable institutional alternative. When the floodgates were opened, the masses streamed out; and the West stepped in.

PART II

PATTERNS OF POPULAR COMPLIANCE
AND COMPLAINT

THE GDR lacked the degree of popular legitimacy with which the Third Reich was inaugurated. The mere existence of the Wall underlines this very obvious fact; without it, the GDR was simply not a viable independent state, as events after 9 November 1989 were to prove. Nevertheless, it is the central thesis of this book that popular discontent alone was not sufficient to fell the system. The effective containment of widespread individual discontent over a period of time actually contributed to the longevity and domestic stability of the GDR. Grumbling was increasingly restricted to the private sphere. To some extent, patterns of at least outward conformity developed over time, despite widespread worries and grumbles, and lack of real inner commitment. This incorporation of individuals in state-controlled frameworks such that they effectively acquiesced in their subject status was nevertheless a rather fragile achievement, which could not be taken for granted. Certain areas of society were less easily co-opted; but, even so, the regime nevertheless to a considerable degree succeeded in atomizing discontents, ensuring that much popular disaffection and protest remained largely spontaneous, isolated, and politically without serious effects.

Part II, then, explores the varying patterns of political orientation of the East German people who were *not* pillars of the regime, functionaries or protagonists in the structures of power. Many black-and-white depictions of the GDR tend to categorize the dictatorship rather simply, in terms of oppressors and victims, rulers and repressed. That the GDR was ultimately based on force is not in dispute. But what is infinitely more interesting than a simple repetition of this fact is the recognition that the dictatorship not only succeeded in co-opting people in a variety of ways, but that in other respects it failed to spread its tentacles effectively into every last area of life.

There were manifold ways in which East Germans retained areas of relative freedom of action (*Handlungsspielraum*), distanced themselves from the regime's demands, even to some extent constituted brakes on its activity. And 'resistance', in a more general, pervasive sense—the manifold refusals of everyday life, the retention of standards and morals which challenged the pressures imposed from above—sustained patterns of alternative culture which ultimately helped, under specific historical circumstances, to explode the regime from within.

5

THE CREATION OF A NICHE SOCIETY?
CONFORMITY AND GRUMBLING

THE Germans have long had a reputation, whether deserved or otherwise, for political obedience.[1] Allegedly, Germans—more than any other nation—tend to be rather conformist and to elevate obedience to authority above the dictates of conscience or civic courage (*Zivilcourage*). While this generalization about a supposed national character is clearly oversimplistic, certain variants enjoy some currency with respect to East Germany. It is frequently maintained that, among Eastern European states, the population of the GDR was the most docile in character, the least 'uppity' (*aufmüpfig*), a fact supposedly requiring some explanation. One not entirely flattering version, current for quite a while among some West Germans, was that all those with initiative and spirit fled the GDR while it was still possible, prior to 1961. A rather more academic and scholarly approach to the question was popularized in the notion of a 'niche society', which gained widespread currency with the publication of Günter Gaus's book, *Wo Deutschland liegt*.[2] On this view, East Germans came to terms with the pressures and demands of their regime by leading a double life of outward conformity combined with private authenticity. The net effect was stabilizing, even

[1] The fact that prejudices about a set of German national characteristics are by no means either dead or without influence in high places was underlined by the leaked memorandum by Charles Powell, private secretary to the then British Prime Minister Mrs Thatcher, of a meeting at Chequers on 24 Mar. 1990, reprinted in Harold James and Marla Stone (eds.), *When the Wall Came Down: Reactions to German Unification* (London: Routledge, 1992), 233–9. The six academic participants present at the meeting distanced themselves from the bald presuppositions about 'attributes' which supposedly formed 'an abiding part of the German character', including '*angst*, aggressiveness, assertiveness, bullying, egotism, inferiority complex, sentimentality . . . [A] capacity for excess, to overdo things, to kick over the traces . . . [A] tendency to over-estimate their own strengths and capabilities . . . [T]he conviction . . . [of] a deep moral and cultural superiority . . .' (234). But such views clearly held some sway among British politicians at the time of unification, as the later remarks—which were to occasion his resignation—of the then Secretary of State for Industry, Nicholas Ridley, revealed.

[2] Günter Gaus, *Wo Deutschland liegt* (Munich: Deutscher Taschenbuch Verlag, 1986; first published by Hoffmann and Campe Verlag, 1983).

though the conformity was less than enthusiastic. This hypothesis is certainly very suggestive, and has the advantage of integrating analysis of political structures with social history; but, as we shall see, it requires a considerable degree of historical qualification.

This chapter will, then, seek to explore the extent to which at least a degree of popular compliance, if not active support, for the GDR was achieved, and will examine the history, nature, and preconditions of the alleged 'niche society' in which many East Germans appear to have led relatively sheltered lives. The following chapters will trace the extent to which many East Germans were in fact far less docile, less obedient to authority, less prepared to conform, than had previously been evident, at least as far as Western observers were concerned.

The claims of the state and the worries of everyday life

A primary aim of the East German regime was to produce good socialist personalities, wholeheartedly committing their energies to the greater good of the community and the socialist state. In contrast to the *laissez-faire* attitudes of Western capitalist democratic states, the East German regime operated a proactive social psychology, assuming that social engineering could actively change character types, attitudes, and personalities. The goal of producing the 'new man' (*den neuen Menschen*) was pursued through a variety of means, which shifted in emphasis over time. Policies were to a degree mutually contradictory—and none, in the event, was ultimately successful.

The regime pursued a combination of policies for the transformation of personality. First, there was the materialist view—to be found in Marx—that an alteration of the material conditions of existence would inevitably lead to an alteration in social consciousness. Thus the abolition of the capitalist socio-economic system and class structure would supposedly entail a corresponding change in consciousness on the part of the people. Such a view lay at the heart of a large part of East German denazification policies, for example. Since the communists adhered to a structural theory of fascism, they could argue that once the material base for Nazism had been abolished, Nazi views and attitudes would go away—and thus the former 'small Nazis' who were willing to throw themselves into the building of socialism could be readily accepted as members of the new society. Changes in relationship to the means of production were not always enough, however, as the SED soon discovered.

The regime subsequently devoted a considerable amount of time to analysing and seeking to affect the attitudes of different social classes. A range of social policies were directed at particular groups, providing sops for material discontent at different times. Organizational measures were also employed to try to foster a sense of community spirit, of working for a larger whole and a better future, in order to transform perceptions of the role of individuals in society. As we have seen, the whole of society was deeply penetrated and structured by state institutions and organizations, from work brigades to women's groups, from activities in the FDJ to the League of Culture or the German–Soviet Friendship Society. There was simply no escaping, in an organizational sense, the experience of 'belonging to the community'. Not that this necessarily had the desired effects either, as we shall see.

At the same time a rather different, more idealist view complemented the strictly materialist approach with respect to social conditions determining consciousness. This idealist view could also be found in Marx: the notion that the ruling ideas of the age were the ideas of the ruling class. In the GDR, which was considered for the most part to be in a process of (variously defined) stages of transition, it was necessary to employ a battery of ideological means of education, indoctrination, and propaganda to change people's views. State control of education was a priority right from the earliest stages in the Soviet zone of occupation: denazification of teachers was infinitely more thorough than that of doctors, for example; the abolition of denominational schools, the squeezing out of religious education, and the reorganization of the education system were major priorities. Ideological influence and the induction of a Marxist-Leninist world-view began in kindergarten, and could not be escaped, in the guise of compulsory weekend schools, evening courses, and comparable activities, even in adult life. State control of the media led most people to a generally cynical view of the newspapers, although Erich Honecker continued to take this very seriously and maintained close personal control over the contents of the official SED newspaper, *Neues Deutschland*, to the very last. Those who skipped the slogans in the press could hardly ignore the banners in the streets, across public buildings, hung from motorway bridges: the ubiquity of ideological proclamations was part of the physical as well as mental landscape of East German socialism. Censorship operated for books and magazines, with varying degrees of severity at different times; but the battle over television was finally given up, there being no foolproof means of stopping people from tuning their sets to Western channels. The possibility of watching Western television, which became ever more widespread from the 1970s, meant that there was an alternative source of information and debate which somewhat counterbalanced the regime's own attempts at complete, blanket ideological influence.

Much of the SED's efforts were wasted: the realities of everyday life tended to belie the propaganda put out by the regime. For at least the first few years after the collapse of Nazism, personal worries tended to predominate.

For one thing, there was a widespread reaction against involvement in any sort of politics, against sticking one's neck out again, in the light of the recent experience of punishment for having supported the previous regime. This might nevertheless be tempered with pressures to engage in new political compromises, more for pragmatic reasons of personal advantage than genuine political commitment. Many leapt to join new political parties to disguise their previous political records; there then followed the predictable witch-hunt of tainted individuals in various organizations. And in any event the choice of party might reflect considerations other than the party's ideology and policies. As one perceptive observer living in the Soviet zone put it at the time:

I intended never again to get involved politically, but let myself be signed up as a member of the SPD, as I did not like the Sovietized KPD, and the CDU, which is a resort of former members of the Stahlhelm, inactive Nazis, and other people keen to run with the tide, seems to me less than viable. In the SPD, which is basically made up only of former members, mainly farmers and workers who never joined the NSDAP, they are very cautious in relation to newcomers such as myself.[3]

This particular new convert to the SPD was very soon disillusioned by the merger and the communist domination of the new SED; it was all too clear that the Russians dominated the German communists, and the latter, with Russian backing, dominated former SPD members. More generally, the gaps between rhetoric and reality were only too obvious in the following years. For many ideologically uncommitted East Germans, politics became a matter solely for cynical manipulation or critique.

Furthermore, in the devastated conditions of the first years after defeat, sheer personal survival was the main preoccupation for most people.[4] This

---

[3] Correspondence between Max Berger and Hans Arnold Plöhn, Institut für Zeitgeschichte (IfZ), ED 170, letter of 21 Nov. 1945.

[4] Cf. e.g. the autobiographical accounts collected in the Institut für Zeitgeschichte, Munich; e.g. Walburg Lehfeldt, 'Wie konnte das geschehen? Erlebnisse einer Deutschen in Polen und in der russischen Besatzungszone, 1932–1950' (IfZ, MS 348), 93–155, which makes no attempt at answering the question posed in the title of 'how could it happen', but rather provides innumerable details of the hardship and sufferings, the begging and illnesses, the

was a period when millions were resettling from lost homes in the eastern territories, when returning prisoners of war were seeking to be reunited with often scattered or decimated families, when there were intense personal traumas and tragedies to be resolved. There were around 3.6 million refugees in the Soviet zone in 1946, seeking food and shelter, competing with local communities for scarce resources. Added to the strains of social integration of populations with often very different dialects, cultural, and religious characteristics, was sheer hunger, exacerbated by the fact that the winter of 1946–7 was one of the harshest of the century. *Hamstern*, a combination of bartering and scavenging for food, was a major preoccupation for the vast majority of people, often alongside the problems of accommodation in conditions of great overcrowding and simply seeking to keep warm. These were essentially existential concerns, rather than questions to do with specific political ideologies. And as one socialist, Dr Karl Schultes, who was still actively working in the Soviet zone, put it in October 1947 in a letter to a friend in America: 'The economic misery and the sheer lack of food, quite apart from the massive coal deficit, will make it extremely difficult for the democratic forces to win over the population.'[5]

Material concerns were accompanied by more general worries about the future of Germany. Rumours were rife, making rational planning for the future relatively difficult. For example, in February 1946 the rumour was circulating in the area of Lübtheen in the Soviet zone that the English would soon come and oust the Russians, so that people were less willing to commit their energies to building up the economy according to Soviet plans, with deleterious effects on agricultural production, general *Aufbauwilligkeit*

---

attempts to gain enough food and outwit the allegedly plundering and raping Russians, before a final flight to Bremen in West Germany in 1950. Similarly, Dr Karl Lerp, 'Erinnerungen aus meinem Leben. Für seine lieben Geschwister und Geschwisterkinder aufgeschrieben' (IfZ, ED 173), describes how the years from 1920 to 1939 were 'unsere glücklichsten und sorglosesten Jahre'; indulges in a degree of self-pity about how his weight dropped from 70 to 50 kg while interned by the British, to some extent compensated for by the very interesting company with whom he shared his internment (including the former Croatian envoy who had many intriguing tales to recount of meetings with Hitler, Goebbels, and other party bigwigs); and then gives nothing but practical and personal details concerning the reconstruction of his life in the Soviet zone after his release. This kind of partly self-pitying, partly self-heroizing tone is found in innumerable biographical and autobiographical accounts of the period, and relates to the simultaneous lack of adequate 'reckoning with the past'. For a more literary version, see e.g. Christian Graf von Krockow's rendering of his sister's experiences in *The Hour of the Women* (London: Faber and Faber, 1991, trans. from the original German *Die Stunde der Frauen* by Krishna Winston).

[5] IfZ, Nachlass Karl Schultes (Bundesarchiv Signatur NL 185, IfZ, ED 188/5), letter of 25 Oct. 1947.

(willingness to build for the future), and so on.[6] To quote Schultes again, this time in a letter to a friend in Palestine:

... Germany's situation and future is really so uncertain that I am afraid there will still be considerable difficulties and reversals. For with the situation as it is today, the democratic idea cannot seriously consolidate itself and grow roots. Right from the start, it is severely discredited by the variety of opinions and heavy foreign burdens, but above all by the great material distress of the population.[7]

Uncertainty about the future, combined with material distress, could hardly provide firm foundations for any sort of stable political reorientation for the mass of essentially apolitical Germans.

Even after the formal creation of two separate and opposing states in 1949, there were for many years continued rumours about the immediate possibility of another war. Throughout the 1950s, whether rightly or wrongly, people saw the future of the 'German question' as still wide open. This only began to change after the building of the Wall, and was eventually consolidated by the conclusion of *Ostpolitik*.

Hopes were often raised, only to be dashed, with sometimes unexpected consequences as far as popular opinion was concerned. After rising expectations with Western triumphs in the Korean War and hopes of a mass demonstration in the elections of 1950, disappointment set in. The Americans, rather than Hitler—or even the Russians—seem to have been the focus of considerable popular criticism at this time, for apparently leaving East Germans in the lurch. As a report on popular opinion in the 'eastern zone' of October 1950 put it: 'Along with a sense of complete helplessness goes, increasingly, a feeling of having been abandoned ... [the blame for division] is not placed with Hitler or total defeat in war, but rather, above all, with the compliant politics of Roosevelt *vis-à-vis* Stalin, which led to the Potsdam Agreement, and thus to the surrender of the whole of eastern Europe to the Russian system.' The sentence could often be heard that 'The Americans delivered us up to the Russians, and the West shoved us off ...'.[8] This feeling of having been effectively abandoned by the West was consolidated after the Geneva Conference. As a Western report on opinion in the zone suggested, the population were experiencing 'a deep sense of disillu-

---

[6] Berger–Plöhn correspendence, letters of 3 Feb. 1946 and 29 June 1953. In the wake of the June Uprising of 1953, there was a rumour in the same area that reunification would come soon, but the precondition would be a currency reform, with the consequence that people were spending all their savings on consumer durables in the expectation that money would rapidly become as worthless as in 1923. Similar rumours continued to circulate well into the 1950s, including in the confused months of 1956.

[7] Nachlass Schultes, ED 188/6, letter of 2 Dec. 1947.

[8] IfZ, Fg 44/2, 'Ostzonaler Stimmungsbericht nach den Wahlen vom 15.x.1950'.

sion. Above all, any trust in the USA has been completely shattered . . . In general therefore, there is an air of resignation and passivity.'[9]

War and peace continued to be major worries of the East German people, related of course very closely to questions of the standard of living and relations with the West. With the alleged benefit of hindsight, it is sometimes difficult to imagine oneself into the mind-set of those who, in the 1950s, very vividly feared the imminence of another world war. Yet the records show that this was a major fear for many East Germans. It perhaps became of declining salience in the period of stabilization and improvement in relations between the superpowers and the two Germanies in the late 1960s and 1970s; it reappeared with a vengeance in the unofficial peace initiatives from the late 1970s and through the 1980s.

When the Nationale Volksarmee (NVA, National People's Army) was founded in January 1956, there appears to have been widespread disapproval. An analysis by the trade union (FDGB) opens with the typical introductory paragraphs stressing how everyone allegedly supports the NVA 'for the reason that our Republic and our achievements are most dangerously threatened by the fascist and militarist forces of West Germany'.[10] It then goes on to reveal the real extent of popular disquiet. 'A large proportion of the population are wavering, because among many colleagues there is still a lack of clarity about the real character of our National People's Army.' Fears of loss of family members were combined with a dislike of the notion of Germans shooting on Germans, and a well-founded suspicion that rearmament was at the expense of popular living standards. Individual examples of specific comments are given from a number of factories: 'If everyone rearms and we form an army, then there will only be war and we don't want war'; 'Who is going to pay for the rearmament, and what about our standard of living that we were promised'; 'We don't want German to shoot on German, and if we form an army, what will happen then'; 'As usual it's the small fry who will have to pay for it, while the big fish will be drinking to their own good health'. In a factory manufacturing bras in Karl-Marx-Stadt (Chemnitz), which employed around 280 mostly older women workers, many of whom had lost their menfolk in the Second World War, there appears to have been almost total hostility: 'We destroyed all the weapons in 1945, now they are being made again. We are not going to give up our sons.' In another report, young people and the intelligentsia are identified as holding pacifist sentiments in

---

[9] Ibid., 'Die politische Lage in der DDR' (n.d., probably 1955).

[10] FDGB, 2672, Information No. 4, 'Stimmung der Werktätigen zur Schaffung der Nationalen Volksarmee' (20 Jan. 1956).

principle; women as fearing most for their husbands and sons.[11] And, of course, the majority of non-communist East Germans would have infinitely preferred a united Germany. As one individual put it, 'We would rather have "free elections" in the whole of Germany than a people's Army'.[12] The widespread popular conversion in the Federal Republic to faith in NATO and strong Western defences against the perceived threat of communism was not paralleled in East Germany.

The national question was obviously of almost overriding concern. With the passage of time West Germans were progressively ever less interested in the East, prepared to turn westwards, become good 'Europeans' and forget about the 'other Germany'. While in the 1950s reunification ranked as one of the most important problems for West Germans, by 1983 less than 5 per cent accorded it such significance. The decline was more marked among young people than old.[13] This was not true for those left stranded on the wrong side of the Iron Curtain. Attempts to retain links with relatives in the West, to receive visitors and gifts from the West, to gain visas and hard currency for travel in the West, were constant aspirations for large numbers of East Germans. Given the imbalances in size of population and patterns of migration, only one-third of West Germans had relatives in the East, while as many as two-thirds of East Germans had relatives in the West.[14] Lack of political freedom was clearly also a massive factor in popular opinion. This lack of freedom was not so much, or not solely, a question of political forms—a significant proportion of the German electorate had after all voted for the dismantling of Weimar democracy—but rather a question of personal freedom to travel, to discuss, to make choices. 'National' identification was hence not only a matter of a sense of national identity, which faded far faster in the West than the East, but also a matter of the desire for freedom.

Given the material affluence of the West, grumbling about the standard of living was of course virtually inseparable from the national question. As one would-be wit among the workers is alleged to have complained: 'Before, we had a princely state and workers' prices—now we have a workers' state and princely prices.'[15] Throughout the entire history of the GDR, people made unfavourable comparisons with the standard of living in the West. This was the driving force behind western migration in the 1950s, and, combined

[11] FDGB, 2672, Information No. 6.   [12] Ibid., Information No. 4.

[13] D. P. Conradt, *The German Polity* (London: Longman, 3rd edn., 1986), 49.

[14] Lutz Niethammer, 'Erfahrungen und Strukturen. Prolegomena zu einer Geschichte der Gesellschaft der DDR', in Hartmut Kaelble, Jürgen Kocka, and Hartmut Zwahr (eds.), *Sozialgeschichte der DDR* (Stuttgart: Klett-Cotta, 1994), 100.

[15] FDGB, 2672, Information No. 10.

with a dislike of the repressive atmosphere of the GDR, provided a continued motive for people to abandon homes, homeland, families, and all that was near and familiar, in favour of a risky escape to an uncertain future, right through until the mass refugee flights of the summer and early autumn of 1989. The population haemorrhage at times of porous borders— until 1961 and in the summer and autumn of 1989—of course posed an explicit challenge to the legitimacy of the regime, ultimately eventuating, in the context of other factors, in its final collapse. But for the best part of forty years material shortages were taken for granted as an unavoidable aspect of life, and, well aware of the population's material disquiets, consumerism was a repeated tactic of the rulers to attempt to allay popular discontents.

On the other hand, East Germans were not entirely undifferentiated in their opinions: there was not simply a blanket condemnation of the East and adulation of all things Western. Some opinion poll surveys carried out by specialized institutes of opinion research for the SED are highly revealing in this respect. Since these surveys were carried out not for publication, but rather for identification of real problems which the party sought to address, there are no obvious attempts to dress up the results in the regime's typical tones of blatantly dishonest optimism when information was intended for public consumption. With all due caution with respect to popular suspicions and the sorts of answers people in a dictatorial regime are likely to give to opinion poll questions, the results are nevertheless of considerable interest.

In 1969, on the basis of a survey of 11,419 schoolchildren aged between 14 and 19, the Institute of Marxism-Leninism of the Central Committee of the SED found that around three-quarters of young people 'recognize with no reservations or with only weak reservations our values and goals, 10 to 20 per cent have, despite a basically positive attitude, rather greater reservations, and 5 to 10 per cent have a negative attitude of rejection'. The results of the 1969 survey confirmed those of previous years since the building of the Wall.[16] Younger classes of schoolchildren were on the whole more positive in their opinions than older; and children at the EOS (the equivalent of academic sixth-form colleges) were more positive than those at the less academic, vocational schools (POS). As the report notes, the 'usual hypothesis' (which they allege they wish to discard but is clearly introduced for serious consideration) runs along the following lines:

[16] IfGA, ZPA, IV A 2/2021/370, 'Kurzfassung über Probleme und Folgerungen zur Bewußtseinsentwicklung Jugendlicher in der DDR, die vom Zentralinstitut für Jugendforschung anläßlich der "Umfrage 69" vorgelegt wurden', 2, 3.

'Younger pupils are less aware of problems, "naïver" than older ones, pupils from EOS schools behave in a more goal-oriented manner, pretend more, are less honest than children in vocational schools . . . Attitudes towards the army, the party, work with the FDJ, community work, and critical engagement with bourgeois ideology and mass media are always more negative in vocational schools than in the EOS.'[17]

The report notes some interesting patterns of differentiation in the opinions of the young people who were surveyed. For example, 86 per cent professed to be 'proud' of the GDR and 90 per cent 'claim to love the GDR as their fatherland', for a variety of reasons—among which the GDR's economic performance and political circumstances did not feature strongly. Only one-third of young people were prepared to respond positively to the suggestion that the development of the standard of living, or the 'opportunities for free political activity' might be a reason for GDR patriotism, while nearly three-quarters (73 per cent) gave as a reason 'secure career prospects and the variety of possibilities for development'.[18] In response to a question about the GDR media, the survey found that: 'The most positive attitudes relate to sports programmes. Political information is judged in much less positive terms. Only 40 per cent are completely of the opinion that radio and television give accurate information on important political events.'[19] As many as two-thirds (67 per cent) openly admitted they preferred Western media (including the dreaded pirate pop station of the 1960s, Radio Luxemburg, clearly the epitome of Western decadence as far as the SED were concerned) over GDR offerings.[20] Such wide contrasts suggest that children were not simply giving the positive answers they assumed would be expected, but were to some considerable degree responding fairly honestly—and with some perceptiveness of realities.

This sort of open-eyed and realistic differentiation is evident also in opinion poll surveys of adults in a range of occupations carried out in the 1970s, with very comparable results. For example, an opinion poll carried out among agricultural workers in February 1976 asking whether the GDR or the Federal Republic was 'better' on a range of aspects found that only just over a third (36.4 per cent) were prepared to say that personal income was better in the GDR than the FRG, compared with 80.3 per cent who thought that social security (soziale Betreuung) was superior in East

[17] IfGA, ZPA, IV A 2/2021/370, 'Kurzfassung über Probleme und Folgerungen zur Bewußtseinsentwicklung Jugendlicher in der DDR, die vom Zentralinstitut für Jugendforschung anläßlich der "Umfrage 69" vorgelegt wurden', 3.
[18] Ibid. 8.   [19] Ibid. 10.   [20] Ibid. 11.

Germany.[21] Less than half those surveyed would concede that work productivity, leisure, and housing were better in the GDR (44.4, 44.6 and 47.6
per cent respectively); the rest for the most part diplomatically divided their
responses between the 'I can't say' and 'no answer' categories rather than
daring to suggest that conditions in the FRG were of the same standard or
better than conditions in the GDR. In 1977, similar surveys found nearly
three-quarters (72.3, 70.4 per cent) agreeing that 'basic material security
(*Sicherheit der Existenz*)' was better in the GDR, and comparable proportions (71.4, 74.3 per cent) agreeing that the GDR was better in respect of
social security in the sense of welfare provisions (*soziale Betreuung*), while
a mere quarter to a third of those surveyed (27.1, 29.2 per cent) could bring
themselves to agree that personal income was better.[22] When asked in 1976
to rate whether certain facilities were 'good', 'satisfactory', or 'unsatisfactory', only 37.1 per cent of residents of the surveyed areas felt that shopping
facilities were good, and a paltry 13.7 per cent were prepared to pretend
that 'gastronomic facilities' in their area were good, over half (51.7 per cent)
quite honestly reporting that they were 'unsatisfactory'.[23]

These sorts of answers suggest that most East Germans, whether still at
school or at work, had a fairly clear picture of the advantages and disadvantages of living in the GDR, sufficiently strong to be reflected, even if with
some distortions due to the constrained circumstances of a non-liberal
regime, through the opinion poll surveys of their Big Brother state. For all
the distortions, it is quite clear that considerable numbers of East Germans
had well-grounded grumbles about the conditions of life in the GDR. But
most of them on the whole kept their grumbling muted and with the passage
of time were increasingly prepared to go along with the regime in some form
of passive conformity to its structures and rituals. It was this combination
of conformity and grumbling, *Anpassung und Meckern*, which, eventually,
gained for the GDR the label of a 'niche society'.

Achieving conformity? Compliance and the 'niche society' in the 1970s

By the 1970s, it was common to see well-organized mass parades and mass
demonstrations on the occasion of public holidays, such as May Day, or the

---

[21] IfGA, ZPA, IV B 2/2.023/51, Institut für Meinungsforschung beim ZK der SED, 'Bericht
über eine Umfrage zu einigen Fragen der sozialistischen Landwirtschaft (Bereich Tier-
produktion)' (27 Feb. 1976).   [22] Ibid. (24 May 1977).
[23] Ibid., IV B 2/2.028/40, Institut für Meinungsforschung beim ZK der SED, 'Bericht über
eine Umfrage zum gesellschaftlichen Leben und zur Arbeit der Nationalen Front in den
Wohngebieten' (7 July 1976).

anniversary of the death of Rosa Luxemburg and Karl Liebknecht. As well as those actively participating—marching past in FDJ uniform or whatever, carrying the official banners—there would be the well-behaved crowds who turned out to stand on the pavements and cheer the marchers along. For most of those participating, this would be a classic case of outward conformity. One turned up with one's work brigade, was seen to be there by the boss, and after a decent interval disappeared to the beer garden to have a drink with colleagues and friends. It was also, as Stefan Wolle has suggested, a form of mass public humiliation (*Demütigung*), a visible obeisance to one's lords and rulers.[24] These rituals were a public display of subordination, of subject status. And it was in these public rituals that the first open challenges to authority were to come in the later 1980s, with the carrying of unofficial banners in the Olof Palme peace march of 1987.

It took some time before this mass conformity, this outward and visible sign of willing subordination to domination, could be achieved. It also took considerable organizational work on the ground. A report dated 14 May 1956 from the Plauen SED leadership to the Central Committee of the SED complains that the participation in the demonstrations of 1 May was smaller than in the previous year, due to poor organization. It comments that 'Among the demonstrators there lacked, above all, the necessary enthusiasm[!]' and adds that there was even evidence of 'enemy activities', with swastikas being hung on garden fences, and 'small quantities of leaflets, particularly anti-Soviet propaganda' being repeatedly dropped via balloons.[25] Similarly, a report on party work in Berlin in 1955 bemoans the 'great gaps in the political-organizational leadership of the masses by the party. This was particularly evident in the demonstrations on the occasion of 8 May. Party organizations were not even able to prevent a relatively large exodus from the marching ranks of demonstrators.'[26] Given the context—the ruins, the rubble, the grey and dismal atmosphere a mere ten years after the end of the war—it was scarcely surprising that there was little spontaneous enthusiasm expressed in parades. Achieving outward conformity was more a matter of party discipline and control of the masses than

[24] Stefan Wolle, 'Der Weg in den Zusammenbruch: Die DDR vom Januar bis zum Oktober 1989', in Eckard Jesse and Armin Mitter (eds.), *Die Gestaltung der deutschen Einheit* (Bonn: Bundeszentrale für politische Bildung, Schriftenreihe Band 308, 1992), 75–6: 'In the annual rhythm of the calendar the party paid homage to itself. The stupid rituals strikingly symbolized the rigid inflexibility of the system. The essential heart of the secular liturgy consisted in the collective humiliation of the masses in face of their rulers. The goal, as with every liturgy, was, so far as possible, to exclude all individuality and critical rationality.'

[25] IfGA, ZPA, IV 2/5/968, report of 14 May 1956.

[26] SAPMO-BArch, IV 2/5/975, 'Einschätzung der Lage und des Standes der Parteiarbeit in Berlin' (20 May 1955).

inward conviction on the part of the population. In general one could suggest that the 1950s were characterized by sufficient uncertainty about the future, combined with the still open border with West Berlin, for most people to maintain a relatively low-profile, wait-and-see stance with little impetus to put oneself out in visible conformity.

The niche society did not so much reflect any real change in attitudes and values, a diminution in what might be called justifiable grumbling, and a growing acceptance of the *status quo*. Rather, it was a product of changing circumstances, changing conditions of action, which produced changes in people's expectations and patterns of behaviour. There never was a 'golden age' in the GDR when the subordinate masses were genuinely content to leave politics to a well-meaning but all-powerful élite and to retreat into private niches, cultivating their gardens (literally as well as metaphorically, given the ubiquitous popularity of the allotments, or *Schrebergärten*, in the GDR as elsewhere in much of eastern central Europe). In so far as there was the appearance of such a situation, it was more or less precisely what the regime under Honecker was aiming at; failing complete commitment to communist ideology and goals, passive conformity and leaving politics to the party was an acceptable compromise. And this compromise was, very nearly, achieved—perhaps for the space of two or three years in the early to mid-1970s, let us say 1972–5.

If this sounds unduly precise and ridiculously restrictive, then it is intended, rather pointedly, to highlight a problem of analysing this phenomenon. What one is pursuing here is effectively an absence, a non-event. One is looking for a period when politics ticked over and the people kept quiet. But what the people felt and thought is only captured, in hindsight, through records, documents, which are social artefacts, political constructions, refracting, to some extent distorting or entirely repressing, the complexities of behaviours, values, and attitudes which go to make up the fullness of 'social reality' at any given time. As we shall see in the following chapters, the records on the whole turn out to be far fuller of complaints, acts of insubordination, and political opposition, than ever previously suspected, at least as far as outside observers were aware. So was perhaps the 'niche society' not so much an accurate description of a passive reality than a reflection of the efficiency of East German security and police forces in repressing unrest, and of East German information control in ensuring that news of incipient revolts rarely leaked out? Was it too a partial chimera of changed modes of reporting in the 1970s, when many series (such as the regional and local party reports, and the trade union reports on public opinion) become extraordinarily bland and positive, revealing virtually nothing of the vivid depictions of popular opinions which, for all the framing, nevertheless shine through particularly in the reports of the early years? Is the concept of a niche society, in effect, a result of the report-writers in the 1970s telling the rulers what they wanted to hear? Or, on the contrary, is the very prevalence of this *Schönfärberei* in the 1970s rather an indication of the stabilization of the system and the lack of serious worries on the part of the report-writers or their recipients?

In other words, there are some real methodological problems with seeking to identify when, if at all, any sort of a 'niche society' existed in the GDR, let alone trying to write its history. But despite these problems, the issues can be addressed. First, as suggested at the start of this section, patterns of mass conformity—at least on the occasion of public demonstrations—did develop. More people were prepared to adopt modes of behaviour of outward conformity in the 1970s than the 1950s. Thus the history of outward conformity can be written. Secondly, the 'niche society' never encompassed the whole of the population. It can be used as a shorthand phrase to summarize certain aspects of life among certain sections of the population in the GDR. As we shall see in the following chapters, significant groups never conformed, although modes of nonconformity, resistance, and opposition were very diverse and changed over time. The extent to which significant sections of the population were prepared to conform also varied at different times. The conditions under which this preparedness broke down will be the subject of a later chapter; here, we shall be concerned with the construction of widespread popular compliance, not the unexpected collapse of popular obedience in the final months of the GDR's life.

In so far as a 'niche society' existed, it was essentially constructed in the course of the 1960s and 1970s, for a variety of different reasons and with variations according to class and generation. The construction of a 'niche society' was moreover more a matter of transforming the structural frameworks in the context of which people led their lives, and at the same time transforming popular expectations, understandings of 'normality', and related behavioural patterns, than of achieving any genuine ideological conversion of the population. Moreover, the 'niche society' was not a stable construction (although once popularized in Western textbooks, it became a stable element of Western interpretations). It reached its high point around the mid-1970s; but the very factors which had gone to produce a degree of stabilization in the system themselves inaugurated a new lability through heightened hopes and expectations which could not subsequently be fulfilled. Let us examine in turn the different elements which served to produce the classic conditions for the niche society and its subsequent shifting.

First of all, there were important external preconditions for the spread of conformity. The stabilization of the GDR's international status was a key prerequisite. In 1961, the building of the Berlin Wall closed off the last escape hole to the West; it was now clear that one would have to make the best of things as they were, at least for the time being. And the duration of the time being began to look ever longer, with the conclusion of *Ostpolitik* in 1972 and the apparent permanence of the division of Germany that the GDR's newly won international recognition as a full voting member of the United Nations in 1973 seemed to entail. People felt that they simply had to live in the GDR as it was; if, after all, it was now officially recognized by what had been characterized as the arch-enemies of the capitalist-imperialist West, then the future of the GDR as a separate state seemed to be rather more definite.

Secondly, there were equally important internal political preconditions. The smooth functioning of the state apparatus and the party system were prerequisites. People only conform to patterns and frameworks if these themselves are accepted as relatively stable facts of life, not subject to perpetual challenge and renegotiation. Moreover, smoothly functioning systems of control help to pressurize and incorporate the population, to produce desired patterns of behaviour and suppress others. As we have seen in Chapter 3 above, by the 1970s the functionary system of organization and grass-roots penetration of society appeared to be rather more effective than in earlier years.

Thirdly, whatever people may actually think about a regime or aspects of its policies, over a period of time they start to develop patterns of behaviour which allow them to live within constraints which they cannot realistically hope to alter. They have to develop a *modus vivendi*. A state which is manifestly built on manipulation and lies, intervention and control, will produce subjects who live a corresponding life of pretence, of *Anpassung*. People, after all, have to live the lives they have, and have only once; they have to create the spaces for a degree of personal happiness, privacy, fulfilment, with corresponding compromises if outward conformity is demanded. More than this, and more positively expressed: a state in which there is only one dominant party will, if it lasts long enough, not only attract careerists and political trimmers, but also more genuinely committed individuals who feel that, if they are to achieve anything at all, they must work through the existing power structures and not against them.

Furthermore, the social history of the GDR produced itself a degree of stabilization. There were some groups who genuinely benefited from the regime's policies in different ways, and thus had something of a stake in the system. First, there were those from relatively disadvantaged backgrounds (children of workers and peasants) who had been given educational opportunities and professional advancement way beyond their expectations. The very real social revolution effected in the early years of the GDR, while antagonizing members of the middle classes and children from religious backgrounds, did give a very real boost to significant numbers of others who were offered opportunities never available to their parents.[27] Secondly, there was the impact of Ulbricht's concern with the 'technical-scientific revolution', and of the economic reforms of the 1960s. Finally, there was the developing impact of generational change. A new generation was coming to maturity which had been more influenced by the GDR than by an early childhood in the Third Reich. For the rising generation, certain features of the sociopolitical landscape began to become the taken for granted parameters of life. One had to go through the motions, grumbling if necessary to relieve one's feelings, but conforming in ever-increasing numbers none the less.

There is also another feature of importance, difficult to capture in documentary evidence but of undoubted significance. This has to do with what might be called the 'normality of everyday life'. People who led most of their conscious lives in the GDR—of whom there was a rising proportion in the population by the 1970s—simply took for granted the rules of existence, the shape and colour of their social, economic, and political surroundings. Without contrasts, without the personal *experience* of something different, it is difficult to define the character of one's own surroundings very precisely. As one East German put it, up until her first experience of West Germany after the fall of the Wall she had not realized the GDR was so grey, the buildings so decrepit, the air so dusty, because she had never known anything different.[28] Her only trip abroad before 1989 had been to Poland, which was visibly very much poorer. Her children, born in the mid-1970s, had experienced a happy childhood, with weekend trips to their country cottage, close to a farm where they could visit the cows, and with a garden in which they grew their own vegetables. They had been on camping holidays in the summer, and had enjoyed the sporting and social activities of their youth groups without ever really questioning the political

[27] See particularly the very suggestive essay by Lutz Niethammer, 'Erfahrungen und Strukturen'.

[28] An East German historian in her early forties, personal discussion, Jan. 1994.

constraints. For families such as this, life in the GDR was simply taken for granted, in much the same way as, for example, millions of Britons might concede that, objectively speaking, their income was lower than that of many Americans, but would not on this account chafe in frustration that they could not afford luxury homes or multiple consumer durables.

These tendencies were reinforced by a number of factors in the early 1970s. Honecker's early years were characterized, not only by the resolution of *Ostpolitik* and the new permanence of the GDR, but also by policies aimed at alleviating conditions in the here and now. In contrast particularly to the Stalinist emphasis on heavy industry characteristic of the 1950s, in the 1970s consumerism became an explicit goal of production. More fridges, washing machines, and television sets were produced; and although waiting lists for new cars remained long, ownership of a second-hand Trabi began to become a not unattainable goal. Social policies were prioritized in the proclaimed 'unity of economic and social policy': improved housing conditions, pensions, and maternity benefits were designed both to enhance the population's sense of well-being and to reverse stagnant or declining population numbers. These policies were combined with a new emphasis on building a sense of 'GDR national identity', now that reunification was no longer the avowed goal of the regime: international sporting successes, emphasis on cultural differences, the renewed appropriation of previously ignored or undervalued aspects of German history, were all brought into play in the attempt to inculcate a sense of pride in the GDR. Hopes of a new era under Honecker, characterized by cultural liberalization, were given sustenance by such proclamations as that of 'no taboos under socialism'. Additionally, the newly recognized GDR's participation in the Helsinki process both reinforced its claim to independent international status and raised hopes of a further liberalization of the regime. The great popular interest shown in Basket III of the Helsinki final act was frequently commented on (rather disapprovingly) in official reports.

But many of these features led only to a short-lived stabilization. Hopes and expectations were raised which could not subsequently be met. Two in particular were of importance as far as the broad masses of the East German population were concerned. One had to do with the standard of living, and expectations of economic improvement; the other related to political liberalization, and specifically the possibility of easier travel to the West and greater access to different media products. The hopes which were raised in the early 1970s led to changed behaviour patterns already in the early 1980s; and they were mightily fuelled by the new signals coming from the Soviet Union in the Gorbachev era. These heightened expectations inaugurated the new lability which was the precondition for the mobilization of the masses in the autumn of 1989.

Raised expectations and heightened lability in the 1980s

The year 1975 can perhaps be seen as a turning-point. The early Honecker years had aroused great expectations; from the mid-1970s, it became increasingly clear that raised expectations would not be fulfilled.

As far as human rights were concerned, both the Federal Republic's new *Ostpolitik* of recognition and *rapprochement* and the Helsinki Final Act played a major role in increasing the GDR's actual openness to the West, and in nurturing hopes of further liberalization. As a summary to Erich Honecker of a report from the Bezirksleitung Dresden (under the leadership of the reform-minded communist Hans Modrow) put it in August 1975:

In the report it is pointed out that, at the moment, the interest of many citizens is still directed too one-sidedly at the sections concerning human contacts and information. These citizens have expectations, above all, concerning further extensions of holiday traffic, tourism, family reunions, marriages, and the import of products of the press. There is widespread support for the demand to call a halt to the arms race. And, according to the report, many young people connect this with illusions of reducing or completely abolishing military service.[29]

Comparable comments come from the Bezirksleitung Schwerin in June 1978:

[It can be] sensed . . . that many citizens have difficulty in the correct evaluation of the specifics of our policies in the interests of peace . . . in this connection the influence of the class enemy is not without effect.

It is still clear that every step towards normal international legal relations between states still leads to illusions with respect to the Federal Republic of Germany, for example concerning travel there or other such matters.

Here we can see that the enemy is still, despite all, using his manifold organizational influences to target citizens, at least as far as problems concerning holiday travel or a sense of nationalism—if only occasionally—is concerned.[30]

The increased cultural and human penetration of the GDR after *Ostpolitik*—the larger numbers of visitors from the West, the massive increase in exposure to Western television and other media—was double-edged in its political implications. On the one hand, it is true that many East Germans now had to view their state as a permanent, internationally recognized entity, and that any end to the division of Germany was now a

[29] SAPMO-BArch, Büro Erich Honecker, J IV A 2/2.030/252, report of 26 Aug. 1975.

[30] Ibid., J IV A 2/2.030/151, letter of 19 June 1978 from Heinz Ziegler, First Secretary, Schwerin, to Erich Honecker.

most unlikely possibility. Unification simply did not seem to be on any realistic political agenda, particularly once the West German CDU came to accept the Social–Liberal coalition's eastern policies. On the other hand, the recognition by the West of the separate existence of an East German state was in part precisely to seek to overcome the barriers to human contact through the Iron Curtain. And this led many East Germans to be both better informed, and to expect continued further improvements in their degrees of freedom and possibilities for contacts with the West.

The economically beneficial *rapprochement* between the two Germanies which was pursued in the early 1980s (and which led to favourable credit agreements which somewhat alleviated the GDR's mounting economic difficulties and international debt mountain) had less welcome domestic political consequences as far as the regime was concerned. As a report from the Bezirksleitung Schwerin put it in April 1986:

There continues to be widespread support for the willingness to engage in dialogue between the GDR and the FRG, from which part of the population is hoping above all for relaxations of travel restrictions and that sort of thing . . . With the variety of contacts between representatives of the party and government of the GDR and the government of the FRG as well as representatives of the SPD, the opinion is frequently expressed that the FRG cannot be that dangerous after all . . .

In typical fashion, the report continues (putting the blame not on the real opinions of the people, but on hostile influences from abroad, which must be countered with the usual weapons of ideological warfare):

In innumerable ways one can sense certain effects of hostile ideological diversions. Therefore it is important, when engaging in face to face ideological work, to put the essence of this dialogue into context, and to demonstrate that under no circumstances can such a dialogue make the antagonistic contradictions between socialism and imperialism disappear.[31]

Similar expectations of the possible results of closer relationships between the two Germanies were clearly raised by Honecker's visit to West Germany of 1987. As a report from Frankfurt-on-Oder put it in October 1987:

The fact cannot be overlooked that among a section of the population of all ages and social classes, there are heightened expectations above all in relation to travel restrictions. This is particularly the case among youngsters, religiously inclined citizens, members of the medical profession and the cultural intelligentsia, as well as tradespeople, artisans, and craftsmen. Such expectations are more or less disassociated from the real situation concerning relations with the FRG and its position with regard to basic questions of the sovereignty and independence of the GDR. Evidence of this is the continuing rise in the number of applications in the third

[31] Ibid., J IV A 2/2.030/240, report of 15 Apr. 1986.

quarter of 1987 for a permanent change of residence to the BRD or Berlin (West), in which connection many individuals express the expectation that it would now be easier to move across to the FRG.[32]

In the context of *rapprochement* between the two Germanies, there was clearly something of an air of expectation, of leavening of the dead weight of separation, of hope for liberalization and increased freedom of movement.

These hopes were given massive impetus, of course, by the accession of Gorbachev to power in the Soviet Union. Widespread expectations of the possibility of increased openness and change within the Soviet bloc countries were sufficiently strong to be reflected even in the most *schöngefärbt* (glossed over and rose-tinted) party reports—an indication, perhaps, that even the local party leaders were becoming increasingly impatient with Honecker's resistance to notions of glasnost and perestroika, and were using their reports to drop broad hints on this front.

For example, the Leipzig party report of June 1987 suggests that although everyone is of course prepared 'to struggle perpetually for the highest daily achievements', nevertheless 'questions are put concerning the realistic nature of tasks set, the continuity of the production process, and the provisions of material and spare parts. At the same time, the question is raised as to whether a more critical approach, such as is current in the Soviet Union, might not help us to progress more quickly.' The report continues to enumerate the very real worries of the population and the local party leadership, concerning energy for heating, lack of quality of goods ('they limit the stability of provisions and lead to irritability among the citizens'), the length it takes to have repairs carried out, the lack of spare parts ('there is increasing criticism of the long waiting periods for fridges because of the lack of thermostats and for vehicle repairs because of a lack of spare parts'), and so on.[33]

A similar commentary comes from Frankfurt-on-Oder in February 1987:

Among comrades and many other politically engaged citizens the speech of Erich Honecker has been understood as a programme for action in 1987. But there are however comments, particularly from members of the intelligentsia, in which comparisons are made with the speeches of Comrade Gobachev . . . For the most part the influence and the intentions of the hostile media are evident here. But there are also voices to be heard from comrades who are unsure of things. . . . Of course superficial comparisons and above all silly assertions are energetically opposed.[34]

---

[32] SAPMO-BArch, J IV A 2/2.030/254, report of 1 Oct. 1987.
[33] Ibid., J IV A 2/2.030/258, report of 11 June 1987.
[34] Ibid., J IV A 2/2.030/254, report of 27 Feb. 1987.

1. Against the ruined skyline of post-war Berlin, organized youth groups, looking rather sullen and miserable, have been marshalled on an official demonstration on the occasion of the 'First *Deutschlandtreffen*', 25–9 May 1950. The somewhat implausible slogan on the banner reads: 'Improved vocational training—undreamt-of opportunities and prospects for upward mobility thanks to the Law for the Furtherance of Youth'.

2. In an official attempt at raising labour productivity through encouraging competitive overwork, President Wilhelm Pieck makes awards at a 'Heroes of Work' ceremony in the Berlin State Opera House, on the 'Activists' Day', 13 October 1950. The slogan behind the dignitaries reads 'Fame and Honour to the Heroes of Work'.

3. Referendum on 3 June 1951 against the 'remilitarization of Germany'—meaning West German involvement in western alliances. Many of the peasant women and children of the village of Drachhausen depicted in this photo had only a few years previously lost their husbands, sons, fathers, in Hitler's war.

4. Suppression of the Uprising on 17 June 1953 by Soviet tanks (Leipziger Strasse, East Berlin).

5. A mere two years after the workers' Uprising of June 1953, somewhat sceptical and disaffected-looking workers listen to a speech by the Minister for Heavy Industry of the GDR, Fritz Selbmann, at a ceremony inaugurating building works on 31 August 1955 at the lignite and coke works, 'Kombinat "Schwarze Pumpe"'. Located near Hoyerswerda, Bezirk Cottbus, this was one of the most important enterprises in the second Five Year Plan.

6. Minister Willi Stoph addresses soldiers and officers of the first regiment of the first Division of the newly founded National People's Army (*Nationale Volksarmee*) in Sachsenhausen, Oranienburg, at the ceremony for the swearing of the oath of allegiance to the 'fatherland', the German Democratic Republic, on 30 April 1956—exactly eleven years after Hitler committed suicide in his bunker in Berlin, having brought the all-German 'fatherland' to ashes and ruins.

7. Two girls at a state youth ceremony (*Jugendweihe*), in March 1958. The *Jugendweihe*, introduced in 1954, was the cause of great controversy between Church and state in the 1950s. The presentation book which the girls are holding, entitled *Weltall, Erde, Mensch* (The Universe, the World, Mankind), presented a materialist view of the origins of the world incompatible with the biblical story of Creation and the preparations for Church confirmation.

Villagers on an official May Day demonstration on 1 May 1960 in Leussow, Kreis Neustrelitz. The flag of the Peasants' Party, the DBD, is visible. This community had just won on the 'Beautiful Village' competition.

Rather disgruntled workers at a *Roter Treff* meeting in a machine factory in Halle, 1960. The top propaganda banner, above the FDJ picture of Karl Marx, reads: 'We, the members of the Youth Brigade "Karl Marx", are competing for the title of honour "Brigade of Socialist Work"'. The lower banner contains the injunction: 'Secure peace through good deeds for the victory of socialism—Beat the militarists and revanchists in Bonn!'.

10. Following the erection of the Berlin Wall on 13 August 1961, houses which were adjacent to the new Wall were cleared and their inhabitants moved out. This photo shows a forcible removal in Bernauer Strasse on 24 September 1961.

11. A parade of the National People's Army opening the official demonstration of 1 May 1962 with a display of military might.

12. Erich Honecker signs the Helsinki Final Declaration in August 1975, seated in a position of honour between the West German Chancellor Helmut Schmidt and US President Gerald Ford.

13. Young Pioneers on a holiday camp in Crimea. Sunshine and friendship were probably more important to these young people than the ideology of their youth organization.

14. The participants at the highly significant 'summit meeting' (*Spitzengespräch*) between representatives of Church and state on 6 March 1978. Erich Honecker (second from the right) met with the Executive Committee of the Conference of Protestant Church Leaders in the GDR. From left to right: Rudi Bellmann, Hermann Kalb, Siegfried Wahrmann, Heinz Eichler, Paul Verner, Manfred Stolpe, Christina Schultheiss, Kurt Domsch,

15. Erich Honecker, Willi Stoph, Horst Sindermann and their wives cast their votes at the local elections on 6 May 1984. The observations of the falsification of local election results five years later, in 1989, was to occasion well-organized protests.

16. The formation of the 'GDR Committee for the 750th Anniversary of Berlin'—a typical attempt at representing the GDR as the crowning culmination of history, and ensuring the co-operation of a compliant state church for legitimation of the regime. On the left (next to a display table with the original founding charter of Berlin), Manfred Stolpe, President of the Consistory of the Protestant Churches, addresses various political dignitaries: Erich Honecker, Horst Sindermann, Erhard Krack, Egon Krenz, Harry Tisch, Günter Mittag (from left to right), with other notables in the background.

17. In a typical attempt to inculcate a friend/foe mentality and emphasize paramilitary socialization, children are invited to meet border soldiers and to play on military vehicles on the 'Day of the Border Troops', 23 November 1986.

18. In a remarkable display of apparent toleration, demonstrators with banners from unofficial peace initiatives (such as the church 'peace weeks') were allowed to walk among official demonstrators on the Olof Palme Peace March of September 1987. This particular section of the March was on the way to a memorial ceremony at the former Nazi Concentration Camp of Ravensbrück.

19. East and West Germany apparently developing an ever more amicable long-term relationship on the occasion of Erich Honecker's visit to the Federal Republic in September 1987. In this photo, taken in Bonn on the occasion of the signing of governmental accords and economic agreements between the two states, Erich Honecker, flanked by his Politburo colleague Günter Mittag, stands side by side with Federal Chancellor Helmut Kohl and his Economics Minister Martin Bangemann.

20. Soviet President Mikhail Gorbachev and his wife are greeted with unusually genuine enthusiasm by East German crowds on their arrival in East Berlin for the fortieth anniversary of the foundation of the GDR in October 1989. Erich Honecker gives a subdued smile in the background; within less than two weeks, he had been ousted from office.

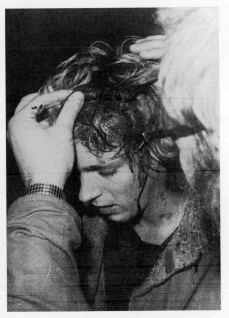

21. Attempting to present an illusion of domestic peace, the regime dealt very brutally with those who dared to 'think differently'. Thousands went on to the streets of East Berlin Berlin on 7 October 1989, during the official anniversary 'celebrations', to demand greater freedom and dialogue; hundreds were brutally beaten up, arrested and detained, like this unfortunate individual at the corner of Dimitroff Strasse and Prenzlauer Allee.

22. A victim of regime brutality, 7 October 1989.

23. After the dramatic
renunciation of the use of force to
suppress the mass demonstration
in Leipzig on 9 October, ever
larger numbers of people dared to
come out on the by now regular
Monday evening marches around
Leipzig's Ringstrasse. This photo,
taken on 30 October 1989, shows
the crowds marching through the
Karl-Marx-Platz.

24. Professor Jens Reich, a
co-founder of New Forum, was
one of the critical intellectuals
who joined with others, both
more and less supportive of the
regime, to address around half a
million demonstrators at an
officially approved mass meeting
in East Berlin on 4 November
1989.

25. The extraordinary courage and active non-violence of demonstrators was an important factor in the character of the 'gentle revolution'. Two young people in this (possibly posed?) photo offer flowers to a uniformed member of the security forces in the course of a demonstration in East Berlin on 7 November—two days before the breaching of the wall.

26. The extraordinary night of 9/10 November 1989, as people—from East and West—climbed ecstatically on to and over the once dreaded Berlin Wall.

27. Not with a bang but a whimper . . . The end of the GDR was symbolized by thousands of Trabis nosing westwards through ever proliferating border crossings and gaps, official and unofficial, in the no longer quite so Iron Curtain.

In Schwerin in December 1988 the same sorts of sentiments are recorded: 'the expectation was frequently expressed that our society should permit more openness and freedom of opinion'; people were following the developments in the USSR, Poland, and Hungary extremely closely. At the same time, increasing numbers of people were expressing their desire to leave the GDR.[35] Within a year of this report being compiled, they were of course—entirely unexpectedly—able to put these hopes and expectations into practice.

It is clear from the above that the West German policies of increasing human and political contacts between the two German states were having noticeable effects on the aspirations of the East German population. So too were the new initiatives taken by Gorbachev in the Soviet Union. Nevertheless, while the Federal Republic recognized the GDR as a legitimate discussion partner, engaging in party political contacts at the highest levels and receiving Erich Honecker as a distinguished guest of state, it could hardly be predicted that the GDR would simply crumble and disappear within the foreseeable future. Indeed, had the Federal Republic recognized the GDR's full sovereignty and ceased to accord automatic rights of citizenship and residence in the West to East German citizens, the GDR might never have crumbled at all—and would certainly not have collapsed so fast. Thus, although there was in certain circles an air of heightened expectation, beginning with developments *vis-à-vis* the West in the early to mid-1970s and encouraged by the new winds blowing from the East in the later 1980s, the prevailing pattern among East Germans was one of general compliance with the rules of the political game which people within the GDR felt they were constrained to play.

How did people conceptualize the kind of double life they were leading? A number of concepts were current. For example, there was the notion of *freiwilliger Zwang*—'voluntary coercion'. If one simply wanted to avoid trouble, it was better to do voluntarily what one was going to be forced to do anyway. Another such phrase was that of *bequemes Schweigen*, having an easy life by keeping quiet. This did not necessarily mean that people were not critical; but such criticism was often expressed in the sublimated form, for example, of political jokes, which allowed a ventilation of feelings and a sense of solidarity among those enjoying the joke while posing little real challenge to the regime. (Question: 'When you die, would you rather go to a capitalist hell or a socialist hell?' Answer: 'A socialist hell of course. You get roasted in the flames of hell in both cases; but in a socialist hell, there is

[35] Ibid., IV B 2/14/70, 'Rat des Bezirks Schwerin, Informationsbericht für Okt./Nov. 88' (6 Dec. 1988).

a shortage of matches, they've run out of wood, and the Devil is not working at the moment.')[36] The circumvention or manipulation of rules, the sense of human solidarity in muted oppression, the retreat into the pleasures and problems of private life, were all modes of long-term survival in what appeared, for most people, to be a permanent political situation. In what was quite clearly an ultimately repressive state, it took considerable courage and conviction to speak out directly on matters of conscience.

All this suggests that the regime's polices of (to put it neutrally) socialization and education, or (more pejoratively) indoctrination, were to little effect, despite the massive resources poured into propaganda. In other words, what we have been examining here is *not* the way in which the state successfully 'indoctrinated' or (less pointedly) 'socialized' its subjects, but rather the ways in which it sought to achieve their outward compliance. And this achievement is in many ways infinitely less remarkable than the other side of the same coin; the conditions under which subjects refused, in different ways, to offer up their compliance, to acquiesce in their own subordination. More important than positive indoctrination in achieving conformity was the paucity or absence of institutional bases for the articulation of countervailing views, for at least a limited form of 'civil society' or supportive non-state-controlled environment in the context of which to debate and critique the regime. This, however, as we shall see in Chapter 8, was to develop in the course of the late 1970s and 1980s. For the most part, discontent and opposition was effectively contained or fragmented. It is to the misfits, the nonconformists, the proponents of different outlooks—in short, to those who, in the now famous words of Rosa Luxemburg, 'thought differently' (*die Andersdenkenden*)—that we now turn.

---

[36] For this and other examples, see Karl-Dieter Opp and Peter Voß, *Die volkseigene Revolution* (Stuttgart: Klett-Cotta, 1993), 91–3; see also Arn Strohmeyer, *Visa-frei bis Hawai* (Frankfurt-on-Main: Eichborn, 1990).

6

MODES OF POPULAR DISSENT

ONE fact was evident throughout the GDR's history: a lot of people did not like the GDR. That there was mass discontent with the political constraints and material shortcomings of life in the GDR is indisputable. This was both externalized and reified in official views, which almost automatically attributed very diverse expressions of protest to the 'class enemy' (usually expressed as an individual, with references to the *Klassenfeind*, the *Tätigkeit des Klassengegners*), allegedly steered from the imperialist-capitalist West. But in reality there were many, often quite conflicting, bases of discontent within the GDR itself, frequently sparked by unfavourable comparisons between West and East but certainly based more on authentic experience than on manipulation by alleged enemy agents.

There was clearly a major difference between the Third Reich and the GDR in this respect. The Third Reich was at least in origin carried on a tidal wave of enthusiasm which, even if never characteristic of a majority of the population, was sufficiently widespread and genuine to provide Nazism with a basis of popular support never enjoyed to such an extent by the communist regime in the GDR. The early years of the Third Reich were, moreover, characterized by improvements in living standards for many sectors of the population, combined with a return to full employment, a restoration of a degree of national pride, and a sense of movement upwards and onwards. At least among significant sections of the population these trends, combined with a carefully tended presentation of Hitler as the charismatic Führer, did much to provide a real basis of support for the regime. There was nevertheless a significant proportion of the population in Nazi Germany who, right from the start, were characterized rather by degrees of disgruntlement, grumbling, and partial or sporadic nonconformity.[1]

[1] On patterns of popular opinion and political culture in the Third Reich, see particularly the seminal works by Ian Kershaw, *The Hitler Myth* (Oxford: Oxford University Press, 1987); *Popular Opinion and Political Dissent in the Third Reich* (Oxford: Clarendon Press, 1983); *Hitler* (Harlow: Longman, 1991); and also e.g. Detlev Peukert, *Inside Nazi Germany* (London: Batsford, 1987).

The task for the communists in East Germany after 1945 was far more difficult in some respects than that of Hitler after 1933. The extent of basic political/ideological disagreement was far greater, the extent of popular support far less. What is interesting, however, is that even with this far greater reservoir of popular discontent, there were no serious political implications as far as regime stability was concerned. The agonized questioning about lack of adequate resistance in the Third Reich appears almost misplaced, almost irrelevant, when one considers how little practical effect the far greater reservoirs of discontent had under the East German dictatorship. It is a sobering thought that both dictatorships ultimately fell only under the impact of altered external circumstances: in the case of the radical, expansionist, warmongering Third Reich, defeat in world war; in the case of the artificially created, militarily subordinate GDR, the withdrawal of Soviet preparedness for military intervention and the collapse of the protective Iron Curtain.

The debate on resistance in the Third Reich has led to an increasingly sophisticated theoretical discussion about what can be held to have constituted resistance, and the extent to which acts of nonconformity can be put under the more general heading of 'opposition' or the German term of 'withstanding (*Widerstand*)'.[2] This sort of behaviour in effect only became politicized because the regime treated such evasion of its total claims as intrinsically political.[3] Martin Broszat in particular has proposed the notion of *Resistenz*, or 'immunity', to relate to the degree of failure of the regime to penetrate certain sections of society and achieve its claim to total conformity. Given the ambiguities of the term 'resistance' in English (which carries both the medical sense of immunity or resistance to infection, and the rather more active sense implied by the notion of opposition), both the debate and the terminology have proved somewhat difficult to carry over into Anglo-Saxon equivalents. But whatever the difficulties of translation, there is a well-defined area of enquiry. This has to do with those aspects of social behaviour which in their *effects*, even if not in the motives of the individuals concerned, constituted to a greater or lesser extent obstacles to the regime's realization of its objectives. In this sense, such nonconformity

---

[2] For a sensitive analysis of the responses of the German people, see Martin Broszat, 'The Third Reich and the German People', in Hedley Bull (ed.), *The Challenges of the Third Reich* (Oxford: Clarendon Press, 1986); and for an excellent recent summary of the state of debate, see Ian Kershaw, *The Nazi Dictatorship* (London: Edward Arnold, 3rd edn., 1993), ch. 8, ' "Resistance without the People"?'

[3] For a thoughtful conceptual discussion, see particularly Ian Kershaw, ' "Widerstand ohne Volk?" Dissens und Widerstand im Dritten Reich', in Jürgen Schmädeke and Peter Steinbach (eds.), *Der Widerstand gegen den Nationalsozialismus* (Munich: Piper, 1985).

was—whether or not intended as such—a form of resistance to the demands of the state.

Given the very recent opening of the East German archives, it will clearly be many years before the debates on dissent and resistance in the GDR reach the level of conceptual sophistication, empirical saturation, and substantive detail characterizing the historiography of Nazi Germany. The main focus of historians' attention so far with respect to opposition has been on major flashpoints such as 1953, on well-known dissident intellectuals, and on the oppositional movements of the autumn of 1989, subjects which will be treated in subsequent chapters. This chapter seeks to open up some of the rather more inchoate, but no less important, forms of popular dissent or 'resistance' in the broader sense to the regime's demands. It is clear that much nonconforming behaviour was not explicitly regarded or consciously intended as such: it was not directly aimed to be effective against the regime, but was rather a form of reaction against the demands imposed on the individual. It was on the whole primarily self-protective, with respect to the defence of an individual's own personal values or interests, rather than actively oppositional in intent.

There were certainly parts of East German society that the state was unable to reach: that enjoyed a degree of immunity, or resistance in the medical rather than political sense, to infection by official propaganda. Immunity might be based in cultural and religious values, in individual aspirations, in clashes of material interest, or a complex combination of these. The degree of resistance was affected, too, by the social and political context of refusal to conform or rejection of the regime's demands, and by the state's changing responses to such rejection.

Strong religious faith, supported by local pastors, communities, and the institution of the Church, proved to be a major 'protective' factor (to continue the medical metaphor), as we have seen in Chapter 4 above, although the degree to which this protection could be sustained depended very much on local political circumstances. The persistence of the power of the Church as an institution, and religious beliefs as a coherent alternative to the communist, atheist world-view, posed a continuing problem for the authorities, and lay behind the attempts to co-opt the Church which were symbolized in the Church–state agreement of 1978. There were also other, often less ideologically explicit, bases of refusal: disaffection and an inclination to drop out, for example, among young people who did not like the pressures for social participation, political conformity, military service, and comparable activities, but who did not quite know where else to turn. Seeking to develop an adequate youth policy was a perpetual concern of the regime, which never succeeded in the ultimately unattainable goal of achieving 100 per cent conformity among youth. Conflicts over material interests were a perpetual source of possible political confrontation, given the lack of adequate bases for genuine representation of workers' interests in what was officially the 'workers' and peasants' state'. And, whatever the degree of satisfaction of material concerns, some socio-economic groups appeared less compliant or open to propaganda than others.

There is no attempt at any comprehensive catalogue of forms of nonconformity here, since the aim is to open up areas of enquiry rather than to present what would be a premature typology. Nor are definitive answers proposed to the very important question of the effects of such dissent on the efficiency and long-term survival chances of the system. But the hypothesis is proposed that, although all forms of dissent represented both a failure on the part of the regime to achieve its professed goals, and a degree of what might be called 'disturbance' in the system, ultimately the rather widespread nonconformity discussed in this chapter was relatively efficiently dealt with by the East German authorities, so that its net effect was not, under most circumstances, seriously destabilizing. Similar efficiency was evident in the suppression of the more active forms of opposition discussed in the following chapter. In contrast, the new social and political currents of the 1980s, analysed in more detail in Chapter 8 below, while carried by only a tiny minority of activists, proved in the end to be far more politically important than did the infinitely more widespread patterns of popular disaffection which are the subject of attention here.

Splutterings from below: strikes and disturbances

It might be expected that committed Christians, or hangovers of the old petty bourgeoisie, or the perennially rebellious and experiment-happy youth, might naturally present some problems as far as conformity was concerned.[4] But what of the workers in the self-professed 'workers' and peasants' state'? Perhaps somewhat ironically, the most active and potentially counter-productive (from the regime's point of view) expressions of discontent appeared in the protection, not so much of cultural values or personal authenticity, as of more purely material interests. Nor was it only workers who were prepared to express quite openly their lack of respect for the regime. In this section, we shall look at explicit manifestations of popular unrest and localized conflicts with at least certain aspects of the regime's policies and practices.

[4] The following section has been published, in slightly different form, as part of an article in *Contemporary European History*, 2: 3 (Nov. 1993), 265–82.

It has frequently been assumed that the East Germans were on the whole a remarkably quiescent population. With the exception of the strikes of June 1953 (of which more in the following chapter), until the opening of the archives it had appeared that there was very little active unrest among the East German labour force. But it is now clear that these assumptions were mistaken. East German workers were far more rebellious in the defence of their interests than had previously been assumed. And again, because of the nature of the regime, there was an intrinsic relation between *any* form of protest, over however apparently trivial and localized an issue, and the assumption on the part of the authorities of a wider political purpose or implication.

The evidence of workers' unrest and of splutterings of revolt is far greater than ever previously imagined.[5] The opening of the files of the trade union organization, the FDGB, has made a veritable gold-mine of detailed information available. In addition to very detailed general reports on trade union matters, including periodic reports on the moods of different groups of workers and the spread of popular opinion on a variety of topical issues, the FDGB kept very detailed files on *besondere Vorkommnisse*, or unusual incidents of particular interest. These ranged from (often quite serious) industrial accidents and problems of health and safety at work, to wildcat strikes, lack of work discipline, acts of insubordination, and ultimately of course the activities of the ubiquitous *Klassenfeind*. The reports are particularly interesting, and probably—once the terminology and ideological perspective are appropriately translated or interpreted—rather accurate guides to the extent and character of unrest among the workforce. These reports were on the whole confidential, even highly confidential (*streng vertraulich*), not intended for widespread circulation, let alone public consumption. Thus there was no need for unnecessary beautification (*Verschönerung*), although many of the general reports (but not those on *besondere Vorkommnisse*) start with the usual optimistic statements before engaging with the more critical material.[6] The authorities had a vested interest in identifying very

---

[5] See the very brief and patchy discussion in Karl Wilhelm Fricke, *Opposition und Widerstand in der DDR* (Cologne: Verlag Wissenschaft und Politik, 1984), ch. 6, 101–4. Fricke's discussion could at that time only be based on snippets gleaned from occasional newspaper reports (e.g. extrapolating from reports of fines or prison sentences passed on offenders) and a little educated guesswork: as Fricke himself says, the 'sparse news reports' can only provide 'a highly incomplete picture' (101). He comments that 'there were also occasional threats of strikes and work stoppages in the seventies and early eighties' (104), but has no detailed material to analyse.

[6] This becomes particularly true from the early 1970s onwards, when the general reports cease to have much use as a real reflection of public opinion, and act rather more as the mouthpiece of the trade union functionaries who might wish to make use of spurious reported comments to bring certain considerations to the attention of the central trade union leadership, less in touch with opinions at the grass roots. Certainly in the 1950s, however, and through the

precisely the causes and sources of unrest, since the intention was to deal effectively with any untoward activities: to stamp out or remove ringleaders, to remove the bases of justified grievances, to ensure that the public face of harmony and quiescence was maintained. Although not 'scientific', in the sense of technically sophisticated public opinion surveys, the trade union reports provide the nearest equivalent to what one would find in local and national newspapers in a more open and pluralist society. Every little incident and accident is there, reported of course from a certain point of view, the biases inherent in which have to be taken into account when using the material.

What then do these reports show? Some of the everyday concerns and opinions on current affairs have been discussed in the previous chapter; here, we shall focus specifically on evidence of political discontent and more particularly on the forms of *expression* of this discontent.

Unofficial work stoppages—the downing of tools, walking out on the job—was obviously a very effective means both of expressing dissatisfaction and directly affecting the functioning of the regime by striking at the very heart of its economic efficiency. Increasing productivity was a constant aim of the regime, reiterated through innumerable competitions for increases in work productivity (*im sozialistischen Wettbewerb*) and reinforced by the stereotypical stony-faced images of powerful labourers overfulfilling their quotas to the greater glory of socialism. But such exploitation of the labour force depended on a very delicate balance of pressure and nego-tiation over wages, tariffs, and productivity levels. This balance could, very easily, be upset; nor was it the only factor affecting people's willingness to work.

Strikes were, therefore, not necessarily *political* in either origins or inten-tion; however, since they posed a challenge to authority in the 'workers' and peasants' state', they were very often interpreted and treated as political events. Reading through the reports of unofficial work stoppages, it be-comes apparent that the most common causes were comparable to those dealt with through more institutionalized channels of interest representation and conflict resolution in democratic societies. A very common reason for downing tools was precisely that which sparked off the June Uprising in 1953: the raising of work norms. With inadequate equipment, and short-ages of materials, workers very often found it difficult if not impossible to

1960s, there is a very real sense of the genuine opinions and word-for-word comments of real people coming through what is often very lively reporting from the grass roots. The files on *besondere Vorkommnisse* continue to reflect very accurately the extent and character of disturbing incidents right up into the 1980s.

produce more; and when corners were cut on safety standards, industrial injuries often resulted.[7] Differential pay rates, inadequate working conditions, unfair treatment of individuals, attempts to stamp out previously lax practices, poor food or food which had been heated too early for the late shift, disputes over beer bottles—these and other major and minor irritations in everyday life at the workplace often gave grounds for unofficial work stoppages of greater or lesser duration.[8] Frequently the initial dispute was exacerbated by the imbibing of considerable quantities of alcohol; it is quite striking how often accounts of *Sauferei* (excessive drinking) crop up in the reports.[9]

Once a fully-fledged confrontation was under way, it was often discovered that the individuals concerned had 'Western contacts' (not very surprising, since a majority of the population had friends and relatives in the West); this was then interpreted as putting a political gloss on the strike, rendering what originated as a work dispute into something altogether more sinister. For example, in November 1961 three workers at the VEB Waggonbau Goerlitz left their shift, started drinking, and eventually became too drunk to return to work. On investigation, all three were found to have close connections with West Berlin, and were therefore arrested.[10] Often, too, workers would threaten to strike for higher wages, making comparisons with better conditions in the West, and would argue that the FDGB did not truly represent workers' interests, so why should they pay union dues, which only went into the pockets of functionaries; such comments, too, were clearly 'political' and were treated as such.[11]

[7] Cf. Archiv der Gewerkschaftsbewegung Berlin, FDGB Bundesvorstand (cited as FDGB). File no. 5414, report of 8 Aug. 1968, on an explosion on 11 July 1968 at a PVC production factory of the VE electro-chemicals combine in Bitterfeld, which left 32 dead and 238 injured within the factory (of whom 8 died later), and 2 dead, with many more injured, outside, as well as having long-term health risks (heart and circulatory problems) after imbibing the gases released. The *Produktionsdirektor* himself blamed the explosion on the emphasis on ever higher productivity at the expense of safety measures.

[8] See e.g. FDGB: file no. 15/1470/6447, letter of 28 Dec. 1961; file no. 3023, reports of 25 Sept. 1964, 20 May 1965, 7 July 1966, 9 Aug. 1967, 29 Nov. 1967, 26 June 1969 (in which the cook who was responsible for the poor food which occasioned the strike was eventually dismissed, after trying to mislead the investigation by producing an atypically good meal); 29 July 1969, 7 Aug. 1969 (food produced too early had gone off in the heat by the time the late shift were able to take a meal break), 16 Apr. 1970, 27 Oct. 1975, and others.

[9] See e.g. FDGB, file no. 15/1470/6447, report of 13 Dec. 1960: 45 workers in the *Töpferei* section of the VEB Steinzeugwerk Krauschwitz downed tools at 8.30 a.m.; while most of these returned to work by 11 a.m., 10 got so drunk that they were unable to return all day. Cf. also report of 23 Nov. 1961 on problems of work discipline, excuses for failing to show up for work or to leave early, and excessive drinking.

[10] FDGB, file no. 15/1470/6447, report of 11 Nov. 1961.

[11] See e.g. FDGB, file no. 2672 (1956), Information No. 7, 1–2. There is some evidence that workers' production brigades fulfilled at least some of the functions which the official trade

On occasion, however, investigation would reveal that workers' protests were to an extent justified, and realistic measures would be taken to attempt to rectify the causes of industrial unrest. It was sometimes the local functionaries, rather than the workers, who were at fault; for example, one report comes to the unequivocal conclusion that 'the roots of industrial conflicts show clearly that, now as previously, trade union leaders continue to tolerate slovenliness, bureaucratism, and heartlessness'.[12] Another investigation of a dispute over wage payments, work contracts, and the regulation of working conditions revealed that 'the colleagues who have downed tools do not seek to exert pressure on the organs of state, but merely want to force the factory director to clarify working conditions in the factory'. The latter, it was noted, had been sacked from previous positions because of drunkenness, and 'even during the investigative discussions . . . the factory director was drunk'.[13]

It is noticeable, however, that after 1953 these strikes remained purely localized. They arose over local issues, local sources of friction, and they were relatively rapidly and often quite efficiently dealt with at a local level. Despite the comments reported from the Stahl- and Walzwerk Brandenburg, where pictures of Ulbricht and Grotewohl had been defaced, to the effect that 'it is no wonder that a 17th June occurs, because the atmosphere in the factory is so miserable, and this shows that in socialism too there are crises',[14] there were no further mass uprisings after 1953. This was very largely because the central authorities themselves were not in such public disarray over policy as they had been in the run-up to June 1953. There were no ambiguities, no splits in orientation, to be explored and exploited; there was little chance of achieving much. Partly, too, the workers became more resigned to their fate. They had learnt lessons from the defeat of 1953. As one worker from the Cottbus railway station put it: 'Just stop talking about striking, everyone who strikes has to be locked up. I was also locked up on 17/6/1953.' And another Cottbus worker pointed sadly to the lack of external support for domestic unrest: 'We can't strike, no one supported us either on 17/6.'[15]

union organization was structurally unable to fulfil. The brigade appears to have provided a centre of communication and a mediating body between workers, who felt it genuinely represented their interests, and state representatives seeking to impose party policies. See Jörg Roesler, 'Die Produktionsbrigaden in der Industrie der DDR. Zentrum der Arbeitswelt?', in Hartmut Kaelble, Jürgen Kocka, and Hartmut Zwahr (eds.), *Sozialgeschichte der DDR* (Stuttgart: Klett-Cotta, 1994).

[12] FDGB, 15/1470/6447, report of 7 July 1966, 5.   [13] Ibid., report of 9 Aug. 1967, 3.
[14] FDGB, file no. 2677, report of 4 Aug. 1961, 16.
[15] FDGB, file no. 15/1470/6447, report of 17 Jan. 1961.

Workers did not need to strike to indicate disquiet. Acts of industrial sabotage were extremely common. The reports are full of indications of a critical, disgruntled, non-cooperative stance, expressions of which might range from the cutting of cables or the emptying of functionaries' petrol tanks to the defacing of pictures of political figures.[16] There were also more subtle means of insulating oneself from the all-pervasive ideology of the state even while at work. In the VEB Weimarer Porzellan in Blankenhein, when a speech on the foundation of the National People's Army was carried on the factory radio system, women in the printing section indicated their disapproval by wrapping shawls, scarves, and headscarves around their ears, while in the neighbouring painting department the workers struck up a 'whistling concert' to drown out the noise of the radio.[17]

There were many other ways, too, of making more directly political protests. Youth disaffection was often explicitly political as well as cultural. A report of December 1956, in the backwash of the Hungarian uprising, notes that young people are holding 'hostile discussions while enjoying considerable quantities of alcohol, including comments such as "it would have been better if the counter-revolution in Hungary had been successful"'; in *Fach-* and *Hochschulen* there were 'perpetually hostile comments about the situation in Hungary'.[18] Despite such intensive debates, many spontaneous expressions of protest reveal a degree of ideological confusion—or operation on the principle that 'my enemy's enemy is my friend': to demonstrate against the GDR, any symbol to which the GDR was officially opposed would do. Thus Western democracy and Nazism were virtually equated, both being seen as opponents of communist rule,[19] and the daubing of swastikas and favourable references to Hitler and Nazism were as common as demands for political freedom and favourable references to Adenauer.

Swastikas and other appeals to the Nazi period were a recurrent symbol of unrest, clearly designed to antagonize the authorities. In 1956, in the context of the Hungarian crisis, there were numerous incidences of swastikas being daubed on walls, often accompanied by the slogan 'SED—No!'[20] At the beginning of August 1961, a week before the erection of the Berlin Wall, a large number of rough, uncomplimentary leaflets (*Schmierzettel*)

[16] See e.g. FDGB, 2672, Information No. 8, *passim*.   [17] Ibid., Information No. 10, 5.
[18] SAPMO-BArch, IV 2/5/732, report of 21 Dec. 1956.
[19] This was of course an ironic mirror image of the officially propagated view that West Germany, far from marking a clean break with the past, as the GDR allegedly did, was rather the natural homeland of former Nazis and represented the 'capitalist-imperialist' successor to the preceding 'fascist' Nazi state.
[20] IfGA, ZPA, IV 2/5/968, report of 25 Jan. 1956, 5.

with swastikas were found in the Wella-Ventile factory.[21] In 1967, at the Radebeul-Zitschewig secondary school (*Oberschule*) in the Dresden-Land district, pupils of classes four and six had taken to greeting each other with 'Heil Hitler!' and 'Heil to our Führer!' One pupil had stolen a red warning flag, and embellished it with a self-drawn swastika; others had somehow acquired SS-Stahlhelm helmets, which they were openly flaunting.[22] In 1969, in Parchim, eleven different instances of graffiti including swastikas were reported, some with additional slogans, such as 'Russians out of Czechoslovakia'.[23] In March 1970, in the *Walzwerk* department of the VEB Edelstahlwerk Freital, there was a *Hakenkreuzschmiererei* (daubing of swastikas) with a 'Sieg Heil!' added for good measure.[24]

Most of these were simply designed to irritate and antagonize the authorities. Occasionally there were attempts to bring together former Nazis, or to influence the young, or there were expressions to the effect that things had been better in the old days. An SED report of January 1956 tells us that the owner of the Hotel Goldener Löwe in Plauen had been arrested, 'because there have yet again been unpermitted gatherings [literally 'riotous assemblies'—*Zusammenrottungen*] of former active fascists in his restaurant, who intend to found a so-called "League of Former Fascists" and who have already been meeting regularly in the restaurant, singing fascist songs, etc.'[25] In the context of the foundation of the National People's Army, a worker is reported as saying 'Build homes instead of barracks. We fought for a better cause in the fascist army than today.'[26] A report of March 1961 complains that 'in the Magdeburg district it appeared that older colleagues were exerting a negative influence on youngsters, in that they were reporting their wartime experiences . . . in the most glowing colours. In the Kraftwerk Thälmann, Leipzig, youth were also under a bad influence and expressed the opinion that "they would have been better off in the Nazi Reich".'[27] A schoolteacher was dismissed in 1969 for uttering such comments as 'I would have preferred to live under Hitler, he understood how to give youngsters ideals and mobilize them for his goals'.[28] A member of the FDGB in Leipzig was found to be spreading such phrases as 'I'll make Hitler youths out of you yet' and 'I will found my own party and then all the Comrades will be put into a Concentration Camp'.[29] In December 1970, the postmaster in

[21] FDGB, file no. 2677, report of 4 Aug. 1961, 16.
[22] FDGB, file no. 3023, report of 1 Feb. 1967.   [23] Ibid., report of 17 June 1969, 2.
[24] Ibid., report of 13 July 1970, 1.
[25] IfGA, ZPA, IV 2/5/968, report of 9 Jan. 1956, 4.
[26] FDGB, file no. 2672, Information No. 4 (20 Jan. 1956), 5.
[27] FDGB, file no. 2677, report of 14 Mar. 1961, 5.
[28] FDGB, file no. 3023, report of 20 Jan. 1969, 2.   [29] Ibid., report of 12 Aug. 1970, 2.

charge of the Nordhausen 2 district was found, not only to have been stealing goodies from packages arriving from the West, but also to be in possession of a copy of Hitler's *Mein Kampf*.[30] Such examples could readily be multiplied; in all areas of the GDR, disgruntlement could easily be expressed through appeals to better times gone by.

Disgruntlement could also be expressed through comparisons with the West, and the authorities were as irritated by graffiti supporting Adenauer as Hitler. In 1956, on the occasion of President Wilhelm Pieck's birthday, a plaque congratulating him was unofficially embellished with a further phrase: 'And we congratulate Adenauer the leader of the workers of all Germany.'[31] When Adenauer died in 1967, the flags were flown at half-mast in three secondary schools in Berlin-Köpenick, and at one of them there was a demand for a minute's silence in Adenauer's honour.[32]

An extraordinary ideological mixture is revealed in a report, dated June 1967, on political troublemaking in the VEB Kranbau Eberswalde. Three ringleaders are spreading the views that: 'During the Second World War, Walter Ulbricht stayed behind the front and betrayed Communists' (i.e. pro-communist); 'We are not free in the GDR, but rather we are walled-in citizens (*eingemauerte Bürger*)' (pro-freedom); and 'Eichmann (this refers to the war criminal) [*sic*] should be given a posthumous order of merit for his deeds in the Second World War' (pro-Nazi).[33]

Immunity or *Resistenz*, refusals, and rejection

There were many more general pockets of immunity inherited from the pre-1945 period. Many Germans simply could not stomach the Sovietized slogans, methods, and goals of the new regime. Very large numbers of older Germans—in both East and West—had difficulties coming to terms with the forcible division of their nation, and could not accept even the basic legitimacy of the GDR. Former Social Democrats often were not able to make their peace with the SED, finding the Marxist-Leninist notion of party discipline and democratic centralism anathema to their conception of socialist democracy. A number of social and economic groups—particularly among the old economically independent middle classes rather than the newly promoted cadre intelligentsia—found their very existence threatened by the regime's policies.

The resistance, in the sense defined above, of such groups to penetration by even the most dedicated communist party activists, was a matter of great

---

[30] Ibid., report of 16 Dec. 1970, 3.   [31] FDGB, file no. 2672, Information No. 7, 4.
[32] FDGB, file no. 3023, report of 26 Apr. 1967.   [33] Ibid., report of 20 June 1967.

concern to the regime. It is documented in official reports with meticulous care under such euphemistic headings as 'Unklarheit', 'Unverständnis', and 'Zurückhaltung' (lack of clarity, misunderstanding, remaining withdrawn); such terms indicate that there is still the possibility of salvation—or at least enlightenment—of the relevant individuals and groups, who are not yet to be numbered among the 'hostile-negative forces', the enemies of the state.

The extent of such 'confusions' and 'failures of understanding' is revealed, for example, in a detailed analysis of party work in Karl-Marx-Stadt (Chemnitz) compiled in preparation for the elections of 17 September 1961.[34] Following the usual optimistic and dishonest opening ('On 17 September 1961 the population of our town made an unambiguous declaration of commitment to our party and government'), the report proceeds to a very clear dissection of its degrees of support or otherwise in different social groups. Even as far as the working class is concerned, the picture is mixed: 'Among sections of the working class, particularly workers in private enterprises and also, to some extent, in those in joint state/private control, there is still a lack of clarity over the character of the two German states. That is expressed in the lack of understanding for the fact that at present no travel permits can be issued for travel to West Germany.' Peasants had not yet been convinced of the benefits of collectivization of agriculture: 'A considerable proportion of the collectivized peasants today still maintain the position that an increase in market production can be better achieved through individual work patterns.' While some sections of the intelligentsia (particularly those who owed their rise to the state's policies) were beginning to be more positive, others were less inclined to support the regime: 'Those sections of the intelligentsia such as doctors in private practice, artists, and also sections of the freelance intelligentsia, often maintain considerable reserve in expressing their political opinions in discussions and open meetings.' It was particularly difficult to reach certain sections of the middle classes, particularly independent traders and artisans, who in general still suffered from 'great lack of clarity and lack of commitment to the politics of our party and government'. Women seem to have been among the least readily persuadable groups: 'We have a lot of ground to make up concerning political work among the female intelligentsia, female peasants on collective farms, and among female employees in private enterprises and joint private/state enterprises.' Finally, despite allegedly locating a few favourably inclined pastors, the report has to conclude that

[34] SAPMO-BArch, IV 2/5/961, 'Abschlußanalyse der Volkswahlen 1961 der SED-Stadtleitung Karl-Marx-Stadt' (23 Sept. 1961).

'despite this positive development, it is evident that a large proportion of those who did not vote are from groups of the population with religious commitment'. The balance sheet appears complete—and it hardly amounts to a resounding popular endorsement of the regime's policies or powers of persuasion.

Inevitably, with the passage of time, certain of the older enclaves and social groups started to decline in proportionate numbers. The small independent traders and property owners were decimated through government policies, the older generation by simple mortality. Other groups were, as we have seen above, brought around gradually to patterns of at least outward compliance in the following years. Infinitely more disturbing for the regime was its failure to capture the loyalties of youth, to influence the rising generation which did not necessarily have prior loyalties to alternative, institutionalized belief systems but simply refused to be persuaded into supporting the communist cause.

Youth was a perpetual problem for the SED. The Western rock concert at the Reichstag of 1977, listened to by thousands of rock fans on the other, eastern side of the Brandenburg Gate and followed by mass arrests on Alexanderplatz, was but a very late and visible sign of a persistent undercurrent of unrest among East German youth, a loose and implicitly subversive interest in all things Western as far as music, clothes, and popular culture were concerned. And youth were also often at the forefront of spontaneous political unrest. But the most striking feature of the political role of youth in the GDR was perhaps the way in which the regime's own policies simultaneously succeeded in labelling anything that was not completely conformist as politically relevant (whether or not it was intended as such) and in the process actually producing a degree of disaffection which might not have been so pronounced under a less interventionist regime.

The reports from a wide range of sources, right through from the 1950s to the 1980s, are full of complaints which in essence are exceedingly similar, pointing to ever repeated patterns of behaviour among young people, although the particular forms of expression, the cultural symbols and idols, were of course subject to change with changing fashions. As in virtually all other areas of life, the SED's attempts to exert total control, attain total conformity, were often not only inherently doomed to failure but were also at times quite ludicrous. Arguably, too, the SED's interventions and policies actually made things worse: although a slight rise in conformity overall can be documented for the mid-1970s, a rise in general youth disaffection and 'asocial behaviour' seems to have been quite considerable in the 1980s.

In the late 1950s, Elvis Presley appears to have been the main idol and attraction for large numbers of young East Germans. According to a report of December 1959, 'Rock 'n' Roll' fan clubs combined their musical enthusiasms with strong political views: 'The "Rock 'n' Roll fans" are those most frequently encountered', who 'combine their "demands" for Rock 'n' Roll with depraved ravings against our leading comrades'.[35] As, for example, a Stasi report in late November 1959 had recorded: 'on 27.11.59 at 21.45 o'clock a horde of youngsters, around 80 individuals, came roaring down the Alaunstraße in the direction of Luisenstraße and cried out "We want our old Kaiser Wilhelm, we don't want W. Pieck, Grotewohl, and W. Ulbricht, we want Rock 'n' Roll". At the moment around 15 people are in custody.'[36] On 7 October 1959 in Leipzig a group of about forty youths attacked five students 'and swore at these, calling them Sheriff-helpers. Only when the students said that they were not auxiliary police volunteers (VP-Helfer) did the others let them go.'[37] Comparable 'gang activities (Bandentätigkeit)' and 'similar groups of "Presley-fans"' were reported in Erfurt, Magdeburg-Süd, Gera, Pößneck, Saalfeld, Lobenstein, Jena, Greiz, Bitterfeld, Frankfurt-on-Oder, Mühlhausen, Berlin, and Weimar.[38]

Most incidents of Bandentätigkeit appear to have involved fairly universal patterns of behaviour among young people: listening to Western music, getting drunk, and then being involved in a variety of lesser pranks, more serious acts of vandalism and violence, and/or what was deemed to be immoral behaviour. What was specific to the GDR was that these activities were associated with 'Western influence', and much youthful fooling around was hence labelled 'agitation hostile to the state (staatsfeindliche Hetze)'. In this way, expressions of high spirits and unguarded opinions could readily become politicized by virtue of the regime's interpretations and interventions.

For example, in the late summer of 1961 eighteen pupils of the EOS Jüterbog went to an organized camp at the Baltic Sea with pupils from the Karl-Marx-Oberschule in Leipzig. The almost inevitable in such a situation came to pass. In the disapproving tones of the report which was sent to the relevant department of the Central Committee of the SED in Berlin: 'The schoolgirls and boys drank copious quantities of alcohol, stayed on the dance floor until late in the night with no supervision, and engaged in immoral activities in the tents. In the course of this they made friends with the pupils from Leipzig.' Being the GDR, matters did not stop here. The

---

[35] SAPMO-BArch, IV 2/16/230, 'Einschätzung der gegenwärtigen Bandentätigkeit und strafbaren Handlungen die gegen den Staat gerichtet sind...' (4 Dec. 1959).
[36] Ibid., report of 30 Nov. 1959.   [37] Ibid., report of 5 Dec. 1959.
[38] Ibid., report of 4 Dec. 1959.

young people engaged in a ritual burial ceremony, burying a bottle which contained pictures of Walter Ulbricht and other communist leaders under the heading '*Schweinemischfutter* (pigswill)'. The joke continued with daily flag ceremonies (*Fahnenappell*) over the grave, accompanied by anti-Soviet songs, and the use of the Nazi 'true German greeting' and the 'aryan greeting'. Friendships made at camp were sustained subsequently: 'On 23 and 24/8/1961 Leipzig pupils were in Jüterbog or Jüterbog pupils were in Trauenbrietzen, respectively. There was, it is true, no "flag ceremony" on these occasions, but again there was a lot of drinking and dancing to tape recordings of Bill Haley and Presley.'[39] And all this, in the absurd interpretation of the SED, was deemed to be deeply hostile and dangerous to the state, *staatsfeindlich*.

Youth in Dessau were also considered to be guilty of behaviour 'hostile to the state and characteristic of the class enemy'. On the way back from the sports field they had 'disparaged' the 'refrain of the workers' battle song "Auf auf zum Kampf" and had sung the following text: ". . . we have sworn loyalty to Adolf Hitler, we offer Adenauer our hand". Pop songs were also rewritten by them and they sang "We want to have Hindenburg and Hitler again".' The 'ringleader and instigator' of this subversive chorus was allegedly a 16-year-old apprentice, 'who additionally incited murderous hatred against Comrade Walter Ulbricht . . . He expressed the following: "Walter Ulbricht is the Concentration Camp Commandant of the GDR and should be stood against the wall".'[40]

Such sentiments were shared by others. Apprentices at the VEB Elektro Kohle Lichtenberg were so bored with their lessons that, as a way of passing the time, they invented a new party under the name '*Eigentumsbildende Partei Deutschlands*' (*EPD*), which one could only join if one could claim to have committed five murders. Candidates for membership had to present plausible stories. One suggested murdering Walter Ulbricht, burying him in Marx-Engels-Platz, and building a toilet on top. According to the young people involved in this exercise, 'allegedly they came to engage in this because of the boring nature of the teaching. The whole thing had only been a joke.' Nevertheless, the authorities took it more seriously. All were arrested and charged 'for violation of § 19 of the state legal code (activity hostile to the state, character assassination)'.[41] A similar 'provocative incident' which was taken sufficiently seriously to find its way into the Central

---

[39] SAPMO-BArch, IV 2/905/27, 'Bericht über die Vorkommnisse an der Erweiterten Oberschule Jüterbog' (4 Oct. 1961).

[40] Ibid., 'Mitteilung der BL Halle v. 29.11.1961 über feindliches Auftreten von Jugendlichen aus Lernaktiven des RAW Dessau' (13 Dec. 1962).

[41] Ibid., 'Information über Feindarbeit unter Lehrlingen im VEB Elektro Kohle Lichtenberg' (14 Feb. 1962).

Committee files was the graffiti on a bench in the physics classroom of the Schleusenweg-Oberschule, Kleinmachnow, in July 1962. This read: 'Who has eaten an Ulbricht-Schnitzel yet?—No one, because the swine is still alive.'[42] And the records, collated with typical ponderous care in the central party files, are full of comparable incidents.

Clearly these young people participated in general cultural trends and age-specific interests, as well as expressing quite spontaneous disaffection with political constraints in the GDR. But their activities were typically put down by the SED leadership to 'enemy activities' and malign Western influences seeking to persuade youngsters to leave the GDR. Equally typically, the SED drew the usual organizational conclusions: 'The FDJ leadership reacts in a most inadequate manner to incidents of this type . . . There is insufficient coordination with the relevant local organs . . .' The assumption as usual is that more organization and control will deal with the problem of youth disaffection.

But one problem appears to have been that many young East Germans simply did not like being over-organized: SED efforts were hence on the whole counter-productive, the proposed cure exacerbating rather than alleviating the symptoms of the disease. Resistance to organization was apparent already to the rather frustrated and overstretched party organization in the 1950s. A report of October 1955 on the inadequacy of party youth work in Berlin, for example, notes that: 'The greatest deficiencies . . . consist in the insufficient links, the insufficient influence, and the insufficient work with working-class youngsters.' It continues, with an evident degree of battle-weariness:

A further great deficiency consists in the fact that there is no goal-oriented and appropriately planned educational work. This is hindered to a very large degree by the constant campaigns and activities which perpetually absorb the energies of the whole apparatus of functionaries and main office-holders. This is also particularly evident in the opinions of many youngsters, who express the view that, when the FDJ comes to them, it is only because it wants something, for example participation in demonstrations, public meetings, etc.[43]

And although the party and FDJ organization was more smoothly functioning by the later 1960s, the situation with respect to youth preferences appears to have improved, from the party's point of view, only very little. As a report of 1969 complained: 'It cannot be acceptable that c.85% claim that it is not in the FDJ group, but rather in [spontaneous, non-organized] *leisure*

---

[42] SAPMO-BArch, IV 2/905/27, letter of 13 July 1962.
[43] SAPMO-BArch, IV 2/5/975, 'Zu einigen Fragen der Jugendarbeit in Berlin' (10 Oct. 1955).

groups that their needs are fulfilled. This undoubtedly points to the fact that many youngsters satisfy their interests and needs *outside of the youth organization*, in leisure groups which are not educationally directed and controlled, and thus are frequently exposed to negative influences.'[44] Fear of being exposed to 'negative influences' was of little use, however, given that 'positive' influences appeared to be of declining salience for young people in any event: the same report bemoaned the increasingly critical opinions young people had of their teachers, with declining respect for authority evident in the course of the 1960s (a phenomenon which was of course not restricted to the eastern side of the Iron Curtain).

There is some evidence that positive attitudes towards the GDR among young people improved during the 1970s, only to decline again in the mid-1980s, well before the autumn of 1989.[45] But the behaviour of young people seems to have been just as prone to pranks, particularly under the influence of alcohol, as it ever was, while interest in Western culture, Western clothes, and Western music increased rather than waned during this period.

The notion that even members of the FDJ would conform to the serious, dedicated stereotype of official propaganda was always somewhat far-fetched. There were frequent incidents occasioning official censure of FDJ members. For example, in 1970 at the Ingenieurschule Köthen, a member of the FDJ local leadership and of the SED expressed his view 'that the FDJ is not very different from the Hitler Youth organization'. On the occasion of an official visit of a delegation of Russian young people in November 1974, members of the hosting FDJ group drowned out the Russian song that was played in their honour, called their guests 'Russian swine' and other insulting epithets, and even the FDJ secretary was found, along with all the rest, to be 'in an inebriated condition'. (The typical recommendation at the end of this report referred to the need for more careful preparation, party discipline, and care in cadre selection.) During the showing of the Soviet film *Blockade* in the Palast-Theater Görlitz in September 1975, the school-children and FDJ groups present showed less than appropriate reactions: 'During certain scenes in the film, for example the appearance of Hitler, fascist tank attacks, the torture of Soviet women and so on, there was applause on the part of certain FDJ members. FDJ functionaries and teachers who were present did not do anything to stop this applause.' Similar

---

[44] IfGA, ZPA, IV A 2/2021/370, 'Kurzfassung über Probleme und Folgerungen zur Bewußtseinsentwicklung Jugendlicher in der DDR, die vom Zentralinstitut für Jugendforschung anläßlich der "Umfrage 69" vorgelegt wurden' (1969), 12. Emphases in the original.

[45] Cf. Karen Henderson, 'The Search for Ideological Conformity: Sociological Research on Youth in Honecker's GDR', *German History*, 10: 3 (Oct. 1992), 318–34.

scenes occurred during the showing of this film in Dresden on 13 November of the same year. Comparably irreverent attitudes were evidenced after a training session with air pistols for FDJ members in the Betriebsberufsschule Kleinwanzleben, when a number of young people in the dining-room decided a suitable target for further unofficial shooting practice would be the ubiquitous picture of Erich Honecker on the refectory wall.

Students appear to have been little better behaved. In July 1974, twenty to thirty students, typically somewhat inebriated 'as a result of the enjoyment of alcohol', started making a great deal of noise, throwing water out of the windows of the student residence and swearing at the Volkspolizei, accompanied by raucous singing of the West German anthem.[46] The behaviour of youth groups on organized holidays to other communist bloc countries was also closely monitored, and incidents such as the singing of 'enemy songs' ('Deutschland, Deutschland über alles') or of the official GDR national anthem to scurrilous alternative lyrics ('Risen up from the bed and oriented towards the night potty') were duly recorded for the SED Central Committee's attention. 'Contacts with FRG-citizens' encountered while on holiday were noted, as was 'rowdy behaviour', 'leaving the travel group without permission', and other incidents occurring during the package tours such as rapes, illnesses, and deaths—of which there appear to have been a startling number, sufficient to have caused major public outcry and detailed investigation in any Western democracy.[47]

The behaviour of these young people, while less than perfect, was ultimately sufficiently within bounds for most of them to proceed with conformist career patterns after, perhaps, some form of official rebuke, reprimand, or more serious form of discipline. But there were increasing numbers of young people who began to drop outside the bounds of social conformity altogether. These were the so-called 'asocials', the drop-outs, the *Aussteiger*, adherents of alternative cultures and lifestyles, punks, rock fans, drug addicts, and alcoholics—to name a *very* disparate list. Some clearly collapsed, in a rather unthought-out way, into drowning their sorrows in drink (not, it must be noted, a phenomenon unique to communist societies); at perhaps the opposite end of the spectrum, others chose much more explicitly to signal their differences with the regime by outward appearances, hairstyles, and clothing. Many of these groups were as much at odds with each other as with the regime; indeed, one of the ways in which the authorities sought to slur or tarnish the image of some oppositional groups was to lump them together with a wide range of others of quite different

46 SAPMO-BArch, vorl. SED 18017.
47 Ibid.; see also SAPMO-BArch, vorl. SED 21403.

cultural or political complexions. From the state's point of view, of course, they all had in common the fact that their nonconformity presented an outward and visible symbol of the regime's failure in achieving 100 per cent uniformity and compliance.

There are inevitably a proportion of 'misfits', those designated as 'deviant', in any society: the very definition of deviance is an integral part of the way in which dominant groups construct and seek to maintain distinctive norms and values, and the ways in which subcultural groups develop alternative identities and mount challenges to prevailing norms. Labels such as 'personal inadequacy', 'mental illness', and so on are particularly hard to apply in the political context of a dictatorship. In the current state of research, it would be premature to try to define more precisely the extent to which the GDR produced increasing numbers labelled as 'deviant', or to quantify and explain the proportions of those who turned to drugs, to alcohol abuse, or, in a very different pattern, to alternative styles of clothing and music, as a direct or indirect result of political malaise. Impressionistically, it appears that behaviour signalling rejection of the state's demands for conformity was on the increase in the last decade or so of the GDR's life.[48] In a very general way, it may be observed that many of the subcultural currents of the later GDR are clearly symptomatic, at the very least, of a regime which had failed in its aim of convincing the entire population of its merits: the mere existence of visible nonconformity was an effective challenge to the demands of the state.

Such nonconformity was not able, however, to achieve very much—unless one is able to develop empirical means for identifying and assessing a somewhat nebulous notion of personal happiness or fulfilment for those who found they were able to refuse to conform. The characters in East German fiction, such as the chief protagonist in Ulrich Plenzdorf's *Die neuen Leiden des jungen W.*, do not give much grounds for optimism on this front. Most of the inner life of those whose conformity was not absolute, in so far as it is revealed in those literary depictions which passed the censor's scissors, appears on the whole constrained and gloomy. Personal difficulties and disintegration are more common than individual fulfilment. No doubt in due course sociological, anthropological, and criminological research will

---

[48] Although it was perhaps not—given the very different political conditions—on a scale comparable to trends in the proliferation of alternative cultures in Western societies from the late 1960s. Serious and explicit comparison of rates of drug and alcohol abuse would quite possibly show higher rates in the West for drugs than the East, where alcohol was a more readily available form of anaesthetic against the miseries of everyday life, but the implications of such comparisons would have to be treated very sensitively. 'Deviance' is too complex and wide-ranging a theme to be entered into in detail here.

aid historians in assessing the degree to which these impressions are genu-inely suggestive or rather wide of the mark. In the meantime, however, such retreatist modes of nonconformity on the whole appear rather to have preserved a degree of authenticity for the individual than to have expanded any capacity for action.

All the forms of protest or 'resistance' we have considered in this chapter were, in a sense, localized actions: expressions of discontent, not elements of an organized movement to achieve change. Whether one considers the protection of older value systems or the construction of new lifestyles, the expression of material grievances or the spontaneous ventilation of anger and irritation, these phenomena of resistance, retreat, and rebellion on a small scale serve only to underline the regime's failure to achieve total conformity. In other words, there were gaps and holes, even in the already somewhat retreatist compliance of the niche society. But some of the gaps—ranging from the persistence of Christianity to the wearing of Western jeans—came to be at least tolerated, if never quite happily accepted, by the regime. Other irritations, particularly those to do with material discontents, could to some extent be addressed through appropriate measures of social policy, although often at the expense of productivity or the long-term economic viability of the system. In so far as any of the forms of resistance discussed in this chapter had destabilizing political effects, they were of a creeping, long-term nature, the extent of which must be the subject of further, more detailed exploration.

There were, however, potentially more explosive moments in the history of the GDR: moments when the regime felt it was necessary to put the security forces on maximum alert. As the autumn of 1989 was to show, eruptions in one Soviet bloc state could have serious implications for all the rest. The East German uprising of 1953 was the first in a series: there were further upheavals in Hungary in 1956, Czechoslovakia in 1968, and Poland at intervals until the Solidarity movement of 1980–1 occasioned the intro-duction of military rule. It was quite possible that any of these movements for some liberalization in the Eastern bloc countries could have spin-off effects in others, and the GDR authorities were justifiably worried about the dangers of infection. There were, too, moments of domestic red alert, as in August 1961. Let us turn now to the more obvious flashpoints in East German history, examining the more serious cracks and fissures in the outward façade of Prussian obedience and East German stability.

PART III

CHALLENGES TO DOMINATION

As we have seen in Part II, there were wide areas of society which the regime failed fully to co-opt. Despite the growth in outward patterns of obedience and compliance, notable particularly from the early 1970s, there was still a degree of rumbling below the surface; but these rumblings remained largely private, muted, without serious political effects. Under most conditions, most people in the GDR felt they were constrained to make the best of a bad job, and hoped for the possibility of improvements in the not-too-distant future. Even the young people who engaged in the kinds of youthful escapades described in the previous chapter generally became more docile as they took on adult responsibilities.

Occasionally, however, there were more direct challenges to the regime. While the vast majority of the population were prepared to adopt the patterns of grumbling conformity, alleviated on occasion by explicit but short-lived and largely individual expressions of disaffection, under certain circumstances there was more coordinated opposition. The two key moments in the GDR's history which stand out in this respect are, of course, 1953 and 1989; in between, there were other moments of crisis for the regime which it succeeded in weathering with less visible disruption.

It is important at the outset to note the great differences between 1953 and 1989. The origins of the two crises were very different; one sparked by changing domestic policies of the regime, the other generated in part by the radically altered character of the international situation and the outer parameters of the GDR's existence, combined with a longer growth of organized domestic opposition. The aims and the methods of demonstrators were quite different in each case: the first spread quite rapidly from virtually spontaneous and largely economistic discontents into broader political demands, while the latter involved a highly articulated and complex set of organized political pressures which had been building up over the preceding decade. The responses of the authorities evinced interesting similarities and differences in the two cases: in both 1953 and 1989, the demonstrators were able to exploit weaknesses and differences of opinion at the top; but while in 1953 the ultimate response was repression by force, backed by Soviet tanks, this was not a viable option, for a variety of reasons, in the different circumstances of 1989.

And in between? A recent book on popular opinion in the GDR is entitled (roughly translated) 'Decline and Fall in Stages' (*Untergang auf Raten*).[1] This does not appear to me to be an apposite characterization: 1989 cannot be read off from 1953; there was not a constant, if latent, state of civil war obtaining in the intervening thirty-five years. Force might have remained the ultimate resort for the authorities, but it was not constantly employed; there were many more subtle means of co-option and muted coercion available to the authorities in the period between the Stalinism of the 1950s and the renewed open repression of the later 1980s. Moreover, the popular discontents and pressures of 1989 were new phenomena, not simple continuations of 1953.

The undoubtedly pivotal year of 1968 proves to be exceedingly interesting, for, in a sense, it reveals the extent to which the regime had actually *stabilized* by the later 1960s, and demonstrates the relative efficiency of the regime's responses to political unrest at this time. If one needs a metaphor for describing the periodization of the GDR's history, it is certainly not a 'decline and fall' setting in from 1953, but perhaps, rather, a '*rise* and fall', from the baseline of 1953 to a period of comparative tranquillity in the early 1970s, with new waves of destabilization setting in from the mid-1970s onwards. These new waves encompass a range of components: the growing economic problems which, arguably, originated not so much in any non-viability of a centrally planned economy in principle, as in the changing international economic situation and concomitant rising indebtedness in the GDR from the oil crises of 1973 onwards; the increasing permeability of the GDR towards the West from *Ostpolitik* and Helsinki onwards, and the implications of this for domestic political organization and expression; and finally, the implications of Gorbachev's reforms for the situation in Eastern Europe generally and expectations of reform among both political élites and the people in the GDR in particular.

There was, then, a brief 'golden age' for the GDR in the early 1970s; and it was in principle possible that reforms might be effected which would improve the quality of life in the here and now for East German citizens.

[1] Armin Mitter and Stefan Wolle, *Untergang auf Raten* (Munich: C. Bertelsmann Verlag, 1993).

The early anger and repression of the 1950s was replaced by a more smoothly functioning if drab and oppressive system in the 1960s and 1970s, and was enlivened by growing attempts to stretch the boundaries of the possible and affect the character of the regime on the part of a few courageous souls in the 1980s. And, paradoxically, as we shall see, while those early challenges which directly opposed the regime were in the main counter-productive, serving on the whole to strengthen the system of domination, the later, more subtle attempts to reform the GDR from within were ultimately key factors in its final downfall.

Part III, then, seeks to anatomize the character of changing political challenges to communist rule in the GDR, and explores the ways in which the organization and orientation of dissent interacted with patterns of response from above to produce different political outcomes under changing circumstances over the four decades of East German history. It is to the changing patterns of political opposition in the GDR—to the activities and aspirations of the often tiny minorities of those who not only thought differently, but were prepared to organize and act on their beliefs—that we now turn.

7

THE FRAGMENTATION OF POLITICAL OPPOSITION

'OPPOSITION' in Eastern European societies is a complex phenomenon. It may mean many different things, depending on who is designating what views, for what purposes: the spectrum thus ranges from principled factionalism within ruling communist parties, through a variety of theoretical critiques from the sidelines, to outright rejection of the aims and methods of the system in its entirety.

In examining the history of the GDR, it is important to bear several distinct questions in mind. What forms of political opposition were present, and what were the organizational and structural, as well as ideological, characteristics of different types of opposition? My analysis would suggest that patterns of organization were at least as important as ideas in determining the degrees of impact made by different forms of opposition: being 'against the system' might mean virtually nothing, if it was an isolated and easily suppressed expression of discontent. Moreover, in seeking to explain the failure of any form of opposition prior to 1989, it is just as important to examine the responses of authorities as the forms and aims of opposition. Patterns of political reaction and repression by the regime were arguably equally important in influencing the outcomes of oppositional outbursts.

As we shall see in this and subsequent chapters, in many respects there were vast differences between 1953 and 1989. Throughout the existence of the GDR, there were critical voices from a range of directions. But the history of East German opposition is essentially one of increasing isolation—until the sea changes of the 1980s, which form the subject of the following chapter.

Before examining the history of East German opposition in crisis moments, however, a few comments must be made on the subject of the dissident intelligentsia. Prior to 1989, key intellectual critiques of prevailing political oppression gained widespread attention and interest in the West, and the articulate ideas of East European intellectuals came almost to be equated with 'opposition' in communist states. Yet dissidents have notably spoken with multiple voices: united in opposition, divided with respect to positive alternatives. As in other communist states, dissident intellectuals in the GDR proposed a range of alternative solutions to the problems of 'actually existing socialism'. From Harich's police state, through Havemann's socialism with a human face, to Bahro's notions of a new communist league, a variety of options were aired for discussion.[1] Characteristic of most dissident intellectuals in the GDR was, however, a commitment to some form of Marxism—though not to the neo-Stalinist Marxist-Leninism of the ruling SED—and a degree of asceticism that was unlikely to have mass popular appeal.[2]

There was rather widespread interest among intellectual circles in alternative political views in the early and mid-1950s; but the story is essentially one of a degree of accommodation and intimidation as the 1950s proceeded. The show trials of the early 1950s, the purges of those who opposed Ulbricht's line in 1956–8 (Karl Schirdewan, Fred Oelßner), and the arrest and imprisonment of individuals such as Walter Janka of the Aufbau-Verlag, or Gustav Just of the journal *Sonntag*, who were somewhat stunned by the lack of support from their erstwhile friends, combined with other trends to reduce the extent of at least visible support for such alternatives.[3]

From the later 1950s, dissident intellectuals in the GDR—in contrast to other East European states—were isolated with relative ease by the regime: censorship, imprisonment and (in the case at least of Wolfgang Harich) ultimately expiation, house arrest (Robert Havemann), and of course exile to the West (Wolf Biermann, Rudolf Bahro), were relatively successful measures for reducing the popular impact of intellectual heretics. The slow changes in the character of the professional classes, which may be described as an effective co-option of the intelligentsia, combined with a degree of material security and escapism for the masses, to render the few East German dissidents more easily isolated than their counterparts in other East European states, such as Poland or Czechoslovakia.

The often rather puritanical positive ideas of these intellectuals may have had little popular support: nevertheless, their more general sense of dissat-

---

[1] See e.g. in English: Rudolf Bahro, *The Alternative in Eastern Europe* (London: New Left Books, 1979); Robert Havemann, *An Alienated Man* (London: Davis-Poynter, 1973); U. Wolters (ed.), *Rudolf Bahro: Critical Responses* (New York: M. E. Sharpe, 1980); Roger Woods, *Opposition in the GDR under Honecker, 1971–85* (London: Macmillan, 1986).

[2] Cf. my slightly longer discussion in *The Divided Nation: Germany 1918–1990* (London: Fontana, 1991; New York: Oxford University Press, 1992), ch. 11.

[3] For autobiographical accounts, cf. Walter Janka, *Schwierigkeiten mit der Wahrheit* (Reinbek bei Hamburg, 1989), and *Spuren eines Lebens* (Berlin, 1991).

isfaction with prevailing conditions in the GDR was shared by very many others. As we have seen, genuine enthusiasm for the regime was hardly a hallmark of popular opinion under actually existing socialism. While most people, most of the time, were successfully incorporated with a degree of grumbling acquiescence, on occasion a greater or lesser number were prepared to take the risk of more explicitly challenging the regime. What then was the distinctive character of active popular opposition in the GDR? What were the aims of people participating in demonstrations, how was popular opposition organized, and how was it dealt with by the political authorities? Why was it that, to all outward appearances, there seemed to be so little active popular opposition for over a third of a century—from the suppression of the 1953 uprising to the revolutionary autumn of 1989? Parts of the answers to these questions have been given in previous chapters: here, we shall be concerned with the political flashpoints themselves.

A failed revolution? The uprising of June 1953

The road running from the Brandenburg Gate—symbol of the division of Germany—through West Berlin's leafy park, the Tiergarten, is called the Strasse des 17. Juni. For many years, 17 June was a national holiday in the Federal Republic, celebrated as the day on which democracy-loving East Germans rose in a heroic but ultimately unsuccessful attempt to overthrow the communist dictatorship and reclaim their freedom. For West Germany, 1953 went down in post-war history as the year when the GDR inaugurated the first in what was to be a series of risings against Soviet hegemony: 1953 was thus the prelude to 1956, 1968, 1980–1, and ultimately 1989. For the West, 17 June symbolized the struggle for German unity in freedom and democracy.

In the GDR, the uprising of 17 June 1953 was seen somewhat differently. Desperate attempts were made by the SED at the time to represent the troubles as essentially provoked by Western *agents provocateurs*, counter-revolutionaries, and fascists seeking to overthrow the achievements of socialism, with no real basis among the East German people themselves. When these somewhat far-fetched attempts foundered, the date was virtually lost from official histories of the GDR. But it was not lost from the memories of the officials who authorized its excision from the textbooks: part of the continuing paranoia of the East German leadership, even into the late 1980s, was based in the shock of 1953 and the ever-present fear of its repetition. Unofficially, too, the date marked a deep caesura in people's perceptions and memories; it had a profound impact on patterns of political orientation and action. Yet without any analytic overview, it was more a matter of a collective memory and symbolic talisman: the notion that 'there would be another 17 June' was a constant refrain in collective political culture in subsequent decades, passed on by those who were directly involved to those who had never participated in the events. The implications were various: the hinted threat of another popular uprising was often more than counterbalanced by deep resignation based in recognition of its ready suppression by force and the lack of support from the West. 'The 17 June' thus took on a political force beyond the historical realities of the events of June 1953 themselves.

Despite ever more detailed documentation of the background and course of events, the evaluation of this key moment in East German history remains contentious.[4] Some East German historians—curiously echoing the Cold War views of older Western historians—claim June 1953 as a failed revolution, a mass popular uprising suppressed only by the force of 'Russian bayonets'; others reject such a view as oversimplistic, arguing for further research and debate. What then were the causes and what was the character of the June upheavals? And what were the consequences of this widespread revolt?

It is quite clear that popular unrest in the GDR in the preceding months was indeed both widespread and very diverse. Any attempt to label the uprising under a single heading will inevitably fail to capture the multiple dissatisfactions, and the ways in which these interrelated, overlapped, and snowballed as events proceeded. One cannot retrospectively impose a simplicity and unity of purpose that was not there at the time. A debate which counterposes economic dissatisfaction (economistic strikes in favour of better living conditions) to political demands (anti-communism, unification with the West) similarly fails to capture the ways in which these were so closely interrelated as to be almost inseparable. Indeed, the very fact that the character of the political regime actually determined the nature of social and economic policies makes an attempt to separate the two aspects—'purely

---

[4] For pre-1989 West German academic interpretations (as distinct from the political uses made of the uprising), see e.g. the classic analysis by Arnulf Baring, *Der 17. Juni 1953* (Stuttgart: Deutsche Verlags-Anstalt, 1983; orig. 1965); documents and commentaries in Ilse Spittmann and Karl Wilhelm Fricke (eds.), *17. Juni 1953. Arbeiteraufstand in der DDR* (Cologne: Verlag Wissenschaft und Politik, 1982; Edition Deutschland Archiv); and Christoph Kleßmann, *Die doppelte Staatsgründung* (Göttingen: Vandenhoek and Ruprecht, 1982), 277–82. Since the opening of the archives, there is new material in Armin Mitter and Stefan Wolle, *Untergang auf Raten* (Munich: C. Bertelsmann Verlag, 1993), ch. 1, who present 1953 as essentially the beginning of the end of the GDR; Manfred Hagen, *DDR—Juni '53* (Stuttgart: Steiner, 1992); and Torsten Diedrich, *Der 17. Juni 1953 in der DDR. Bewaffnete Gewalt gegen das Volk* (Berlin: Dietz Verlag, 1991).

economistic' or 'political-revolutionary'—quite artificial. Moreover, the lack of prior planning and co-ordination of dissent meant that many of the demands were in the nature of articulation of grievances as the occasion arose. And behind everything, of course, there lay the prevailing uncertainty about Germany's future. Unique to the GDR, in contrast to other communist states, was its status as part of a nation divided initially by military occupation; any East German communist political élite arguing for a degree of liberalization would essentially also be arguing itself out of a job and indeed out of a state. This was a key problem for humanistic Marxists opposed to Ulbricht's hard-line views: in any genuinely open system, there would very soon have been no GDR at all for them to reform (as reform socialists were to find in 1989–90).

Nevertheless, demands for political change and for German unity did not provide the originating spark for the strikes and mass demonstrations of 17 June. More important were domestic social and economic policies, combined with the inept and to some degree uncoordinated manner in which they were announced and introduced.

The background lay in the rapid changes of policy of the preceding twelve months. In the summer of 1952, the SED had announced the 'Building of Socialism' at the II Party Conference, with a range of concomitant dramatic changes in a variety of aspects of life in the GDR. Although the alleged aim of the SED was German reunification—in contrast to the West German rush to integration in a (West) European Defence Community—in effect the measures of the summer of 1952 were orientated towards more radical transformations of East German social and political life.

In May 1952 the *Sperrzone*—a restricted strip along the inner-German border—had been created, with forcible evictions of 'unreliable' elements of the local population and increased fortification of the border. The defensive forces were built up, with the decision on 1 July 1952 to form the Kasernierte Volkspolizei (KVP) out of the previous HVA units, as well as building up air and water police forces. The rapid build-up of the defence forces was partly paid for by exports of machinery and chemicals to the USSR, partly by savings on social insurance and welfare, higher property and income taxes, and reduced consumption levels for the general population.[5] In August 1952, with the foundation of the paramilitary Gesellschaft für Sport und Technik (GST), pressure on young people to conform to the friend/foe mentality was increased. In the following months a concerted campaign against alleged enemies within was waged. The

[5] Cf. Diedrich, *Der 17. Juni 1953 in der DDR*, ch. 1.

aggressive attacks on perceived 'enemy agents' were of course not specific to the GDR, but, in the wider context of political trials in other Eastern European states (most notably the Slansky trial in Czechoslovakia), served to heighten domestic tensions in the GDR. Alongside visible political trials of individuals and organizations went a more generalized pressure on everything 'social democratic', as well as an intensification of the campaign against young Christians in the Junge Gemeinde. Even members and functionaries of the allegedly loyal bloc parties were suspected of being 'enemy agents'. Paranoia and political repression were clearly the priority of the day.

At the same time, other measures were taken to transform the structures of the state and the economy. In July, fourteen districts or *Bezirke* were created (making a total of fifteen with the pre-existing *Bezirk* of East Berlin), to increase central government control over what had previously been the rather larger and relatively autonomous *Länder*. In the autumn and winter of 1952–3, the pace of agricultural collectivization was forced, leading many peasants to flee to the West, and causing shortages and difficulties with the food supply in towns. The flight of refugees gathered pace, more than doubling from 110,000 in the second half of 1952 to somewhere between 225,000 and 426,000 in the first half of 1953 alone.[6] This only exacerbated more general economic difficulties caused by a range of factors, including prior economic restructuring and dismantling, as well as more recent losses of revenue, difficulties with imports of raw materials, and diversion of material and human resources to the building up of the police and military forces. Living conditions were seriously deteriorating in early 1953. The solution, it appeared to the political leadership, was to press ever harder on the industrial workers, attempting to get them to produce more for their wages. One particular element in this broad policy was the proposed 10 per cent increase in work norms, announced in May and fixed to come into effect on 30 June 1953.

All this was more or less guaranteed to create mass discontent. It was hard enough for the party workers to try to put these policies across to a sullen and recalcitrant population; but the final blow came when Moscow indicated its disapproval of the SED line. Following Stalin's death in March 1953, the new Soviet leadership inaugurated a 'New Course'. With the ending of the Korean War, there were indications of increased Soviet willingness to treat with the Americans and the British in a summit. There were also internal changes in the USSR, with a measure of political decentralization and a focus on the production of consumer goods. Changes in

---

[6] The lower figure is given in Baring, *Der 17. Juni 1953*, 35–6; the higher figure is from Diedrich, *Der 17. Juni 1953 in der DDR*, 42.

Moscow inevitably unsettled the East German regime. Within the SED itself, there was some political uncertainty, incipient factionalism and jockeying for position: in the context of Soviet criticisms of Ulbricht's policies, alternative political views were more openly articulated by Herrnstadt and Zaisser, supported by Beria in Moscow, in what began to look like the opening of a struggle for the party leadership. The Soviet leadership began to indicate its concern over the SED's hard-line policies within the GDR, and in early June SED leaders (Ulbricht, Grotewohl, and Oelßner) were summoned to Moscow to be instructed in the new line they should take. The rapid collectivization of agriculture should be halted; traders and craftsmen should be given more opportunities; the middle classes were to be won over with a range of concessions.

In the event, without any prior discussion in the Central Committee or the broader membership of the SED, the Politburo rather abruptly issued a Communiqué on 9 June, openly admitting its mistakes and accepting the Soviet-imposed change of course—with the exception of the raised work norms, which were simply not mentioned. Following its confirmation by the Council of Ministers, the Communiqué was published in *Neues Deutschland* on 11 June, and caused widespread consternation. Party workers were shattered: they could hardly believe that they now had to preach the opposite of what they had been struggling to support over the previous months. All the efforts and arguments seemed to have been wholly in vain; their exhaustion, their exposure to popular attack, their valiant attempts to defend the apparently indefensible, all now appeared to have been flung to the winds in an abrupt and unexpected political volte-face at the top.[7]

The people were for the most part even more incredulous. The wildest rumours began to fly: Ulbricht had been arrested and deposed, Pieck was dead, the Kasernierte Volkspolizei was to be disbanded, the borders would be opened, the Americans and British were coming, the former private landowners and capitalists were to be invited back.[8] Peasants and larger farmers were particularly pleased that they were now 'free' and would no longer have to join collective farms (LPGs); and agricultural workers on LPGs stopped work, for fear that returning former owners would punish them. There were speculations that civil war was imminent. In Havelberg, one women left a *Gaststätte* happily waving a bunch of flowers and pro-claiming the Nazi slogan, 'Heim ins Reich! (Home into the Reich!)'.[9] Others

---

[7] Cf. the discussion of functionaries' responses in Ch. 3, above (p. 65), and the reports in SAPMO-BArch, IV 2/5/530, e.g. the report of 20 June 1953.

[8] SAPMO-BArch, IV 2/5/543, Information No. 23 (15 June 1953).

[9] SAPMO-BArch, IV 2/5/544, DFD report of 15 June 1953.

simply did not believe the news, or no longer knew what to believe. As one woman in Potsdam put it, 'And here we are, supposed to have confidence in the SED. First of all they make a great mess of everything, then they try to pull out of it all. First they say they want to get rid of capitalism, and now they make a big deal of it again.' Others were even more sceptical, considering the changes of policy to be merely tactical manœuvres pending a reversion to the previous line: 'That's all just peasant-baiting . . . to search out the dim-wits.'[10] Grumblings were overheard on a bus to the effect that similar criticisms of the previous line had long been aired by many people, but that those making the criticisms had been called reactionaries. One person then commented that if ordinary people admitted having made mistakes they were punished, but if the party leaders admitted their mistakes, what did they get? To which the answer was heard—a pay rise.[11]

It is clear from all the reports on the mood of the population in the days after the publication of the Communiqué that there were widespread heightened expectations of major changes ahead: there was a mood of excitement, apprehension, anticipation, in the days preceding the uprising itself. The strikes and mass demonstrations of 17 June were not, then, without a much broader context of discontent and expectation of change. But the specific trigger for the downing of tools was the refusal of the regime to retract the raised work norms in the light of the wider change of course.

The workers had protested against the retention of the raised work norms, and an editorial in *Neues Deutschland* (under the editorship of Herrnstadt) seemd to give their cause some support. But the FDGB newspaper *Tribüne* defended the norms on 16 June, only exacerbating the workers' frustration. On 16 June construction workers on the Stalinallee joined forces with workers from a hospital building site in Friedrichshain to march to the trade union headquarters to demonstrate. Thence they proceeded to the House of Ministries, where, following a lengthy wait, they were met by conciliatory but ineffective responses on behalf of the regime from Brandt, Selbmann, and Havemann. Unconvinced by reassurances from these individuals, the workers became more emotional, and the character of the protest began to change. There were calls for a general strike the following day, and cries were heard such as 'butter instead of cannons', emphasizing a preference for enhanced living standards instead of militarization.[12]

[10] SAPMO-BArch, IV 2/5/544, VdgB report of 12 June 1953.
[11] Ibid., FDJ report of 15 June 1953.
[12] Quoted in Diedrich, *Der 17. Juni 1953 in der DDR*, 64.

Of particular interest with respect to the course then taken by what was able to become a mass uprising was the relative incompetence of the political and repressive authorities in seeking to quell popular unrest. On 16 June the Soviet military commander refused a request for Soviet military aid; on 17 June he agreed it for the purposes purely of securing the zonal boundaries in Berlin. Members of the SED leadership, not expecting demonstrations to spread beyond Berlin, were fearful of reliance on their own police force, to which so much effort and resources had been devoted in the preceding year. According to Diedrich, Ulbricht doubted the political reliability of his own repressive forces: Ulbricht 'had expressed . . . doubts about the political reliability of the KVP if there were any intervention, and had thought that any attack by the KVP-units should be reserved only for the most extreme situations'; there were 'doubts about political reliability and the fear that the soldiers might show solidarity with the workers'.[13] A report signed by Schirdewan at 7 a.m. on 18 June indicates some of the practices that the police and security forces had been indulging in: 'Party organizations in the Volkspolizei and the State Security forces must currently orient their educational work towards ensuring that the armed forces show strength [the word with Nazi connotations, Härte, is used here] and under no circumstances capitulate under pressure and give up their weapons ([as happened in] Schmölln, Leipzig, Gera, Niesky, Wismut, Magdeburg).'[14] Nor were the supposedly loyal political forces much more reliable; in many areas, regime functionaries were themselves as unsure and as perplexed by the changes of course as the demonstrators. In some, they even seem to have agreed with the strikers' demands: in Kreis Wernigerode, for example, the LDPD leader was supporting the strikers, while several mayors were following the same line in a Bürgermeisterversammlung (mayors' gathering) in Kreis Beeskow.[15] This was hardly a recipe for the rapid and efficient quelling of popular disaffection.

But the demonstrators themselves were relatively lacking in clear leadership and purpose, and seemed to have no coordinated response to the equally uncoordinated reactions of the authorities; the result was a confused escalation of the situation. Demands made early in the morning of 17 June at the House of Ministries for the retraction of work norms, the dropping of prices, the resignation of the government, were met with little or no response, serving only to exacerbate expectations, frustration, and anger, leading to uncoordinated scuffles and incidents, and eventually mounting but unplanned levels of violence. By mid-morning, traffic in Berlin had been

[13] Ibid. 66, 67.   [14] SAPMO-BArch, IV 2/5/530, report of 18 June 1953, 7.00 a.m.
[15] Ibid., report of 18 June 1953, 10.50 a.m.

brought to a standstill because of the volume of crowds milling in the streets. At midday, the first warning shots were fired.[16] At 12.30 p.m. Soviet tanks began to roll openly; half an hour later, the Soviet military commander declared a state of emergency in Berlin. In the course of the afternoon, the character of the Berlin demonstrations changed. Many people withdrew from the scene, while those that remained became more violent; social protests were increasingly supplemented with political slogans and demands. By the evening, the Soviet troops had regained control in Berlin, following the total failure of the GDR's own police forces to maintain order. In the absence of any effective political or coercive response on the part of the GDR's rulers, it was ultimately the display of Soviet military force that rescued Ulbricht's regime from ignominious disarray.

A similar picture of uncoordinated protests and confused responses emerged across other areas of the GDR. Workers turned up for work, discussed the situation, elected an *ad hoc* strike leadership, and set off to demonstrate. As demonstrations proceeded, additional numbers of other employees, students, housewives, passers-by joined in, and the actions became ever less coordinated, ever more spontaneous. By the afternoon of 17 June, in the context of rumours that the government had resigned, more political demands were in evidence, including the freeing of political prisoners. Apart from prisons, targets of demonstrators included public buildings of the party and government, and of affiliated organizations such as the FDGB and FDJ, largely as expressions of anger and outrage rather than for strategic purposes. Apart from general demands for the deposition of the regime and the resignation of the leaders, political goals were unclear.[17] There was little evidence of any serious attempt to gain control of the media or transport and communications generally, nor were there efforts to seize caches of weapons from the security forces. In the course of the afternoon and early evening—as new waves of demonstrators joined in towards the end of the day—clashes with police and Soviet troops became more violent, particularly in the major centres of unrest, most notably Magdeburg, Halle, and Leipzig.

---

[16] Cf. SAPMO-BArch, IV 2/5/530.

[17] It should not automatically be assumed that all demonstrators were necessarily in favour of the democratic political system of the Federal Republic of Germany at this time, even if they were in favour of reunification. After all, as the Allensbach Institute of Demoscopy opinion polls showed, even in the mid-1950s around half of West Germans had authoritarian and monarchist sympathies, harking back to the Kaiserreich or the peacetime years of the Third Reich in preference to the years since 1949. It was only in the early 1960s that a majority of West Germans began to be in favour of democracy as such, and even then more for pragmatic reasons relating to the economic miracle than for reasons of principle.

Only in Görlitz and Bitterfeld was there a greater degree of broader regional and political organization evident. In Görlitz an alternative democratic government was formed, with plans for election of a town council, and an attempt to gain control of communications. Former SPD members appear to have been very active here. But, even in this case, Soviet troops were ultimately able to quell the unrest.[18] And even at 11.30 in the morning there were panic reports from the Bezirksleitung Halle to the effect that 'the situation in Bitterfeld is extremely serious, demonstrators have stormed the district leadership offices of the FDJ and the administrative offices of the district council, demolished the furniture, and they are still at it'.[19] Elsewhere, the demonstrators appeared to have milled aimlessly on the streets, unsure how to put their power of numbers into effect. But all over the GDR, the reports give the impression of a situation rolling totally out of the control of local functionaries, on the one hand, but with demonstrators acting without any strategic plan or consolidation of their positions, on the other. In the end, and in the absence of any serious intervention from Western authorities (the official communist story of Western *agents provocateurs* notwithstanding), power really was only the power of the Soviet tanks.

The demonstrations of 17 June eventually began to peter out. The following days were not without incident; there were sporadic strikes, demonstrations, and isolated incidents across the GDR for several weeks. The main areas continued to be the large industrial conglomerations, although throughout the uprising there had been more unrest in rural areas than has previously been realized, particularly in areas with some local industry.[20] The general mood was in the main subdued (*abwartend*): there were few indications of any real change of heart, nor of any greater support for Ulbricht's regime, even after the increased work norms, which had sparked off the mass demonstrations of 17 June, had actually been retracted, and other measures to increase consumer satisfaction were introduced. Although accounts which suggest that the regime had 'lost the confidence of the population' tend mistakenly to presuppose some earlier golden age when the East Germans had genuinely trusted their rulers, nevertheless a visible rift had been revealed which was not so easily healed over. At the

---

[18] Diedrich, *Der 17. Juni 1953 in der DDR*, 126–32.   [19] SAPMO-BArch, IV 2/5/530.
[20] Cf. ibid., report of 18 June 1953, 7.00 a.m.: 'Incidents in villages have been on the increase. This is particularly the case in country areas where there are also industrial working-class elements.' There were also continued moves to try to get out of LPGs: in some areas there had already been 'unrest already for several weeks, which was given further impetus by the situation in Berlin', ibid., report of 18 June 1953, 'Bericht über die Lage auf dem Lande'. Cf. also Diedrich, *Der 17. Juni 1953 in der DDR*, 148.

very least, people were more frightened of the consequences of expressing discontent, and less hopeful of any positive outcome, than they might have been before.

Moreover, even many party workers were less reliable after 17 June than before: as a report of 20 June from the Leipzig area complained, comrades were making remarks such as 'We are not members of the SED but of the SPD'. There still appeared to be some confusion about the leadership and the future: a report from the Abteilung Agitation, under the rather abruptly apt heading 'Alarming Signs', revealed that 'There are reports from Suhl, Erfurt, and Schwerin that teachers are taking pictures [of political leaders] down from the walls on the basis of false rumours. The same thing occurred in the educational centres of the National Front in Erfurt, and in offices of the railway service in the Schwerin district.'[21] Nor had the behaviour of some members of the police forces improved much: on 21 June it was reported that 'there are complaints from the Bezirk Erfurt about the unprofessional conduct of the border police, who in some villages are engaging in often drunken night-time rioting'.[22]

Ulbricht's regime drew the appropriate conclusions in the following days and months. Well over 6,000 people who had been involved in the uprising were arrested. Not only were strikers and the alleged ringleaders of the uprising punished; so too were those thousands of SED members and functionaries who had revealed 'social-democratic' sympathies and failed to sustain the official line in the face of uncertainty. There was a massive purge, not only of the dissident factions at the top of the SED—Herrnstadt, Zaisser, and the Justice Minister Max Fechner—but also of the party ranks throughout the GDR. The police forces were strengthened and restructured in the interests of maintaining internal security and rapid intervention. *Kampfgruppen der Arbeiterklasse* (workforce combat groups) were built up in factories as a reliable on-the-spot force to be deployed in moments of unrest. Emergency plans were developed. And measures were taken to increase the efficiency of the State Security service (Stasi), such that the repressive and coercive apparatus would never be caught unprepared again. In 1989, of course, it was not so much domestic force itself which was lacking, but the political will and Soviet approval for the use of force—a complete reversal of the situation in 1953. Finally, an ironic outcome of these troubles was the consolidation of Ulbricht's own position at the helm; any change in the leadership would have looked like capitulation to the demonstrators, while, with the fall of Beria in Moscow, the fate of

[21] SAPMO-BArch, IV 2/5/530, report of 20 June 1953 from Abteilung Agitation.
[22] Ibid., report of 21 June 1953.

Ulbricht's rivals was effectively sealed. Inner-Politburo opposition was more easily suppressed in 1956–8 than in 1953; and popular revolt was contained within bounds by more rapid repression. Within less than four years of its founding, the GDR was set on the relatively hard-line course that was to characterize it, albeit in changing forms, for the following thirty-six years.

Flashpoints which failed to ignite: 1956 and 1961

Despite minor incidents on the anniversary of 17 June in the following couple of years, there was little evidence of any concerted movement to repeat such a major challenge to the regime. As one party report, compiled on the evening of 17 June 1955, put it: 'The way in which today has unfolded shows that the class enemy has not succeeded in exerting influence on the workers in order to misuse them for provocatory activities.'[23] Leaving aside the typical externalization of opposition in the form of an alien and singular 'class enemy (*Klassengegner*)', the report quite accurately assesses the very minimal degree of active popular protest, despite grumblings, rumblings, and a higher than usual degree of absenteeism from work in certain areas. The odd incident was reported: a transport worker at the S-Bahnhof Hermannstrasse was accosted with the words 'You old SED-swine, why are you working today?'; a total of only forty-four workers stayed away from thirteen factories in the Kreis Köpenick. But isolated incidents and patchy absenteeism amounted in effect to a pattern of discontent without organization or strategy.[24]

The year 1956 promised something more, however. As in 1953, there were major political upheavals emanating from the Soviet Union. Three years after Stalin's death, at the XX Party Congress in the Soviet Union the new leadership under Khrushchev denounced Stalin's political excesses and rejected the personality cult. Although the 'secret speech' by no means amounted to a blanket condemnation of Stalinism or Stalin's record in its entirety—there were many notable omissions and this was scarcely a far-reaching confession of political repentance in principle—it nevertheless signified a major turning-point in communist history. If it was a turning-point in the Soviet bloc, however, it proved to be a turning-point where East Germany found it rather tortuous even to attempt to turn.

In the months following the XX Party Congress, Ulbricht's disavowal of Stalinism in particular and the personality cult in general proved somewhat

[23] Ibid., IV 2/5/975, report of 17 June 1955, 6 p.m.
[24] Ibid., reports of 17 June 1955, 10 a.m. and 2.30 p.m.

lukewarm and effected in a rather mechanistic manner. Yet, as in the months following Stalin's physical (rather than metaphorical or political) death in 1953, with the Soviet denunciation of Stalinism hopes were raised for major changes ahead. In both Poland and Hungary there were widespread popular upheavals, in the latter case only suppressed by—yet again—Soviet tanks. The Suez crisis provided a further element in the general air of international instability and expectation of change.

The air of unrest rippled across to the GDR, most notably manifesting itself in one of the centres of the 1953 uprising, Magdeburg. In the Magdeburg district generally there were clear indications of widespread unrest. There was an increase in incidents of sabotage, arson, the spreading of leaflets and propaganda, and the number of refugees fleeing the Magdeburg area rose by nearly 50 per cent from 2,300 in August 1956 to 3,230 in September. There were all manner of means of indicating disaffection. In early September 1956, for example, the VEB Bau-Union received bricks from the Ziegelei Druxberge with swastikas or SS runes burnt into them.[25] All sorts of often mutually contradictory rumours were abroad, including the notion that entire villages were to be removed and woods to be cleared for Russian troops and military areas, as well as the conflicting rumour that all Russian troops were to be cleared from the area west of the Elbe by the end of the year, and the Americans would come in their place. The district party leadership was distinctly rattled in its evaluation of developments: 'The activity of the class enemy continues to be strongly expressed in activities such as the daubing of hostile slogans, swearing at and threatening state and party functionaries, and expressions of hostility against our state.' The concluding sentence of a report on 'enemy activities' in the first half of October could hardly be more revealing of the popular mood: 'Enemy activities, which are increasingly evident, include new elements, particularly anti-Soviet incitement, open and provocative incitement against functionaries and members of our party as well as against our development as a whole, and, not least, ever more frequent incidents of sabotage in industry and agriculture.'[26]

But there was no repetition of 1953. In the town of Magdeburg itself, there were strikes reminiscent of June 1953. These strikes remained limited to a few factories. Although they were reported in the Western press, the East German authorities seem to have done a remarkably good job of

[25] SAPMO-BArch, IV 2/5/731, 'Bericht über Feindtätigkeit im Bezirk Magdeburg' (5 Sept. 1956).
[26] Ibid., IV 2/5/732, 'Bericht über die Feindtätigkeit im Bezirk Magdeburg in der Zeit vom 1.10.56–15.10.56' (18 Oct. 1956).

suppressing the news within the GDR itself and suggesting that any Western media reports were pure propaganda. This was in marked contrast to 1989, when Western television coverage of events throughout Eastern Europe and the GDR ensured that demonstrators in all areas of the GDR (with the partial exception of the far south-eastern corner, which had only limited reception) were extraordinarily well informed. In the mid-1950s, by contrast, rumour, word of mouth, and the less compelling non-visual medium of the Western radio stations were the main means of rather incomplete communication. In late October 1956 there were rumours circulating, largely on the basis of Western radio reports, that 'there are strikes in Magdeburg'—countered by the SED as a 'falsehood (*Lügemeldung*)'.[27] The rumour failed to gain sufficient ground for much in the way of coordinated sympathy strikes.

The responses to the unrest in Hungary and Poland were rather mixed, too. Very few East Germans appeared to have believed the official line that 'imperialist machinations' were the cause of the uprisings. Most considered that a lower standard of living and a desire for national freedom from the Soviet yoke were the main causes of popular resistance. There was evidently considerable sympathy with these views. Some even seem to have voiced the opinion that if the GDR had a truly national path to socialism (as outlined by Ackermann in 1946), they would be prepared to join a German communist party. Others were less sympathetic, and there was some evidence of what might be called traditional anti-Polish sentiments, particularly with respect to the Polish capacity for hard work (or otherwise) such as: 'The Poles are already downright lazy anyway, and they can't conduct their affairs independently in any case.'[28] Nor had tensions concerning the Oder–Neisse border been overcome at this time: there were complaints that the 'eastern provinces' (*Ostgebiete*) should not have gone to Poland, that Upper Silesia should be returned, and anti-Soviet sentiments were compounded by the view that 'West and East Prussia have always been quintessentially German territory'.[29] The main concerns of many disaffected East Germans appear, however, to have remained restricted to their own standard of living, and in particular to the questions of doing away with ration cards and reforming pensions. There was also a degree of nervousness about the possibility of repeating 1953. As one report concluded: it appeared that 'a large section of the population is rather unwilling to express any opinion on

[27] Ibid., reports of 24 Oct. 1956 and subsequently.
[28] Ibid., IV 2/5/731, 'Bericht über die ersten Diskussionen zu den Vorfällen in Poznan' (3 July 1956).
[29] Ibid., IV 2/5/732, report of 26 Oct. 1956.

the counter-rev. [*sic*] in Hungary and the provocations in Poland'; many were saying that it should not come to another '17.6.' in the GDR, and that 'the workers in Hungary have learnt nothing from the events in the GDR on 17.6.53'.[30]

How should one evaluate all this? The degree of uncertainty and unrest was certainly high, but there was little indication of any positive political programme for change. The reasons for unrest were many and various, and by no means uniformly pro-democratic in the Western sense in any event. Commentators should beware of casting those who were critical of communist repression at the time in an over-favourable light. As will be evident from some of the sentiments quoted above, many of the attitudes which were current merely a decade after the end of the war were quite consistent with Nazi and indeed long-standing, pre-Nazi, sentiments about the alleged 'inferiority' of the Germans' eastern neighbours, and were further informed by a degree of nationalist sentiment about loss of German *Lebensraum* in the east. This stands in very stark contrast to the concerns of demonstrators in the late 1980s, as we shall see. Nor was there any degree of political organization or coordination of expressions of unrest. The main lesson of 1953 seemed to have been learnt: that a spontaneous uprising without Western support would lead only to repression. Thereafter, popular opposition as such remained relatively isolated: expression without effect, a message without a strategic medium.

Very much the same moral holds for the story of popular responses to the building of the Berlin Wall in August 1961. This was of course much more of a domestic occasion for discontent, directly affecting the lives of millions of East Germans, rather than a change emanating from elsewhere. But nevertheless, yet again the most notable feature of popular responses was the very lack of concerted opposition to what was effectively perceived as a *fait accompli*. Although there were of course signs and symptoms in preceding days, the act itself, on the night of 12/13 August, was accomplished with amazing efficiency: Berliners awoke to find that there was very little they could do. The erection and strengthening of the fortified border—first rolls of barbed wire, then concrete slabs and road blocks, all guarded by ranks of armed guards, and finally the more permanent Wall itself (which was further strengthened and streamlined in subsequent years)—were effected with remarkable speed and efficiency. Given the memories of 1953 and 1956, there was little that people—as individuals—could do.

[30] SAPMO-BArch, IV 2/5/732, report of 26 Oct. 1956.

But this was perhaps precisely the point: people reacted as individuals, not organized groups. We have seen, in Chapter 3 above, the discomfort which many functionaries felt with the measures taken by the leadership; expressions of similar discomfort were accentuated among those who had less reason for restraint in their opinions.

On 13 August itself, there was clearly a need for maximum physical security at the border. A short report on the period 9.30 to 11.30 a.m. complained that the Volkspolizei was having to take the brunt of discussions with the population, and that too few party workers were in evidence; seventy 'agitators' were immediately dispatched to the Wollankstraße border crossing-point in question. At the Brandenburg Gate, there were similar problems at first: in the absence of adequate numbers of party agitators, the army and Volkspolizei were too preoccupied by conversations with members of the public to ensure adequate security.[31] From these and other reports it appears that it was mainly young people who were detaining the security forces in conversation.

Some people were of course taking the opportunity—in so far as it still existed—to escape to the West. Many sought to jump from windows of houses and flats on streets forming part of the border; others tried various means of crossing the barbed wire and concrete barrier itself. Inevitably there were casualties, as there were in later years when people still sought to tunnel under, vault over, circumvent, or penetrate an increasingly sophisticated barrier to the West. The adventure stories of individuals secreted in suitcases or car boots, of those who swam underwater to freedom and those who floated over the Wall in home-made air balloons or flying machines powered by bicycle pedals, are testimony to the determination of hundreds to seek to escape what now seemed to many of them more a prison than a homeland. Increasingly, too, there were those who simply put in applications for an exit visa in the hope that within a matter of months or years some exchange agreement would be arranged.

But in the aftermath of the immediate shock, reactions were condemnatory with little practical effect. The numerous reports compiled by the SED and its affiliated organizations reveal a picture of panic shoppping (*Hamsterkaufen*) and wild rumours. There was a widespread notion that there would soon be a currency reform, with compulsory currency exchange, and that it would be wise to be rid of one's money beforehand. There was a run on banks as well as shops. A very lively fear of imminent

[31] Ibid., IV 2/5/433, report of 13 Aug. 1961.

war was widely prevalent, lying behind much of the general panic. In the following days comments were reported such as 'There is soon going to be a war; one really has to make some advance provisions for this'; 'I refuse to take up any weapon, I'm certainly not going to shoot at my West German brothers'; 'Now they've really constructed a concentration camp. No one can get in or out.'[32] What is striking about all these reports, however, is the spontaneous, individual, and generally helpless nature of the reactions.

The regime had the power to control, but not the power to persuade. There were, it is true, some individuals in Berlin who initially welcomed the end to the privileged life of *Grenzgänger* (although others, such as 'cleaning ladies', allegedly complained of increased journey times to work and handed in their notice), but the overwhelming bulk of reported reactions was concerned with the wider implications of the measures.[33] There were innumerable *Schmierereien* with revealing slogans such as 'Kommunisten raus, Deutschland für Deutschen, SED-nee (Communists out, Germany for the Germans, SED-no)' which implicitly identified SED leadership with foreign domination and appealed to nationalist German sentiments.[34] Over three weeks after the sealing of the border, on 6 September, the party leadership in Karl-Marx-Stadt was still complaining that 'it has been impossible to quash the rumour current among housewives that the measures in Berlin will lead to war'.[35] A week later, people in Karl-Marx-Stadt were still complaining that the measures taken were 'too sharp', and that they would only serve to deepen the division of Germany.[36] Even in late September, the intelligentsia had clearly still not been convinced. Comments were reported along the lines of: 'The government's measures of 13.8.61 have made the Iron Curtain even more impenetrable, the risk of war has increased' and 'there should be free elections in the whole of Germany'. Nor were the middle classes any clearer in their understanding of the official line: 'significant sections of the middle classes expressed their lack of understanding for the measures of 13.8.61. There were opinions such as, the measures in Berlin are too hard—the risk of war is increased in this way.'[37]

In the event, of course, the erection of the Wall inaugurated a greater period both of international stability as far as central Europe was concerned

[32] SAPMO-BArch, IV 2/5/433, reports of 11 Aug. 1961, 17 Aug. 1961, 21 Aug. 1961.

[33] Cf. ibid., 'Situationsbericht der Parteileitung der Akademie der Wissenschaften im Berliner Raum' (16 Aug. 1961).

[34] Ibid., report of 18 Aug. 1961.   [35] Ibid., IV 2/5/961, report of 6 Sept. 1961.

[36] Ibid., report of 11 Sept. 1961.   [37] Ibid., report of 23 Sept. 1961.

(the attentions of the superpowers turning elsewhere) and of domestic stability in the GDR. Economic, social, and generational changes began to combine with an increasing efficiency in the functioning of the political system. Nevertheless, for many East Germans the national question remained rather open, and hopes of liberalization and change were by no means extinguished.

The revolution which did not take place: 1968 in the GDR

The year 1968 has been seen as particularly significant.[38] The Western world—from Berkeley to Berlin, via Paris and the LSE—was rocked by student movements advocating enhanced democracy, non-violence (the generation of slogans such as 'flower-power' and 'make love not war'), and the radical critique of structures of repression. With the rediscovery of the ideas of the young Marx in the 1960s, many left-wing intellectuals in the West drew great encouragement from developments in the so-called Prague Spring of Czechoslovakia. The attempts of the reformist Czech leader, Alexander Dubček, to bring about a more decentralized, liberalized, and democratic form of state socialism seemed a highly attractive alternative to the political repression of post-Stalinist regimes in the Soviet bloc. And the forcible suppression of the young green shoots of this short-lived experiment in liberalization, with the invasion of Warsaw Pact troops in August 1968, proved a decisive, shattering experience for many democrats across the world.

At the time, however, to all outward appearances, the GDR had remained as quiescent as ever. The acknowledged expert on opposition in the GDR, Karl Wilhelm Fricke, recounted a few incidents of protest and the trials and punishments of a few protesters, from which he deduced that the real numbers of those demonstrating 'may perhaps have reached three figures'; but, on the basis of the snippets which reached Western observers' eyes, it was not possible to provide much more detail than this.[39] Even an East German author, in a better personal position to comment, referred only to 'the couple of slogans which for the first time in decades were to be seen on the walls of houses, and the few leaflets that were distributed . . .'.[40]

[38] The following section, in slightly different form, has been published as part of an article in *Contemporary European History*, 2: 3 (Nov. 1993), 265–82.

[39] Karl Wilhelm Fricke, *Opposition und Widerstand in der DDR* (Cologne: Verlag Wissenschaft und Politik, 1984) 149.

[40] Wolfgang Rüddenklau, *Störenfried. ddr-opposition 1986–89* (Berlin: BasisDruck, 1992), 16.

We are now able to refine and qualify the received view of outward tranquillity. The extent of popular unrest and of splutterings of revolt was far greater than ever previously imagined. The population of the GDR was not as docile, as obedient to secular authority, as had previously been thought—but nor were all expressions of political unrest as purely pro-democracy or pro-reform socialist, as ideologically straightforward or as intellectually coherent, as has been represented in hindsight.

On the basis of analysis of the documents of the State Security Police (Stasi), the central party archive of the SED, and the Berlin city archives, Stefan Wolle has built up an intriguing picture of the character and extent of oppositional political activity, particularly in Berlin, in the late summer of 1968. Acts of protest were not restricted to students and intellectuals, but rather emanated from all quarters of the population, ranging from the offspring of high SED functionaries, through the circles of the academic and creative intelligentsia, right into all levels and areas of the industrial workforce. As far as generation was concerned, young people—predominantly aged between 18 and 25—seemed particularly active.[41] In Wolle's view, the ideals of reform communism were too abstract to find much resonance among large sections of the population; nevertheless, the Stasi and the SED were correct in their suspicions 'that there was considerable sympathy in the population for a reform-socialist course'.[42]

This picture may be extended, refined, but also in important respects qualified, on the basis of the material in the central trade union archives. These records confirm a picture of very widespread protest. It is certainly true that acts of protest did not come solely, or indeed even predominantly, from members of the intelligentsia. It is less clear, however, that popular protests indicated widespread sympathy for 'reform socialism' in particular, rather than a desire for political freedom in general.

A very interesting analysis of the situation was undertaken by the trade union leadership at the end of the first week of September 1968.[43] This report provides detailed evidence that all over the GDR there were oppositional activities and expressions of protest. In numerous places, workers were refusing to sign the official Declaratory Acts

[41] Stefan Wolle, 'Die DDR-Bevölkerung und der Prager Frühling', Aus Politik und Zeitgeschichte. Beilage zur Wochenzeitung Das Parlament, B36/92 (28 Aug. 1992), 35–45; see esp. 41–3.

[42] Ibid. 45. See also Mitter and Wolle, Untergang auf Raten, ch. 4.

[43] FDGB, file no. 5414 (Präsidiums- und Sekretariatsbeschlüsse des Bundesvorstandes der FDGB betr. Besondere Vorkommnisse 1960–1985), 'FDGB Bundesvorstand. Beschluss des Sekretariats vom 16.9.68. Nr. S 640/68', relating to an analysis of the situation, dated 6 Sept. 1968.

(*Willenserklärungen*) supporting what were euphemistically called the 'measures taken by the five socialist countries'—the suppression of the Czech liberalization movement by force. In Berlin, for example, eleven production collectives of the Baustelle Stadzentrum Berlin refused to sign, as did a production collective from the VEB Stahl- und Blechkonstruktion. In the Forschungszentrum Berlin-Adlershof, handwritten demands for 'Freedom for Vietnam—Freedom for Czechoslovakia' were being circulated. In one factory, the Levy-KG Berlin-Lichtenberg, there were demands for a sympathy strike.[44] In another, a trade union functionary was himself a co-initiator of a protocol that demanded the withdrawal of East German troops from Czechoslovakia.[45] Similar refusals to sign the document supporting the measures were reported from Cottbus, Frankfurt-on-Oder, Rostock, Magdeburg, Halle, Gera—indeed all over the GDR.

Youth seem to have played a very active part in the protests. 'Youngsters' are repeatedly mentioned in the report as being withdrawn, opposed, influenced by Western propaganda. In Rostock, the report speaks of the 'spreading of enemy rumours, including among youngsters'; in Magdeburg, 'apart from enemy arguments . . . there was a spreading of rumours and youngsters displayed partly a wait-and-see attitude, partly a negative response to the measures'; in Halle 'youths appeared with news from the Western media and referred to the inadequate and misleading information produced by our radio and television stations'.[46] In Mühlhausen, and in Erfurt, there had been 'illegal gatherings (*Zusammenrottungen*) of youngsters, who had been chanting the demand "We want our freedom"'—to which there had been a rapid response by the authorities ('Any further developments . . . were prevented by our organs').[47] 'Illegal gatherings of youngsters' are also reported to have taken place on the railway stations of Magdeburg and Stendal.[48] In Erfurt, apart from 'enemy propaganda', there is a noticeable increase in the influence of the Church on young people, with invitations to lectures and discussions.[49] In analysing particular concentrations of activity, the report concludes that: 'It is characteristic of developing activities of the class enemy, that youngsters take the lead.'[50]

The intelligentsia seem to have been scarcely more supportive of the government, although—interestingly, given the more prominent role they have often been allotted in general accounts of 'opposition'—their lack of support appears to have been rather muted, characterized more by passive disapproval and withdrawal than by active protest. There is a report from

[44] Ibid. 5.   [45] Ibid. 6.   [46] Ibid. 7.   [47] Ibid. 4.
[48] Ibid. 12.   [49] Ibid. 5.   [50] Ibid. 9.

Halle that: 'Among members of the intelligentsia there were misunderstand-ings concerning the measures and the role of Dubček. Sometimes the opinion was expressed that the measures were in contravention of interna-tional law.'[51] At the Ilmenau Technical College (TH), ten of the twenty-seven academic colleagues refused to sign the official document. In Dresden, 'in the circles of the intelligentsia and in the health services there was a tendency to withdrawal and refusal to sign the Declaratory Acts'.[52] Of 180 students at a meeting in the student residence of the University of Greifswald, only twenty were prepared to support the invasion of Czechoslovakia.[53] But all sections of the population appeared to be affected in one way or another. In the Dresden, Bautzen, and Dippoldiswalde districts, there was panic shopping. Comparisons were being drawn with 1938. In the border areas, there was very noticeable 'anti-Soviet incite-ment'.[54] Women appeared to be particularly upset if their menfolk were serving in the army.

Typical opinions are reported: this is just like Hitler in 1938; the GDR should remain neutral; 'Let the Czechs seek salvation their own way, why should we get mixed up in it'; 'When the Russian whistles, the others have to dance'; 'If the Russians want to be our friends, they should give Silesia and the other territories back to us'; 'There is no counter-revolution in Czechoslovakia'; 'Why should the National People's Army take part in the invasion, the GDR is itself a country under Soviet occupation', and so on.[55] The mood which comes across in this very wide-ranging and detailed report is quite complex. It is one of general apprehension, of fear of what might come; questions are raised about the responses of Western countries, about whether NATO might also march into Czechoslovakia, about why the Western communist parties of France, Italy, and Sweden were opposed to the measures. Questions are also repeatedly raised about the likely re-sponses of Romania, Yugoslavia, and China. The panic shopping is indica-tive of deep-seated uncertainty about the future. A lot of dissatisfaction with the Ulbricht government is expressed, and there is very widespread support for freedom of the press and public opinion. But it is not all straightfor-wardly pro-democracy.

Indeed, the ideological mixture, the conjuncture of apparently mutually incompatible positions, is perhaps what is most striking about the unrest among the population. This is revealed in the most astonishing juxtapo-sitions, as in the following paragraphs summarizing the situation, which are worth quoting in full:

[51] FDGB, file no. 5414, 7.   [52] Ibid. 6.   [53] Ibid. 12.
[54] Ibid. 6.   [55] Ibid. 2, 3, 8.

—increased daubing of swastikas, SS runes, graffiti in toilets, factories, on buildings, streets and squares. Mostly this graffiti consists of slogans such as 'Long live Dubček—Freedom for Czechoslovakia—Russians and Germans get out of Czechoslovakia—It is just like 30 years ago'. . . .

—provocative expressions and incitements against our state, against the Soviet Union and leading personalities (particularly against Comrade Walter Ulbricht).

For example four youths in the Zentrum-Warenhaus Erfurt described Soviet soldiers as 'pigs and pig-Russians'. There were such graffiti as 'Long live Dubček, down with Ulbricht', 'Dubček has got more people supporting him than Ulbricht has in the GDR', 'Ulbricht is Hitler number 2'. Tearing up of pictures of leading personalities of the GDR and singing of fascist songs.[56]

Similarly, youth at a camp-site in Graal-Müritz, in the Rostock area, demonstrated against the GDR by 'singing fascist songs and carrying around a picture of Hitler'.[57] The singing of fascist songs, daubing of swastikas and SS signs, at the same time as upholding demands for political freedom, appears at first sight quite extraordinary, although clearly both were designed as expressions of protest against the 'anti-fascist' state of the GDR. The West German flag could serve the same purpose: on Neustädter railway station, two GDR flags were torn down, while at the Wasserbohrstelle Gehrendorf two black-red-gold flags without the GDR emblem were raised.[58]

There were a great variety of forms of expression of protest. Slogans, graffiti, anonymous telephone calls threatening leading functionaries, demands for sympathy strikes or at least a downing of tools for *Gedenkminuten* (a minute's silence), and attempted escapes from the GDR were all common. So were acts of sabotage or attempted sabotage. A cable belonging to the Soviet army was hacked through in Dresden. The long-distance gas pipe from Czechoslovakia to the GDR, providing energy to Dresden, was damaged on the Czech side of the border. A telephone cable was cut through on the line from Dessau to Halberstadt. Many other instances of sabotage, including arson, are also reported from a whole range of different areas.[59]

A major form of protest was the distribution of leaflets. Interestingly, however, there is only one mention of an alleged organization behind the leaflet: in Haldensleben leaflets were found proclaiming 'Here speaks the Peace Party of Germany and calls out loud, German communists out, your mothers are waiting at home' (there is a stylistic flourish in the original, which rhymes but does not quite scan: 'Deutsche Kommunisten raus, eure Mütter warten zu Haus').[60] There are numerous other reports of *Flugblattaktionen* (leaflet actions), but without details of their contents.

[56] Ibid. 8.   [57] Ibid. 12.   [58] Ibid.
[59] See generally the detailed reporting ibid. 4–13.   [60] Ibid. 9.

Leaflet actions are mentioned not only in the special report discussed above, but also in the more general trade union reports. On 30 August, for example, it is reported from Karl-Marx-Stadt that 'in the Centrum-Warenhaus leaflets were discovered which called for a collection of signatures to protest against the measures of the five socialist countries. Similar leaflets were found in the letter boxes of employees. . . . the daubing of graffiti, the distribution of leaflets, the writing and shouting of incitements and slogans, continue unabated.'[61] At the same time, of course, the news reporting of the Western media was of very great importance, perhaps rendering the contents of GDR home-grown communications of slightly lesser importance. Subsequent general reports repeatedly stress, for example, that people do not believe the official version of events reported in the GDR press, but rather, through following Western television and radio, believe that the movement for liberalization in Czechoslovakia has more to do with people's desire for freedom than with the alleged activities of Western *agents provocateurs*.[62]

It is now clear that all over the GDR, in all regions and among all classes and groups of society, there were strong, if very variegated, reactions to the events of the summer of 1968. Countless numbers of ordinary individuals were willing to risk disciplinary actions, arrest, and possible imprisonment, by refusing to sign official documents, by demanding sympathy strikes or *Gedenkminuten*, by spreading leaflets or daubing graffiti, by making symbolic demonstrations of their opposition to the Ulbricht regime. The apparent quiescence of the population was due more to rapid, effective intervention and suppression than to lack of public arousal. What then, to summarize, were the main reasons why there was no visible uprising in the GDR in 1968, despite this seething, widespread popular unrest below the surface?

Essentially, there were two major aspects in which 1968 differed from both 1953 and 1989. On the one hand, the character of popular unrest itself was somewhat different. Unlike 1953, 1968 was sparked, not by changes of policy *within* the state, but rather by events elsewhere. The unrest was not therefore rooted in immediate and widespread dissatisfaction with the economic and social policies of the East German regime itself. Nor was it overlaid with the political uncertainties about the duration of division which were characteristic of the early 1950s. The building of the Wall, the New Economic System, and the stabilization of political structures had accomplished much as far as domestic 'making do' was concerned: the

---

[61] FDGB, file no. 2684, Information No. 13 (30 Aug. 1968), 3.
[62] See ibid., Information No. 17 (5 Sept. 1968), 5, and Information No. 18 (6 Sept. 1968).

population was well on the way to the characteristic patterns of grumbling conformity so notable in the 1970s. The unrest was more purely and directly political, and more specifically focused, than had been the case in 1953, when the very diversity of discontents provided much of the explosive and widespread force of the uprising.

Furthermore, in 1968—as in 1953, but unlike 1989—protests were very much in the nature of spontaneous, individual or local, easily isolated acts: outbursts of disapproval, rather than organized movements for change. Political dissent was certainly very widespread, but it was essentially reactive in nature: people knew what they wanted to protest *against*, but they had no organizational networks or strategies for seeking to exert influence on the government or to effect positive alternative policies. This was no longer the case in the later 1980s, when—as we shall see—the political organization of dissent was very much more advanced, programmes for change more explicit.

Secondly, and in contrast to 1953 and—in rather different ways—1989, there were in 1968 no major differences of opinion as far as the political élites were concerned. Working in close conjunction with the SED leadership, the State Security Police was able to suppress all forms of resistance before they were able to achieve much by way of visible impact (in the jargon of the regime, they did not become *öffentlichkeitswirksam*): individuals were arrested, leaflets were collected up and destroyed, graffiti were rapidly removed from walls. The responses of the authorities were rapid, coordinated, and effective. There were no visible splits in the higher ranks of the SED, no differences in opinion over appropriate responses between SED and Stasi, no seeking of dialogue with dissenters: simply suppression. In the wake of this experience, the surly silence and social compromises of the 1970s were surely rational reactions.

This chapter has sought to present a brief insight, based on an analysis of the new material now available, into some key features of popular political opposition in the GDR. This analysis suggests that active popular discontent in the East German dictatorship was far more widespread than previously supposed. Opposition to the GDR existed throughout its history, and was expressed explicitly, in acts of industrial sabotage, work stoppages, leaflet distribution, defacing of the regime's symbols and pictures of leading functionaries, daubing of swastikas, slogans, graffiti, and numerous other means of displaying general insubordination. Particularly widespread and previously unsuspected levels of popular unrest were evident, not only in the well-known incidents of 1953, but also in 1968, when the GDR had previously been seen as a rock of quiescence in the stormy seas of both Western and Eastern Europe. Thus attempts to explain the relative stability of East German communist rule, in contrast to Poland and Czechoslovakia, in terms (at least partly) of the alleged docility of the masses, are misplaced. In so far as docility is to be found, it may perhaps be better sought among the technical and cultural intelligentsias—those who indicated their disapproval by at best a passive withdrawal, a compromise conformity and critique within bounds, or a flight to the West.

For the greater part of the GDR's history, however, élites were able to exert effective control over the rumblings of discontent from below, which remained for the most part easily isolated and uncoordinated. It was not these popular expressions of outright hostility to the regime which ultimately brought it down, but rather—ironically—attempts to improve the GDR from within: that is, it was not opposition, so much as a form of reformism, which contributed to the beginning of the end of the GDR.[63] What needs further examination now are, rather, two separate sets of developments: on the one hand, the key changes in the nature of political dissent, and the emergence of a more widespread and better organized activism for change within socialism, in the course of the 1980s; and on the other, the significant changes in the attitudes, concerns, and responses of the authorities, in particular the SED, in the context of changing domestic and international conditions. Together, these developments helped to determine the way in which the GDR came to an end as much at the hands of a revolution from above as of one from below and one from without—and at the hands of some of those who wanted to improve, rather than destroy, the functioning of actually existing socialism on German soil.

[63] Of course the beginning of the end was only that—the *beginning* of the end. With the opening of the borders, the masses reappeared on the political scene, in the shape of a mass exodus to the West, to ensure that the notion of a reformed GDR would remain an unattainable mirage. Thus popular opposition to the GDR, which had failed to shake its foundations for four decades, was under altered circumstances able ultimately to deal its final death blow.

8

THE GROWTH OF POLITICAL ACTIVISM

THE East German regime *never* succeeded in quelling dissent, discontent, or opposition. What was new about the 1980s was not the 'growth of opposition'—as so often argued—nor even the growth of discontent, but rather a combination of other factors. These include: the changing organizational forms and cultural orientations of a growing minority of political activists, who were seeking, not to overthrow the regime, nor even to escape from the GDR, but rather to improve it from within; the changing domestic political context of their actions, including both the growth of structural spaces within which to act, and the changing responses of the state to what they denigrated as 'hostile-negative forces (*feindlich-negative Kräfte*)'; and, finally, changing aspects of the international context.

These factors of course interrelated, and it is a difficult task to disentangle, for analytic purposes, the interweaving strands of a complicated story. The present chapter will proceed both thematically—to illustrate different aspects of the development of political activism in the 1980s—and chronologically, in order to show the ways in which the developing goals and organizational strategies of activists interrelated with the changing modes of intervention and response of the political authorities (party, state, Stasi), with the Church leadership caught in the crossfire between the demands of communist authorities, would-be reformers, and God.

Broadly, the decade from the late 1970s to 1989 can be divided into three main periods. The meeting between Honecker and Church leaders on 6 March 1978 marked a key turning-point as far as the structural context of political action was concerned.[1] In the years that followed, the state consciously *used* the Church leadership as an indirect means of seeking to control dissident activities. At the same time, of course, dissidents themselves used the free spaces provided by the Church for more open discussion, and for experimentation with new forms of debate and organization. While the state was conscious of—and highly exasperated

[1] See Ch. 4 above.

by—the fact that the Church leadership did not seem able to exert very effective discipline, it nevertheless felt it right to allow more time for Church leaders to do what they could.

The mid-1980s—perhaps from 1984 to 1987—form a transitional period. The state appeared to have achieved much of what it was aiming for: the demoralization of the peace movement, the exile of many dissidents, the co-option of a compliant Church leadership prepared to adopt a conciliatory, indeed obsequious role (as exemplified in the person of Manfred Stolpe). But, at the same time, new currents were emerging: the rise to power of Mikhail Gorbachev in the USSR gave new heart to those yearning for reform in Honecker's GDR, and dissident spirits within and outside the Church began increasingly to bridle against the conservatism and caution of some of their leadership. Grass-roots groups for reform began to proliferate, to create organizational networks and new forms of publicity, in what can be viewed as an emerging, if very limited, 'civil society'.

Finally, from late 1987 matters took a very different turn, on both sides of the equation: ever more aware that Church leaders were losing what little control they had ever exerted over dissident movements, the state resorted to more open and visible repression, more obvious use of heavy-handed tactics by the Stasi. But the forces for reform had by now developed more sophisticated organizational forms and tactics for pressurizing from below, and the last two years of the GDR's history, prior to the autumn of 1989, were characterized by increasing instability and political polarization.

At the same time as the growth of a political activism, however, it should be emphasized that the vast majority of East German citizens continued in the patterns of conformity, grumbling, and making do which have been described in previous chapters. The new political activism was characteristic only of a very small minority—a few handfuls—of citizens. Their activities and organizations grew up in the interstices of East German society, alongside continued patterns of obedience, retreatism, and disparate discontents. Yet, in contrast to an earlier era, in curious ways the concerns of political activists were shared by some members of the political élite, at least at lower levels and in provincial areas if not at the centre or top of the party hierarchy. As we shall see, the developments of the 1980s played a key role in the pattern of the 'gentle revolution' of the autumn of 1989.

Contexts and conditions of emergence

A (Western) report on the mood in the 'Eastern zone' (the GDR) of mid-November 1950 comments on the very striking generational differences in political opinion, and concludes rather pessimistically that 'seen like this, the implementation of bolshevist ideology in the Eastern zone appears to be merely a matter of generations. And this is food for thought for a lot of very serious people from Plauen to Rostock.'[2] In the event, the opposite was the case. The generation of 20- to 40-year-olds—metaphorically, the children of Ulbricht, not Hitler—were at the forefront of the new political initiatives which became increasingly prominent from the late 1970s.

Specific policy issues—peace, the environment, human rights—engaged the attention of a growing minority of young adults from the late 1970s. But a broad spectrum of social-cultural orientations lay behind these particular policy concerns. A new generation was coming to maturity, young adults who had been born and bred in the GDR, and who increasingly questioned *not* the right to existence of a separate East German state, but rather the quality of life in a continuing GDR. Among these, a significant if comparatively tiny minority had refused to conform, even while at school: they had resisted pressures to undergo the *Jugendweihe*, or to participate in the FDJ; they had sought alternative service as *Bausoldaten*, or refused conscription altogether; they had uttered remarks critical of the regime, or shown too much interest in the Western media or Eastern European reform movements. Since the penalty for nonconformity was often non-admittance to institutions of higher education and the restriction of career opportunities, many such young adults had found that the only educational paths and professional careers open to them that were commensurate with their talents and interests were within the Church.[3] The study of theology might still be possible if medicine or journalism were ruled out; a career as a pastor or as a Church employee in some capacity or another might be open while becoming a teacher or doctor would be wholly impossible under the political circumstances.

Thus the regime itself was producing a distinctive generational cluster of nonconformists who, for structural reasons, very often came together on common ground, in a common cultural space, in the penumbra of East German Protestantism. These were young adults who were committed to a degree of honesty, open debate, and discussion which had prevented them

---

[2] IfZ, Fg 44/2, 'Ostzonaler Stimmungsbericht nach den Wahlen vom 15.X.1950'.

[3] This was the case with Rainer Eppelmann, for example. Cf. *Der Spiegel*, 47: 38 (20 Sept. 1993), 63: 'Only after a period of service as a *Bausoldat* did Eppelmann decide . . . to become a pastor—not out of any religious fervour, but rather on the basis of more pragmatic considerations: "I asked myself, what can you become, for a contented or even a happy life in this country? The only answer which occurred to me was: pastor . . . It was clear to me that only the study of theology was able to offer me a little mental freedom." '

from exercising their talents in other walks of life: instead, they were peculiarly concentrated in the environs of the Protestant Church.

The new nonconformists—whether or not they were committed Christians—were characterized, too, by participation in a particular sub-cultural milieu. This might be characterized as a combination of continuing currents that had prevailed among Western youth in the later 1960s— emphasis on peace, the symbolism of flowers, communal sharing—with a certain puritanism and Christian overtones. The flavour is captured, for example, in this invitation to a 'peace workshop' on 27 June 1982:

Beginning of the WORSHIP SERVICE at 10.00 a.m.

Programme for participation for children and adults until 5.00 p.m.!

You can BRING WITH YOU:

Your musical instruments—songs—poems . . .
Desires, anxieties and ideas.

FOOD for yourself, and for someone who has nothing

and a FLOWER IN YOUR HAIR OR BUTTONHOLE[4]

Music, flowers, the honest sharing of ideals and anxieties as well as food, were characteristic of what was essentially a social and cultural, as well as narrowly political phenomenon.

Many of these young adults had just gone through the process of facing up to the dilemmas of whether or not to conform with respect to education, military service, career prospects; many too had young children, and were increasingly horrified at the ways in which their own offspring were being indoctrinated and pressurized even while still in the crèche or kindergarten. This was a generation which had not experienced the Nazi dictatorship, had nothing to cover up in its own past, and no personal reasons to be particu-larly respectful of the older generation of wartime communists. The latter were by now perceived as ageing, ossified, out of touch with reality. On the contrary, as far as the future for themselves and their children was con-cerned, the new generation of nonconformists had everything to play for; and it was their earnest desire to ensure that, so far as possible, they would change the GDR for the better. In their darker moments, many feared that if they did not have the courage to pressurize for change, there might indeed be no tomorrow. As Bärbel Bohley once put it, when threatened that she would have to face the consequences if she continued to engage in 'illegal

---

[4] BP, O-4 766. Capitals and underlining as in original.

activities': she would also have to face the consequences if she did *not* speak out against the increasing militarization of society.[5]

Those involved in the new movements of the late 1970s and 1980s were generally concerned with a whole bundle of closely interrelated issues, and many of the same individuals were actively involved across a range of campaigns. Given the political circumstances, it was virtually impossible to separate critiques of specific policies from a critique of the whole nature of social life and the pressures for conformity operative in the East German dictatorship. As an open letter of students at the Katechetischen Oberseminar Naumburg of January 1981 put it:

In our society, images of the enemy are constantly being created in order to arouse hatred and readiness to engage in violence. This hinders a positive attitude towards peace. Thoughtlessly going along with all this for reasons of fear or for personal advantages furthers this trend and makes us accomplices. Therefore we support all attempts to point out that, through such behaviour, Christians and non-Christians withdraw from their responsibilities for society.[6]

It was above all a deep sense of moral and social responsibility, and the courage to speak out and to seek realistic changes and improvements, which characterized the new activists of the 1980s. After *Ostpolitik*, with international recognition of the GDR, the continued existence of the GDR was essentially taken for granted by most people in both Germanies (with the rather curious exception of the East German leadership, who continued to be plagued by paranoia with respect to Western perceptions and intentions, even in 1987—retrospectively, an *annus mirabilis*—on the occasion of the Berlin 750th anniversary celebrations and Honecker's ceremonious welcome on his trip to the Federal Republic). The brief period of apparent cultural liberalization in the early 1970s, the official commitment to the Helsinki Declaration of 1975, and the generally reformist flavour of Honecker's initial emphasis on social policies and pragmatic improvements in living conditions, stimulated hopes in many quarters for a real possibility of some change towards a more democratic form of 'actually existing socialism' in the GDR. And these hopes were not purely passive: increasingly, social critics sought to make use of official declarations to pressurize the regime to live up to its public word. A process of *Gratwanderung*—tightrope walking—became more widespread: instead of ineffective

---

[5] IfGA, ZPA, IV B 2/14/69, 'Aktennotiz über ein Gespräch mit Frau Bohley, Bärbel, 15.9.83'. The compiler of this report was a state functionary who had no interest whatsoever—quite the reverse—in presenting Bärbel Bohley's courageous stance in a favourable light.

[6] MfS, ZAIG, Z 3100, No. 23/81 (12 Jan. 1981), Anlage.

mouthing of slogans or expressing discontent through unofficial work stoppages, people began to develop strategies of pushing the state towards an expansion of limits, of changing the boundaries of the politically possible. It was this, above all, which distinguished the political activism of the 1980s from the disparate discontents of earlier decades.

Moreover, these political activists were operating in a wholly new situation, with respect both to the domestic political context and the international situation. The Church–state agreement of 6 March 1978 appeared to signify that the boundaries of the politically possible had indeed begun to shift. But the Church–state agreement meant a number of quite different things, depending on perspective.[7] In the event, the activists were able to make use of the new-found spaces for discussion and organization within a rather ambivalent Protestant Church. Mindful of outward appearances and public image in the era of Helsinki, the state too sought to make use of the Church leadership as an indirect means of controlling dissent. Caught in the middle, the Church itself played a highly ambiguous role, as we shall see. Internationally, the new Cold War of the early 1980s, and the subsequent thaw and movements towards reform in Eastern Europe under Gorbachev from the mid-1980s, were important factors in the development of domestic dissent in East Germany. Within these broader contexts, reformist tendencies and incipient social and political movements within the GDR underwent their own processes of cultural and organizational development and change.

The controlled ventilation of dissent, 1978–1984

The period from 1978 to the mid-1980s is characterized by considerable state use of the Church leadership to seek to allow a 'controlled ventilation of dissent', in which protests and relatively open discussions could take place within the context of religious meetings on church premises, but the state impressed on Church leaders the importance of restricting the influence of these gatherings and ensuring that they did not transgress certain clearly defined rules. At the same time, however, the very possibility of more open and free debate attracted many more young people into churches—for reasons having at least initially very little to do with the Christian faith—and contributed to something of a snowball effect. The result was ultimately to be the proliferation of groups, in the mid-1980s, and the eventual loss of control of these new movements by both the Church authorities and,

---

[7] Cf. the detailed discussion in Ch. 4 above.

eventually, even the more openly repressive state by the closing years of the decade.

It is important now to distinguish between a number of different aspects of what has just, rather globally, been referred to as 'the state'. As far as appearances were concerned, there were three separate instances of authority, intervention, and control: first, the state functionaries proper—those holding governmental offices, at the national, regional, or local levels; secondly, the closely related SED hierarchy; and thirdly, the—less visible—levels of the State Security Police, or Stasi. There was a circuitous route of observation, intimation, and ultimately veiled intimidation, culminating finally in meetings of Church leaders (having been themselves subjected to a degree of pressure from party and sometimes Stasi functionaries) with dissidents to seek to deflect their original intentions or to exert some control over the events which did take place. 'Social forces' (*gesellschaftliche Kräfte*) might also be deployed to exert a degree of indirect influence. It is important to note, however, that the Stasi was almost certainly involved, in an essentially *directive* (rather than simply reactive or servicing) capacity, in all aspects of observation, intervention, and control of dissent.[8]

The earliest forms of organized political activism were largely concerned with issues of peace and the militarization of society. Pacifist voices had always been heard in the GDR. We have seen, in previous chapters, the popular fears of war in the 1950s, and the stand of the Church with respect to the introduction of military service in 1962. The creation of an alternative form of service as 'construction soliders' (*Bausoldaten*) in 1964 had in the event served to bring together individuals concerned with defence issues, with around 220 to 240 young men opting for this rather longer period of service—which also marked them out as nonconformists, with associated career disadvantages—each year. Many of these former *Bausoldaten* maintained contacts with each other long after their period of alternative service was over. In 1972 the first *Friedensseminar* (seminar for peace) organized by former *Bausoldaten* took place in Königswalde; by 1979, the numbers attending had swollen to 125 (given the political circumstances, a quite considerable figure) and the seminar had to move into church premises to find adequate space for discussions. In the course of the 1970s, other circles for the discussion of peace issues (*Friedenskreise*) also began to be formed. More broadly, state policies of militarization, and the official cultivation of a friend/foe mentality, with West Germans designated not as relatives but as

---

[8] Cf. the discussion of the Stasi as 'nerve system and brain of the party' in Ch. 2 above.

the arch-enemy, had long been a cause for concern among many East Germans.

Incipient peace initiatives were given added impetus by the changes in the international context of the late 1970s. In 1979, the Western decision to station nuclear missiles on German soil frightened Germans, both East and West, and inaugurated a new period of more intense campaigning from the grass roots on both sides of the Iron Curtain. The Soviet Union's invasion of Afghanistan in 1979, and the new chill in superpower relations in the early 1980s after the thaw and *détente* of the 1970s, exacerbated by the Cold War rhetoric of the Reagan administration in the USA, made the prospects of a Third World War appear ever more possible. Many people, both Christians and non-Christians, sought to protest against the new climate, and to influence the decisions of their governments in a more pacifist direction.

To speak of an unofficial peace movement in East Germany is misleading. There was no single 'movement' as such; rather there were a number of different initiatives, some more spontaneous than others, some more organized and continuous than others, some seeking contacts and publicity in the West or elsewhere in Eastern Europe while others eschewed such potentially risky contacts. A number of key occasions, issues, and developments stand out; at the same time there were longer processes of development, subcurrents, and—as we shall see—what might be called events which did not take place. The relationships of the political authorities and the Church leadership to these initiatives were complex. Both had, in different ways and for different reasons, an interest in seeking to allow the expression while containing the political impact of such pressures for peace.

The state's own official peace movement was directed against NATO missiles, and sought to represent the East German army and the Warsaw Pact troops as simply defensive forces, designed to protect peace. In so far as the Eastern European peace initiatives supported Western peace movements, they were a useful aid in undermining the NATO side of the military balance; and there was some hope that grass-roots movements might put sufficient pressure on Western democratic governments to effect genuine changes in policy. The communists thus had a vested interest in Christian voices for peace which would aid the undermining of the Western will to increase military spending and provision. On the other hand, such energies must not be deployed against the Warsaw Pact's weaponry; moreover, it was essential that the party retain control over *any* movement in the GDR, and not allow any genuine development of organizational pluralism or open discussion. Purely from the political point of view—the aim to quell any initiative not controlled by the party—the unofficial peace initiatives of the late 1970s and early 1980s were an implicit challenge to the hegemony of the SED.

The Church leadership was caught between the demands of conscience and the state. On the one hand, many individual Church leaders and pastors felt passionately that they must speak out for peace; on the other hand, the more cautious or diplomatic members of the Church leadership felt that any expression of concern must be kept within the bounds imposed by the state, to ensure, first, that the campaign could continue, and secondly, that the newly confirmed freedom of religious practice in the GDR should not be put in jeopardy. Thus the leadership at the same time both facilitated and limited incipient peace initiatives. And the state made use of this indirect mechanism of control to avoid the overt appearance of outright repression, while ultimately retaining—at least until the mid-1980s—the upper hand in what was a very delicate balance.

The opposition to the introduction of military education as a compulsory subject in schools, announced in April 1978, was completely unsuccessful. But it gave many people courage to continue to voice their concerns. Bishop Werner Krusche of Magdeburg and Bishop Armin Härtel of Dresden voiced their opposition to this, as did many less prominent churchpeople. Although the 'construction soldier service' was unique among Eastern European states, many pacifists felt that even this did not go far enough for those who had conscientious objections to military service of any kind, even without bearing weapons. In 1981, Pastor Wonneberger of Dresden proposed the notion of 'social peace service' (Soziale Friedensdienst, or SoFD), which, although rejected by the state, remained a campaigning issue for many peace activists.

'Blues masses' and peace prayers began to be a recurrent feature in the programmes of many churches, particularly (in association with Pastor Eppelmann) in the Samariterkirche and the Erlöserkirche in Berlin. Numbers attending very often reached 800–1,000. Although these events achieved no tangible or immediate changes in regime policy, they fostered new cultural currents among young people. Prayers for peace were complemented by discussions on more general social problems, such as the Leistungsdruck, the pressure to conform and succeed, felt by many young people. The need for better interpersonal relationships, for changing the nature of society rather than succumbing to pressures or dropping out, began to be articulated.[9] Here we can see the outlines of a culture of political activism, to be distinguished from the currents of conformity or retreat so prevalent in earlier years.

[9] See e.g. the reports on the blues masses in BP, O-4 766.

The early 1980s saw the beginnings of the politicization of the peace movement, with individuals beginning to link whole society problems with the question of peace. There were also growing links between secular intellectuals (Marxist dissidents) and members of the Church, broadening the spectrum of dissent. For example, in 1982 the dissident intellectual Robert Havemann and the pastor Rainer Eppelmann co-operated in producing their joint Berlin Appeal calling for peace. This by no means elicited universal approval, even among peace activists; many saw it as unnecessarily provocative and politically counter-productive. Despite sympathizing with Eppelmann's 'disquiet and concern', 'concern and impatience', the Berlin-Brandenburg Church leadership withdrew their support on 13 February 1982, commenting that 'the current political and military constellation must be considered much more precisely than is done in the Appeal'.[10] Many pastors rejected it 'because it puts in jeopardy the relationship which has developed between the Church and the state', as a report from Bezirk Cottbus put it.[11] Others, however, such as Pastor Wonneberger in Dresden, continued to try to collect signatures for the Berlin Appeal.

A Stasi report on a peace forum in the Dresden Kreuzkirche, led by Wonneberger, provides interesting insights into the complex processes of influence and control which were at work. On this occasion, Bishop Hempel, in response to a question about whether the Church leadership in Saxony agreed with the decision of the Berlin-Brandenburg Church not to support the Appeal, replied that the Church had to work within clear limits:

This means in practice that political freedom is of great value and we should work for it wherever we can. But external freedom and freedom in the inner sense are not the same thing, and above all not for the Church. This means that as far as working for political freedom in the structural, external sense is concerned, my understanding is that the Holy Scriptures have, for the sake of Christ, set clear limits for the Church. I can well believe that, on the one hand, that is a great disappointment for you, but on the other hand it is, ultimately, the essential strength of the Church.[12]

This theological formulation—separating freedom of spirit from freedom in the secular sphere—was rather typical of the more conservative Church leadership, and was of course in a tradition with which German Protestants,

---

[10] MfS, ZAIG, Z 3201, No. 82/82 (16 Feb. 1982), which includes a copy of the Stellungnahme of the Berlin-Brandenburg Church.

[11] IfGA, ZPA, IV B 2/14/69, 'Rat des Bez. Cottbus, Informationsbericht für die Monate Feb. und März 1982' (13 Apr. 1982), 2.

[12] MfS, ZAIG, Z 3202, No. 85/82 (19 Feb. 1982).

inheriting the legacy of Luther and Kant, were very familiar. Typical, too, were the suggestions made by the Stasi at the end of this report for exerting further influence over the undesired activities of Pastor Wonneberger: on the suggestion of the Stasi, a regional state functionary (the *Stellvertreter für Inneres beim Vorsitzenden des Rates des Bezirkes Dresden*) would speak to the President of the Regional Office of the Landeskirche of Saxony, President Domsch, who would in turn speak with Wonneberger. The Stasi were assured that the regional Church leadership would 'continue to work on disciplining Wonneberger and would let him know that he must not exceed the boundaries of his competence as a pastor'.[13] But despite such efforts, the new initiatives were not so readily suppressed.

At the same time, peace initiatives were beginning to spread as a broader social movement with an incipient mass base. The first *Friedensdekade* (peace week, in fact lasting a period of ten days) was held in the autumn of 1980, adopting as its symbol the 'Schwerter zu Pflugscharen (swords into ploughshares)' badge. Initially printed by a Church printing press in Herrnhut as a bookmark on linen paper, and thus not subject to censorship, the swords into ploughshares symbol had impeccable communist credentials. The picture chosen to accompany the biblical quotation was a depiction of the statue donated by the Soviet Union to the United Nations building in New York, and could thus hardly be objected to by the East German authorities. What they did object to, however, was the way in which this symbol caught on as a badge of protest. Worn as an armband by increasing numbers of young people who wished to express their discontent with the official state-sponsored peace movement, the symbol became an outward sign of a growing wave of incipient political unrest within the GDR, and thus could not politically be tolerated.

The state made this very clear by the winter of 1981-2. The symbol was explicitly forbidden in relation to the Dresden Peace Forum of February 1982. By April 1982, the Church in Saxony explicitly renounced any responsibility for people who continued to wear the symbol. In a letter entitled 'We can protect you no longer (*Wir können Euch nicht mehr schützen)*' Church leaders suggested that it was time to rethink tactics, and that the meaning of the symbol now had to be reconsidered in the light of political circumstances.[14] Many activists replaced their swords into ploughshares badges with a sign equally irritating to the authorities: a blank patch sewn on to the arm where previously the armband had been. This was of

---

[13] Ibid.
[14] The letter is reprinted in Klaus Ehring and Martin Dallwitz (eds.), *Schwerter zu Pflugscharen. Friedensbewegung in der DDR* (Hamburg: Rowohlt, 1982), 65-7.

course totally beyond any non-ludicrous form of state repression. But the effect was probably only one of a brief lifting of spirits among activists rather than anything more substantial.

From 1980 onwards, however, peace weeks (*Friedensdekaden*) became a regular annual event. These were regional gatherings, with programmes of activities lasting for ten days, with a predominantly religious flavour but clear political overtones and implications. They served to provide continuities within the unofficial peace movement, and to facilitate networks and contacts among activists in different areas of the GDR. They thus performed a very important organizational function, as we shall see, which was to distinguish the political activism of the 1980s from the disparate discontents of previous decades. But they also facilitated the state's overview of dissident activities, and were relatively easy to control by the state. *Friedensdekaden* were organized under the close oversight of the Church authorities—and, through them, of the state.

There were concurrent organizational developments. In the spring of 1983, at a peace seminar in Berlin, a number of peace groups came together to form a network, or *Netzwerk*. Several peace activists began regular meetings under the heading *Konkret für den Frieden*, and an organizational committee—the *Fortsetzungsausschuß*—was formed to coordinate future events. Local groups retained autonomy, and there was no single leadership figure in these activities. It was thus relatively difficult for the state to seek to behead these proliferating movements, although the Stasi scored considerable success in devastating particular local groups.[15]

The cross-fertilization between Christians and non-Christians was evident too in the growing unofficial women's movement of the early 1980s. Following the introduction in March 1982 of a new law on military service stipulating the mobilization of women, in 1983 the group known as *Frauen für den Frieden* (women for peace) was founded. Early activities included a demonstration under the rubric of '*Fasten für das Leben* (fasting for life)' in August 1983. Among leading individuals were Bärbel Bohley and Ulrike Poppe, both of whom were arrested for their activities later in 1983. Bohley was quite explicit that she was prepared to make use of the Church for protection so long as it was necessary, but not to engage in undue compromises to its authority. As she put it in a meeting of women's peace groups

---

[15] Cf. e.g. Wolfgang Rüddenklau, *Störenfried. ddr-opposition 1986–89* (Berlin: BasisDruck, 1992), and Vera Wollenberger, *Virus der Heuchler: Innenansichten aus Stasi-Akten* (Berlin: Elefanten-Press, 1992), on the breaking-up of the Friedenskreis Pankow by what became known as 'Lutzis' (since a remarkable number of Stasi infiltrators rather clumsily adopted the same cover name of 'Lutz').

on 14–15 September 1984: ideally, she would like 'to break with the "tutelage and regulation" of the Church'; but she had no idea 'whether and how an "independent women's group" outside the Church could exist'.[16] As we shall see, however, by the later 1980s the tensions between Church and some groups had developed to such an extent that many did, effectively, operate to a large degree outside the Church, except in those areas where individual pastors were favourably inclined.

In addition to longer-term strategies, there were many individual events or demonstrations, some of which were repressed or diverted, others of which took place but with greater or lesser degrees of publicity. Those which became known to Western observers at the time—such as the peace demonstration in the Frauenkirche in Dresden on 13 February 1982, or the demonstration in Jena on Christmas Eve 1982[17]—represent only the tip of a very much larger iceberg, the true extent of which will only become known as the archives are extensively trawled. A few examples to indicate the range of activities which did or did not take place must suffice to illustrate the multiple political seethings below the apparently tranquil surface of an outwardly stable state.

Individual events included planned demonstrations on specific occasions. Some were suppressed before they could begin: in March 1982, for example, the Junge Gemeinde in Jena planned activities to commemorate the anniversary of the bombardment of Jena. Appropriate state pressures were put on Bishop Leich, who was persuaded to forbid the planned commemorative service.[18] A more successful unofficial demonstration did, however, take place the following year, without the protection of the Church, on the occasion of the 38th anniversary of the bombardment of Jena on 18 March 1983. A 'hostile-negative group of individuals' appeared in a 'provocative' manner 'with public impact' at the official demonstration of approximately 15,000 participants. The thirty or so 'hostile-negative' forces bore homemade banners bearing such slogans as 'Make peace without weapons!', 'Disarm yourselves!', 'Get rid of war toys!', 'Militarization out of our lives', 'We want social peace service!', and the by now wholly provocative 'Swords into ploughshares!'[19] In the church service of the same evening, Bishop Leich adopted a notably pro-state stance, emphasizing that there were boundaries which must not be overstepped. People would simply have to

[16] MfS, ZAIG, Z 3396, No. 368/84 (27 Sept. 1984).

[17] Cf. Ferdinand Kroh, 'Havemann's Erben—1953 bis 1988', in id. (ed.), *'Freiheit ist immer Freiheit'. Die Andersdenkenden in der DDR* (Frankfurt-on-Main and Berlin: Ullstein Sachbuch, 1988).

[18] MfS, ZAIG, Z 3206, No. 133/82 (18 Mar. 1982).

[19] Ibid., Z 3290, No. 101/83 (21 Mar. 1983).

come to terms with the lack of a social peace service (SoFD), a dissident could not make use of the service to collect signatures for a petition to Honecker, 'the church is not for purposes of advertising'. Leich concluded that 'it is necessary to have confidence in the state'. The indirect pressures of the Stasi, via state functionaries, on the Church dignitary had achieved the desired effect, although they had not succeeded in suppressing initiatives from below.

Similarly, demonstrations were planned for the anniversary of the Hiroshima bombing on 6–7 August 1983. Actions were planned for Jena, Berlin, Halle, Schwerin, Neubrandenburg, Karl-Marx-Stadt, and elsewhere. The final comment which follows the Stasi's analysis of the plans is very revealing of its *modus operandi*, and demonstrates yet again the role of the Stasi as nerve system and brain centre of the state: 'Measures were introduced in all the affected districts and areas to investigate these plans further and, in conjunction with the relevant state organs and social forces, either to prevent the planned activities, or to exert influence in such a manner as to ensure that the course of events unfolded without any disturbance, or to reduce them to purely religious activities.'[20]

Some events simply did not take place at all. One such, which for its sophisticated simplicity deserves to make up in historical fame what it lost in publicity at the time, was a plan for a symbolic act of 'mass death' at the eleventh moment of the eleventh hour planned by a number of independent peace groups and the Initiative Frauen für den Frieden for 22 October 1983. The individuals involved intended simply to lie down in front of the Red Town Hall (Roter Rathaus) in East Berlin's central square, Alexanderplatz, at five minutes to twelve precisely, and have the contours of their bodies outlined in chalk on the pavement. They would remain until removed by security forces. In the event, the demonstration never took place. Sixty-four people were individually prevented from participating; in the words of the Stasi report, they were 'rounded up, interrogated, and taught a lesson (*belehrt*)' before ever reaching the site of the planned demonstration, while a further sixteen were arrested on the spot before anything had begun.[21]

Perhaps most important were the emerging currents of discussion, debate, and the establishment of organizational forms with a degree of continuity and longevity under the protection—and constraints—of the Church. The small peace circles themselves helped many young East German adults simply to learn to express themselves more freely, to articulate their own ideas in public, in ways which the pressures of GDR education and social

[20] MfS, ZAIG, Z 3300, No. 258/83 (28 July 1983).
[21] Ibid., Z 3324, No. 361/83 (21 Oct. 1983), and No. 362/83 (24 Oct. 1983).

institutions did not allow. As Vera Wollenberger was later to put it, for example: 'It is for me today still one of the most important outcomes of the work in peace circles that the participants learnt to express their opinions freely and openly. Most of them had not only to overcome their timidity about talking in front of a lot of people, but also their fear of saying openly what they were thinking.'[22] From these small, local circles sprang broader and larger initiatives.

The proliferation of dissent in the mid-1980s

The middle years of the 1980s were marked by a number of new features. Groups became more specialized, focusing on particular issues; and there were attempts to coordinate the activities of groups in different areas through networks which transcended local and regional boundaries. There were also increasing efforts to create some limited form of 'public sphere' through the production of illicit *samizdat* literature—a phenomenon which had been markedly absent in the GDR for the most part of its history (in contrast to neighbouring Eastern bloc countries), partly because of the relative ease of publication in West Germany. By 1987, too, it became apparent that many individuals and groups were increasingly irritated with the more conservative Church leadership, and were seeking to free themselves from the protection of the Church, which now appeared more constraining than enabling. The state, too, became aware that the Church's allotted role as the controller of dissent was no longer (or not yet?) being adequately fulfilled, and the Church leaders appeared to have ever less control of the development of dissidence. As the political activists became ever more bold and organized, so the state came to use more overt means of control, bypassing an apparently ever more ineffectual Church leadership. These developments were to come to a head in the winter of 1987-8.

Networking and specialization

The idea of networking had been present already in the peace movements of the later 1970s and early 1980s, and there were quite explicit views in some quarters about the forms it should take. A Stasi report gives a very succinct summary of the viewpoint articulated at a peace seminar in March 1983:

EPPELMANN and TSCICHE [*sic*] reckon that conditions have developed to the point that 'networking' through the formation of a 'community of solidarity' should be taken in hand. In their view, this should take place not through a hierarchical but

---

[22] Wollenberger, *Virus der Heuchler*, 17.

rather a federal structure. In this way, the possibility would be avoided that any state measures against the main actors would cripple the organization. In the framework of the planned 'community of solidarity' it is intended to introduce processes of 'alternative further social development'. In this way, alongside the intended exchange of experiences and information, those who are involved in this community should be guaranteed protection, help, and solidarity. The assumption was made that the goals to which the 'solidarity community' aspired would provoke the resistance of Church leadership bodies, and that the realization of these goals would only be possible beyond the boundaries of the Church. In this sense they had to be more daring.[23]

Similarly, in a meeting on 14–15 September 1984, women's peace groups from all over the GDR met in the Evangelical Community Centre in Wörmlitz-Böllberg/Halle. In the view of a Stasi report, this meeting was

to be evaluated as a first attempt, analogous to meetings of representatives of so-called peace circles and environmentalist groups in the GDR, to bring together the so-called women's groups which have recently been formed, and which are quite varied as far as their social structure and political goals are concerned. It is intended to get them to agree on common basic positions, to draw them more strongly into public visibility, to exchange experiences of their political impact, and to orient them towards further activities.[24]

That the women's movement was relatively rapidly successful in these aims becomes clear from a report on the second GDR-wide meeting of women's groups on 29–31 March 1985 in Berlin. Despite previous typical discussions between state representatives and Church leaders, the Stasi's expectations were 'not in the least fulfilled', in particular because of the attitude of 'tolerance and inconsistency . . . on the part of Generalsuperint. KRUSCHE'. As a result, in the light of various Stasi reports

the second supra-regional gathering of so-called women's groups in the GDR is to be evaluated as a further significant step of sufficiently well-known hostile-negative forces to bring together women's groups effectively for purposes of inspiring and organizing a so-called inner opposition, agreeing on unified political and organizational basic positions, and orientating themselves towards further activities.[25]

In the Stasi's view, the women's movement had 'qualitatively and quantitatively reached a higher stage of development'—praise indeed from this source, supreme master as the Stasi was of the art of political organization.

The notion of networking, in very loose political forms—informal contacts, liaison between essentially leaderless, autonomous regional and local groups—became a common feature of the development of a variety of forms

---

[23] MfS, ZAIG, Z 3332, Information No. 86/83 (7 Mar. 1983), 7–8.
[24] Ibid., Z 3396, No. 368/84 (27 Sept. 1984).
[25] Ibid., Z 3450, No. 152/85 (29 Apr. 1985).

of political activism in the middle years of the 1980s. This was a key organizational characteristic which distinguished the dissent of this decade from the more isolated and spontaneous popular protests of earlier years, and made the proliferation of grass-roots dissent less easy to deal with as far as the state was concerned. For the time being, the state's main strategies remained those of Stasi observation, infiltration, and intervention, as well as the use of the Church authorities as a means of control.

In addition to networking, however, the groups were themselves becoming increasingly specialized in their work, and distinct from one another in a variety of ways. The general wave of concern about peace began to crystallize into a number of more distinctive groupings and orientations, focusing on different aspects of policy. The Bundestag decision of 22 November 1983 that nuclear missiles were to be stationed on German soil (followed by the arrival of the first Pershing missiles the very next day) had a depressing effect on unofficial peace initiatives, one of whose main aims had now been defeated. And, in preparation for Honecker's planned, but ultimately aborted, trip to West Germany in 1984, there was a relaxation of restrictions on travel visas and a consequent spate of emigrations to the West in the period from February to May 1984. The combination of the defeat on the issue of nuclear missiles in central Europe and the so-called *Ausreisewelle*, which robbed the incipient alternative political initiatives of many potential supporters and activists, produced a widespread mood of resignation.[26] But the response was ultimately to pursue new strategies and to focus on other avenues of possible change. The broad issue of human rights in the GDR, and the need for specialized pressure groups focusing on particular areas, came to the forefront of concern.

Human rights initiatives

At the *Friedenswerkstatt* in Berlin on 29–30 June 1985, the possibility of setting up a GDR-wide seminar on human rights was discussed.[27] This was to discuss not only issues relating to peace, but also matters which directly affected individual activists, such as their effective *Berufsverbot* or ban on appropriate professional careers. A planned meeting in the autumn of 1985 to discuss this new initiative was, after Stasi pressures, forbidden by the Treptow church in which the meeting was to be held. In the event, the participants in the new initiative—who had disagreed already over tactics in

[26] Cf. Kroh, 'Havemann's Erben'; and Rüddenklau, *Störenfried*, 49–51.

[27] Cf. MfS, ZAIG, Z 3467, No. 286/85 (3 July 1985); and Wolfgang Templin and Reinhard Weißhuhn, 'Initiative Frieden und Menschenrechte. Die erste unabhängige DDR-Oppositionsgruppe', in H. Müller-Enbergs, M. Schulz, and J. Wielgohs (eds.), *Von der Illegalität ins Parlament. Werdegang und Konzept der neuen Bürgerbewegungen* (Berlin: LinksDruck Verlag, Christoph Links, 1991).

relation to the banned meeting, and whose disagreements were exploited and exacerbated by the Stasi informers in their midst—subsequently split into two groups.[28] One later became known as Gegenstimmen; the other was the Initiative Frieden und Menschenrechte (IFM), formally founded in January 1986.

The IFM conceived itself as the first truly independent political group, outside the Church.[29] In retrospect, it was perceived as the first group 'which openly articulated its role as political opposition',[30] and thus was essentially forced into operating *outside* the Church, which still maintained the role of a Church within socialism. Rather than making use of church premises—with all the associated compromises and constraints—the IFM met in private homes, and attempted to make use of privately owned writing materials and copying machines.

The IFM consciously adopted less cautious strategies, seeking to publish open letters, petitions, and appeals, sometimes jointly with Church or peace groups and sometimes independently. A nice example of its activities is the open letter of 20 July 1986, from Hirsch, Grimm, and Templin jointly with Pastor Rainer Eppelmann, to the Council of Ministers of the GDR. This protested against the Wall, demanded greater freedom to travel, improvements in communications, East–West contacts, the freedom of information, culture, and literature. The letter was firmly grounded in astute political tactics, appealing to the officially acknowledged leadership of Moscow: 'The "new thinking and acting" demanded by the General Secretary of the CPSU is demonstrated first and foremost by both sides refraining from whipping up fear and suspicion and by demolishing barriers of all sorts.'[31] Gorbachev was essentially being used as a legitimatory means of appealing to the Honecker leadership: Gorbachev was less an instigator of these political initiatives than an occasion for strengthening the case of the would-be reformers in East Germany. The IFM also fostered contacts with the West, and sought publicity in the Western media, as well as linking up with similar groups elsewhere in Eastern Europe.

The basic aims of the IFM were focused on the issue of *domestic* social peace: on the democratization of society, the establishment of the rule of law, the right to strike, the establishment of independent courts, and guarantees of the freedom of speech, of the press, of organization. Socialism—even with a human face—was not a professed goal or explicit plat-

[28] Cf. Wollenberger, *Virus der Heuchler*, 67–70.
[29] See Templin and Weißhuhn, 'Initiative Frieden und Menschenrechte', on which this and the following paragraphs are based.
[30] Ibid. 154.   [31] BP, O-4 766.

form of the human rights activists in the IFM. Membership was left delib-
erately informal: anyone who signed a petition or joined in an activity was
deemed to 'belong'. There was no hierarchy or structure, and after the early
period in which there were three spokespeople—Peter Grimm, Ralf Hirsch,
and Wolfgang Templin—there were no formal positions in what remained
essentially a very small group. Active membership was probably only in the
region of thirty individuals. Several participants in the IFM were to be
founder members of Neues Forum, including Bärbel Bohley, Katja
Havemann, and Katrin and Frank Eigenfeld, while others were subsequently involved in other movements of the autumn revolution (Ulrike
Poppe in Demokratie Jetzt, and the Stasi IM Ibrahim Böhme in the Social
Democratic Initiative, for example).

The IFM produced the first truly *samizdat* publication of the GDR,
Grenzfall, on 19 June 1986 (previous quasi-political publications, such as
the ten-page 'information paper' *Schalom*, having been produced under the
auspices of the Church and stamped with the censorship-evading mark,
'Only for inner-Church use').[32] This first issue of *Grenzfall* was distributed
at the 1986 *Friedenswerkstatt* on 29 June 1986 in Berlin Lichtenberg,
despite the state's previous attempts at influencing the proceedings through
Church leaders. The Stasi report on this occasion notes rather grumpily
that, despite previous discussions with the Berlin state functionary responsible (Genosse Hoffmann), Generalsuperintendent Krusche's influence on
the gathering was minimal: his and others' 'influence on the way in which
the occasion went off was ... characterized by inconsistency and lack of
determination'. Templin, Hirsch, and Grimm were thus able to distribute
the '1st edition of an information leaflet with the title "Grenzfall" ' which
was an 'attempt ... to construct a "GDR-wide" information network for
all those active in the work of a political underground'.[33] In the later, post-
1989 view of Templin and Weißhuhn, the monthly publication of *Grenzfall*
proved to be 'a stimulus for further publications and independent periodicals within and beyond the Church, in other words a stimulus for the
development of a second public sphere, which was characteristic of the new
quality of activity and of networking of the groups in the second half of the
eighties'.[34]

By September 1987, human rights issues—particularly in connection with

---

[32] Cf. the exemplar of 17 Sept. 1984 in BP, O-4 766. On 12 Nov. 1984 Generalsuperintendent Krusche was officially warned of the dangers of permitting another issue of
Schalom to be produced.

[33] MfS, ZAIG, Z 3524, No. 313/86 (2 July 1986).

[34] Templin and Weißhuhn, 'Initiative Frieden und Menschenrechte', 154.

the desire to leave for the West—had become sufficiently burning that a new group was formed dealing solely with human rights, the Arbeitsgruppe Staatsbürgerschaftsrecht der DDR (Working Group for GDR Citizenship Rights). Although many individuals associated with this themselves desired to leave for the West, one of the main activists, Wolfgang Templin (also a founder member of the IFM), was more concerned to remain in the GDR and work for the improvement of human rights within the system. The tensions between those seeking exit, and those pressurizing for change within the GDR, were to grow in the ensuing months. Many political activists felt that demonstrations for reform were being effectively hijacked by people seeking to have themselves arrested and exiled—the quickest way of going west. Similarly, the Church leadership was caught between its professed aim of persuading people to stay and build a better GDR, and helping those in need of advice, care, and confession at times of personal distress and doubt. The advice centres which the Church set up were a perpetual focus of SED criticism, since the dual functions—individual counselling while yet supporting the view that it was better to stay than to leave—were often incompatible.

Peace initiatives between Church and state

Peace initiatives continued of course to be a major focus of concern—and a cover or pretext for a range of parallel and related discussions. There were a variety of types of meeting and demonstration, including meetings of local peace circles (*Friedenskreisen*), joint meetings under the heading of *Konkret für den Frieden*, regional peace workshops (*Friedenswerkstätte*), and the annual peace weeks (*Friedensdekaden*). Although the middle years of the 1980s represented something of a trough with respect to the peace movement, narrowly defined, these gatherings sustained a certain momentum of organization and discussion which was to prove important in the genesis of 1989.

The *Friedenswerkstatt* of 1985, for example, was not initially expected to be of much import, according to a report of a preliminary discussion on 11 June 1985 between the *Stellvertreter des Oberbürgermeisters für Inneres*, Comrade Hoffmann, and, on behalf of the Church, Manfred Stolpe and Generalsuperintendent Krusche: 'Stolpe explained that, for the planned peace workshop he feared, not fireworks (*Brisanz*) but rather "boredom". The excited agitation in respect of the peace question was over, and also many "agitators" were no longer in the country. Problems could only arise where Western journalists made a big deal of certain minor incidents.'[35] In

[35] BP, O-4 766, 'Information über ein Gespräch des Stellvertreters des Oberbürgermeisters für Inneres, Genossen Hoffmann, mit Konsistorialpräsident Stolpe und Generalsuperintendent Dr Krusche am 11.06.85'.

the event, there were indeed significantly fewer participants in 1985 than in the previous year: perhaps 1,800 in 1985 compared to around 3,000 in 1984.[36] The discussion was allegedly 'laborious and hard to keep going... The mood in the room corresponded with the general mood, questions were raised, without being able to answer them.' The state concluded that the Church leadership remained predominantly loyal; that negative forces were not gaining in support but were nevertheless becoming more outspoken and seeking to provoke confrontation; and that it must remain the state's strategy to stick to the current course of avoiding open confrontation or the creation of martyrs. It was this strategy of course that was to change in the later 1980s.

The significance of peace workshops was not, however, limited to discussion of peace policies in a narrow sense. They were in the event more important in the function they performed for the airing of a wide range of related topics, and in cross-fertilization between an ever-increasing number of groups. As we have seen, it was at the allegedly relatively unsuccessful 1985 peace workshop that the human rights movements were conceived. Many individuals and groups were able to meet in the context of church-protected peace events in ways which would have otherwise been impossible. The 1986 *Friedenswerkstatt* in the Erlöserkirche in Berlin, for example, attracted around 1,300 participants (a further drop in numbers from the previous year), mostly in their twenties.[37] Stalls were set up on the church premises, representing the following groups: the (pro-regime, officially supported) *Christliche Friedenskonferenz* (Christian Peace Conference, CFK); various peace groups from different areas and churches (Samariter, Erlöser, Pankow, Friedrichsfelde, Potsdam, Weißensee, Kaulsdorf, Pfarr, and Glauben); the *Niederländisch-Ökumenische Gemeinde* (Ecumenical Congregation of the Netherlands); Inkota; *Ärzte für den Frieden* (Doctors for Peace); *Homosexuelle Selbsthilfegruppe* (Homosexual Self-help Group); *Ökologiekreis Zion* (Zion Ecology Circle); *Lesbenkreis* (Lesbian Circle); *Frauen für den Frieden* (Women for Peace); *Wühlmäuse* ('voles'; *wühlen* also has overtones of subversive—underground in the metaphorical sense—activities); *Aktion Sühnezeichen* (Action Sign of Atonement); and the IFM, which had been expressly forbidden. The plethora of groups represented essentially reflected the increasing specialization and proliferation of grassroots activism in preceding years. This peace workshop included discussions of socialist democracy, human rights, and ecological questions, particularly with respect to the Chernobyl disaster.

[36] Ibid., 'Information zur "Friedenswerkstatt" am 30.06.85 in der Berliner Erlöserkirche'.
[37] Ibid., 'Erste Information über den Verlauf des "Friedenswerkstatt" am 29.06.1986 in der Berliner Erlöserkirche, 10.00–18.00'.

The state's report on the 1986 peace workshop drew rather negative conclusions in comparison to the more self-satisfied view of the previous year. Despite the fact that participants tended to seek individual solutions to perceived problems (personal austerity, use of the bicycle rather than the car, for example), the capacity of the Church leadership to control the event was clearly less than adequate. The event showed 'that Church leaders again promised more to state representatives than they were able to deliver'. It was also apparent 'that their influence on the participants in the peace workshop was minimal'.[38] Rather belatedly, the state was discovering that the Church was not organized on the lines of democratic centralism so familiar to SED and Stasi functionaries. It could not be simply assumed that decisions reached at the top would have any impact lower down: the Church could not, in fact, prove to be as useful as had been assumed as a coordinated (*gleichgeschaltet*) arm of the state.

The planned *Friedenswerkstatt* of 1987 was in the event forbidden, following pressures put on Günter Krusche in Berlin. Krusche's increasing compliance with the state—notwithstanding his helpfulness to individual dissidents—had already been evident in earlier years. A state report of 1981 on the question of human rights and the Church had at that time differentiated within the Church leadership and singled out Stolpe and Krusche as the most 'positive': 'Among the contributions currently available, the ones from OKR Stolpe and Dozent Günter Krusche are the most constructive.'[39] In the ensuing years Krusche and—to a much greater extent the always compliant Stolpe—had been learning the arts of cultivating a good relationship with secular authorities, even if this meant adopting a relatively heavy-handed stance towards activists within the Church.

Controversies over particular events and developments were reflected in wider theological controversies within the Church. What should be the role of the Church within socialism? Some Church leaders sought to emphasize that the Church was about salvation, not politics. Others found neat formulations for the difficulty of their role in opening church doors to all of God's creation while at the same time sustaining the Church's compliant and therefore relatively privileged role in relation to a state which certainly held the ultimate power of coercion. As Bishop Werner Leich put it: 'The Church is there for everyone, but not for everything.'[40] There were great differences

[38] BP, O-4 766, 5.

[39] BP, O-4 1943 (Feb. 1981), 'Zu einigen Problemen der gegenwärtigen Auseinandersetzung um die Menschenrechte unter besonderer Berücksichtigung der Haltung der Kirchen'.

[40] Quoted in Josef Schmid, 'Die politische Rolle der Evangelischen Kirchen in der DDR in den achtziger Jahren. Gratwanderung zwischen Opposition und Anpassung', in Müller-Enbergs, Schulz, and Wielgohs (eds.), *Von der Illegalität ins Parlament*, 357.

in different areas: the Church in Berlin-Brandenburg was constantly in confrontation with grass-roots groups, whereas in Leipzig and Saxony groups were on the whole less aggressive and cultivated better relationships with the local Church leaders.[41] Similarly, some Church leaders, such as Heino Falcke of Erfurt, were much more favourably inclined to reformist currents from below than were others, such as the very pro-Honecker Bishop Horst Gienke of Greifswald.[42]

In response to the ever more frustrating compliance of key members of the Church leadership with the state's directives and pressures, certain Christians decided to break away from the hierarchy's control. In May 1987, the formation by Vera Wollenberger and others of the 'Church from Below' (*Kirche von Unten*) was announced in the underground pamphlet *Fliegende Blätter* as an autonomous Church within the Church, on the grounds that 'the Church has built up a structure and hierarchy which curtails all spontaneity, personal initiative, and self-determination on the basis of alleged objective pressures'.[43] Along with other developments in the summer and autumn of 1987, this marked the beginning of the end of the state's experiment in using a *gleichgeschaltete* Church as a means of exerting political control.

But, in the meantime, the situation remained in the balance: in a sense, the compliance and continued commitment of the Church to maintaining a good relationship with the regime was the necessary precondition for the slow, admittedly constrained but nevertheless protected, nurturing of distinctive cultural and political currents. In addition to the activities of local peace groups, for example, there continued to be the well-coordinated annual peace weeks (*Friedensdekaden*). Each year, from 1980 onwards, the Church organized these peace weeks under a specific theme.[44] Reading

[41] As one dissident put it: 'We in Saxony have quite a good relationship with the Church leadership . . . Of course we don't let them exclude us, but we don't exclude either (Natürlich lassen wir uns nicht ausgrenzen, aber wir grenzen auch nicht aus)'. Quoted ibid. 357; see generally 357–8.

[42] Cf. IfGA, ZPA, IV B 2/14/69, Rat d. Bez. Erfurt, 'Beurteilung der Probstei Erfurt der Evangelischen Kirche der Kirchenprovinz Sachsen, Dr Heino Falcke': Falcke is criticized for his support of Solidarność, Konkret für den Frieden, and even Gorbachev[!]; he allegedly wants the GDR leadership to 'take over Soviet practices on the path to social renewal. His destructive utterances against official GDR policies of dialogue, peace, and security moved in this direction . . .'

[43] Quoted in Kroh (ed.), '*Freiheit ist immer Freiheit*', 48.

[44] 9–19 Nov. 1980: 'Frieden schaffen ohne Waffen'; 8–18 Nov. 1981: 'Gerechtigkeit Abrüstung Frieden'; 7–17 Nov. 1982: 'Angst Vertrauen Frieden'; 6–16 Nov. 1983: 'Frieden schaffen aus der Kraft der Schwachen'; 1–12 Nov. 1984: 'Leben gegen den Tod'; 10–20 Nov. 1985: 'Frieden wächst aus Gerechtigkeit'; 9–19 Nov. 1986: 'Friede sei mit Euch'; 8–18 Nov. 1987: 'Miteinander leben'; 6–16 Nov. 1988: 'Friede den Fernen und Friede den Nahen'.

through the materials collated in preparation for these annual gatherings, what is perhaps most striking is the highly religious tone, flavour, and content of the documents. The biblical references, prayers, and expressions of a Christian world-view are overwhelming: the power of prayer is clearly rated more highly than overt political organization. But there is also a sense of humour and recognition of worldly realities: the 1987 *Friedensdekade*, for example, produced a postcard with a cartoon of a mouse, at ankle height between two large pairs of aggressively confrontational jackboots, hopefully holding up a placard saying 'Frieden' (peace) and a flower.[45] This slightly anxious but intrinsically optimistic mouse, determinedly demonstrating its position against all the odds, stood as a symbol of what the Christian peace activists were seeking to do.

Friedensdekaden no doubt were of great individual interest to participants, whose personal faith and commitment must have been considerably strengthened in meetings with others. But at the same time these meetings were on the whole relatively easily controlled by the state, through the Church leadership.[46] With prior pressures exerted by state and SED functionaries, combined with a critical presence of Stasi and police officials, and the adequate distribution among the participants of 'reliable social forces', it was possible at the very least to ensure that any critical voices were not *öffentlichkeitswirksam* (had no public impact), that there were no public disturbances or *besondere Vorkommnisse* (notable incidents), and that there were no reports in the Western media. Even better from the regime's point of view, it was on occasion possible to ensure that in place of 'system-indifferent' comments (which did not distinguish on the *Animal Farm* lines of 'NATO weapons bad, Warsaw Pact weapons good'), some positive case could be articulated in favour of actually existing socialism. The observation and control processes thus veered between damage limitation exercises and the attempt to influence events in a 'positive' direction, as desired by the state.

The state's attempted harnessing of the Church is well expressed in a comment on preparations for the 1985 *Friedensdekade*: 'In the period of preparation and working up materials for this year's peace week, realistic forces in the leadership groups of the BEK and the regional Churches were able to achieve a further incorporation of the peace week in the overall framework of constructive Church peace activities. In this way, the leeway for the negative forces was further limited . . .'[47] For the most part, these

---

[45] BP, O-4 1431.

[46] Cf. the reports in BP, O-4 1432.

[47] BP, O-4 1433, 'Information zur sechsten Friedensdekade des Bundes der Ev. Kirchen in der DDR, vom 10.11.1985–20.11.1985'.

preparations reaped the appropriate reward. In some areas attendances were low, and the course of events was 'objective, calm, and accorded with state expectations . . .'. State organs were 'geared towards immediate intervention so that during the peace week the existing good state/Church relationship would not be burdened, but rather secured and enhanced'. Occasionally church services attracted only older, regular members of local congregations; and interest in some rural areas appears often to have been close to non-existent.[48]

Nevertheless, the odd event escaped even the closest state control. On 12 November 1985, for example, in Eppelmann's church in Berlin, West German journalists and television reporters witnessed the singer Stefan Krawczyk performing songs with lyrics critical of the fortified borders and travel restrictions of the GDR. On the same occasion, the invited Pastor Tschiche's 'massively demagogic and clearly antisocialist' lecture distinguished three possible modes of response to prevailing political circumstances, worth quoting for its highly apposite analysis of the alternatives open to citizens of the GDR who were not blinded by regime propaganda:

—retreat into the inner sphere (niche society)
—infiltration of social institutions in order to alter structures (but has the disadvantage that it might in the process stabilize conditions),
—rejection of current structures, search for new lifestyles, freeing oneself from dependence, training in the 'upright walk', publicly resisting those in power. (The speaker identified himself with this course of action.)[49]

It was precisely because small numbers of people chose the third option, in preference to the widely prevalent first and second forms of response, that the stability of the GDR began to be shaken in the course of the 1980s. And in 1988–9 increasing numbers opted for the third approach, at the same time as the Church leadership and the state began to lose control.

Environmentalist movements

Closely related to concerns about the threat of nuclear war were worries about the use of nuclear energy in power stations—a worry which was mightily fuelled by the Chernobyl disaster of 1986, on which more below. But environmentalism was not limited solely to the threat of nuclear annihilation from whatever source: there was increasing evidence of the ad-

---

[48] Cf. the Neubrandenburg report on the 1984 *Friedensdekade*: 'In rural areas the "peace week" plays virtually no role at all' (BP, O-4 1433).
[49] BP, O-4 1433, 'Schnellinformation über gravierend negative Aussagen in der Veranstaltung der Samaritergemeinde zur Friedensdekade am 12.11.85' (Abt. Kirchenfragen, Berlin, 13 Nov. 1985).

verse consequences on human health and longevity, on perinatal mortality rates and the incidence of chronic diseases, of the regime's general disregard for health and safety issues if these were to be at the expense of economic growth. The evidence of mounting environmental damage was so severe that in 1980 the state itself founded the official *Gesellschaft für Natur und Umwelt* (GNU, Society for Nature and the Environment) to deal with growing public concern. But at the same time it sought to suppress the evidence which formed the basis for any rational response: in 1982 the state issued an order banning the publication of any data relating to the increasingly deleterious environmental situation.

Even without any hard facts, individuals living in the GDR could readily be distressed by the sheer visibility—and not only visibility, but also smell, even taste—of environmental pollution. One environmentalist, Michael Beleites, comments that it was not only contact with Church groups that awoke his concerns about the environment. Even as a child and youth, the contradictions were all too evident: 'The puddles at the marsh, in which the toads spawned, were always covered with a dull film of dust, the nightly song of the nightingale was drowned by the permanent droning of the turbines from the power station and the din of briquette moulding, and the scent of the summer meadows in blossom was mixed with the smell of gas from the smouldering works.'[50] And any Western visitor to the GDR would have been struck by the ubiquitous smell, flavour, even taste on the tongue, of brown coal (lignite) dust, and by the almost lurid, incandescent glow of chemical pollution afflicting the sky in the most polluted areas, such as the region around Bitterfeld and Halle.[51]

For all the state's official concern about the environment, the real strategy of the SED in the 1980s was to try to co-opt, deflect, or destroy unofficial environmentalist movements while continuing to pursue economic growth at the expense of environmental concerns. As one state document put it:

---

[50] M. Beleites, *Untergrund. Ein Konflikt mit der Stasi in der Uran-Provinz* (Berlin: BasisDruck, 1992), 32.

[51] After the fall of the communist regime, one wit daubed the following slogan on the crumbling walls of the inner courtyard of a typically gloomy and decrepit tenement building in Berlin, which by most Western standards would have been designated unfit for human habitation: 'Ruinen schaffen ohne Waffen' (make ruins without weapons, a pun on the previous peace movement slogan, 'Frieden schaffen ohne Waffen'). For further details of environmental pollution in the GDR, cf. Joan DeBardeleben, '"The Future Has Already Begun." Environmental Damage and Protection in the GDR', in M. Rueschemeyer and C. Lemke (eds.), *The Quality of Life in the German Democratic Republic* (New York: M. E. Sharpe, 1989).

We must assume that certain economically necessary measures (particularly in the exploitation and opening up of resources) cannot be realized without pollution or destruction of the environment. Then there will be . . . reactions from the population . . . Especially since environmental consciousness is growing among broad circles of the GDR population and ecological questions will continue to form a focal point of ideological disputes.[52]

Western scholars have previously assumed that environmentalist movements were in some way less politically threatening than the peace movement, since state and environmentalists allegedly had common interests on which they could co-operate. It was thought that purely technical considerations allowed ecologically concerned citizens to work alongside environmental experts—who were often state functionaries—on common projects.[53] It is now clear that this was far from being a straightforward, self-evident arrangement based on questions of technical expertise. Rather, it was a politically motivated strategy for the *channelling* and political *containment* of the energies of environmentally aware citizens, specifically designed and executed by the state with characteristic cynicism. The East German authorities sought to deflect environmentalists into small-scale, time-consuming, narrowly focused, and state-controlled projects, and to bring them under the wing of the state-sponsored environmental society, the *Gesellschaft für Natur und Umwelt.*

One of the state's main concerns, reflected in innumerable documents, was the desire to ensure that all discussions were to remain 'objective' (*sachlich*), putting the state's interpretation of the 'facts' and separating any concern over environmental issues from possible public 'defamation' of the GDR, or independent political organization from below.[54] Their greatest fear was the political impact of uncontrolled environmentalism:

But precisely in the effort to understand the essence of the ecology problem and to arrive at basic pronunciations on how to overcome it, a range of politically false and negative declarations are arrived at on the basis of petty bourgeois starting points, neutral or system-indifferent basic positions, and a markedly bourgeois conception of democracy.[55]

The 'familiar politically negative forces within and outside the Church' were trying to 'misuse' this: 'in relation to the question of environmental protec-

---

[52] BP, O-4 799, 'Information zur weiteren Arbeit gegenüber dem Kirchlichen Forschungsheim Wittenberg' (3 Dec. 1985).
[53] Cf. Merrill E. Jones, 'Origins of the East German Environmental Movement', *German Studies Review*, 16: 2 (May 1993), 235–64.
[54] Cf. e.g. BP, O-4 799 (4 Aug. 1988), 3.
[55] Ibid., 19 Nov. 1984, 5.

tion they are attempting to revive the notion of the Church as watchman *vis-à-vis* the state.'[56] The Church leadership and synods had been forced to consider environmental issues, which now appeared to be firmly on the agenda for discussion. It was the task of the state, in conjunction with the Church leadership, to ensure that the 'realistic-loyal' (i.e. pro-state) forces retained the upper hand, and that a process of polarization and isolation of 'hostile-negative forces' was set in motion.

In the event, intervention in the environmentalist movements achieved varying degrees of success. The main Church environmentalist movement, embodied in the Kirchliche Forschungsheim Wittenberg (KFH), directed by Dr Peter Gensichen, was to a considerable degree co-opted and its importance as a centre of dissidence defused. Other environmentalist currents were more successful in resisting the influences of Stasi and state, but were nevertheless split and savaged by Stasi policies. None, however, was completely destroyed, and the organizational networks and political strategies and experience built up in the course of the 1980s were to prove important when the opportunity for change finally came in 1989.

A case-study of the Kirchliche Forschungsheim Wittenberg proves extremely instructive in examining and illustrating the methods and tactics employed by state, party, and Stasi, and the conditions of their success. The combination of sophisticated techniques of observation and influence with a relatively compliant personality and a high-profile but potentially easily threatened Church institution in Wittenberg led to a higher degree of success, as far as the SED was concerned, than was possible with the more thorny problems of the less institutionalized groups led by more prickly personalities in Berlin.

The ecclesiastical research institute in Wittenberg had been founded as long ago as 1927, as the *Forschungsheim für Weltanschauungskunde*, to explore the relationship of Christianity to nature. In 1971, theologians and Church leaders asked the KFH to bring environmental issues more directly into its remit, and in 1974 Dr Peter Gensichen began work on these questions at the institute. As Director of the KFH from 1975, Gensichen became increasingly active, not just as a researcher but also as a publicizer and organizer. As a state report put it: 'With the arrival of Dr Gensichen . . . the thematic scope of the institution began to change. Alongside a continuing interest in traditional themes (evolution and faith in creation), questions of ecology and environmental protection began to be

[56] BP, O-4 799 (19 Nov. 1984), 6.

more strongly highlighted.'[57] In 1980 the institute produced a pamphlet entitled 'The Earth Is To Be Saved (*Die Erde ist zu retten*)'; and from 1980 onwards, it produced what was essentially the first ecological newsletter in the GDR, the semi-annual 'Letters' (*Briefe*). Gensichen also mounted a travelling exhibition shown in churches, and organized a number of meetings (in April 1983, June 1984, and April 1985) to which representatives from all over the GDR travelled, as well as demonstrations of alternative, ecologically sound lifestyles, such as the annual weekend entitled 'Mobile Without a Car (*Mobil ohne Auto*)'.

The GDR authorities were clearly concerned about the potential of this centre, and adopted a number of strategies to observe and influence the development of its activities. At the same time, they sought to work on the Director of the KFH to ensure that he would, indirectly, carry out much of this political work for them:

It is necessary to strengthen the realistic positions of Dr Gensichen by commentaries and discussions on technical and political questions of environmental and nature conservation, in their totality as well as in relation to specific questions (in so far as this is possible), and in relation to philosophical and ethical problems in this area; and to encourage the acquisition of new insights [by Dr Gensichen], with the objective of ensuring that the insights attained in this way are reflected in the work of the KFH and so become effective in Church politics.[58]

In 1984, Peter Gensichen had still been evaluated as 'not very constructive'. For example, in the context of a discussion on environmental questions, Gensichen had tried 'on the basis of the alleged non-publication of the number of foggy days in the Halle area to demonstrate that, through the refusal to release information, insecurity and anxiety grew among the population'.[59] The state had to some extent 'put in train a process of growing awareness on the part of Dr Gensichen'. Nevertheless, 'at the same time it became clear that it is necessary to engage in well-directed political-ideological work with Dr Gensichen, to help him to reach further insights'[!].[60] Despite the fact that 'Dr Gensichen, and with him the KFH, continue to cling to a range of politically false and problematic orientations and methods'—in particular, 'the continued goal of coordinating Church ecology groups'—on the whole developments suggested 'that he, and with

[57] Ibid., 'Information zur Tätigkeit des Kirchlichen Forschungsheimes Wittenberg (KFH) und Schlußfolgerungen für die staatlichen Reaktionen gegenüber dem Forschungsheim' (19 Nov. 1984). Cf. also Jones, 'East German Environmental Movement'.

[58] BP, O-4 799, 'Information zur weiteren Arbeit gegenüber dem Kirchlichen Forschungsheim Wittenberg' (3 Dec. 1985), 2.

[59] BP, O-4 968, Information of 31 Aug. 1984. OKR Ziegler, Präses Wahrmann, and Präses Böttcher, by contrast, 'belonged to that group of realistic Church office-holders...'

[60] BP, O-4 799 (19 Nov. 1984), 10, 11.

him the activities of the Kirchliche Forschungsheim, are capable of being influenced in our direction'. Again and again this report stresses the need to emphasize 'co-operation on practical or related matters (*sachlich und sachbezogene Zusammenarbeit*)' as the best means of co-option.

The close co-operation of the Stasi and the state and Church functionaries is clearly demonstrated by subsequent developments. A Stasi report of May 1985 on a meeting of environmental groups in the KFH on 26–8 April 1985 comments favourably on Gensichen's rather cautious line, and his aversion to engaging in any overly provocative activities. The report makes the usual final suggestions: that there should be appropriate meetings between state (not Stasi) and Church functionaries at the relevant levels, to prevent the 'hostile-negative forces' from creating new structures, to continue 'the process of differentiation', to isolate the most radical spirits, and to involve other 'confessionally involved persons in practical measures' of environmental work under state and party control.[61] By March 1986, the allotted state functionary was clearly doing his best:

The discussion had the general objective of making contact with Dr Gensichen and creating a basis from which further political influence on him would be possible, in other words, to generate confidence. For this reason, certain questions were not pursued further, nor was he forced into foregrounding any statements of position.[62]

In August 1986, although the state functionary felt that it was clearly necessary to continue to work on Gensichen, the latter was in any event of his own accord requesting further discussions.[63]

By the spring of 1986, the role of the KFH appeared to be moving in the state's desired direction, partly as a result of Gensichen's apparent pliability and caution. A Stasi report on the meeting of representatives of environmental groups of the Protestant Churches which met at the KFH on 18–20 April comments on improvements since earlier years:

This sort of annual meeting has been held since 1983 and up till now revealed the intentions of reactionary forces in the Church and other hostile-negative forces of bringing together 'environmentalist groups' organizationally in the sense of a so-called alternative environmentalist movement and of creating a degree of internal unity.

This no longer appeared so threatening in 1986:

It has become clear that the constructive and offensive policies of the party and government in environmental questions, and the state's related conception of incor-

---

[61] MfS, Z 3458.
[62] BP, O-4 799, 'Vermerk zu einem Gespräch mit Dr Gensichen, Leiter des Kirchlichen Forschungsheim, am 7.03.1986 in Wittenberg' (17 Mar. 1986), 5.
[63] Ibid., 'Vermerk zu einem Gespräch mit dem Leiter des Kirchlichen Forschungsheimes Wittenberg, Dr Gensichen, am 27.08.1986 in Wittenberg' (9 Sept. 1986).

porating Christians with an environmental consciousness and commitment, have found a positive response among the vast majority of Church 'environmental groups'.[64]

Gensichen appeared to be acting entirely in the state's interests by this time. He advised against the groups becoming involved in the *Konkret für den Frieden V* activities planned for 1987; rather, it should be left to individuals to decide whether they wanted to participate or not. He also advised against confrontation with the state: for example, there should not be a large cycling demonstration (*Radsternfahrt*) but rather a number of smaller, less noticeable actions. No decisions were taken as to whether there should be a follow-up meeting in 1987. The publication of the environmentalist periodical *Anstöße*, which until 1985 had been produced by the KFH, should be moved to Berlin. All in all, the Stasi were rather pleased with their indirect influence on what was happening:

Through the consistent implementation of the state's plan for incorporating environmentally conscious and committed Christians, the ground was increasingly swept
from under the feet of even those hostile-negative forces who were trying to misuse
the 'environmental work' of the Church for the formation of hostile-negative groupings and the construction of an alternative conservation movement.[65]

The report concludes with a very typical proposal about the strategies necessary to continue to influence matters in the desired directions. Measures include: the continued engaging of Christians in state-run activities and organizations; the use of 'confessionally committed people' to influence environmental activities into the directions desired and controlled by the state, for example under the aegis of the *Kulturbund*; and to continue 'the process of differentiation' and isolation of the 'hostile-negative (*feindlich-negative*)' forces in the Church. While the former two strategies appear to have been relatively successful, the latter badly misfired as far as the state was concerned.

By 1987, the attempts of the state to influence Gensichen were quite clearly having the desired effect. One report concludes that 'in the two-hour discussion Dr Gensichen appeared visibly more receptive and active than in previous meetings. Altogether, the discussion proceeded in an open and constructive atmosphere.'[66] The report's final suggestions—apart from de-

---

[64] MfS, ZAIG, Z 3512, No. 225/86, 'Erkenntnisse im Zusammenhang mit einem erneuten Treffen von Vertretern sogen. [*sic*] Umweltgruppen evangelischer Kirchen in der DDR von 18. bis 20. April 1986 im Kirchlichen Forschungsheim Wittenberg/Halle' (14 May 1986).

[65] Ibid.

[66] BP, O-4 799, 'Vermerk zum Gespräch mit Dr Gensichen, Leiter des Kirchlichen Forschungsheimes in Wittenberg (KFH), am 28.05.1987, 15.00 bis 17.00 Uhr im Kirchlichen Forschungsheim' (12 June 1987), 6.

tailed tips on following up certain leads given by Gensichen in the course of the discussion—include the need to keep working on Gensichen.

It is not suggested here that Gensichen was in any way compromised by these discussions; he was probably not even fully aware of what lay behind many of them. This is in all probability a case of a genuinely committed, environmentally concerned Christian who was prepared to listen to what he considered to be reasonable arguments on specific issues. His own expertise, in combination with his institutional responsibilities, led him to adopt what was in the end the sort of moderate strategy which the state found least threatening and most easily controlled. This was not the case with some more radical spirits, who pressed their environmental concerns from rather more marginal positions in the Church.

The main competitor to the KFH was the Umweltbibliothek (UB, or Environmental Library) founded in the summer of 1986 in the East Berlin Zionsgemeinde. Two of the founders had suffered a ban on their careers (*Berufsverbot*) as a result of nonconformist behaviour, and were found employment as janitor and caretaker by Pastor Hans Simon at the Zionskirche—a very typical illustration of the ways in which dissenters found themselves in the environs of the Church. Originally conceived as a communication and information centre, collecting data and publications on environmental matters (with help from the West in the person of Roland Jahn, a peace activist who had been deported in 1983), from August 1986 the UB produced its own publication, the *Umweltblättter*.

The UB was by no means an entirely harmonious organization. There were internal tensions with respect to both strategic considerations and personality differences, which were adroitly exploited by Stasi infiltrators (IMs).[67] The suggestion made by Carlo Jordan in October 1987 that a network of local groups should be founded met with considerable opposition, and led ultimately to a split in the movement. On 10 January 1988 a number of individuals founded a loose association known as the *Arche*, with a new publication entitled *Arche Nova*, seeking to create a network within the GDR and the cultivation of contacts with Western and other Eastern European environmentalist movements. Other environmentalists disliked and disapproved of this more open confrontation with, or provocation of, the East German state.

Nevertheless, the proliferation of groups was associated with a related growth of political debate and the expansion of an incipient 'public sphere', the precondition for the emergence of a nascent 'civil society' in the East

---

[67] Cf. Jones, 'East German Environmental Movement'.

Germany of the 1980s. Many groups sought to produce publications, vehicles for a broader debate (comparable in importance, perhaps, to the expansion of publication of newspapers and periodicals in the eighteenth century, the classic period of the emergence of a 'bourgeois civil society' in Germany). The publication of *Grenzfall*, for example, by Templin, Hirsch, and Grimm was explicitly conceived as an attempt to create an information network for subversive forces across the GDR.

Moreover, the inescapability and ubiquity of environmental concerns was brought home to increasing numbers of people by the Chernobyl disaster of 26 April 1986. The relatively anodyne reporting of this event in the GDR media (which sought to propagate the view that no East German nuclear reactor could possibly suffer the same fate, due to allegedly greater technological prowess and efficiency) was counterbalanced, of course, by the extensive coverage of the after-effects of Chernobyl beamed over to the GDR on West German television. There was simply no possibility of disguising the seriousness of the disaster or covering up its consequences. Environmentalists and peace activists joined forces in producing a document under the heading 'Tschernobyl wirkt überall (Chernobyl Has Effects Everywhere)', and a petition protesting to the government. International links also became more important to many activists: there were first contacts with the Eastern European movement Greenway in 1986, and in September 1987 some East Germans attended a Greenway meeting in Cracow, Poland. But the environmentalist currents emerging in the GDR were by no means necessarily political allies of one another.

The degree of success of the Stasi in splitting the environmentalist movements is, for example, illustrated by the negative comments made by Gensichen on the UB in 1988:

His criticisms concentrate on lack of objectivity, cheap publicity stunts, lack of technical substance, and not least a lack of religious/theological substance. All their activities amount to nothing much, as far as he is concerned. This is also evident in the style of the 'Umweltblätter'. He ... knows that there are forces active in the 'Umweltbibliothek' who really only want to use the Church as a cover. At the moment there are apparently quite enormous disputes between them ... In his opinion the Umweltbibliothek will, sooner or later, fall apart as a result of internal quarrelling.[68]

A degree of—perhaps?—jealousy was evident in a further negative comment: 'Unfortunately, because of the events at the Zion Church and the Western media coverage, the impression had arisen that the Um-

[68] BP, O-4 799, 'Vermerk zu einem Gespräch mit dem Leiter des Kirchlichen Forschungsheimes Wittenberg Dr Gensichen am 19.5.1988 in Wittenberg' (24 May 1988), 1.

weltbibliothek embodied the real environmental work of the Church in the GDR.'[69] Clearly by this time Gensichen himself was entirely 'objective' (*sachbezogen*) in the state's sense.

But the splitting of the movements had neither removed their basis, nor prevented their growth. If anything, Stasi strategies had ultimately aided a process of political education, as more and more East Germans learnt the complex arts of self-organization and political pressure group work under dictatorial conditions. They learnt techniques of information gathering and dissemination, they created bonds and—sometimes fragile—friendships across localities, and they developed some vision of what would make a better society. Much of this vision was vague and general in character— more open government, more democratic participation, more concern for peace and the environment, more respect for the dignity of human individuality and difference. The specifics of policy and political platforms did not emerge until the autumn of 1989: what was important at this time was the growth of coherent, articulate, widespread pressure for reform. Perhaps most importantly, the political activists of the 1980s acquired the courage of their convictions, to use the Quaker phrase.[70] Their concern was sufficient to engage in major personal risks in the pursuit of a better future.

Moreover, there were some grounds for realistic hopes in this respect. Following the accession of Gorbachev to power in 1985, many believed that the GDR too would begin to engage in a process of domestic restructuring and democratization. Despite the obvious resistance of Honecker and the old guard to any real policies of change—and the oft-repeated dismissive remarks about 'neighbours changing their wallpaper', summarizing the official view that there was absolutely no need for change in the GDR— there were nevertheless brief glimpses of apparent liberalization in the mid-1980s. Particularly in the period leading up to Honecker's visit—with all due pomp and ceremony, as respected head of state—to West Germany in 1987, there were public measures designed to emphasize just how liberal and open the GDR allegedly was. The early months of 1987, for example, saw a wave of visas for Western visits and emigration, allowing unpre-

---

[69] BP, O-4 799, 'Vermerk zu einem Gespräch mit dem Leiter des Kirchlichen Forschungsheimes Wittenberg Dr Gensichen am 19.5.1988 in Wittenberg' (24 May 1988), 2.

[70] And despite their tiny numbers, certain Quakers were rather active in these movements: Hans Misselwitz, the Quaker husband of Pastor Ruth Misselwitz of the Friedenskreis Pankow, for example, fostered contacts with Western Quakers such as Eva Pinthus. So did many reformist members of the establishment Protestant Church who had an interest in active methods of non-violence; even at the leadership level, Bishop Heino Falcke of Erfurt was open to such currents. Many characteristics of peace circles—the egalitarianism, openness, and emphasis on active non-violence—have distinctive Quaker overtones and parallels.

cedented numbers of East Germans to travel to the West on pretexts which in previous years would not have merited any consideration. The Berlin 750th anniversary celebrations of 1987 were similarly designed to foster the view of the GDR as a forward-looking, progressive, and increasingly tolerant society.

The culmination of this period came with the Olof Palme peace march of September 1987. For the first time in East German history, unofficial placards were carried alongside the official banners of the state organizations. The authorities were clearly somewhat ill at ease with this unprecedented experiment in pluralism. As the First Secretary of the Bezirksleitung Potsdam put it, when evaluating the section of the march from Ravensbrück to Sachsenhausen on 2 to 4 September 1987, the whole situation was extremely difficult to handle. Determined to ensure that, under the spotlight of international publicity on this most sensitive lap of the international march, nothing should go amiss, the Potsdam First Secretary requested the Church leaders to remove the unofficial banners from view. Given the fact 'that the grass-roots groups simply take no notice of injunctions coming from leading Church personalities', this was unsuccessful; he then made a direct appeal to individual banner-bearers to drop out (even less successfully), and at the same time sought to ensure that official party and mass organization banners were displayed in full prominence.[71] The party's own standard-bearers appear to have had a little difficulty on occasion in exercising a degree of tolerance, but in the event the march went very peacefully and, on some accounts, rather fruitfully.[72]

The experiment could have been a harbinger of incipient liberalization within the GDR, in the broader context of Honecker's Western visit and the joint paper between the SED and the West German SPD. Had Honecker chosen to retire gracefully in the autumn of 1987, the history of the GDR might have been written a little differently (although it is likely that its ultimate end would have been much the same). Certainly Honecker's own role in history would have been evaluated less harshly. But, in the event, the brief thaw very soon came to a dramatic end. The wave of hope accompanying the Olof Palme peace march—evident among many SED functionaries as well as dissident political activists—was soon dashed by the events of the following months. From late 1987 until the summer and autumn of 1989,

---

[71] SAPMO-BArch, IV B 2/14/70, 'Zur politischen Wertung des im Bezirk Potsdam verlaufenden Abschnittes des Olof-Palme-Friedensmarsches von 02.09 bis 04.09.1987 von Ravensbrück nach Sachsenhausen aus kirchenpolitischer Sicht'.

[72] Cf. also Gerhard Rein, *Die protestantische Revolution 1987–1990* (Berlin: Wichern Verlag, 1990), 19–23.

the fragile balance of compromise and accommodation began to tip, until finally events swung out of control, beyond even the capacity of the apparently omnipotent and omniscient Stasi to salvage. It is to the combination of repression and resistance which characterized the closing two years of the East German communist dictatorship that we now turn.

Repression, resistance, and destabilization, 1987–1989

The political activists had been a force for destabilization and change within the GDR throughout the 1980s; in the closing two years their voices were heard more forcibly, their actions were less easily contained and constrained. The retreatist majority of the population, on the other hand, had for the most part been relatively quiescent politically, although throughout the 1980s (and particularly in 1984 and 1987) there was a constant stream of people applying for visas to leave for the West. Those seeking to leave by less orthodox routes were, however, deterred by the very real risk of death if caught trying to escape over the border illegally. Both sorts of disaffection became very much more important, in different ways, in the course of the two years from late 1987 to the autumn of 1989. And, at the same time, the forces of repression in the final years of the GDR became very much more open and confrontational: the situation was becoming more tense, or *zugespitzt*.

A convenient starting date for this last period of destabilization is provided by a particular incident, which nicely illustrates the change in climate after the moment of hope in the late summer of 1987. On 24 November 1987 a raid by the Stasi was carried out on the Umweltbibliothek. This was to be what is conventionally called a 'set-up': the Stasi had arranged, through an IM, that a copy of *Grenzfall*, the publication of the non-Church-based IFM, would be printed that night, illegally, on the Church-owned printer of the UB. Then, when the premises of the UB were raided, this illegal material would be found and appropriate charges brought. The raid went ahead as planned: unfortunately for the state, however, the Trabi which was to bring the incriminating material to the UB premises—owned by the Stasi informer, but clearly more sympathetic to the dissidents' cause—broke down on the way and failed to deliver the material in time.[73] The UB and the IFM publicized the raid, which proved to be more embarrassing than helpful for the SED and the Stasi.[74]

[73] Jones, 'East German Environmental Movement', 252–4.
[74] Stefan Wolle describes this as constituting the first 'cracks in the concrete of state socialism'; Stefan Wolle, 'Der Weg in den Zusammenbruch: Die DDR vom Januar bis zum Oktober 1989', in Eckard Jesse and Armin Mitter (eds.), *Die Gestaltung der deutschen Einheit* (Bonn: Bundeszentrale für politische Bildung, 1992), 78.

The consequences were to shift the relations between state and activists into a new gear. Activists mounted public demonstrations of support for those who had been arrested, including *Mahnwachen* (vigils of admonition or warning). The immediate effect was the return of Church property and the release of those who had been arrested, although in the longer term the Stasi determined to destroy the UB. A partial success from the state's point of view was scored when some environmentalists split from the UB to form the *Arche* in January 1988. The activities of this group were partially subverted by the tactics of certain IMs who were members, such as Henry Schramm of Halle, while another Stasi IM, Pastor Erler in Leipzig, successfully subverted attempts to establish a UB in Leipzig comparable to that in Berlin.[75] But on the whole the effect of the incident was to polarize the situation and to arouse dissident forces into more concerted political efforts and open demonstrations of protest. An invisible threshold of overcoming internal barriers of fear and seeking new ways of moving forward was gradually being crossed.

There are a number of as yet unexplained and curious features of the incidents of late 1987, suggesting some lack of coordination or communication between the Stasi and state authorities. For example, the lawyer acting for the dissidents, Wolfgang Schnur (who was later revealed as a Stasi informer) announced on 4 December at a large meeting in the Zionskirche that the Generalstaatsanwaltschaft had said that the proceedings against the arrested activists were to be suspended; the Staatsanwaltschaft, however, denied this.[76] Clearly somewhere an intended deal had not quite been clinched in time for public announcement.

Similarly, there is a degree of mystery over events surrounding an earlier meeting in the Zionskirche. Young people leaving the church after a concert service on 17 October were attacked by a group of neo-Nazis, described in the report compiled for the then security chief Egon Krenz as '30–40 "Skinheads" dressed in black' yelling slogans such as 'death to the Red Front (*Rot Front verrecke*)', 'Jews out of German churches', 'Jewish swine, Jewish sows (*Judenschweine, Judensäue*)', and 'Sieg heil'.[77] While Egon Krenz's office collated an extensive file on the issue, dissidents were somewhat disconcerted by the lack of any visible police intervention or control of these 'rowdies' and suspected that the neo-Nazis were acting, if not at the

[75] Jones, 'East German Environmental Movement'.
[76] SAPMO-BArch, Büro Egon Krenz, IV 2/2.039/312.
[77] See ibid., IV 2/2.039/191, for a report on the concert itself at which two *Punkmusikformationen* (Firma from East Berlin, and Element of Crime from West Berlin) had performed to around 300 young people, without official permission and advertised only through word of mouth; and ibid., Büro Egon Krenz, Abteilung für Sicherheitsfragen, IV 2/2.039/313, on neo-Nazi activities.

behest, then at least with the implicit or even explicit approval, of the Stasi, whose work of intimidation of dissidents they appeared to carry out rather well.[78] It was all the more incensing, therefore, when Vera Wollenberger found herself and others involved in the *Mahnwachen* implicitly coupled with neo-Nazis in an article in the relatively mass circulation newspaper *Junge Welt* on 12 December 1987. Wollenberger took the unprecedented step of suing the editor for defamation.[79]

In a climate of increasing tension, some individuals involved in the by now incipient citizens' movement (*Bürgerbewegung*) determined to make use of the annual Luxemburg–Liebknecht parade in January 1988 to demonstrate their concern for greater freedom in the GDR. The problem of demonstrating for change within the GDR was, however, increasingly complicated by the concomitant movement of those seeking a fast exit to the West, who were to some extent hijacking dissident activities for their own ends. The former sought, through subtle tactics of pressure and demonstration, to effect changes within the GDR, while the latter had a vested interest in more dramatic gestures designed to have themselves arrested and exiled—the most rapid means of successfully leaving for the West. There were increasing tensions within dissident groups, as suspicions were aroused—often either instigated or nurtured by Stasi IMs—as to the underlying motives of different individuals with respect to the likely effects of proposed tactics.

In the event, in January 1988 a somewhat uncomfortable quotation from Rosa Luxemburg—'Freedom is always the freedom to think differently (*Freiheit ist immer die Freiheit der Andersdenkenden*)'—which was excluded from the official SED canon of the communist heritage was nevertheless displayed on a dissident banner. Despite the state's extensive preparations to ensure that the demonstration was not subject to any unwonted political disturbance, the dreaded *Öffentlichkeitswirksamkeit* (public impact) of dissident activities was achieved.[80] But the repressive

[78] Cf. Wollenberger, *Virus der Heuchler*, 83–4: 'As we discovered afterwards, the Volkspolizei . . . had installed observation points in side streets, but had not intervened or only intervened too late . . . The links between Stasi, army, police, and neo-Nazis have not yet been investigated . . . But after the Skinhead attack [I had] several more experiences of meetings of the citizens' movement being threatened by neo-Nazi attacks, and these threats often led to the Parish Council of the relevant congregation withdrawing permission for meetings out of fear of the consequences of such an attack.'

[79] Ibid. 87–90.

[80] On the security preparations, including plans to remove potential demonstrators from the crowds, cover up unofficial placards, and hand over individuals to MfS forces, see the report of the then Berlin party boss, later would-be reformer-in-waiting, Günter Schabowski, to the then security chief Egon Krenz: 'Maßnahmen zur Sicherung eines störungsfreien Verlaufs der Kampfdemonstrationen am 17. Januar 1988', SAPMO-BArch, IV 2/2.039/312 (14 Jan. 1988).

response was massive. Large numbers of people were arrested; many were held without charges being brought for considerable periods of time, and the most prominent dissidents were sent into exile, willingly or unwillingly.[81]

This was in fact the beginning of the end. Ever larger numbers of people became involved in organized, non-violent demonstrations of sympathy and solidarity with the dissidents who had been treated so harshly on this occasion. Candlelit meetings, concerts, and vigils in churches became a standard method of demonstrating opposition to the repressive measures of the state. In Leipzig, for example, Monday prayer services became an important regular event—long before they were to become the highly public starting-point for street demonstrations in the autumn of 1989. All over the GDR, there was a growing sense that, somehow, there would have to be changes; and that people were increasingly willing to organize, discuss, and pressurize for change.

The relations between Church and state—the implicit compromise in the by now overstretched 'spirit of 6.3.78'—began to break down. Although Manfred Stolpe continued to play an essentially obsequious role, acutely irritating to individual dissidents (although the consequences may well have been beneficial for the citizens' movement in the longer term), other Church leaders began more openly to voice their concerns.[82] As the Thuringian Bishop Leich, for example, put it in a circular letter of 1 February 1988, there were widespread fears following the Luxemburg–Liebknecht demonstration that the state was resisting necessary processes of renewal and change: that hopes had been aroused by developments in the USSR and that citizens had a right to express their feelings on this matter. 'Many had hoped

[81] Cf. the personal account of her own imprisonment and the less than straightforward manner in which her case was dealt with (through the involvement of senior Church personnel and the Stasi as well as the legal system) in Wollenberger, *Virus der Heuchler*. Wollenberger's own situation was complicated by the fact that both her own husband, Knud, and her defence lawyer, Wolfgang Schnur, were Stasi informers and therefore hardly acted to represent her interests. See also Krenz's total and entirely uncritical justification of the mass arrests, the proceedings against Hirsch, W. and R. Templin, B. Bohley, S. Krawczyk, F. Klier, and Werner Fischer, and the compulsory exile of 53 persons, in a paper he drafted for party organizations, 'Zur Festnahmen von Personen wegen des begründeten Verdachts landesverräterischer Beziehungen', SAPMO-BArch, IV 2/2.039/312.

[82] Cf. e.g. the record of Stolpe's discussion with the Hauptabteilungsleiter beim Staatssekretär für Kirchenfragen concerning the permission for Bärbel Bohley and Werner Fischer to re-enter the GDR in the summer of 1988. Stolpe was personally to ensure that there would be no 'media spectacle' or 'victory celebrations' and 'that Bohley and Fischer will refrain from any activity hostile to the state and not return to their earlier environs'. Clearly over-estimating his own capacity to influence the actions of these individuals, Stolpe 'explained that he would personally intervene to ensure a calm and discreet treatment of [Bohley and Fischer's] return to the country'. SAPMO-BArch, IV 2/2.039/312 (5 July 1988).

that there would be some movement in the situation in our society. Instead of this, nothing is happening.' Leich went on to emphasize that while the Church could not support particular political positions, it would support individuals in need, whatever their views. To those in trouble in Berlin, he stated: 'You must know that we are on your side and will not leave you on your own. We will also not allow ourselves to be distanced from the peace and environmentalist movements in our congregations.' It was essential that 'the readiness to engage in dialogue should grow anew' between the state, the Church, and society.[83]

But it was precisely this 'readiness for dialogue' that the top political leadership of the GDR was resisting. Throughout 1988 Honecker and his close associates continued to pursue the policy of pretending that all was well and that suppression of alternative views—including even censorship of the Soviet magazine *Sputnik*, carrier as it was of notions of perestroika and glasnost—would ultimately ensure an end to all the troubles. Even the alleged reformers-in-waiting appeared to be paralysed by inbred habits of communist party discipline and horror of the ultimate political crime of factionalism: there is little sign in the records of this time of the supposed will to reform retrospectively claimed by a number of communists after the *Wende*.[84]

The Luxemburg–Liebknecht demonstration of January 1989 was successfully navigated, from the point of view of the state, and a number of other potentially destabilizing initiatives were successively repressed by the ever more vigilant Stasi.[85] Less easily disguised were the well-orchestrated observations of the rigging of results in the May 1989 local elections. Establishing to their own satisfaction that the standard massive returns in favour of the SED were fabricated, dissident groups mounted a campaign of monthly demonstrations against this manifest dishonesty, which came to symbolize the more general lack of democracy and legitimacy of the entire dictatorship. At the same time, however, events elsewhere were providing the conditions for more widespread demonstrations of the relative lack of popular legitimacy of the GDR.

In the first week of May 1989, while dissidents within the GDR were

[83] SAPMO-BArch, IV B 2/14/70, 18th Rundbrief (1 Feb. 1988).

[84] Cf. e.g. the files in the offices of Günter Schabowski and Egon Krenz, both of whom have subsequently cast themselves in a somewhat favourable and reform-minded light.

[85] Cf. e.g. the report of an attempted silent demonstration (*Schweigemarsch*) in Leipzig on 15 Jan. 1989: at 4 p.m., around 150 to 200 people were involved in an unofficial gathering (*Zusammenrottung*) in a market square, apparently intending to start on a march. This gathering was successfully broken up by 5.15 p.m., with 53 arrests by security forces. All those arrested were subsequently released the same evening. The whole thing 'hardly made any public impact (*kaum öffentlichkeitswirksam*)'. SAPMO-BArch, IV 2/2.039/312, Bez. Leipzig (16 Jan. 1989).

monitoring the election procedures, a newly reformist leadership in Hungary was beginning to dismantle its border fortifications to the West. Hungary had always had more permeable borders than the GDR: given the material preconditions for travel in a hard currency zone, Hungarian citizens were relatively easily able to take their holidays in the West, as the ubiquity of tiny Hungarian caravans (more or less solid tents on wheels) jostling beside the more luxurious and capacious Bürstners, Adrias, and Dethleffs in West European campsites clearly demonstrated. By the early summer of 1989, the Hungarian government was toying with a move, not only to a more market-oriented economic system (with which Hungary had long experimented) but also towards a more pluralist political system and more open borders. On 2 May the Hungarians began to dismantle their border with Austria; in the following weeks, increasing numbers of holidaying East Germans took the opportunity to escape to the West. By August, the situation was rapidly developing out of control: East Germans were not only exiting in increasing numbers through the Hungarian–Austrian border, but also, under the spotlight of international television cameras, seeking refuge in the grounds of the West German embassies in Prague, Budapest, even East Berlin itself, in the hope of rapid escape to the West. On 11 September, Hungary formally opened its borders to the West, permitting East Germans to leave without visas. The consequence, of course, was to create a leak in the seal separating the communist bloc from the West; and with this, of course, a crack in the last remaining physical defence of communist rule in the GDR.

The suddenly renewed nightmare of a massive haemorrhage of citizens, almost forgotten since the erection of the Berlin Wall in 1961, represented a major challenge to the Honecker regime. It was a challenge to which the gerontocracy proved unable to rise. The international embarrassment of a leadership seeking to prepare for the fortieth anniversary celebrations of the GDR was immense; it was exacerbated by Honecker's own illness and personal incapacity to respond. Given the manner in which, over preceding years, Honecker had successfully isolated the top leadership and immobilized his immediate political subordinates, the regime seemed incapable of any flexible or effective response to a situation of increasingly serious proportions.

The moment was clearly ripe for the nascent movements for democratization within the GDR. In late August, the first initiatives were taken to found an East German Social Democratic Party; its call to supporters was published on 26 September, while it was officially founded as a party on the symbolic date of 7 October. Other incipient political groupings also declared their programmes and aims in the course of the early autumn weeks.

Democracy Now published its programmatic pamphlet on 12 September; Democratic Awakening was founded on 1 October. Most important, however, was the collective movement, New Forum (Neues Forum), which understood itself not as a political party, but rather as a (constitutionally permissible, at least in theory) association (*Vereinigung*), intended to open up the public sphere for open discussion and debate. The founding document of New Forum, proclaimed on 10 September, urged the importance of free and open discussion of the manifold, often contradictory, imperatives of policy and public welfare, arguing that the time was ripe for the energies of citizens to be directed to the issues of the day:

Communication between state and society is visibly disrupted in our country. Evidence of this ranges from the widespread sense of being fed up (*Verdrossenheit*) through the retreat into private niches to mass emigration . . . The disrupted relationship between state and society cripples the creative potential of our society and hinders the solution of pressing local and global tasks. We fritter ourselves away in bad-tempered passivity and yet we have so many more important things that we could be doing for our life, our country and humanity.[86]

It was precisely this mobilization of ever-increasing numbers of formerly passive citizens that was to bring movement into the system in the coming weeks.

[86] Quoted in C. Schüddekopf (ed.), '*Wir sind das Volk!*' (Hamburg: Rowohlt, 1990), 29.

9

THE END OF A DICTATORSHIP

MASS MOBILIZATION AND REGIME IMPLOSION, AUTUMN 1989

No revolution, historically, has been a simple matter. In no case is it sufficient to seek to explain only the growth of popular discontent: dislike of prevailing political conditions has never been a sufficient explanation even of an isolated revolt, let alone a successful revolution. As argued above, dislike of the GDR was relatively constant throughout its forty-year history, and does little to elucidate its final collapse.[1] While every revolution is in a very real sense unique, there are certain recurrent features. *All* successful revolutions appear to be characterized by a particular combination of factors. One of these is the growth of a revolutionary movement which at crucial moments is capable of mobilizing large numbers of people to mount a serious challenge from below. But equally important is the question of élite claims to power and exertion of effective rule. Historically, notable revolutions—including the English Revolution of 1640 and the French Revolution of 1789—have originated, not with a challenge from below, but rather with splits among ruling élites (although of course emerging splits are often simultaneously exploited and exacerbated by growing challenges from below).[2] The course taken by revolutionary developments may also depend crucially on international circumstances. In the East German case, the state was characterized by a lack of national legitimacy and the artificial nature of its construction and dependence on the Soviet Union:

---

[1] It is therefore not sufficient to emphasize this factor as the final explanation of the revolution, although this sort of emphasis is prevalent in many essays on the GDR; cf. e.g. David Childs's essay in Janet Wharton (ed.), *German Politics and Society from 1933 to the Wende* (Nottingham: INGASA, 1992).

[2] For a path-breaking comparative analysis of the conditions for successful social revolutions, see Theda Skocpol, *The State and Social Revolutions: France, Russia, China* (Cambridge: Cambridge University Press, 1979). For my own analysis of the historiographically rather contentious English Revolution, see M. Fulbrook, *Piety and Politics: Religion and the Rise of Absolutism in England, Württemberg and Prussia* (Cambridge: Cambridge University Press, 1983).

thus it was peculiarly fragile with respect to changes in the international system.

The period from late 1987 onwards was more polarized, more unstable, than at any time since the early 1950s. Some of the reasons for instability were strikingly similar to those of the early 1950s; other factors were markedly different. As far as the international context was concerned, there was a new lability, a new willingness to rethink the post-war settlement, on the part of the Soviet Union. Under Gorbachev, the German question was open again, in a way in which it had not been since the rejection of the Stalin notes and the incorporation of the two parts of Germany into their respective NATO and Warsaw Pact military alliances. As far as the East German political élites were concerned, it would be exaggerating to suggest that there was the degree of open factionalism and political or ideological difference characteristic of the newly 'unified' Socialist Unity Party of the early 1950s; but there was in more muted form a new climate of uncertainty, dissatisfaction with Honecker's resistance to reform, and the sense that change was on the agenda, although the manner and timing of any shift could neither be predicted nor openly plotted. At the same time, however, the repressive forces were infinitely larger, more sophisticated in their techniques of observation and control, and more efficient in their capacity to repress. A key difference, however, lay in the character of dissent. Popular opposition to the regime in the 1950s had been diverse, largely spontaneous, and easily isolated. In the late 1980s, while the vast majority of the population had in many respects found a *modus vivendi* of grumbling conformity, there was a new and ultimately crucial leaven in society: a network of organized groups, who, for all their internecine differences, for all the state infiltration and control, were determined to set in motion realizable processes of democratization and reform. It was this peculiar combination which was to eventuate in the 'gentle revolution' of the autumn of 1989.

The roles of different elements and historical actors at different phases of the GDR's collapse have contributed to the complexity of the debates over whether or not the GDR experienced a revolution from below, an implosion from above, or a collapse from without. Is the beginning of the end of the GDR best explained in terms of the 'growth of political opposition'; or by a palace revolution or leadership coup followed by communist abdication from power; or by the end of the Cold War and the loss of the protective Iron Curtain imprisoning an unwilling population? Different accounts have tended to emphasize one or another factor.

Clearly the end of the GDR has to be understood in terms of a combination of factors: any explanation must be couched in terms of the ways in which challenges from below interacted with responses from above in the context of unfolding international circumstances. When one analyses the course of events in the GDR, however, it would seem that the pressures from *below* and from *outside* were in fact of paramount importance. The 'implosion' of the regime, or the effective abdication of the domestic élites, came largely as an initially unintended reaction to what had become an increasingly uncontrollable situation.

The Soviet Union effectively renounced the GDR. This was the crucial precondition for its eventual demise. Since this chapter will explore in more detail the unfolding of domestic politics, it is important to stress this point at the outset. In the later 1980s, in the context of increasing domestic economic (and hence social and political) difficulties within the USSR, leading Soviet strategists began to moot the possibility that hegemony over the Eastern European states could and should no longer be sustained. The cost was effectively greater than the benefits. As Martin McCauley has demonstrated, between 1986 and 1988 the Gorbachev leadership 'came to the momentous conclusion that a military presence in [Eastern Europe] reduced rather than enhanced Soviet security'; and in 1987, in a development completely at odds with the official line in the GDR, the Soviet leaders began to entertain the idea that there was, after all, only *one* German nation.[3] At the same time, the Moscow leadership began to explore the possibility of removing Honecker from power. It is of course not suggested here that the Soviet intention at this stage was anything more than the replacement of Honecker by a more reform-minded leader, who might introduce a degree of restructuring and debate in the GDR; nevertheless, this introduced an element of movement and uncertainty in the situation.

The consequences of these shifts in Soviet policy under Gorbachev were multiple. Domestic movements for change within Eastern bloc countries were enthused and motivated by hopes that processes of glasnost and perestroika might be set in motion within their states. Reformist currents were particularly strong in Poland and Hungary, with very immediate effects on the character of the Iron Curtain. The Soviet Union, operating its new 'Sinatra doctrine' ('letting them do it their way') remained content to look on, without intervening; there were no invasions of Soviet tanks, no closing of the borders with displays of force. And the very incapacity— exacerbated by serious physical illness, necessitating surgery and hospitaliz-

[3] Martin McCauley, 'Gorbachev, the GDR and Germany', in G.-J. Glaeßner and Ian Wallace (eds.), *The German Revolution of 1989: Causes and Consequences* (Oxford: Berg, 1992), 164.

ation in July and August 1989—of Erich Honecker in the face of these crises only confirmed Gorbachev's irritation with the East German leader and his rising sense of the need for renewal and reform in the GDR leadership. Renewal and reform did not of course at this stage mean the renunciation of the GDR; but that was the ultimate effect of the train of events which were set in motion by the snowballing crises of the summer of 1989.

Within the GDR, dissident hopes had for long been fuelled by the notion of a post-Honecker, pro-reformist leadership. These hopes were moreover not limited to those of dissident persuasions: within the leadership of the SED itself, a process of differentiation was developing—if only in very muted form—which culminated ultimately in the replacement of Honecker by Egon Krenz. As we shall see, this proved in the end to be a 'last revolution from above': the lack of national legitimacy of the GDR, and the existence of another Germany according automatic rights of citizenship to fleeing East Germans, swept away the ground from under the new leadership's feet. Within weeks, the domination of the SED, which had held sway so effectively for forty years, was in ruins. The will for power—and with it the capacity to exert effective authority—collapsed with the crumbling of the physical boundaries to this artificial state. All that remained, in the succeeding months, was the negotiation of the manner and speed of the collapse, the sealing of the USSR's renunciation of its creation, and the conditions of East Germany's effective take-over by the West.

Bearing this wider context in mind, let us proceed to examine in more detail the role of different domestic political currents in the unfolding story of the demise of the GDR.

The mobilization of the masses

Up until the late summer of 1989, there had been, as we have seen in previous chapters, several forms of popular response to the regime. There was the very small minority of activists, engaged in their discussion groups and mini-campaigns for changes on particular issues; the retreatists who were prepared to take the risks entailed in applying for exit visas or seeking some means of more rapid escape, including, of course, those seeking to leave for the West in increasing numbers as the borders became more permeable; and the very much larger numbers of essentially passive subjects, who made do with a grumbling quiescence and constrained conformity. In late September 1989, there were stirrings of change. The leaven of dissident groups began to raise the bread of the largely subordinate masses, slowly at first, but with gathering strength over the ensuing few weeks. Unspoken taboos, internalized self-censorship, inner fears and constraints were overcome, in a process of learning, as the Germans put it, an *aufrechten Gang*— learning to walk upright, one's head held high. A new element entered East German politics: increasing numbers of East Germans began to change from being passive subjects to active citizens.

The accounts of this period rightly stress the emotion and atmosphere of the heady few weeks from late September to early November: a period when the masses emerged on to the streets of the GDR, demonstrating peacefully for change in their own society; when, in a sense, they finally came to assert that it *was* their society, they *they* were the 'people' in whose best interest the party had claimed to rule. There was a complex interplay, in the space of a few short weeks, between, on the one hand, the growing self-confidence and overcoming of fear on the part of the masses, guided and supported by the political activists in the environs of the Church, and, on the other, the growing uncertainty and incapacity to initiate effective responses on the part of the authorities. The implicit social contract of conformist subordination below and largely non-violent repression above had been broken; ever-growing numbers were no longer willing to act the role of obeisant subjects, while the willingness to put into effect the perpetual threat of open, violent force came increasingly under question. At the same time, increasing numbers of those who had previously sustained the regime in a variety of official capacities began to dare to say openly that, in effect, the Emperor had no clothes. The binding spell of mutual complicity in mass deceit began to be broken.

The demands of the New Forum for legal recognition played a role in mobilizing the masses on to the streets; but the demonstrations were larger than this, and the long prehistory of political activism with a puritanical flavour played a major part in the course of what became known as the 'gentle revolution'. Moreover, there was a mutual shaping of action and response: the very non-violence of the demonstrators served to defuse the possibility of violent repression by the authorities; while at the same time the loss of the external cordon of force, the Iron Curtain, made the issue of internal use of force all the more central. Violence would have to be employed directly against the population on the ground, now that it could no longer be employed indirectly, at one remove, through their effective imprisonment in their own country. Immediate and visible repression was either imperative—or obsolete, if the claim to be the people's regime were to be rendered real.

Throughout the summer months, there was a growing ferment of ever more open discussion and debate about the sense of crisis in the GDR. People turned up to work, not knowing from one day to the next which of their colleagues would have fled in the meantime; they debated with family and friends whether they, too, should take the opportunity to flee while the possibility was there—on the historically not unfounded assumption of a possible clampdown on the lines of 1953, 1956, and 1968. The exodus of thousands of East Germans from their homeland prompted those who remained to question more urgently whether they themselves should leave or stay; and, if the latter, what they should or could do to help to make the GDR a place in which people would be willing, voluntarily, to stay. There was no longer any possibility of repressing public debate; of retaining the complicity of the niche society.

This was perhaps the crucial mobilizing factor. Private grumbles—which had been mounting in insistency in the later 1980s—over material and existential problems in the GDR now became publicly articulated and expressed. The regime's attempts at *Verschönerung*—the Potemkin village images beloved of Mittag and Honecker—could no longer be sustained. Although the precise extent of the GDR's indebtedness was not known, and what figures existed were suppressed, public attention was increasingly focused on the ever more visible problems of economic stagnation, even collapse, and, in particular, on the increasingly evident environmental pollution and decay.[4] The exodus to the West then in some ways lifted the taboo on open debate; private grumbles could no longer be isolated, ignored, denied. There was also, too, perhaps for the first time since 1953, a perception that coordinated protest might have the capacity to effect real change; in this sense, there was a key shift in the perception of opportunity structures, rather than solely in the level of discontent as such.

Even those who had served, through their functions, to sustain the regime in an official capacity began publicly to articulate the need for more open debate. The Evangelical Synod meeting in Eisenach emphasized, in its closing declaration of 19 September, the urgency of dialogue: 'In order not to obstruct the way into a just, democratic, internally and externally peaceful and ecologically sustainable society, an open dialogue involving the whole of society has now become urgent. This entails also an opening up of

---

[4] Cf. Karl-Dieter Opp and Peter Voß, *Die volkseigene Revolution* (Stuttgart: Klett-Cotta, 1993), 84–95. The highest source of dissatisfaction in their survey appears to have been the environment (93).

currently existing political structures.'[5] On 20 September, even the leader of the LDPD, Manfred Gerlach, openly stressed the need for new ideas and new thinking to deal with the ever more evident crisis facing the country: 'The GDR needs people who question, are impatient, are curious; it needs everyone who bridles at "normality" and in this way helps to discover and implement new ideas.'[6] But although two of the pillars of the system of domination—the Church and one of the bloc parties, whose leader was one of Honecker's eight deputies and hence closely implicated in the structures of power—openly acknowledged the time for dialogue, this was not yet true of the ruling SED, which publicly maintained a steadfast silence, pretending that all was for the best in the best of people's republics. It was to take considerable pressure from below to nudge the SED into concessions and acknowledgement of the need for reform.

The small circles and groups of reformers which had been growing over the preceding years began, in the late summer and early autumn, to develop into a proliferating set of firmer political organizations, each with its own rather broad statements and visions, arguing most basically the need for dialogue. The New Forum, the Social Democratic Initiative, Democracy Now, Democratic Awakening, and a variety of other newly formed and often quite minuscule groups, built on the experiences of the preceding years to network, organize, and pressurize for change.[7] At the same time, a quite new phenomenon emerged: the almost inchoate growth of a sense among at least some of the people that they were, after all, and after decades of subordination, a significant force in their own land.

In a demonstrative, politically effective sense, the public mobilization of the masses as a power on the streets can be dated from events in Leipzig on 25 September. Leipzig was an important trade and university city, with a degree of debate and openness to the world comparable to Berlin, facilitated by the regular Leipzig trade fairs and their local implications in terms of provisions and news. There was also a history of local political concern, building on dissident intellectual circles in the 1950s as well as reactions to specific events such as the demolition of the University Church in 1968. The Monday evening services in the Leipzig Nikolaikirche had been a regular event over a considerable period, dating back as far as the introduction of

---

[5] Reprinted in Günter Fischbach (ed.), *DDR-Almanach '90* (Stuttgart: Bonn Aktuell, 1990), 241.

[6] Ibid. 242.

[7] For documents relating to these and other opposition groups up to the end of Nov. 1989, see e.g. G. Rein (ed.), *Die Opposition in der DDR* (Berlin: Wichern, 1989).

regular Monday peace prayer services in relation to the Swords into Plough-shares campaign of 1982; they continued to be a regular, if often muted, feature in subsequent years. In the late summer of 1989, their significance increased dramatically.

On the occasion of the peace prayers on 25 September, a new phenom-enon developed.[8] As on many previous occasions, those who wanted a rapid exit from the GDR started to demonstrate, chanting 'We want out! (Wir wollen raus!)'. But, on this occasion, a new chant was raised. Against the voices of those seeking to leave were raised the voices of those proclaiming 'We are staying here! (Wir bleiben hier!)'.[9] On this evening, demonstrators on a march around the town sang 'We Shall Overcome' and other songs; there was a growing sense of the power of the people to express peacefully their will to stay, but also the need to engage in dialogue, to effect changes. Those who were choosing to stay were at the same time emphasizing the need for the party to listen to the people, not to suppress them and expect unquestioning obedience to the diktat of the party.

From then on, the Monday Leipzig demonstrations became a growing political factor; it was remarkable how fast the weekly cycle became a significant factor in the making of a peaceful revolution. The extraordinary regularity, and yet distance, of this cycle, which did not interrupt the normal patterns of a working life ('No strikes: the revolution takes place outside working hours'), was a remarkable feature of the unfolding revolution.[10] The banners and slogans have by now entered the mythology of the revol-ution, most notably the ubiquitous 'Wir sind das Volk! (We are the People)', epitomizing the assertion of self-empowerment by the people. 'Neues Forum zulassen!', the demand for the legalization of New Forum, was another focal rallying cry; 'Keine Gewalt!' was an essential, recurrent reminder to desist from violence—on both sides. The concerns and at the same time the sustaining wit of the people were expressed in a wide variety of often rhyming slogans ('SED—das tut weh!', 'Visa-frei nach Hawaii', 'Mit dem Fahrrad durch Europa, aber nicht als alter Opa') on home-made banners in the following weeks.[11] It is notable that the common theme of these home-

[8] Cf. Opp and Voß, Die volkseigene Revolution, 44; and Reiner Tetzel, Leipziger Ring (Frankfurt-on-Main: Luchterhand, 1990), 7.

[9] See the eye-witness reports in Neues Forum Leipzig, Jetzt oder nie—Demokratie. Leipziger Herbst '89 (Munich: C. Bertelsmann Verlag, 1990), particularly 33, and Tetzel, Leipziger Ring. See also the account in Hartmut Zwahr, Ende einer Selbstzerstörung. Leipzig und die Revolution in der DDR (Göttingen: Vandenhoek and Ruprecht, 1993), 23–6.

[10] 'Gestreikt wird nicht. Die Revolution findet am Feierabend statt', in Tetzel, Leipziger Ring, 33.

[11] Roughly translated as: 'SED—that hurts', 'Visa-free as far as Hawaii', and 'Bicycle tour round Europe, but not as an old grandfather' (a reference to the greater ease of travel for

made banners and slogans was simply the desire for greater democracy, freedom, and dialogue, rather than any specific social or economic demands. But the most important thing was less the articulation in words of specific views, let alone policy proposals, than the mere fact of ever larger numbers of people daring to come out on the streets and march, together, without violence.

Slowly, too, people in other cities and towns across the GDR began to follow the Leipzig example—beamed to them on Western television news, in contrast to 1953 when it was extremely difficult to collate accurate news and to coordinate strategies across different regions—and began to come out, in smaller numbers, but with similar restraint and dignity, to assert their right to be heard. The accounts of demonstrations in late September and early October emphasize the complexity of the motives and emotions of those daring to come out on the streets at this time. Some demonstrators had attended the relatively 'safe' church services—under the protection of the church premises, to which they had grown accustomed during the 1980s—and then, strengthened by the hymns, the prayers, the words of pastors, had walked out into the dangerous territory of the public domain to face the uncertainties of Stasi and police surveillance, as they embarked on their open defiance of the ban on mass demonstrations (denigrated in official terminology as *Zusammenrottungen*). Others had flocked to the churches and found they were already full: they either waited outside or joined other services in nearby churches. Services at the Nikolaikirche in Leipzig, for example, were soon complemented by concurrent services in two neighbouring churches, before the congregations met for the common march. Other participants were initially bystanders, watching out of interest as the train of demonstrators marched by: they were urged to join the march, as demonstrators chanted 'Gorbi! Wir bleiben hier! Neues Forum zulassen! Reiht euch ein! (Gorbi! We are staying here! Legal recognition for New Forum! Join in with us!)'.[12] There was an air of expectation, of excitement mixed with apprehension; people knew that 'something was happening', and wanted to watch; they were often then pulled into a bodily, physical commitment from which it was hard to extricate oneself, and became at the same time emotionally, psychologically involved and changed in the complex process of total mobilization.

pensioners). For further examples, cf. Opp and Voß, *Die volkseigene Revolution*, Tetzel, *Leipziger Ring*, and Zwahr, *Ende einer Selbstzerstörung*.

[12] Evidence of a 24-year-old student, Dirk Barthel, on the way in which he became involved in the Leipzig demonstration of 2 Oct., reprinted in Neues Forum Leipzig, *Jetzt oder nie—Demokratie*, 45–6.

For, once in, it was difficult to get out: chains of uniformed police and Stasi officers in civilian clothing separated demonstrators from escape routes; police vans were ready in side streets to block off exit routes and to take those arrested into custody. As one demonstrator put it, 'We . . . set off with a mixture of determination, courage, and doubt. We are flanked on both sides by a strong police presence, I start to become frightened.'[13] There was, however, a momentum of mounting solidarity, as people sought to help those who had been struck by batons or mishandled by policemen, and to surge forward in a disciplined crowd seeking a degree of safety in numbers, infused with a real sense of the power of the people, 'a courageous mass of people (eine mutige Menschenmenge)'.

The retreat from the use of repression and force by the authorities, however, was by no means a predetermined matter. In late September and early October, it looked as if the incipient revolution could very easily become yet another in the history of failed revolutions in Germany, a tale of martyrs felled by brutal and efficient state repression. What then determined the responses of the authorities to the pressures for change which were being articulated with increasing forcefulness on the streets of this formerly apparently so quiescent state? Why were SED and Stasi so helpless in the face of mass popular unrest, despite the massively increased numbers of those working in the state security apparatus, and in stark contrast to the smooth, effective repression of unrest in 1968? What really lay behind the façade of the would-be reformers who soon appeared on the stage of the GDR to represent the SED in the weeks of crumbling communist rule from late September to early December? In short, as Erich Mielke subsequently rather plaintively put it, 'How did it come about that we simply gave up our GDR, just like that?'[14]

The renunciation of repression?

There are several strands and stages to the story of the collapse of rulership and the implosion of the East German dictatorship.

First of all, there was the issue of whether or not to use force to repress the growing popular unrest. Here, several elements appear to have played an important role, including: the reliability (or otherwise) of the troops on the ground; the political assessments and persuasions of regional functionaries; and central orders from above. In a situation essentially driven from below, the orders from above were more a last attempt to set a stamp of

---

[13] S. Gradt, in Neues Forum Leipzig, Jetzt oder nie—Demokratie, 46.
[14] Erich Mielke, 'Spiegel-Gespräch', Der Spiegel, 46: 36 (31 Aug. 1992), 39.

authority on what was happening on the ground than a prime determinant of changing policies. Moreover, the character, not only of the demonstrations, but of the crisis facing the country as a whole, played a role in the very widespread decision to desist, ultimately, from violence. It was no longer possible to misrepresent demonstrators as 'rowdies', *agents provocateurs*, or the misguided victims of Western campaigns to undermine the GDR. For once, it was widely recognized that the causes, and not merely the symptoms, of popular unrest would have to be addressed. The old labels, techniques, and strategies, developed to perfection in the arcane manuals and practices of the Stasi, were simply no longer applicable.

In the early phases of the autumn, the deployment of force was a major strategy of the regime in the attempted suppression of visible popular unrest. Around eighty people were arrested in East Berlin on 7 September, for protesting against the falsification of the May election results. On 18 September, around a hundred people were arrested in Leipzig for seeking to take part in a demonstration after the regular Monday evening service in the Nikolaikirche. Eleven people who had participated in the Nikolaikirche services were sentenced to up to six months' imprisonment; two dozen others were given fines ranging up to 5,000 Marks. On 2 October in Leipzig, water cannons, batons, and dogs were used to frighten and disperse demonstrators. Several demonstrators sustained serious injuries as a result of clashes with the security forces. On 4 and 5 October, as special trains brought would-be refugees from the embassies in Prague and Warsaw across the territory of the GDR to the West, demonstrators were dealt with quite brutally by security forces, and there were violent clashes in Dresden and Magdeburg. On the weekend of 7–8 October, the occasion of the blatantly dishonest anniversary 'celebrations' staged by the Honecker leadership for the visit of Gorbachev to Berlin, popular demonstrations were suppressed only through massive police and Stasi interventions with numerous arrests and the very physical intimidation of participants.[15]

In preparation for the expected ever larger turnout at the by now regular Monday Leipzig demonstrations, on 8 October Erich Mielke ordered a state of red alert for the GDR's security forces. It is worth reprinting the order at some length, to reveal the inimitable (and virtually untranslatable!) flavour of the Stasi view of the world at this stage:

Because of the enemy's unrestrained campaign of incitement, slander, and massive intervention attempts, the political-operative situation inside the GDR has very significantly worsened of late.

[15] Cf. e.g. the account in Zwahr, *Ende einer Selbstzerstörung*, ch. 4.

There has been an aggravation of the nature and associated dangers of the illegal mass gatherings of hostile, oppositional, as well as further hostile-negative and rowdy-type forces aiming to disturb the security of the state as well as public order and security and in this way to bring about an endangering of the socialistic state and society of the GDR.

For the consistent and effective suppression and repression of all behaviour and activities in this connection I hereby order:

1. A state of 'full alert' according to Directive No. 1/89, Para. 11, for all units until further notice. Members of permanently armed forces are to carry their weapons with them constantly, according to the needs of the situation . . .

Sufficient reserve forces are to be held ready, capable of intervention at short notice even for offensive measures for the repression and breaking up of illegal demonstrations . . .

3. All appropriate and available IM/GMs [unofficial and societal collaborators of the Stasi] are immediately to be brought into play in capacities appropriate to the situation . . .

6. Political-operative resistance work in the armed organs as well as in the workers' combat groups is to be strengthened through directed measures on the part of the relevant service units.[16]

This state of full alert was clearly explicitly designed as a massive operation for the suppression, by violent means if necessary, of the growing demonstrations which posed an ever-increasing threat to the stability of the GDR. But, in the event, the East German revolution did not develop into a civil war or a massively bloody period of struggles. The turning-point came on the very day following the issue of Mielke's effective licence for massacre. A number of elements played a role in the ultimately essentially non-violent outcome.

A major factor was the very peaceful, positively non-violent, character of the demonstrations. The slogan 'Keine Gewalt! (No Violence)', frequently chanted on marches, was directed as much at the participants themselves as at the forces ranged against them. As one participant in a demonstration reported, 'At the end [of a speech by a representative of New Forum] the speaker calls out for presence of mind: "Don't damage anything, resist any kind of provocation that could lead to violent conflicts!" '[17] Had the demonstrators initiated violence, the response would have been massive. A directive of 16 October was quite clear on this: '[The command] is to be observed that a direct intervention of police forces and means will only occur when persons or property are attacked or other serious incidents of

[16] MfS, 'Mielke an Leiter der Diensteinheiten' (8 Oct. 1989), repr. in Armin Mitter and Stefan Wolle (eds.), 'Ich liebe euch doch alle!' Befehle und Lageberichte des MfS, Jan.–Nov. 1989 (Berlin: BasisDruck, 1990), 201–2.　　　　[17] Tetzel, Leipziger Ring, 36.

violence take place.'[18] It was a source of some irritation to Mielke that the demonstrators proved so disciplined, so restrained: as he put it on 7 November, two days before the opening of the Wall, it was evident 'that demonstration organizers—to some extent supported by Church forces—are increasingly taking their own measures to hinder any sort of provocation (their own orders, prematurely breaking off events, creating human chains to protect MfS property)'.[19] Demonstrators were determined to emphasize their desire for dialogue, for a chance to be heard and to engage in democratic debate; a vital aspect of this was to refuse to be pulled into violent confrontation.

A second factor of considerable importance was the reliability—or otherwise—of members of the police, auxiliary troops or workers' armed brigades, and other forces on the ground. A somewhat ambiguous but highly suggestive body of evidence points in the direction of a crumbling of the willingness on the part of the troops to obey orders and employ force against the demonstrators. The Magdeburg SED leadership sought to downplay the alleged unwillingness of security forces to engage in confrontation: 'At the same time, leading oppositional forces are trying, even in public meetings, to create the impression that the security forces who have to intervene doubt whether what they are doing is right.'[20] On the other hand, the Stasi central headquarters had rather precise figures tending to confirm the opposition's claims. As a Stasi report of 15 October noted:

In the course of the action, the readiness of various combat group units to engage in battle and intervention was markedly hindered, as was their political-moral condition, by various incidents, modes of behaviour and appearance.

This was above all expressed in

—individual collectives and combat troops refusing to intervene as intended,
—resigning from the SED and from the combat groups
—refusing to obey orders.

According to reports currently available, for example, 188 combatants have resigned from the combat groups of the working class and 146 combatants refused to follow orders to intervene when these had been given.

The main centres in which combatants have resigned from the SED and the combat groups are the Bezirke Karl-Marx-Stadt (136), Leipzig (18), and Magdeburg

[18] Repr. in Roland Pechmann and Jürgen Vogel (eds.), *Abgesang der Stasi. Das Jahr 1989 in Presseartikeln und Stasi-Dokumenten* (Braunschweig: Steinweg-Verlag, 1991), 254.

[19] Repr. in Mitter and Wolle (eds.), *'Ich liebe euch doch alle!'*, 251.

[20] SED Bezirksleitung Magdeburg (16 Oct. 1989), repr. in Pechmann and Vogel (eds.), *Abgesang der Stasi*, 258.

(15). The most frequent refusals to obey orders were found in Leipzig (85), Karl-Marx-Stadt (28), and Magdeburg (27).[21]

One participant in the Leipzig demonstration of 2 October reported on the basis of personal experience: 'The young conscript police have an almost despairing, uncertain expression on their faces. I let myself be pulled along, go up to them: "You wouldn't ever shoot at us, would you?" "But we've only got rubber truncheons!" And then they call to each other: . . . "I've only got another couple of days, then I'm going to be marching along with them!" '[22] One of the enduring visual memories of the television coverage of the autumn revolution must be the extraordinary, almost palpable psychological power of the people as they overcame their fear, attained the courage of their convictions, and physically approached uniformed troops to engage them in dialogue, offer them flowers, and suggest they should break out of their allotted roles and recognize the common humanity which bound together the East German citizens across the imposed, external divides of repressors and repressed. The indirect influence of strong cultural strands of the Protestant tradition (such as the Quaker teachings of 'that of God in every man' and the active desisting from violence) cannot be overlooked in this connection, however secularized through the prisms of the new social and cultural currents of the minority movements in the GDR of the 1980s, now reaping their harvest in influencing the masses.

For all the complexities and the partial breakthroughs and setbacks which characterize any real sequence of historical developments, there was a particular, significant turning-point in the decision to engage in dialogue rather than repression as far as the authorities were concerned. This turning-point came on 9 October, the day after Mielke had issued the red alert described above. The Leipzig demonstration of 9 October was the largest yet; it was accompanied by massive preparedness on the part of the security forces for a clampdown of Chinese proportions.[23] Yet, in the course of the evening, the decision to refrain from forcible intervention was taken, and officially ratified by the then security chief Egon Krenz in Berlin. From then on, the momentum of growing mass mobilization and the overcoming of fear was to snowball, accompanied by the ever more speedy collapse of authority above. This key turning-point has been the subject of considerable discussion. Subsequently, Egon Krenz sought to take the acclaim for the decision. In fact, the main initiative appears to have been taken by regional

[21] Mitter and Wolle (eds.), 'Ich liebe euch doch alle!', 221.

[22] S. Gradt, repr. in Neues Forum Leipzig, Jetzt oder nie—Demokratie, 47.

[23] Cf. the very moving account of participants' fear, and attempts to boost their courage in the strength of numbers, in Tetzel, Leipziger Ring, 15–19.

and local functionaries of the SED in conjunction with Leipzig Gewandhaus Orchestra Director Kurt Masur. Their joint declaration was read out over loudspeakers and in effect gave the demonstrators an assurance of safe conduct; the security forces were held off, the demonstration allowed to proceed in peace. With Krenz's somewhat belated ratification of this policy of—at least implicitly—conceding the right to demonstrate, a major watershed had been passed.

On the other hand, the use of repression in principle had by no means been definitively renounced. The Stasi documents from the subsequent weeks reveal that tactical retreat and regrouping by no means implied any final concession of total defeat. The war was simply to be fought, for the time being, by other means.

The collapse of the will to rule

A second major watershed was of course the palace revolution itself: the replacement of Honecker by Krenz, effected on 17–18 October 1989. This palace revolt appears to have been entirely designed as a 'holding operation'. There was widespread frustration at Honecker's resistance to Gorbachev-style reforms, his increasing distance from—and unwillingness even to recognize—the mounting problems faced by the country, and his evident incapacity to deal with the refugee crisis and challenge to the very legitimacy of the GDR in the summer of 1989. These factors led to the coup against Honecker in October 1989.

On 17 and 18 October 1989, Erich Honecker was ousted from his position as General Secretary of the SED, and associated state offices, first in a closed meeting of the Politburo itself and subsequently in a plenary session of the Central Committee. At the latter, he was able to use the face-saving formula adopted eighteen years earlier by Ulbricht, of ill-health.[24]

The palace revolution was followed by the phase of seeking to negotiate change and reform—but with the ultimate intention of retaining power, regrouping, and ensuring a strong position from which reforms might later be amended or even rescinded. It is now increasingly clear that the appearance of reform was precisely that: an appearance. All the concessions of late October and early November 1989—up to and including the opening of the Berlin Wall on 9 November—were designed in a typically manipulative and cynical fashion, with the overriding aim, not of extending genuine democ-

---

[24] Cf. the text of Honecker's resignation, quoted in Krenz's own self-serving and anodyne account: E. Krenz, *Wenn Mauern fallen* (Vienna: Paul Neff Verlag, 1990), 17–18.

racy but rather of clinging to power under altered colours. There was at this stage absolutely no intention of any real renunciation of the SED's claim to total domination. All appearances of 'pluralism' were simply designed as the best tactical means, under less than ideal circumstances, of continuing to exert effective total control by the SED.

On the other hand, however, there are signs that already during this phase, when the top leadership was still clearly determined to hold on to power, there were nevertheless increasing difficulties in the exercise of that power.

Certain political leaders in the provinces appear to have been ever less sure of the appropriate way forward. However cynical the Krenz leadership may have been about projecting the appearance of willingness to reform, there are indications that in some areas there were more genuine impulses in this direction.[25] Such appears to have been the case in Leipzig, and also in Dresden, where local SED leaders started discussion with a 'Group of 20' representing the citizens.[26] There are, however, some difficulties in the evaluation of the evidence. Local leaders' willingness to negotiate with Church leaders as an alternative to employing force was nothing substantially new nor startlingly significant: this technique of using the Church to mediate between the state and the people had of course been employed for years, even if there were some differences in the forms employed (particularly the constitution of the Group of 20) in October 1989. That it contrasted with more heavy-handed alternatives, particularly the open use of brute force, is of course clear; what is less clear is whether it was yet another tactic for the party to cling on to power or whether it genuinely represented a willingness to engage in real, irreversible processes of democratization. At this stage, the former seems more likely than the latter.

Nevertheless, whatever the motives of those leaders prepared to engage in dialogue rather than repression, there was a clear effect on the snowballing process of mass mobilization. With the lowering of the risks, ever more people found the courage to come out and march. And permitting the previously unpermitted gatherings of people, for whatever cynical or genu-

[25] Cf. e.g. Peter Przybylski, *Tatort Politbüro. Band 2: Honecker, Mittag und Schalck-Golodkowski* (Berlin: Rowohlt, 1992), 121 ff.

[26] Cf. Daniel Friedheim, 'Regime Collapse in the Peaceful East German Revolution: The Role of Middle-Level Officials', *German Politics*, 2: 1 (Apr. 1993), 97–112. There are, however, some problems with the interpretation of the material presented in this article. Friedheim's research project entailing retrospective interviews with middle-ranking officials does not seem likely to elucidate the truth of the matter, since retrospectively these officials will of course cast their actions in a pro-democratic light.

ine combination of motives, was also a highly significant concession by a regime which was clearly losing control of developments.

Moreover, would-be reformers among the co-opted intelligentsia, who had previously maintained a relatively subdued or constrained presence in the GDR, began to join the more outspoken dissident intellectuals and enter on to the political stage. The bandwagon was also joined by some of the more pro-Gorbachev spirits in the SED. The culmination of this convergence of currents was reached in the—officially permitted—mass demonstration on East Berlin's Alexanderplatz on 4 November, with speeches from individuals as diverse as the writers Christa Wolf, Stefan Heym, and Christoph Hein, representatives from the Church and from New Forum, including Jens Reich, and those who had previously been pillars of the political establishment, such as LDPD leader Manfred Gerlach, the former Stasi spy chief and deputy Minister for State Security Markus Wolf, and Politburo member Günter Schabowski.

The rising tide of pressures for reform and change led, in the following days, to waves of changes and concessions from above: a proposal for a new travel law was published on 6 November, allowing permits for travel abroad for up to thirty days a year; the entire Council of Ministers resigned *en bloc* on 7 November; on 8 November the Politburo followed suit. The Central Committee confirmed Egon Krenz as General Secretary, and nominated a new Politburo, including some reforming spirits such as the previously excluded Dresden party chief Hans Modrow. But for all the beheadings and concessions, the SED's desperate attempt to cling on to power remained. The *Wende* was at this stage one of appearance and personality, not one of policy and principle.

The real loss of the will to rule came only *after* the opening of the Berlin Wall. This itself has been the subject of much speculation. Was the breaching of the Wall on the night of 9 November a historic act, or a spectacular blunder? When the evidently weary government spokesman, Günter Schabowski, was handed a small piece of paper at the end of a lengthy press conference in the late afternoon announcing new travel regulations, he read it out without observing the embargo and date on which the new regulations were to come into effect. The response was electric: Schabowski was overwhelmed by questions from reporters. Did the new regulations mean that the Berlin Wall no longer retained its original functions? What would now be its status? Schabowski was somewhat at a loss for answers. More importantly, perhaps, the guards at the Wall were equally at a loss: they had not been prepared for the wave of popular excitement which was soon to greet them. Hearing the news, people thronged to the Wall. Incapable of dealing with the ever-increasing crowds in an orderly, bureaucratic fashion, and instructed to avoid bloodshed at all costs, the border guards gave up the struggle and abandoned themselves to passive observation of the orgy of humanity, joy, and euphoria as the night of dancing and drinking champagne on the top of that most inhumane symbol of repression wore on.

Yet only eight days earlier, this had been the very thing that East Germany's new 'reforming' leader, Egon Krenz, had been determined to avoid. In his discussion with Gorbachev in Moscow on 1 November 1989, Krenz had commented, in connection with preparations for the planned mass demonstration of 4 November: 'Measures must be taken to prevent any attempt at a mass breakthrough across the Wall. That would be awful, because then the police would have to intervene [with force] and certain elements of a state of emergency would have to be introduced.'[27] In effect, Krenz was implying that any attempt to breach the Wall would necessarily entail the kind of forcible repression he had taken such pains to distance himself from since the turning-point of 9 October.

This discussion between the reformist leader of the Soviet Union, Mikhail Gorbachev, and the newly would-be reformist leader of the GDR, Egon Krenz, is altogether highly revealing.[28] Krenz was clearly determined to curry favour with Gorbachev: according to his own account, Krenz allegedly only made his decision to challenge Honecker for the leadership when he saw that Erich Honecker 'did not understand or did not want to understand the statements of Comrade Gorbachev'.[29] In a wide-ranging discussion of internal differences within the SED over previous years, Krenz portrays himself less as Honecker's hard-line crown prince (which he was) than as the protector, almost guardian angel, of Gorbachev's preferred candidate, whom Honecker sought to oust from party office, Hans Modrow. This attempted shift in image is comparable to that relating to the savage use of force to suppress pro-democracy demonstrators in Tiananmen Square (applauded by Krenz) and desisting from the use of force in Leipzig on 9 October (for which Krenz sought to take the credit).

[27] SAPMO-BArch, IV 2/2.039/329, 'Niederschrift des Gesprächs des Genossen Egon Krenz, Generalsekretär des ZK der SED und Vorsitzender des Staatsrates der DDR, mit Genossen Michail Gorbatschow, Generalsekretär des ZK der KPdSU und Vorsitzender des Obersten Sowjets der UdSSR, am 1.11.1989 in Moskau', 31.

[28] Not least for the very frank personal comments made by Gorbachev on other politicians. He has an astute thumbnail evaluation of West German Chancellor Helmut Kohl, for example: Kohl is in Gorbachev's view 'no intellectual luminary, but rather a petty bourgeois. These are the social strata which understand him best, too. But he is, nevertheless, a skilful and obstinate politician', in some ways comparable to former US President Reagan.

[29] SAPMO-BArch, IV 2/2.039/329, 41.

But it is also quite clear from the Krenz–Gorbachev conversation, and from other documents from Krenz's office at this time, that Krenz was determined to introduce reforms only in so far as they would serve to rectify the currently unstable situation and regain the 'trust' of the people. A Politburo memo of 3 November 1989, for example, betrays a sense of loss of control, a loss of initiative; but nevertheless concludes that the party must 'united, with closed ranks, do justice to its leadership role . . . and so [win back] the confidence' of the people. At even this late date, the Politburo is still debating whether the party is prepared to be dictated to 'by the street', and 'whether members of the defence and security organs must now expose themselves "non-violently" to every attack'.[30] On 6 November, the party propaganda department evaluated the mass demonstration of 4 November. Concessions should indeed be made, but not to the extent that they might endanger the leading role of the party, or represent any real loss of the party's power: 'The demand for free elections can in principle be supported, since it corresponds to the basic principles of our socialist constitution, nevertheless this must not entail opening the door to bourgeois party pluralism[!].' However, 'demands for abolition of the leading role of the SED are totally unacceptable to us as communists. But concrete steps and measures are to be mentioned, which indicate the way in which the SED wants to win back lost trust through a democratic renewal of its party and earn its democratic legitimation through its achievements.'[31]

The conclusions reached are characteristically cynical and manipulative. The central party leadership recognized the need to conduct local dialogues in different ways, according to local circumstances. Comrades were actually *instructed* to appear to differ and deviate from the official party line, in order to gain the trust and confidence of the population: 'Involved comrades must be prepared, not to proclaim the word of the party, but rather to give the appearance of being thoughtful and realistic, in order to win back our credibility . . . [!]'.[32] Other sources emphasize the need to find the most intelligent local functionaries, who are capable of projecting an image of independent thought. The SED party archive collected photographs of party functionaries coming out on balconies to meet and debate with demonstrators, no doubt with a view to the appropriate historical gloss in the course of time.[33]

[30] IfGA, ZPA, IV 2/2.039/317, Politburo Information of 3 Nov. 1989.
[31] Ibid., Abteilung Propaganda, 'Erste Einschätzung der Demonstration und Kundgebung am 4. November 1989 in Berlin' (6 Nov. 1989), 3, 4.
[32] Ibid. 5.
[33] Cf. the interesting commentaries attached to the backs of some of these photographs in the SED Bildarchiv in Berlin.

It was only during the phase from mid-November to December 1989, that the real loss of the will to power was experienced—although at different rates among different groups. Initially, the SED leadership thought that their tactics of appearing willing to engage in reforms might have worked, as far as pressures from popular demonstrations were concerned. A report of 13 November noted with some satisfaction that, since the border crossings had been opened, the numbers on demonstrations had declined and internal pressures appeared to have eased somewhat.[34] But the SED itself, particularly at the grass roots, was in disarray: the functionary system was beginning to collapse. Reports from the provinces in the weeks immediately following the opening of the Wall emphasize the extent to which party members and local functionaries are 'deeply shattered (zutiefst erschüttert)' about the revelations of corruption among former Politburo members and ministers in the Volkskammer.[35] Gone are the days of bland reports signifying nothing: suddenly, there are cries from the heart. The party apparatus on the ground was seizing up and ceasing to function; the leadership at the top no longer had a base from which to exercise its claim to power.

A few excerpts must suffice to give some impression of the mood among the party apparatchiks in the week or two following the fall of the Wall and the waves of revelations of corruption in high places.[36] From Leipzig, on 14 November, in the context of rising numbers resigning from the party, comes the plea to Krenz: 'I beg you, take the opportunity and send words of encouragement and comfort to the hundreds of thousands of comrades, who could do nothing about it and believed that they were serving a good cause. Say again, clearly, that they bear no blame for this.' From the First Secretary in the Bezirksleitung Schwerin, on 16 November: 'Fears about the fate of our party are rising . . . triggered above all by the revelations of the bitter truth at the tenth sitting of the Central Committee of the SED and the parliamentary meeting of last week. Irritability and anxiety are increasing, and people are afraid that our party no longer has firm ground under its feet.' Functionaries were resigning their positions, members leaving the

[34] SAPMO-BArch, IV 2/2.039/317, 'Information der operativen Führungsgruppe. Betreff: Lage auf dem Territorium der DDR' (13 Nov. 1989).

[35] On the parliamentary investigations into corruption, see e.g. Volker Klemm, Korruption und Amtsmißbrauch in der DDR (Stuttgart: Deutsche Verlags-Anstalt, 1991). He suggests (12), that the committee set up by the Volkskammer on 13 Nov. 1989 was intended mainly to fulfil an alibi function—to act as a form of lightning conductor for popular outrage and emotion, disguising the facts of continuities in power and the more general functioning of the system as a whole. If this was indeed the intention, then it backfired spectacularly.

[36] The following quotations are extracts from a series of letters to Krenz from Bezirksleitung First Secretaries, collected in SAPMO-BArch, Büro Egon Krenz, IV 2/2.039/317.

party *en masse*, no decisions could be reached or carried out. 'It is all happening at great physical and psychological cost. This cannot be kept up for any length of time.' Less than a week later, the situation in Schwerin appeared merely to have deteriorated: 'The psychological situation in the party apparatus, particularly however in the district leadership offices, is strained to the utmost. Many comrades are desperate, crippled in their actions, shaken and deeply disillusioned . . . The current lack of any conception among the party leadership is bringing matters to a head. The shattering truth, daily expanded, has had a devastating effect, comrades are tearing themselves to bits, suicidal thoughts are on the increase . . .' On the same day, the First Secretary of Bezirksleitung Rostock wrote to Krenz about the 'psychological pressure and moral terror against functionaries of our party'. And two days later, on 24 November—only two weeks after the opening of the Wall—the Cottbus Bezirksleitung wrote that it was virtually no longer possible to make the party apparatus function on the ground. The end of SED domination was marked by the loss of its functionaries' will to rule.

The end of a dictatorship

When did the East German dictatorship really come to an end? The end of the GDR itself has a clear date: the two Germanies were formally united as a new political entity, an enlarged Federal Republic of Germany, on 3 October 1990; the GDR narrowly missed the embarrassment of a forty-first anniversary four days later. But the communist dictatorship had crumbled long before this, and had been successively replaced by a variety of political forms.

The first shift was marked by the movement of the balance of power away from the SED leader and Chair of the Council of State to the previously politically subordinate position of Prime Minister and Chair of the Council of Ministers—i.e. from the party to the government. On 1 December 1989 the Volkskammer formally deleted the party's leading role from Article 1 of the Constitution. Since, however, this role had only been enshrined in the Constitution since 1968 (by which time the party had of course enjoyed nearly half its total lifetime of power), it can hardly be taken as the decisive point of no turning back. Even during the following winter months of round table discussions with representatives of oppositional groups, there were still well-founded suspicions that much of the apparent change might be readily reversible should conditions prove favourable. The dreaded Ministry for State Security, for example, was initially replaced by the Office for

National Security, which evinced a remarkable degree of continuity in aims and personnel with its predecessor. It was only after a massive storming of the Normannenstraße Stasi headquarters in mid-January 1990 that the citizens' movements began to assure themselves that the multi-headed hydra was beginning to be brought under some genuine democratic control; even so, in subsequent months there were innumerable ways in which evidence was destroyed and distorted, arousing suspicions of continued networks of influence and control over the Stasi's legacy.

In many respects, the March 1990 elections mark the formal end of the East German dictatorship: for the first time since the creation of the GDR, the population were able to take part in elections in which the number of seats allotted to each party had not been determined in advance. Although many criticisms could be levelled against the (formally legitimate) means of opinion formation and political influence exercised during the pre-election campaign (with massive financial and organizational input from the West, particularly on the part of Kohl's conservative forces supporting the Alliance for Germany), this was a free election in which the population expressed a majority preference for those relatively right-wing forces which seemed to promise the most rapid unification with the West.

There are many factors involved in the manner and pace of the demise of the GDR itself.[37] Once the borders were opened, it could not survive as an independent, viable, socio-economic and political entity; the automatic rights of citizenship entitlement in the democratic West, combined with the infinitely higher Western standard of living, meant a continued flow of refugees and a rapidly deteriorating domestic economic situation. The seizure of the initiative by West German Chancellor Kohl—already on 10 November, when, at the newly opened Wall, he proclaimed 'Wir sind doch ein Volk!', and more specifically in his ten-point plan of 28 November—combined with a window of opportunity in relation to Gorbachev's USSR

[37] For more detailed accounts, see my *The Divided Nation: Germany 1918–1990* (London: Fontana, 1991; New York: Oxford University Press, 1992), ch. 13; Konrad Jarausch, *The Rush to German Unity* (New York and Oxford: Oxford University Press, 1994); A. James McAdams, *Germany Divided: From the Wall to Reunification* (Princeton: Princeton University Press, 1993), chs. 6 and 7; Jonathan Osmond (ed.), *German Reunification: A Reference Guide and Commentary* (Harlow: Longman, 1992); Stephen Szabo, *The Diplomacy of German Unification* (New York: St Martin's Press, 1992); and for a range of reactions, Harold James and Marla Stone (eds.), *When the Wall Came Down: Reactions to German Unification* (London: Routledge, 1992). There are a large number of German publications documenting the collapse of the GDR and German unification: see e.g. *Der Fischer Weltalmanach: Sonderband DDR* (Frankfurt: Fischer, 1990); *DDR-Almanach '90* (Stuttgart: Bonn Aktuell, 1990); G.-J. Glaeßner, *Der schwierige Weg zur Demokratie* (Opladen: Westdeutscher Verlag, 1992); Eckard Jesse and Armin Mitter (eds.), *Die Gestaltung der deutschen Einheit* (Bonn: Bundeszentrale für politische Bildung, 1992).

and helped to force the pace of negotiations at the international level. In the course of the following months, it became increasingly clear to the international community that the German question had to be entirely rethought: an independent East German economy could not be sustained in the face of open borders to the West; West Germany could not afford the social costs and political consequences of a continuing flow of refugees; and in light of a collapsing domestic economy and a rapidly crumbling Warsaw Pact, the Soviet Union was prepared to negotiate for the best possible terms of military and political withdrawal from its erstwhile satellite state. Currency union of the two Germanies on 1 July 1990 served simply to speed up the pace of the GDR's collapse. The unification treaty, the finalization of the two-plus-four negotiations, the broader approval of the participants in the CSCE, the reconstitution of the East German *Länder* and their accession to an enlarged Federal Republic, were but external formalities regulating and legitimating an ongoing process of disintegration and dissolution.

But the communist dictatorship itself had collapsed already before this. All the apparatus and structures of power—the dominance of the SED, the co-option of the bloc parties and mass organizations, the compliance of the Church leadership, the unwilling collusion in subordination of the masses— all these had crumbled, at varying rates and in differing ways, in the preceding months. When the SED itself effected a purge of its leadership and a reorientation of its image at its extraordinary XII Congress in the first week of December 1989, it knew that its historic moment of domination was, effectively, at an end.

CONCLUSION

10

THE PECULIARITIES OF THE EAST GERMAN DICTATORSHIP

How should one seek to understand the dynamics of the development, stabilization, and ultimate demise of the GDR? What specific concepts, and what broader interpretive framework, have most purchase in seeking to explain both the quiet longevity and the rapid collapse of the GDR? A number of hypotheses have been advanced in the course of this book, which must be addressed more explicitly here. And how, in broader terms, should this remarkable experiment be evaluated, both historically and morally? Was the communist project inevitably doomed to fail, foundering on the rocks of its internal contradictions? Were the intrinsically humanistic and emancipatory goals of Marxism inevitably jeopardized by internal contradictions, by an essential *Lebensunfähigkeit* (non-viability)? Or was the ultimate collapse more a matter of unfavourable historical conditions for the communist project?

Clearly these are exceedingly broad philosophical as well as social-historical questions, which—even prior to the collapse of communism in Eastern Europe—have exercised thinkers grappling with the distortions of Marxism-Leninism, Stalinism, and succeeding variants of communist repression, for many decades. No definitive answers can be proposed here. But it is impossible to write about a communist dictatorship, and to define elements of specificity as well as common traits, without at least beginning to engage with these broader issues. If for no other reason, this is the case because explanation inevitably involves evaluation of the actors' own strategies of action, their aims, their policies, and the ways in which they achieved or failed to achieve the desired effects, created new opportunities and pressures, were the witting or unwitting causes of a range of historically important consequences. In a highly intrusive regime which explicitly sought to transform society according to 'scientific principles', above all, these questions cannot be escaped. To seek to explain the history of the GDR is thus inevitably to evaluate the guiding theories and strategies of the key political players: in other words, to confront the issue of the intrinsic viability or otherwise of the communist enterprise. It is also, of course, to evaluate the very real human obstacles to that enterprise, and equally to evaluate the modes of personal preservation, resistance to change, and more active alternative strategies of social and political transformation.

The life and death of the GDR

This book has sought to anatomize patterns of political culture, ranging from, in Part I, those involved in the structures of domination, through, in Part II, those who came to some form of more or less willing accommodation with—or mode of retreatist survival within—the regime, to, finally, the more active challenges to domination analysed in Part III. Some basic theses concerning the life and death of the GDR may now be proposed.

(1) **The people of the GDR *were not* 'as a nation' more docile, more obedient to authority, or more enthusiastic about their regime, than the populations of neighbouring communist states.** Cultural explanations of stability—the alleged docility of the apolitical German—are misplaced. Many people did not like the GDR for a variety of reasons. Throughout the life of the GDR, there were unruly spirits who expressed their discontent in a wide variety of ways. The presence of popular discontent alone can explain neither a revolution nor a lack of revolutionary unrest.

(2) **The political and repressive organs of the GDR *were* on the whole more efficient than comparable organs in neighbouring states.** By 1958, just under a decade after the establishment of the GDR, Ulbricht had succeeded in purging the leading party of reformist spirits; inner-party differences did not subsequently attain externally visible political consequences until the autumn of 1989. Similarly, the functionary system of rule was developed in the course of the 1950s and 1960s to attain a degree of smooth efficiency that was also not seriously destabilized until the later 1980s. The armed forces, police, and internal security apparatus of observation, intervention, and control were, given the paranoid world-view of the political leadership and after the experience of 1953, built up to a quite astonishing degree. For a variety of reasons, this system came to collapse in the autumn of 1989.

(3) **The combination of (1) and (2) meant that, for the most part, the vast mass of the population were, by the early 1970s at the latest, accommodated into political and social structures and organizations ensuring a degree of outward conformity, while expressions of spontaneous unrest were rapidly and effectively suppressed.** There was a remarkably high

degree of interpenetration of state and society, fostering the development of the 'niche society'.

(4) However, new social and cultural currents from the later 1970s, aided by a new structural space for activity under the partial protection as well as limited control of the Church, exerted a degree of pressure for change within the system. The unique structural location of the Protestant Church after the failed attempt at *Gleichschaltung* in 1978 allowed new forms of political activism, with new patterns of political organization, to develop in the 1980s, in a wider context which for a variety of reasons fostered hopes of reform.

(5) As part of a divided nation, the GDR had a unique situation among Eastern European states, which vitally affected every stage of its development and demise. The policies of the Soviet Union had a profound impact on the GDR's creation, its character and continued existence, and its collapse. The policies of the West had a less easily identified but no less important influence on patterns of economic and political change within the GDR, and, of course, on its final disappearance as a state.

Together, these theses help to explain the apparent paradox: that the GDR was, to outward appearances, politically one of the most stable communist bloc states, and that, nevertheless, it collapsed with extraordinary speed and non-violence. Before discussing this substantive interpretation of the GDR's history further, however, it is worth raising for explicit attention the theoretical framework which has been developed here.

Theoretical implications

Traditionally—and put rather crudely—two major aspects of domination have been identified: coercion and consent. Recently social and political theorists working in a variety of traditions have begun to discern difficulties with unreflective notions of coercion and consent. The latter concept in particular began to be examined more closely, as in part a product of socialization—or, from another theoretical perspective, indoctrination, even 'false consciousness'—while hidden coercion began to be found in the apparently most innocent and well-intentioned of institutions (churches, schools, asylums). Nevertheless, underlying a whole range of otherwise quite divergent approaches is the essentially dichotomous assumption that to explain political stability one needs to examine the ways in which the dominated are either coerced into obedience, or in some way brought to believe in the legitimacy of a given political order.

The assumption has thus been that political stability is essentially based on the appropriate inculcation of notions of obedience among the dominated, with sanctions against those who continue to engage in what are socially defined as deviant practices. The essential, underlying question is basically: why is it that the dominated accept their own subordination, and how are they brought to believe in the legitimacy of a given political system characterized by inequalities of power and resources? This general assumption then leads to a variety of specific investigations, in order to determine how the trick is achieved. The focus may be on articulate ideologies or belief systems (intellectual, cultural, or religious heritages), on the more implicit codes of conduct inculcated through socialization (as in Bourdieu's notion of 'gentle violence'), or on the impact of educational, religious, and cultural institutions. The older historiography of Germany tended to focus particularly on an allegedly quiescent German Protestant tradition; more subtle approaches have emphasized the role of social institutions such as schools, the authoritarian, paternalistic family, and the officially sponsored inculcation of popular nationalism. And attempts to integrate analyses of coercion with those of consent have not thus far been entirely successful.[1]

Max Weber, in his classical analysis of modes of domination, constructed his theoretical approach not around the orientations of the dominated, but rather on the claims made by rulers, and the relations between rulers and their functionaries or staffs.[2] Weber argued that regime stability was predicated on the rulers' claims to legitimacy combined with the preparedness of rulers' staffs to support those claims, for whatever mixture of personal motives (not only, or necessarily, including any genuine belief in the validity of legitimacy claims). This very useful shift of attention from those being dominated to those doing the dominating was not, however, complemented by a theoretically integrated social analysis. With the exception of the concept of charismatic domination, Weber did not explore any *intrinsic* relationship between the rulers' claims on the one hand, and the responses of the dominated on the other, seeing these as historically contingent, separate factors. Although the notion of charismatic domination entails an

---

[1] e.g. Alf Lüdtke's very useful reminder of the persistence of extra-economic coercion in capitalist societies nevertheless fails to explain how—if at all—notions of 'self-coercion' become internalized. Despite the claim that through repeated, state-sanctioned use of violence, naked 'power' eventually becomes taken-for-granted 'authority', Lüdtke does not succeed in explaining the social bases of 'resistances' or 'refusals', nor indeed does he satisfactorily show that effective inculcation of self-coercion is any real key to explaining patterns of stability and change. Alf Lüdtke, *Police and State in Prussia, 1815–1850* (Cambridge: Cambridge University Press, 1989); cf. my review of this in *Social History* (May 1992).

[2] Max Weber, *Economy and Society* (New York: Bedminster Press, 1968).

inherent developmental dynamic, neither of Weber's other major concepts of domination—traditional and rational-legal or bureaucratic—does much more than present a classificatory concept of such broadness and generality as to have little real explanatory purchase.[3]

It is now essential to construct a coherent theory of domination which is able to combine political history with social history, and to explore the interconnections between the modes of domination of élites and the acquiescence or otherwise in their own domination of the subordinate groups.

Hegel pointed out that for there to be masters, there have to be slaves: the master–slave relationship is one of symbiosis. Clearly, there are unequal power relationships involved, and this is not all a matter of a confidence trick. But there is a very important insight entailed in this somewhat simplified proposition. Much of life under dictatorships is characterized not by the use of force, nor even by fear of the use of force, but by a symbiotic mode of life, a coming to terms with the parameters of the system and operating within often unwritten rules. Stability is predicated on a form of *Anpassung*, a preparedness to go through the motions, to participate in the rituals and acts of obeisance of everyday life—in short, a willingness to ensure that one actually has as easy a life as is possible under the given political conditions. This is certainly neither a case of coercion, nor of consent: there is no belief in the legitimacy of domination, no positive support of the system in principle, nor is there necessarily a well-justified daily fear of repression. This mode of behaviour does not fit well into the basically dichotomous schemes characterized above. Rather, it is simply a form of often unthinking—even unconscious—conformity, of co-operation with the often implicit rules of the game.

The analysis of the anatomy of the East German dictatorship presented above suggests some more general theoretical propositions, which may now be proposed quite explicitly:

(1) What explains political stability, at least as far as domestic patterns of political culture are concerned, is not so much the existence of genuine popular support or effective ideological indoctrination, nor constant fear of violence and repression, as simply conformity, political passivity, and the fragmentation and easy suppression of dissent.

---

[3] For Weber's ideal types of modes of domination, see in particular his discussion in *Economy and Society*. For an interesting and fruitful application of the notion of charismatic rule to an interpretation of Hitler's power, see Ian Kershaw, *Hitler* (Harlow: Longman, 1991). For a more general brief critique of the applicability of Weber's approach to the course of 20th-cent. German history, see my article 'Legitimacy and Domination: Aspects of Herrschaft in Twentieth-century Germany', in J. P. Stern (ed.), *London German Studies III* (London: Institute of Germanic Studies, 1984).

(2) This unthinking conformity is more likely to be achieved where the system of domination operates smoothly; in other words, where, for whatever combinations of personal motives, the rulers' staffs effectively sustain and reproduce the system of rule.

(3) Conversely, domestic political instability begins to occur when the rules of the game begin to be queried, challenged; and when these challenges occur in favourable structural circumstances. Organization may be as important as ideology.

(4) These challenges will be more effective if the carriers of the system of domination are for any reason divided among themselves or open to possibilities for change.

The key question then becomes *not* 'why do subjects obey?' *but rather* 'under what conditions do which particular groups begin to challenge the rules of the game, and how do these developments relate to the strategies of rulers and their staffs seeking to sustain the system of domination?' The origins and development of dissent and opposition, and their relations to the changing orientations and capacities for action of rulers under different circumstances, thus become the keys to understanding political stability and instability.

These abstract reflections must, of course, be complemented by real historical analysis of real historical configurations, to which we now return.

Reinterpreting GDR history

The relatively long history of the GDR, followed by its very rapid collapse, underlines quite clearly the inadequacy of either a 'history from above' or a 'history from below' taken in isolation; it indicates, too, the futility of a political history which is not informed by social history, or a social history which is not intrinsically linked with political history. And the history of this most intrusive of political regimes illustrates, too, the importance of analysis of mentalities, of conflicting ideals and world-views, in the context of certain changing structural conditions and international contexts.

In so far as any sort of periodization can be traced, the passage of generations certainly made a considerable difference. On the one hand, people began to take the GDR for granted, as an entity that would continue to exist for the foreseeable future—certainly for their own lifetimes and beyond. Thus there was what may be called a 'coming to terms with the present'; a learning of modes of behaviour which would not get one into trouble with the authorities, which would provide one with certain small advantages and benefits. People learnt, in effect, how to operate or play the system, according to often unwritten rules and codes of behaviour. It was this which produced the patterns of outward conformity and apparent docility prevalent in at least the early 1970s. But this conformity was counterbalanced by the retention of a certain inner distance, a recognition of the fact that one was playing a game to which one lacked the requisite inner commitment. Those socialized under the Third Reich might have been particularly adept at playing this game. But a younger generation which had never known anything other than the GDR was often, paradoxically, characterized both by higher expectations of what the state could offer and, in certain respects, even less convinced of its merits. A considerable percentage of youth—a minority, but a sizeable minority—effectively switched off, dropped out, experimented with forms of nonconformity and asocial behaviour. This was not necessarily political, however; the development of the tiny but visible minority of politically active groups in the 1980s was a unique development under specific structural and cultural preconditions. More widespread was a simple failure of the regime even to co-opt people to a passive assent to the overall goals and outer parameters of the state—particularly the lack of freedom to travel—even though there was a degree of differentiated support for at least some specific policies and aspects of life in the GDR. Yet, in the process of the SED's attempts, it did ultimately change patterns of behaviour, expectations, and attitudes.

As far as more active opposition is concerned, the argument has been developed in this book that mass discontent did not necessarily mean the basis for a popular uprising, let alone a successful revolution. What was important was less the simple existence of oppositional opinions or orientations, which existed throughout the GDR's history, than the emergence of new forms of organization and the development of an incipient 'civil society' in the context of changing circumstances and regime responses in the course of the 1980s. And in 1989, it was only relatively slowly, and late, that the masses entered the political scene, when the regime was visibly crumbling from above.

Prior to 1989, there was only one widespread popular uprising in the GDR's history, that of 1953. There was also, throughout, a steady minority of intellectuals who criticized, usually from a Marxist standpoint, the shortcomings of the neo-Stalinist form of regime which existed in the GDR; again, for the most part they were relatively easily isolated. In contrast to the dissident intelligentsias of Poland and Czechoslovakia, they failed to command a broader following among the professional classes, or to create alliances with members of the working classes, let alone the peasantry (which was not exactly in the vanguard of political activity in the other cases either, it may be noted parenthetically). The most critical spirits in East Germany could also, in contrast to those in neighbouring communist states, be readily shipped to the West where continued critiques might command higher royalties but would at least be cut off from immediate political networking and influence among like-minded souls. For all the diversity of forms of intellectual critique and popular discontent during the period until the late 1970s, there was one feature in common: dissent was fragmented. Strikes remained localized, daubing slogans and distributing leaflets was more effective in letting off steam than rallying non-existent troops, private grumbling and a retreat into the small circle of family and friends was often the only means of retaining a degree of authenticity.

A major difference from around the late 1970s was the more effective organization and coordination of dissent. There were, too, significant shifts in the culture, ideology, and practical goals of the most articulate and organized dissenters of the later 1970s and 1980s. The unwitting effect of the regime's treatment of nonconformists was a growing presence of 'those who thought differently' in the environs of the Protestant Church. And an equally unwitting effect of the regime's attempt to 'coordinate' the latter as an institution was precisely to create the limited structural space in which the new subcultural currents could be nurtured, grow, and eventually reach fruition.

It was not only the culture, the character, and the organizational forms of dissent which changed; there were also key developments in the relations between state and society, and in the character and capacity to respond to challenges from below on the part of the authorities. After the initial period of building up the institutions of party, state, and repressive forces in the 1950s and early 1960s, the structures of domination on the whole operated rather smoothly in the GDR. Organizations of party and state worked hand in hand; the functionary system of rule played a key role in a deep, multifaceted, although never quite absolute, penetration of society. Ironically, despite the fact that there was less popular enthusiasm for the GDR than for the Third Reich, the East German regime was perhaps sustained to a greater degree by widespread societal participation in its structures and functioning. The interpenetration of state and society was at a relatively high level, ensuring a considerable degree of structural stability and reproductive capacity. The one—crucial—failure of the regime as far as the system of domination was concerned was the failure, ultimately, of the SED to co-opt the Protestant Churches. The attempt at *Gleichschaltung*, which appeared so near to realization in March 1978, was to backfire extraordinarily badly in the course of the 1980s. If there were key turning-points in the history of the GDR, the Church–state agreement of 6 March 1978 is to be numbered among them. On the whole, however, whatever the difficulties with respect to the economic sphere, the political system of the GDR was for the most part remarkably streamlined and effective, unlike the infinitely more chaotic organization of the 'polycratic' Third Reich.

Nevertheless, the informing mentalities of the founder generation of communists—that unique combination of paternalism and paranoia—were not sufficient to meet the demands of a modernizing society in the changing world of the 1980s. Moreover, for all its streamlined efficiency, the communist system never devised a satisfactory mechanism to ensure a smooth succession to the leadership. Party discipline and the habits of subordination allowed the ageing leadership under Honecker to remain in command for too long, with no means of ensuring any non-destabilizing change at the top. The ensuing differentiation within the ruling groups, the rising frustration in the middle ranks with the inflexible gerontocracy above, the apparent need—evident to all except the immediate Honecker coterie—to engage in at least a limited degree of restructuring (although not democratization in the Western sense, let alone a collapse into the arms of the West), added up in the end to a quite different set of responses to the challenges of the autumn of 1989 than the united front evident in most earlier periods of crisis after the débâcle of 1953. Of course, had the Iron Curtain between Hungary and Austria not been opened, had the masses not acquired the courage of their convictions to come out on to the streets and demonstrate, had Honecker had the sense to retire on grounds of age at what appeared to be a high point of his career in 1987, then a leadership transition might have been effected comparable to that from Ulbricht to Honecker in 1971. In the event, however, the ensuing fall of the Wall was to create such entirely different conditions that the entire edifice of communist rule was to crumble with extraordinary speed within a matter of weeks.

Some aspects of the unique international status of the GDR have been touched on above. The Soviet Union was of such obvious importance in the foundation, development, and death of the GDR that relations between the Soviets and SED leaders have been the subject of constant and highly detailed investigation. With the opening of the archives, it is to be expected that scholarly interpretations will continue to be revised for some time to come. At every stage in the GDR's life, its leaders were in different ways constrained, to a greater or lesser degree, by sometimes conflicting Soviet aims and considerations. These external parameters constituted the outer conditions for the developments in domestic popular opinion explored in this book. The West also served a number of stabilizing functions which should not be ignored: as dumping ground for dissidents and disruptive elements; as highly valuable source of hard foreign currency, essential equipment and materials, and increasingly also of credits; and arguably also as a foil in the ideological warfare of the Cold War period ('where have all the Nazis gone?'). Many commentators have also subsequently criticized Western politicians in the post-Adenauer era for abandoning the Hallstein doctrine and being too willing to talk with the GDR government, thus according it a degree of international legitimacy to which it should not have been entitled.

But Western policies in the 1970s and 1980s clearly also proved in a number of respects to be important in *de*stabilizing communist rule in the GDR. The West inevitably remained an uncomfortable salient point of comparison: the lack of intrinsic national legitimacy for the GDR was compounded by the lower standard of living and the possibility (not always indulged in by the population) of making unfavourable comparisons with the freer and more affluent lifestyle of the West. More particularly, the policy of the Federal Republic towards the GDR from the era of *Ostpolitik* onwards tended to foster the conditions for a degree of openness and debate in the GDR, and made it more difficult for a regime under the post-Helsinki spotlight to clamp down on dissidents in ways it might have liked. Here, the policies of those Western politicians prepared to treat with the GDR authorities appear to have gone just far enough to destabilize, but in the end not so far as ultimately to shore up the regime. The policy of maintaining openness and human contacts was sufficient to encourage the survival of limited spaces for 'thinking differently', but not sufficient to accord final legitimation to the repressive regime (although had the division of Europe remained for long enough, it might possibly at some stage have come to this). West German exponents of *détente* with the GDR never quite dared to amend the provision of their own Basic Law which committed them to the ultimate goal of reunification and proclaimed the entitlement to citizenship in the West of Germans in the East, despite the fact that reunification appeared an increasingly unreal chimera propagated only by revisionist fringes on the far right. Had the Federal Republic acceded to Honecker's desire for full and final recognition of GDR citizenship, a separate East German economy after the fall of the Wall might have been somewhat more viable, sustainable at least in terms of retention of labour power in the medium term, than in the event it proved to be. The existence of entitlement to citizenship in the richer West with open borders for East Germans was the final nail in the GDR's coffin.

Was the GDR inevitably doomed to fail?

If we agree that, at least historically, the Wall was the essential precondition for the GDR's survival from 1961 to 1989, then a further question must be posed. Was the GDR intrinsically non-viable? Teleological views of regimes which have collapsed tend to discern the seeds of later destruction in every aspect of their development, as the historiography of the failed Weimar Republic reveals only too clearly. In the wake of the collapse of the GDR, a similar historiography is already developing. There are a number of hypotheses which may be advanced in seeking to address the question of the GDR's survival chances or, as the Germans so nicely put it, its *Lebensunfähigkeit*.

First of all, there was the multifaceted problem of the GDR's lack of either national or intrinsic legitimacy. The GDR was clearly an artificially created state with no 'national' legitimacy. But, in a sense, this is true of *all* states. Historically considered, the concept of 'nation'—which in popular parlance today seems a 'natural' entity—is itself a relatively recent invention.[4] The notion advanced by nineteenth-century nationalist movements that nations and political states should be coterminous is an even more recent invention. Historically, there are many precedents for the viability, under a wide range of conditions, of states which are either multinational or cover only parts of a nation which is divided among different states. The history of the 'Germans' themselves provides innumerable variants on this theme, as any cursory consideration of Austrian and Swiss history, in addition to the history of 'small Germany' more narrowly defined, will readily suggest. The mobility of borders and frontiers in central Europe has been one of the few constants—if that is the right word—of central European history over the ages. Moreover, a sense of national identity is often forged more by common institutions and experiences *after* changes in political boundaries than as a prerequisite for the stability of those frontiers.

Without entering into the very interesting issue of whether or not two separate national identities were developing among the Germans, East and West, a more general point must be made. It was not so much because the GDR lacked national legitimacy, as that it failed to produce a new, intrinsic legitimacy of its own, that its stability was undermined. The widespread discontent within the GDR, relating both to material shortcomings and to lack of political and physical freedom, was exacerbated in a context in which there was another state offering automatic citizenship entitlement. If

---

[4] For further discussion and a guide to the relevant literature, see M. Fulbrook (ed.), *National Histories and European History* (London: UCL Press, 1993).

large numbers of the GDR's citizens had been dissatisfied and wanted to leave, but had not had the benefit of a richer neighbour which would welcome them in, then the degree and character of domestic instability would have been rather different.

The differences would not all have run in the same direction, however. It is certainly true that the haemorrhage of citizens was exceedingly damaging in the short term, both in the period before 1961 when refugees were predominantly young, skilled, and male, and in 1989 when the refugee crisis both precipitated the regime crisis and ultimately also determined the collapse into the hands of the Federal Republic. But the medium-term effects of the early period of population loss may, somewhat paradoxically, have been on the whole to help to stabilize the system in the 1960s and 1970s. Career chances and the possibility of rapid promotion in skilled occupations and professions were open to those who were prepared (or constrained) to stay in the GDR and to evince the appropriate political conformity or, better, commitment. A generation of functionaries and professionals was hence produced who owed their rapid rise to positions of responsibility directly to the system itself; and who were therefore prepared to engage in compromises, and anchor the system. In the longer term, of course, the rapid rise of this relatively young generation tended to block the chances of those in the following age groups, who hence felt increasingly frustrated and disillusioned with a state populated and run by, it may have seemed, people of relatively mediocre abilities promoted above the level they deserved.

The lack of intrinsic legitimacy relates centrally to the question of the material shortcomings of the GDR. Had the West German economic miracle and affluent consumer society not been the significant comparator—indeed, had West German capitalism not been so spectacularly successful—East Germans might only have compared their situation with the even less successful economies of other Eastern European states (and their own past in the 1920s and 1930s), and have been less discontented on the economic front. But again, some qualifications are in order. The state's interventionist role, and its own self-proclaimed social policies—particularly in the era of 'the unity of economic and social policy' under Honecker—raised expectations among the populace which were not ultimately fulfilled. Moreover, a somewhat post-materialist concern about the environment seems to have taken precedence as an issue in the later 1980s, although here again the West offered a better record.

The economy is a key factor in other respects than popular discontent, important though that is in terms of political consequences. Economic

stagnation, environmental devastation, rising international debt, were decisive issues in the changing mood among the political élites in the course of
the 1980s. The shifting of fronts, the incipient lability within the ranks and
even the higher reaches of the SED, the willingness to treat with notions of
a palace revolution, are all inexplicable—as indeed is the wider context of
Soviet perestroika—without an understanding of the economic problems
of the Soviet bloc in the 1980s. Although the GDR was better cushioned
than its neighbours, for a variety of reasons, not even Western credits from
its affluent twin could stave off the day of reckoning for ever.

This consideration, inevitably, raises the question of whether all command economies are intrinsically guaranteed to fail, and whether the market
system is inherently more rational and successful. Given the background of
periodic recessions, depressions, and slumps, and the fact that the state
intervenes to a greater or lesser degree even in 'market' economies, which
also carry their casualties in terms of unemployment, to adopt the latter
position requires careful qualification. Moreover, it would be overly simplistic to assume that the internal character of the economic system—central
command or market—is the sole or even primary factor determining success
or failure.

Without entering into technical debates in economic history, it is possible
to point to contextual factors which were of major significance in affecting
the economic performance of the Soviet bloc. One was of course the
(admittedly contested) economic implications of militarization in the Cold
War era. Whatever the knock-on effects of arms production and other
military-related activities and expenditures, there can be little doubt that
these activities were detrimental to consumer satisfaction in Eastern Europe.
Similarly, it appears to have been primarily political, not economic,
considerations which brought the economic reforms of the 1960s to a rapid
end in the wake of 1968. On the views of some economic historians, these
reforms held at least the promise of rendering the East German economy
viable and capable of further flexibility and development.

Secondly, the economic difficulties of the 1980s were intimately related to
the wider energy crises of 1973 and 1979, and to the world economic
recession which afflicted not only Soviet bloc countries but also Western
capitalist economies in the 1980s. For a variety of reasons, the East German
economy was less well able to respond to the increasingly unfavourable
international economic conditions of the period after 1973 than were the
struggling, but nevertheless surviving, capitalist economies of Western
Europe. Aid from the Federal Republic meant that the GDR's economic
problems were both alleviated and camouflaged, but the social and econ-

omic policies of Honecker from the reforms of the early 1970s through the microchip madness of the 1980s failed to produce any viable solution to the underlying difficulties and broader challenges. One can plausibly argue that the East German economy was not intrinsically non-viable, but rather that its developing non-viability set in from around 1973. There is also a broader problem here which must be mentioned: given the ways in which, historically, the performance of command economies has been intimately affected by their relations with contemporaneous capitalist economies and polities, the question of the alleged non-viability of a state-controlled economy is one which must remain, at least theoretically, open.

Other factors relevant to the intrinsic viability or increasing inflexibility of the GDR are more specific to its own internal structures (although, to the extent to which these structures were common to other communist states, comparable effects might be observed elsewhere). The character of the system as a whole was such as to foster particular traits and values. Patterns of promotion militated against independent individuals who were prepared to take initiatives, and in favour of those conformists who would unquestioningly obey directives from above and toe whatever happened to be the official line. This official line was itself determined by a small number of men at the top of the apex of political power. By the 1980s, the leadership increasingly cut itself off both from 'reality'—reports to the centre were so glossy as to be effectively meaningless, while the official Wandlitz compound presented an artificial island insulated from experience of everyday life in the GDR—and from the advice of those placed in a better position to know what was really going on. There was, thus, a decline in any real attempts to come to terms with the issues, to grapple with policies, or to address fundamental problems, but rather an increasing resort to a combination of indoctrination and repression. In the closing years of the Honecker era, the police and the Stasi were increasingly seen as the first, not the last, resort of government.

Ultimately, it can be said both that the GDR helped to produce the seeds of its own destruction, although the final outcome was by no means in any way inevitable, and that its history cannot be understood in abstraction from the wider context in which it was created, sustained, and eventually abandoned. The history of the GDR is intrinsically related to the broader history of Europe: to the war unleashed by Hitler, and the consequences of this war; to the Cold War and the competition of systems; to the collapse of the Soviet empire and the relinquishment of its satellites. But the character of the GDR's life and the manner of its collapse equally cannot be explained without an informed understanding of domestic social and political patterns and processes. And when one examines this complex configuration of factors, the thought must occur: a truncated and occupied corner of defeated post-Nazi Germany was hardly the most promising soil in which to plant the seeds of the Marxist vision of a truly human and free society of equals. In the words of the classic joke, when asked the way to a desirable location the respondent replies: 'If I were going there, I wouldn't start from here.'

A 'fourth Reich'? The GDR in comparative context

Comparisons can take many forms. The most frequent forms of comparison in the political cut and thrust of public debates tend to be at the polar extremes: contrasting, or equating. Thus the GDR, throughout its history, was constantly contrasted with its Western, democratic, capitalist twin, the Federal Republic of Germany. This politically motivated contrast was two-sided: the black-and-white character of the debate was found in mirror image on both sides of the Iron Curtain, with only the colour of the evaluation changing as one viewed the pair from one side or the other. Equating was the corollary of contrasting: from the West, the East German dictatorship was often equated with the Third Reich and/or with other communist 'satellite' states; the concept of 'totalitarianism', despite its somewhat chequered history, could perform a useful function for implicit equation in such attempts. From the East, it was West Germany which (under the blanket heading of 'fascism' or 'capitalist imperialism') could be tarred with the slur of continuities with Nazism, although, admittedly, under another outward guise.

Such very crude comparisons, whether of equation or contrast, can readily be ridiculed. They relate, however, to a broader problem. Natural scientists are free to invent a vocabulary which is independent of, and can be neither employed nor challenged by, the inert matter under analysis. But historians and social scientists, in contrast, must use words which also form the language of public debate. Common elements provide a conceptual apparatus for classifying the world according to salient characteristics— freedom or lack of it, to take the prime example at issue here. The very word 'dictatorship', unashamedly used in the title of this book, carries with it a weight of connotations and reverberations. It is therefore vitally important to identify with greater precision what were the defining characteristics of the East German dictatorship, using comparison not as a simplistic tool of global conflation and castigation, but rather as a means towards a more differentiated analysis of a complex reality.

The GDR is often, for largely political reasons, compared with the preceding Nazi dictatorship. In the socio-economic sphere, of course, the GDR effected a very radical revolution. From land reform in 1945, through the progressive expropriation of private property, the step-wise collectivization of agriculture, and state ownership and control of industry and finance, the character of economy and society in the GDR was dramatically transformed. The debates today therefore revolve more around the political patterns in the two dictatorships. What were the similarities and differences in degrees of popular consent or opposition, in patterns of repression and resistance? How do structures of power and patterns of popular political culture compare?

The most useful areas of comparison have to do with the areas in which the dictatorships evince a degree of similarity in seeking to enforce their claims, and the respects in which these attempts were or were not resisted (in the broadest sense) by different elements in the population. The total claims made on citizens by the SED are clearly reminiscent of those of the Third Reich, and have given some basis to attempts to compare the two regimes under the general conceptual heading of 'totalitarianism'. (It is perhaps in this preliminary, categorizing function with respect to regime claims—if at all—that the concept is of some use.) In general, the attempt at total influence on people, and the total transformation of attitudes, was not a realizable goal in either the Third Reich or the GDR. But, in different circumstances in each case, the attempts were not without effects, some more and some less conducive to the stability of the dictatorship.

Any analysis of popular opinion in the Nazi dictatorship must balance a number of conflicting phenomena. On the one hand, Hitler was brought to power by a combination of mass popular support and élite machinations. Key individuals in the closing stages of the Weimar Republic thought that they could effectively make use of this upstart demagogue, Hitler, to their own ends; in the event, of course, they were proved wrong. Nevertheless, the authoritarian élites who helped to destroy the Weimar Republic recognized the genuine popular appeal of Hitler's rhetoric and the power of Nazi political organization. Widespread support for Hitler in the summer of 1932 (37.8 per cent of the vote) was real; and Hitler's popular support probably rose at certain times after 1933, particularly at times of easy foreign policy triumphs. In the peacetime years of the Third Reich, Hitler continued to exert an extraordinary degree of charismatic authority, whipping up popular enthusiasm for the Führer which to a considerable extent compensated for the petty irritations and grumbles of everyday life. Moreover, despite criticisms of some aspects of social and economic policy in the

Third Reich, other features—such as the social activities and sense of community experienced in the Hitler Jugend or Bund deutscher Mädel (the youth organizations for boys and girls)—were genuinely popular in many quarters.

On the other hand, of course, the Third Reich was at the same time a brutal, repressive dictatorship. The first concentration camp, at Dachau, was opened as early as March 1933 for those who did not conform. The SA, the SS, the Gestapo, in different ways epitomized the reality of brute force as the final arbiter in what was still formally a state adhering to the rule of law. People who did not share the quasi-hysterical faith in the Führer or even, more pragmatically, some of the prejudices and goals of the Nazis, lived in a climate of fear, barely daring to voice their hesitations or reveal their nonconformity. Those who did not have the immense personal courage—or sometimes quite futile bravado—to risk open opposition had to retreat into a double life, minimally conforming in public and grumbling in private. And ultimately, in this police state, particularly under the radicalization of wartime conditions, those whose dissent was betrayed—often quite spontaneously by neighbours bearing a personal grudge—had to pay with their freedom, sometimes with their lives.[5]

How does the GDR compare? Quite clearly it lacked the initial, intrinsic popular legitimacy enjoyed by the Third Reich. Imposed under conditions of defeat and military occupation, the rule of the SED never achieved the degree of genuine popular support enjoyed by Hitler. After 1945, it is true, many Germans did share an urgent desire to build a new and better society, to make a clean break with an utterly discredited past. In the later years of the war, disaffection and disillusionment with Hitler had spread far wider than the circles of those intrinsically opposed to Nazism on grounds of principle. But these feelings were counterbalanced by a widespread fear of communism, dislike of the Soviet occupation, and disgruntlement with the political constraints and material shortcomings of the present. And in the GDR of the 1950s there was no equivalent of the economic upswing out of depression in the 1930s, no equivalent of the sense of a return to national greatness to compensate for political repression.

Yet the communists wanted at least the appearance, and preferably the reality, of comparable mass support; they made comparable 'total claims' on individuals; they employed comparable organizational means to try to incorporate people into some wider sense of 'national community'

[5] As many as 5,000 Germans were sentenced to death by the notorious People's Court under Roland Freisler in the closing months of the war alone, in a veritable orgy of political repression for the most minor infringements after the failure of the July Plot of 1944.

(although there were of course major differences between what the communists understood by 'community' and the Nazis' ethnic—racist—definition of the *Volksgemeinschaft*). While the SED never succeeded in developing any genuine leadership cult—despite the ubiquity of pictures of Ulbricht and subsequently Honecker in rooms and offices where once Hitler (and before him the Kaiser) had hung—they did to some degree succeed in obtaining at least the outward compliance of a considerable proportion of society. The correlate of the lack of a genuinely popular enthusiasm for a charismatic leader figure was the existence of a highly organized, smoothly functioning apparatus of power and control. Furthermore, what was accomplished by the sniping of neighbours to the Gestapo in Nazi Germany developed into the most extraordinary system of organized observation and informing in the Stasi state. And despite the lack of intrinsic enthusiasm, as a result of a variety of factors explored above by the 1970s many East Germans had come to some form of *modus vivendi* with a regime which had stabilized in a manner never achieved by the volatile, expansionist, and destructive Third Reich. It should not be forgotten that the Third Reich lasted a mere twelve years; under admittedly very different international circumstances—not all of which were necessarily beneficial to longevity—the GDR lasted forty.

Even the most cursory comparison of the GDR with the Third Reich will tend to reveal a far greater number of differences than similarities, which it would be inappropriate to begin to explore in any detail here. The ease with which this particular case for comparison has been grasped—both after 1945 and after 1989—has had more, perhaps, to do with contemporary political considerations than with the intention of seeking analytical purchase on historical interpretations of dictatorial rule.

The GDR as contemporary history

The GDR is not merely an academic stamping ground for the testing of social and political theories. Real people lived in the really existing GDR; many of them are still seeking to make their lives in the radically altered situation of today.

Given the politically sensitive nature of all contemporary history, explanation and evaluation can easily develop into retribution, recrimination, or self-justification. While academic debates can always flare up into heated ideological battlegrounds—on the pages of learned journals, the English Revolution (or merely revolt?) of the seventeenth century is by no means over—the recent history of Germany is perhaps peculiarly politically sensitive. Heated confrontations with the Nazi past were by no means resolved before they became overlaid, and further complicated, by a new and complex confrontation with the more recent past. History in Germany is so deeply linked in with the characteristically German preoccupation with national identity that there can be a peculiarly sharp quality to even ostensibly 'purely academic' debates. Questions about causes rapidly become questions about the attribution of blame. Explanations of the outcomes of particular struggles, long hence fought in reality, rapidly become renewed battles over the identification of sins of omission and commission.

And—not to put too fine a point on much of the current discussion—was the GDR effectively just as evil as the Third Reich? Should 'destasification' learn its lessons from the lukewarm and patchy denazification carried out after 1945? How should the Germans, once again, overcome a dictatorship? Who should be punished, who reprimanded, who allowed to remain in positions of responsibility and reward, who compensated for injustices suffered? These 'knowledge-guiding interests' inform and underlie many of the current debates, from the parliamentary investigative commission (Enquetekommission des Bundestages) on the one hand to the diatribes of journalists in the popular press on the other.

It must be stated at the outset, very categorically, that while it is not the task of a historian to propose any scale of relative morality, there was no equivalent of Auschwitz in the GDR. It was not a primary aim of the SED regime to destroy—to murder, in cold blood—millions of fellow human beings on grounds of 'race' or identity. Nevertheless, the intrinsic immorality and inhumanity of many communist tactics and strategies—the lies, the deception, the devaluation of personal differences, the elevation of a notional historical goal over individual rights—have been emphasized throughout this book. From the moral point of view of this author, as for many others, this wholesale disregard for certain values, this willing destruction of lives, emotions, careers, this preparedness to deform both human personalities and the physical environment in pursuit of the alleged higher goal of history, are utterly unacceptable. To point out that the GDR was not the Third Reich, at least in respect of mass genocide, is therefore in no way to condone the sins of the GDR. (Nor, it should be added, is it necessarily to turn a blind eye to the inequalities, distortions, and injustices wrought by elected governments in capitalist societies; but they may at least in principle, though not always in practice, be held accountable—precisely the virtue of a democracy—for the consequences of their actions.) The sins of the GDR are, however, more readily understandable, perhaps, than those of the Nazis: there is really no way of comprehending Auschwitz, however much documentation may be gathered, however much explanation and argument may take place. It is somewhat easier to enter the mind-set of those who sought to overcome this disaster and construct a better society, however much one disapproves of the communist world-view and the repressive methods they felt themselves constrained to employ.

Can there be any moral equivalent of the Richter scale for registering degrees of evil? Loss of life is clearly more final than loss of liberty; being deprived of ever having children is more absolute than being deprived of seeing them, of being able only to look forward to occasional visits; killing millions in factories of death is in absolute terms on a larger scale than killing a matter of hundreds for seeking to escape from a drab and repressive state. Unleashing an expansionist war embroiling states and societies across the world is of a quite different order than playing a minor, subordinate role in the subversive tactics and boundary sniping of the Cold War. But, ultimately, the debate on degrees of evil escapes the realms of historical explanation. It is a matter for ethics, political philosophy, individual morality.

All individuals have their own personal values and preferences, their sympathies and hostilities, and what Habermas has popularized, in a somewhat unwieldy formulation, as 'knowledge-guiding interests'. These inevitably colour questions posed, categories used to gather and organize material, and general frameworks of enquiry. Innumerable scholars have come to agree with Max Weber that all historical and social scientific investigation is in one sense doomed to transience, as each succeeding generation poses new questions to the past. Within generations, a plurality of approaches is based on the fact that investigators are also, in some senses, a part of that which is under investigation: human analysis of human societies inevitably entails a degree of self-reflexivity.

It is nevertheless the task of the historian—however personally sympathetic to one cause or another, however hostile to the views or activities of others in the drama—to take a step back and seek to present a sober analysis of all the relevant factors as they are captured in the particular net of categories and concepts. Historians can only seek to understand the ways in which human beings of different ethical, moral, and political persuasions responded to pressures and challenges, sought to accommodate themselves to given conditions, or to transform the circumstances in which they lived.

Whether any of the visions for which the GDR formed the battleground—from that of an essentially humanistic, egalitarian communism, undistorted by the twists of Cold War Stalinism, through that of some form of Christian or democratic socialism—could ever have been achieved, under more favourable circumstances, historical analysis will not reveal. Given the real historical circumstances, and particularly the economic watershed between East and West, which increased to a yawning chasm over the years, a GDR with open borders—a prerequisite for any form of truly democratic socialism—could scarcely hope to survive. The final, ironic outcome, the twist in the tail of the history of the GDR—the ultimate 'lesson of history'—is that intentional action very often produces totally unintended consequences. A degree of humility as well as adherence to aspirations and visions is in order for anyone seeking not merely to understand but also to change the world.

Many commentators have pointed out that the fall of the Wall has served only to reveal the startling persistence of inner walls, walls in the mind. The failures of mutual understanding are remarkable. But with the end of the real Cold War, it is time too to seek to overcome and reject simplistic, black-and-white images of the divided past. The contested history of the GDR, the illumination of its inner life, must be retrieved in all its complexity and contradiction into the double history of the new Germany. Its reappropriation is only now beginning.

SOURCES AND BIBLIOGRAPHY

Abbreviations and note on the archival sources

A considerable amount of renaming, moving, and reclassification of the newly opened East German archives took place during the course of the research for this book. I have cited archival material under the heading of the archive and the classification system in use at the time of my reseach. All translations of quotations from archival sources in the text are my own. The following notes list the main archival sources used, with the abbreviations used in citations in the text.

BP   Bundesarchiv Potsdam: the main state archives of the GDR, located in Potsdam, and now run as a branch of the Federal Archives of Germany. I made use of the files of the Ministry for Church Affairs, and material relating to dissent and oppositional movements.

FDGB   The GDR trade union archive, which at the time of my research was still an independent archive under the auspices of the Johannes-Sassenbach-Stiftung located on Unter den Linden, Berlin. The material from this archive is now in the SAPMO-BArch (see below). I made particular use of trade union reports on popular opinion (*Stimmungen und Meinungen*) and files containing reports on particular incidents (*besondere Vorkommnisse*), as well as more general reports to the FDGB Executive Committee.

IfGA, ZPA   The archive of the Institute for the History of the Workers' Movement in the Central Party Archive of the SED. During the course of my research, this was taken over by the Bundesarchiv to become part of the SAPMO-BArch (see below). A considerable amount of opening up and reclassification of material was under way at the time of my research. I have cited material consulted before the change to the SAPMO umbrella under 'IfGA, ZPA' in view of subsequent reclassifications.

IfZ   The Institute for Contemporary History, Munich. I used this for files relating to the Soviet occupation, for personal correspondence and autobiographical accounts of the early post-war years, and for Western reports on public opinion in the Soviet zone before and after the foundation of the GDR. Prior to the opening of the GDR archives, this was a major source of primary material on East Germany; it was of course rapidly overtaken in importance by the

East German archives, but nevertheless contains many significant holdings.

MfS   The archive of the GDR Ministry for State Security (the Stasi), now run under the auspices of the Federal Office for the Documents of the State Security Service of the Former GDR (or Gauck-Behörde). I sought to follow shafts into this vast labyrinth by reading reports on specific oppositional groups and activities as well as the more general reports of the Central Evaluation and Information Group (ZAIG).

SAPMO-BArch   The Foundation for the Archives of the Parties and Mass Organizations of the GDR under the Federal Archives of Germany. A number of previously independent archives, including the FDGB (trade union) and the FDJ (Free German Youth organization) archives, as well as the SED party archive itself, are now under this umbrella. Much of the material was being reclassified at the time of research; the abbreviation 'vorl.' (*vorläufig*) in some footnotes indicates a temporary classification assigned by the archive.

In the SED archives, I made particular use of the reports from party organizations in different regional and local areas, of sociological surveys and general reports compiled for the use of the Politburo, and of materials located in the files of particular offices (Büro Ulbricht, Honecker, Krenz, Schabowski, etc.), as well as making *Stichproben* (exploratory forays) into other materials kept by this archive. On every visit, new areas had been opened up for researchers to peruse; there is a veritable gold-mine here for further research.

Interviews

When I first conceived the idea for this book, I had no idea that the GDR would collapse and the archives would be opened. I was nevertheless very curious to find out how people experienced life in the GDR, and what effects the regime's propaganda and organizational strategies had on their perceptions and behaviour. I therefore sought to supplement the material available at the time in the West with a number of informal interviews with individuals in the GDR. These were carried out in a relatively unsystematic and unauthorized fashion in the course of a series of 'holiday' visits on tourist visas to the GDR at various times during the 1980s. I made notes after discussions, but never attempted to tape-record any conversation.

The people I spoke to may be divided into a number of categories:

(*a*) 'carriers of the regime' met in the course of official occasions (such as the 1983 Luther anniversary, celebrations for the 35th anniversary of the GDR in 1984, numerous events organized by bodies such as the Britain–GDR Friendship Society, and so on);

(*b*) historians and other academics with whom I came into contact through conferences or by arranged visits;

(c) Christians contacted through Christa Grengel of the central offices of the Protestant Church in East Berlin, and, quite separately, through the Quakers;

(d) individuals contacted through personal networks of family and friends, including people of different generations, social backgrounds, occupations, and political persuasions;

(e) casual contacts met in the course of travelling around.

This cross-section is of course not representative in any stringent sociological sense, and discussions were essentially of a suggestive nature. But active engagement with the views of people living in, and coming to terms with, the GDR in many different ways formed an integral part of the development of the arguments outlined in this book.

Select bibliography of published sources

This select bibliography lists the published primary and secondary sources referred to in footnotes (excluding a few articles and some works of imaginative literature), and a few other works consulted in the course of writing this book. It makes no attempt to represent a comprehensive guide to publications on the GDR, which is currently one of the fastest growing areas of German historiography.

ACKERMANN, A., 'Gibt es einen besonderen *deutschen* Weg zum Sozialismus?', *Einheit*, 1 (Feb. 1946), 22–32.

ANDERT, R., and HERZBERG, W., *Der Sturz: Erich Honecker im Kreuzverhör* (Berlin and Weimar: Aufbau Verlag, 1990).

BAEHR, VERA-MARIA (ed.), *Wir denken erst seit Gorbatschow. Protokolle von Jugendlichen aus der DDR* (Recklinghausen: Georg Bitter Verlag, 1990).

BAHRO, RUDOLF, *The Alternative in Eastern Europe* (London: New Left Books, 1979).

BARING, ARNULF, *Der 17. Juni 1953* (Stuttgart: Deutsche Verlags-Anstalt, 1983; orig. 1965).

BAYLIS, THOMAS, *The Technical Intelligentsia and the East German Elite* (Berkeley and Los Angeles: University of California Press, 1974).

BELEITES, M., *Untergrund. Ein Konflikt mit der Stasi in der Uran-Provinz* (Berlin: BasisDruck, 1992).

BESIER, GERHARD, *Der SED-Staat und die Kirche* (Munich: C. Bertelsmann Verlag, 1993).

—— and WOLF, S. (eds.), *'Pfarrer, Christen und Katholiken'. Das Ministerium für Staatssicherheit der ehemaligen DDR und die Kirchen* (Neukirchen: Neukirchener Verlag, 2nd edn., 1992).

BEYME, K. VON, and ZIMMERMANN, HARTMUT (eds.), *Policymaking in the German Democratic Republic* (Aldershot: Gower, 1984).

BLANKE, THOMAS, and ERD, RAINER (eds.), *DDR—Ein Staat vergeht* (Frankfurt-on-Main: Fischer Taschenbuch Verlag, 1990).

BULL, HEDLEY (ed.), *The Challenge of the Third Reich* (Oxford: Clarendon Press, 1986).

BÜRGERKOMITEE LEIPZIG (ed.), *Stasi Intern. Macht und Banalität* (Leipzig: Forum Verlag, 1991).

BÜSCHER, WOLFGANG, and WENSIERSKI, PETER, *Null Bock auf DDR. Aussteigerjugend im anderen Deutschland* (Hamburg: Rowohlt, 1984).

BUSCHFORT, WOLFGANG, *Das Ostbüro der SPD* (Munich: Oldenbourg, 1991).

CHILDS, DAVID, *The GDR: Moscow's German Ally* (London: Allen and Unwin, 1985).

—— (ed.), *Honecker's Germany* (London: Allen and Unwin, 1985).

Chronik der Ereignisse in der DDR, Edition Deutschland Archiv (Cologne: Verlag Wissenschaft und Politik, 1989).

CONRADT, D. P., *The German Polity* (London: Longman, 3rd edn., 1986).

DÄHN, HORST, *Konfrontation oder Kooperation? Das Verhältnis von Staat und Kirche in der SBZ/DDR 1945–1980* (Opladen: Westdeutscher Verlag, 1982).

DDR-Almanach '90 (Stuttgart: Bonn Aktuell, 1990).

DDR-Handbuch (Cologne: Verlag Wissenschaft und Politik, 2nd edn., 1979).

DDR—Wer war Wer. Ein biographisches Lexikon (Berlin: Ch. Links Verlag, 1992).

DENNIS, M., *German Democratic Republic* (London: Pinter, 1988).

DIEDRICH, TORSTEN, *Der 17. Juni 1953 in der DDR. Bewaffnete Gewalt gegen das Volk* (Berlin: Dietz Verlag, 1991).

DITFURTH, C. V., *Blockflöten. Wie die CDU ihre realsozialistische Vergangenheit verdrängt* (Cologne: Kiepenheuer and Witsch, 1991).

ECKART, GABRIELE, *So sehe ick die Sache. Protokolle aus der DDR* (Cologne: Kiepenheuer and Witsch, 1984).

ECKELMANN, WOLFGANG, HERTLE, HANS-HERMAN, and WEINERT, RAINER, *FDGB Intern. Innenansichten einer Massenorganisation der SED* (Berlin: Treptower Verlagshaus GmbH, 1990).

EDWARDS, G. E., *GDR Society and Social Institutions* (London: Macmillan, 1985).

EHRING, KLAUS, and DALLWITZ, MARTIN (eds.), *Schwerter zu Pflugscharen. Friedensbewegung in der DDR* (Hamburg: Rowohlt, 1982).

ELITZ, ERNST, *Sie waren dabei* (Stuttgart: Deutsche Verlags-Anstalt, 1991).

EVANS, RICHARD J., *In Hitler's Shadow* (London: I. B. Tauris, 1989).

FILMER, WERNER, and SCHWAN, HERIBERT, *Opfer der Mauer* (Munich: C. Bertelsmann Verlag, 1991).

FISCHBACH, GÜNTER (ed.), *DDR-Almanach '90* (Stuttgart: Bonn Aktuell, 1990).

FISCHER, ALEXANDER, and HEYDEMANN, GÜNTHER (eds.), *Geschichtswissenschaft in der DDR*, i (Berlin: Duncker and Humblot, 1988).

Fischer Weltalmanach: Sonderband DDR (Frankfurt: Fischer, 1990).

FLORATH, BERND, MITTER, ARMIN, and WOLLE, STEFAN (eds.), *Die Ohnmacht der Allmächtigen* (Berlin: Ch. Links Verlag, 1992).

FRICKE, KARL WILHELM, *Opposition und Widerstand in der DDR* (Cologne: Verlag Wissenschaft und Politik, 1984).

—— *MfS Intern* (Cologne: Verlag Wissenschaft und Politik, 1991).

FRIEDHEIM, DANIEL, 'Regime Collapse in the Peaceful East German Revolution: The Role of Middle-Level Officials', *German Politics*, 2: 1 (Apr. 1993), 97–112.

FULBROOK, M., *Piety and Politics: Religion and the Rise of Absolutism in England, Württemberg and Prussia* (Cambridge: Cambridge University Press, 1983).

—— 'Co-option and Commitment: Aspects of Relations between Church and State in the GDR', *Social History*, 12: 1 (Jan. 1987), 73–91.

—— A Concise History of Germany (Cambridge: Cambridge University Press, 1990).

—— The Divided Nation: Germany 1918–1990 (London: Fontana, 1991).

—— The Two Germanies 1945–1990: Problems of Interpretation (Basingstoke: Macmillan, 1992).

—— 'New Historikerstreit, Missed Opportunity, or New Beginning?', German History, 12: 2 (1994), 203–7.

—— (ed.), National Histories and European History (London: UCL Press, 1993).

GAUCK, JOACHIM, Die Stasi-Akten. Das unheimliche Erbe der DDR (Hamburg: Rowohlt, 1991).

GAUS, GÜNTER, Wo Deutschland liegt (Munich: Deutscher Taschenbuch Verlag, 1986; orig. 1983).

GELLATELY, R., The Gestapo in German Society (Oxford: Oxford University Press, 1990).

GERLACH, MANFRED, Mitverantwortlich. Als Liberaler im SED-Staat (Berlin: Morgenbuch Verlag, 1991).

GILL, DAVID, and SCHROETER, ULRICH, Das Ministerium für Staatssicherheit. Anatomie des Mielke-Imperiums (Berlin: Rowohlt, 1991).

GLAESSNER, G.-J., Die andere deutsche Republik (Opladen: Westdeutscher Verlag, 1989).

—— Der schwierige Weg zur Demokratie (Opladen: Westdeutscher Verlag, 1992).

—— and WALLACE, IAN (eds.), The German Revolution of 1989: Causes and Consequences (Oxford: Berg, 1992).

GOECKEL, ROBERT, The Lutheran Church and the East German State (Ithaca, NY: Cornell University Press, 1990).

HACKER, JENS, Deutsche Irrtümer: Schönfärber und Helfershelfer der SED-Diktatur im Westen (Frankfurt-on-Main and Berlin: Ullstein, 1992).

HAGEN, MANFRED, DDR—Juni '53 (Stuttgart: Steiner, 1992).

HAVEMANN, ROBERT, An Alienated Man (London: Davis-Poynter, 1973).

HEITZER, H., GDR: An Historical Outline (Dresden: Verlag Zeit im Bild, 1981).

HELWIG, GISELA, and URBAN, DETLEF (eds.), Kirchen und Gesellschaft in beiden deutschen Staaten (Cologne: Verlag Wissenschaft und Politik, 1987).

HENDERSON, KAREN, 'The Search for Ideological Conformity: Sociological Research on Youth in Honecker's GDR', German History, 10: 3 (Oct. 1992), 318–34.

HENKYS, REINHARD (ed.), Die evangelischen Kirchen in der DDR (Munich: Chr. Kaiser Verlag, 1982).

HENRICH, ROLF, Der vormundschaftliche Staat (Hamburg: Rowohlt, 1989).

IGGERS, GEORG (ed.), Marxist Historiography in Transformation: New Orientations in Recent East German History (Oxford: Berg, 1991).

JAMES, HAROLD, and STONE, MARLA (eds.), When the Wall Came Down: Reactions to German Unification (London: Routledge, 1992).

JÄNICKE, M., Der dritte Weg (Cologne: Neuer Deutscher Verlag, 1964).

JARAUSCH, KONRAD, The Rush to German Unity (New York and Oxford: Oxford University Press, 1994).

—— (ed.), Zwischen Parteilichkeit und Professionalität. Bilanz der Geschichtswissenschaft in der DDR (Berlin: Akademie Verlag, 1991).

JEFFRIES, IAN, and MELZER, MANFRED (eds.), *The East German Economy* (London: Croom Helm, 1987).

JESSE, ECKARD, and MITTER, ARMIN (eds.), *Die Gestaltung der deutschen Einheit* (Bonn: Bundeszentrale für politische Bildung, 1992).

JONES, MERRILL E., 'Origins of the East German Environmental Movement', *German Studies Review*, 16: 2 (May 1993), 235–64.

KAELBLE, HARTMUT, KOCKA, JÜRGEN, and ZWAHR, HARTMUT (eds.), *Sozialgeschichte der DDR* (Stuttgart: Klett-Cotta, 1994).

KELLER, D., MODROW, HANS, and WOLF, HERBERT (eds.), *Ansichten zur Geschichte der DDR* (Bonn, Berlin: PDS/Linke Liste im Bundestag, 1993).

KERSHAW, IAN, *Popular Opinion and Political Dissent in the Third Reich* (Oxford: Clarendon Press, 1983).

—— *The Hitler Myth* (Oxford: Oxford University Press, 1987).

—— *Hitler* (Harlow: Longman, 1991).

—— *The Nazi Dictatorship* (London: Edward Arnold, 3rd edn., 1993).

Kleines Politisches Wörterbuch (Berlin: Dietz Verlag, 3rd edn., 1978).

KLEMM, V., *Korruption und Amtsmißbrauch in der DDR* (Stuttgart: Deutsche Verlags-Anstalt, 1991).

KLESSMANN, CHRISTOPH, *Die doppelte Staatsgründung* (Göttingen: Vandenhoek and Ruprecht, 1982).

—— *Zwei Staaten, eine Nation: Deutsche Geschichte 1955–1970* (Göttingen: Vandenhoek and Ruprecht, 1988).

—— 'Was kann die künftige DDR-Forschung aus der Geschichtsschreibung zum Nationalsozialismus lernen?', *Deutschland Archiv*, 25: 6 (June 1992), 601–6.

KNABE, HUBERTUS (ed.), *Aufbruch in eine andere DDR* (Hamburg: Rowohlt, 1990).

KNAUFT, WOLFGANG, *Katholische Kirche in der DDR* (Mainz: Grünewald, 1980).

KOCKA, JÜRGEN (ed.), *Historische DDR-Forschung: Aufsätze und Studien* (Berlin: Akademie Verlag, 1993).

—— (ed.), *Die DDR als Geschichte* (Berlin: Akademie Verlag, 1994).

KÖNIGSDORF, HELGA, *Adieu DDR* (Hamburg: Rowohlt, 1990).

KRENZ, EGON, *Wenn Mauern fallen* (Vienna: Paul Neff Verlag, 1990).

KRISCH, H., *The German Democratic Republic* (Boulder, Colo.: Westview Press, 1985).

KROCKOW, CHRISTIAN, Graf VON, *The Hour of the Women* (London: Faber and Faber, 1991).

KROH, FERDINAND (ed.), *'Freiheit ist immer Freiheit'. Die Andersdenkenden in der DDR* (Frankfurt-on-Main and Berlin: Ullstein Sachbuch, 1988).

KUCZYNSKI, JÜRGEN, *Ein Leben in der Wissenschaft der DDR* (Münster: Westfälisches Dampfboot, 1993).

KUNZE, REINER, *Die wunderbaren Jahre* (Frankfurt-on-Main: Fischer Verlag, 1976).

LANG, JOCHEN VON, *Erich Mielke* (Berlin: Rowohlt, 1991).

LEONHARD, WOLFGANG, *Child of the Revolution* (London: Collins, 1957).

—— *Spurensuche. Vierzig Jahre nach 'die Revolution entlässt ihre Kinder'* (Cologne: Kiepenheuer and Witsch, 1992).

LINKE, DIETMAR (ed.), *'Streicheln, bis der Maulkorb fertig ist'. Die DDR-Kirche zwischen Kanzel und Konspiration* (Berlin: BasisDruck, 1993).

LOEST, ERICH, *Die Stasi war mein Eckermann, oder: Mein Leben mit der Wanze* (Göttingen: Steidl Verlag, 1991).

LÜDTKE, ALF, *Police and State in Prussia, 1815–1850* (Cambridge: Cambridge University Press, 1989).

LUDZ, PETER CHRISTIAN, *The Changing Party Elite in East Germany* (Cambridge, Mass.: MIT Press, 1972).

MAAZ, HANS-JOACHIM, *Der Gefühlsstau* (Berlin: Argon, 1990).

MCADAMS, A. JAMES, *Germany Divided: From the Wall to Reunification* (Princeton: Princeton University Press, 1993).

MCCAULEY, MARTIN, *Marxism-Leninism in the GDR: The Socialist Unity Party* (London: Macmillan, 1979).

—— *The GDR since 1945* (London: Macmillan, 1983).

MAIER, CHARLES, 'The Collapse of Communism: Approaches for a Future History', *History Workshop*, 31 (Spring 1991), 34–59.

—— *The End of East Germany* (Princeton: Princeton University Press, forthcoming).

MEUSCHEL, SIGRID, *Legitimation und Parteiherrschaft* (Frankfurt-on-Main: Suhrkamp, 1992).

—— 'Überlegungen zu einer Herrschafts- und Gesellschaftsgeschichte der DDR', *Geschichte und Gesellschaft*, 19: 1 (1993).

MEYER, GERD, *Die Machtelite in der Ära Honecker* (Tübingen: A. Francke Verlag, 1991).

MIELKE, ERICH, 'Spiegel-Gespräch', *Der Spiegel*, 46: 36 (31 Aug. 1992).

MITTER, ARMIN, and WOLLE, STEFAN (eds.), *'Ich liebe euch doch alle!' Befehle und Lageberichte des MfS Jan.–Nov. 1989* (Berlin: BasisDruck, 1990).

—— —— *Untergang auf Raten* (Munich: C. Bertelsmann Verlag, 1993).

MÜLLER-ENBERGS, H., SCHULZ, M., and WIELGOHS, J. (eds.), *Von der Illegalität ins Parlament. Werdegang und Konzept der neuen Bürgerbewegungen* (Berlin: LinksDruck Verlag, Christoph Links, 1991).

NETTL, J. P., *The Eastern Zone and Soviet Policy in Germany 1945–50* (London: Oxford University Press, 1951).

NEUES FORUM LEIPZIG, *Jetzt oder nie—Demokratie. Leipziger Herbst '89* (Munich: C. Bertelsmann Verlag, 1990).

NIETHAMMER, LUTZ, PLATO, ALEXANDER VON, and WIERLING, DOROTHEE, *Die volkseigene Erfahrung. Eine Archäologie des Lebens in der Industrieprovinz der DDR* (Berlin: Rowohlt, 1991).

NITSCHE, HELLMUTH, *Zwischen Kreuz und Sowjetstern* (Aschaffenburg: Paul Pattlock Verlag, 1983).

Ohnmacht. DDR-Funktionäre sagen aus (Berlin: Verlag Neues Leben, 1992).

OPP, KARL-DIETER, and VOSS, PETER, *Die volkseigene Revolution* (Stuttgart: Klett-Cotta, 1993).

OSMOND, JONATHAN (ed.), *German Reunification: A Reference Guide and Commentary* (Harlow: Longman, 1992).

OSTOW, ROBIN, *Jews in Contemporary East Germany* (London: Macmillan, 1989).

PECHMANN, ROLAND, and VOGEL, JÜRGEN (eds.), *Abgesang der Stasi. Das Jahr 1989 in Presseartikeln und Stasi-Dokumenten* (Braunschweig: Steinweg-Verlag, 1991).

PEUKERT, DETLEV, *Inside Nazi Germany* (London: Batsford, 1987).

PHILIPSON, DIRK, *We Were the People: Voices from East Germany's Revolutionary Autumn of 1989* (Durham, NC: Duke University Press, 1993).

PRZYBYLSKI, PETER, *Tatort Politbüro. Band 2: Honecker, Mittag und Schalck-Golodkowski* (Berlin: Rowohlt, 1992).

REICH, JENS, *Abschied von den Lebenslügen* (Berlin: Rowohlt, 1992).

REIN, GERHARD, *Die protestantische Revolution 1987–1990* (Berlin: Wichern Verlag, 1990).

—— (ed.), *Die Opposition in der DDR* (Berlin: Wichern, 1989).

REISSIG, ROLF, and GLAESSNER, G.-J. (eds.), *Das Ende eines Experiments: Umbruch in der DDR und deutsche Einheit* (Berlin: Dietz Verlag, 1991).

REITINGER, HERBERT, *Die Rolle der Kirchen im politischen Prozeß der DDR 1970 bis 1990* (Munich: tuduv-Verlag, 1991).

REUTH, RALF GEORG, *IM 'Sekretär'. Die 'Gauck-Recherche' und die Dokumente zum 'Fall Stolpe'* (Frankfurt-on-Main and Berlin: Ullstein, 1992).

RÜDDENKLAU, WOLFGANG, *Störenfried. ddr-opposition 1986–89* (Berlin: BasisDruck, 1992).

RUESCHEMEYER, M., and LEMKE, C. (eds.), *The Quality of Life in the German Democratic Republic* (New York: M. E. Sharpe, 1989).

SANDFORD, GREGORY, *From Hitler to Ulbricht: The Communist Reconstruction of East Germany, 1945–6* (Princeton: Princeton University Press, 1983).

SANDFORD, JOHN, *The Sword and the Ploughshare* (London: Merlin Press/European Nuclear Disarmament, 1983).

SASS, ULRICH VON, and SUCHODOLETZ, HARRIET VON (eds.), *'Feindlich-negativ'. Zur politisch-operativen Arbeit einer Stasi-Zentrale* (Berlin: Evangelische Verlags-Anstalt, 1990).

SCHABOWSKI, GÜNTER, *Das Politbüro* (Hamburg: Rowohlt, 1990).

—— *Der Absturz* (Berlin: Rowohlt, 1991).

SCHÄDLICH, HANS JOACHIM (ed.), *Aktenkundig* (Berlin: Rowohlt, 1992).

SCHELL, MANFRED, and KALINKA, WERNER, *Stasi und kein Ende: Die Personen und Fakten* (Frankfurt-on-Main and Berlin: Ullstein, 1991).

SCHERZER, LANDOLF, *Der Erste. Eine Reportage aus der DDR* (Cologne: Kiepenheuer and Witsch, 1989).

SCHORLEMMER, FRIEDRICH, *Bis alle Mauern fallen* (Berlin: Verlag der Nation, 1991).

—— *Worte öffnen Fäuste* (Munich: Kindler, 1992).

—— *Träume und Alpträume* (Munich: Knaur, 1993).

SCHÜDDEKOPF, C. (ed.), *'Wir sind das Volk!'* (Hamburg: Rowohlt, 1990).

SCHWEIGLER, GEBHARD, *National Consciousness in Divided Germany* (London: Sage, 1975).

SKOCPOL, THEDA, *The State and Social Revolutions: France, Russia, China* (Cambridge: Cambridge University Press, 1979).

SOLBERG, RICHARD, *God and Caesar in East Germany* (New York: Macmillan, 1961).

SONTHEIMER, K., and BLEEK, W., *The Government and Politics of East Germany* (London: Hutchinson, 1975).

SPITTMANN, ILSE (ed.), *Die SED in Geschichte und Gegenwart* (Cologne: Verlag Wissenschaft und Politik, 1987).

—— and FRICKE, KARL WILHELM (eds.), *17. Juni 1953. Arbeiteraufstand in der DDR* (Cologne: Verlag Wissenschaft und Politik, 1982).

SPOTTS, FREDERIC, *The Churches and Politics in Germany* (Middletown, Conn.: Wesleyan University Press, 1973).

STARITZ, D., *Geschichte der DDR, 1949–1985* (Frankfurt-on-Main: Suhrkamp, 1985).

Stasi-Akte 'Verräter'. Bürgerrechtler Templin: Dokumente einer Verfolgung, Spiegel-Spezial, No. 1/1993.

STEINLEIN, REINHARD, *Die gottlosen Jahre* (Berlin: Rowohlt, 1993).

STOLPE, MANFRED, *Schwieriger Aufbruch* (Munich: Siedler, 1992).

STROHMEYER, ARN, *Visa-frei bis Hawai* (Frankfurt-on-Main: Eichborn, 1990).

STULZ-HERRNSTADT, NADJA (ed.), *Das Herrnstadt-Dokument. Das Politbüro der SED und die Geschichte des 17. Juni 1953* (Hamburg: Rowohlt, 1990).

SZABO, STEPHEN, *The Diplomacy of German Unification* (New York: St Martin's Press, 1992).

TETZEL, REINER, *Leipziger Ring* (Frankfurt-on-Main: Luchterhand, 1990).

THIERSE, WOLFGANG, *Mit eigener Stimme sprechen* (Munich: Piper, 1992).

TURNER, HENRY ASHBY, *The Two Germanies since 1945* (New Haven: Yale University Press, 1987).

USCHNER, MANFRED, *Die zweite Etage. Funktionsweise eines Machtapparates* (Berlin: Dietz Verlag, 1993).

40 Jahre DDR ... und die Bürger melden sich zu Wort (Frankfurt-on-Main: Büchergilde Gutenberg, 1989).

WALLACE, IAN (ed.), *The GDR in the 1980s*, GDR Monitor Special Series, No. 4 (Dundee, 1984).

WAWRZYN, L., *Der Blaue. Das Spitzelsystem der DDR* (Berlin: Wagenbach, 1990).

WEBER, CHRISTIAN, *Ich bleibe! Alltag in der DDR* (Stuttgart: Quell Verlag, 1989).

WEBER, HERMANN, *Die DDR 1945–1986* (Munich: Oldenbourg, 1988).

WEBER, MAX, *Economy and Society* (New York: Bedminster Press, 1968).

WEHLING, HANS-GEORG (ed.), *Politische Kultur in der DDR* (Stuttgart: Verlag W. Kohlhammer, 1989).

WILKENING, CHRISTINA, *Staat im Staate* (Berlin and Weimar: Aufbau Verlag, 1990).

WOLF, MARKUS, *In eigenem Auftrag. Bekenntnisse und Einsichten* (Munich: Schneekluth, 1991).

WOLLE, STEFAN, 'In the Labyrinth of the Documents: The Archival Legacy of the SED-State', *German History*, 10: 3 (1992), 352–65.

—— 'Die DDR-Bevölkerung und der Prager Frühling', *Aus Politik und Zeitgeschichte. Beilage zur Wochenzeitung Das Parlament*, B36/92 (Aug. 1992), 35–45.

WOLLENBERGER, VERA, *Virus der Heuchler: Innenansichten aus Stasi-Akten* (Berlin: Elefanten-Press, 1992).

WOLTERS, U. (ed.), *Rudolf Bahro: Critical Responses* (New York: M. E. Sharpe, 1980).

WOODS, ROGER, *Opposition in the GDR under Honecker, 1971–85* (London: Macmillan, 1986).

Wörterbuch der Geschichte (Berlin: Dietz Verlag, 1984).

Wörterbuch der Marxistisch-Leninistischen Soziologie (Berlin: Dietz Verlag, 1983).

ZIMMERMANN, H., '"Kirche im Sozialismus"—Zur Situation der evangelischen Kirche in der DDR', *DDR-Report*, 12: 1 (1979).

ZWAHR, HARTMUT, *Ende einer Selbstzerstörung. Leipzig und die Revolution in der DDR* (Göttingen: Vandenhoek and Ruprecht, 1993).

INDEX